MCSA
Windows Server® 2016
Practice Tests:
Exams 70-740, 70-741, 70-742, and 70-743

William Panek

Crystal Pa

SYBEX®
A Wiley Brand

Senior Acquisitions Editor: Kenyon Brown
Development Editor: Kezia Endsley
Technical Editor: Chris Crayton
Senior Production Editor: Christine O'Connor
Content Enablement and Operations Manager: Pete Gaughan
Executive Editor: Jim Minatel
Production Manager: Kathleen Wisor
Book Designers: Judy Fung and Bill Gibson
Copy Editor: Elizabeth Welch
Proofreader: Louise Watson, Word One New York
Indexer: Jack Lewis
Project Coordinator, Cover: Brent Savage
Cover Designer: Wiley
Cover Image: Getty Images Inc./ Jeremy Woodhouse

V10006453_113018

This book is dedicated to Alexandria and Paige. We couldn't ask for better kids.

Acknowledgments

I would like to thank my wife and best friend, Crystal. She is always the light at the end of my tunnel. I want to thank my two daughters, Alexandria and Paige, for all of their love and support during the writing of all my books. The three of them are my support system and I couldn't do any of this without them.

I want to thank all of my family and friends who always help me when I'm writing my books. I want to thank my brothers, Rick, Gary, and Rob. I want to thank my great friends Shaun, Jeremy, and Gene.

We want to thank everyone on our Sybex team, especially our development editor, Kezia Endsley, who helped make this the best book possible, and Chris Crayton, our technical editor. It's always good to have the very best technical person backing you up. I also want to thank Christine O'Connor, our production editor, and Elizabeth Welch, our copy editor.

Special thanks to our acquisitions editor, Kenyon Brown, who was the lead for the entire book. Finally, we want to thank everyone else behind the scenes who helped make this book possible. It's truly an amazing thing to have so many people work on my books to help make them the very best. I can't thank you all enough for your hard work.
—Will Panek

I would like to second Will's sentiments and thank all the same individuals. I would like to personally thank my husband and best friend, Will, because without him I would not be where I am today—thank you! I would also like to express my love to my two daughters, who have always shown nothing but love and support for everything we do.
—Crystal Panek

About the Authors

William Panek holds the following certifications: MCP, MCP+ I, MCSA, MCSA+ Security and Messaging, MCSE-NT (3.51 & 4.0), MCSE 2000, 2003, 2012/2012 R2, 2016, MCSE+ Security and Messaging, MCDBA, MCT, MCTS, MCITP, CCNA, CCDA, and CHFI. Will is also a five-time Microsoft MVP winner.

After many successful years in the computer industry, Will decided that he could better use his talents and his personality as an instructor. He began teaching for schools such as Boston University and the University of Maryland, just to name a few. He has done consulting and training for some of the biggest government and corporate companies in the world, including the United States Secret Service, Cisco, the United States Air Force, and the United States Army.

In 2015, Will became a Senior Microsoft Instructor for StormWind Studios (www.stormwindstudios.com). He currently lives in New Hampshire with his wife and two daughters. Will was also a representative in the New Hampshire House of Representatives from 2010 to 2012. In his spare time, he likes to do blacksmithing, shooting (trap and skeet), golf, racquetball, and ride his Harley. Will is also a commercially rated helicopter pilot.

Crystal Panek holds the following certifications: MCP, MCP+ I, MCSA, MCSA+ Security and Messaging, MCSE-NT (3.51 & 4.0), MCSE 2000, 2003, 2012/2012 R2, 2016, MCSE+ Security and Messaging, MCDBA, MCTS, and MCITP.

For many years she trained as a contract instructor, teaching at such places as MicroC, Stellacon Corporation, and the University of New Hampshire. She then became the vice president for a large IT training company, and for 15 years she developed training materials and courseware to help thousands of students get through their certification exams. She currently works on a contract basis, creating courseware for several large IT training facilities.

Crystal resides in New Hampshire with her husband and two daughters. In her spare time, she likes to camp, hike, shoot trap and skeet, golf, bowl, and snowmobile.

About the Technical Editor

Chris Crayton, MCSE, CISSP, CASP, CySA+, A+, N+, and S+, is a technical consultant, trainer, author, and industry leading technical editor. He has worked as a computer technology and networking instructor, information security director, network administrator, network engineer, and PC specialist. Chris has authored several print and online books on PC repair, CompTIA A+, CompTIA Security+, and Microsoft Windows. He has also served as technical editor and content contributor on numerous technical titles for several of the leading publishing companies. He holds numerous industry certifications, has been recognized with many professional and teaching awards, and has served as a state-level SkillsUSA final competition judge.

Contents at a Glance

Contents at a Glance

Contents

Introduction

This book is drawn from more than 20 years of IT experience and Microsoft testing. We have taken that experience and translated it into a Windows Server 2016 book that will help you prepare for the MCSA: Windows Server 2016 exams.

Microsoft Windows Server 2016 is the newest version of Microsoft's server operating system software. Microsoft has taken the best of Windows Server 2003, Windows Server 2008, and Windows Server 2012 and combined them into the latest creation, Windows Server 2016.

Windows Server 2016 eliminates many of the problems that plagued the previous versions of Windows Server, and it includes a much faster boot time and shutdown. It is also easier to install and configure, and it barely stops to ask the user any questions during installation. In this book, we will show you what features are installed during the automated installation and where you can make changes if you want to be more in charge of your operating system and its features.

The Microsoft Certification Program

Since the inception of its certification program, Microsoft has certified more than two million people. As the computer network industry continues to increase in both size and complexity, this number is sure to grow—and the need for proven ability will also increase. Certifications can help companies verify the skills of prospective employees and contractors.

The Microsoft certification tracks for Windows Server 2016 include the following:

MCSA: Windows Server 2016   The MCSA is now the lowest-level certification you can achieve with Microsoft in relation to Windows Server 2016. It requires passing three exams: 70-740, 70-741, and 70-742.

MCSE: Cloud Platform and Infrastructure   The MCSE certifications, in relation to Windows Server 2016, require that you become an MCSA first and then pass two additional exams. The additional exams will vary depending on which of the two MCSE tracks you choose. For more information, visit Microsoft's website at www.microsoft.com/learning.

How Do You Become Certified on Windows Server 2016?

Attaining Microsoft certification has always been a challenge. In the past, students have been able to acquire detailed exam information—even most of the exam questions—from online "brain dumps" and third-party "cram" books or software products. For the new generation of exams, this is simply not the case.

Microsoft has taken strong steps to protect the security and integrity of its new certification tracks. Now prospective candidates must complete a course of study that develops detailed knowledge about a wide range of topics. It supplies them with the true skills needed, derived from working with the technology being tested.

The new generations of Microsoft certification programs are heavily weighted toward hands-on skills and experience. Microsoft recommends that candidates have troubleshooting skills acquired through hands-on experience and working knowledge.

Fortunately, if you are willing to dedicate the time and effort to learn Windows Server 2016, you can prepare yourself well for the exam by using the proper tools. By working through this book, you can successfully meet the requirements to pass the Windows Server 2016 exams.

MCSA Exam Requirements

Candidates for MCSA certification on Windows Server 2016 must pass at least the following three Windows Server 2016 exams:

- 70-740: Installation, Storage, and Compute with Windows Server 2016
- 70-741: Networking with Windows Server 2016
- 70-742: Identity with Windows Server 2016

Those who have a qualifying certification can take the Upgrading exam "Upgrading Your Skills to MCSA: Windows Server 2016" (Exam 70-743). The objectives for this exam span the three individual exams. This book covers all of the objectives for the Upgrading exam. For details about the exam, visit Microsoft's website at www.microsoft.com/learning.

Microsoft provides exam objectives to give you a general overview of possible areas of coverage on the Microsoft exams. Keep in mind, however, that exam objectives are subject to change at any time without prior notice and at Microsoft's sole discretion. Visit the Microsoft Learning website (www.microsoft.com/learning) for the most current listing of exam objectives. The published objectives and how they map to this book are listed later in this introduction.

For a more detailed description of the Microsoft certification programs, including a list of all the exams, visit the Microsoft Learning website at: www.microsoft.com/learning.

Tips for Taking the Windows Server 2016 Exams

Here are some general tips for achieving success on your certification exam:

- Arrive early at the exam center so that you can relax and review your study materials. During this final review, you can look over tables and lists of exam-related information.

- Read the questions carefully. Do not be tempted to jump to an early conclusion. Make sure you know *exactly* what the question is asking.

- Answer all questions. If you are unsure about a question, mark it for review and come back to it at a later time.

- On simulations, do not change settings that are not directly related to the question. Also, assume the default settings if the question does not specify or imply which settings are used.

- For questions about which you're unsure, use a process of elimination to get rid of the obviously incorrect answers first. This improves your odds of selecting the correct answer when you need to make an educated guess.

Exam Registration

As of December 31, 2014, Microsoft ended its relationship with Prometric, its old testing centers, and all exams are now delivered through the more than 1,000 Authorized VUE Testing Centers around the world. For the location of a testing center near you, go to VUE's website at www.vue.com. If you are outside of the United States and Canada, contact your local VUE registration center.

Find out the number of the exam that you want to take and then register with the VUE registration center nearest to you. At this point, you will be asked for advance payment for the exam. The exams are $165 each, and you must take them within one year of payment. You can schedule exams up to six weeks in advance or as late as one working day prior to the date of the exam. You can cancel or reschedule your exam if you contact the center at least two working days prior to the exam. Same-day registration is available in some locations, subject to space availability. Where same-day registration is available, you must register a minimum of two hours before test time.

When you schedule the exam, you will be provided with instructions regarding appointment and cancellation procedures, ID requirements, and information about the testing center location. In addition, you will receive a registration and payment confirmation letter.

Microsoft requires certification candidates to accept the terms of a nondisclosure agreement before taking certification exams.

Who Should Read This Book?

This book is intended for individuals who want to earn their MCSA: Windows Server 2016 certification.

This book will not only help anyone who is looking to pass the Microsoft exams, it will also help anyone who wants to learn the real ins and outs of the Windows Server 2016 operating system.

What's Inside?

Here is a glance at what's in each chapter:

Chapter 1: Installing Windows Servers in Host and Compute Environments   In the first chapter, we cover questions on how to install, upgrade, and migrate servers and workloads, install and configure Nano Server, and create, manage, and maintain images for deployment.

Chapter 2: Implement Storage Solutions   This chapter asks questions on how to implement server storage and implement data deduplication.

Chapter 3: Implement Hyper-V   We take you through questions on how to install and configure Hyper-V, configure virtual machine (VM) settings, configure Hyper-V storage, and configure Hyper-V networking.

Chapter 4: Implement Windows Containers   This chapter asks questions on how to deploy and manage Windows Containers.

Chapter 5: Implement High Availability   This chapter takes you through questions on how to implement high availability and disaster recovery options in Hyper-V, implement and manage failover clustering, implement Storage Spaces Direct, and manage Virtual Machine movement in clustered nodes.

Chapter 6: Implement Domain Name System (DNS)   In this chapter, you will see different questions that cover how to install and configure DNS servers and implement and maintain IP Address Management (IPAM).

Chapter 7: Implement Network Connectivity and Remote Access Solutions   In this chapter we cover questions on how to implement virtual private network (VPN) and DirectAccess solutions.

Chapter 8: Implement an Advanced Network Infrastructure   This chapter includes questions on how to implement high-performance network solutions and determine scenarios and requirements for implementing Software Defined Networking (SDN).

Chapter 9: Install and Configure Active Directory Domain Services (AD DS)   This chapter shows you questions on how to install and configure domain controllers.

Chapter 10: Implement Identity Federation and Access Solutions   In this chapter we cover questions on how to install and configure Active Directory Federation Services (AD FS), implement Web Application Proxy (WAP), and install and configure Active Directory Rights.

What's Included with the Book

This book includes many helpful items intended to prepare you for the MCSA: Windows Server 2016 certification.

Objectives   These questions are mapped directly with the exam objectives. This will help you prepare for the different exam questions.

Sybex Test Engine   Readers can access the Sybex Test Engine, which includes the assessment test and chapter review questions in electronic format. In addition, there are a total of three practice exams included with the Sybex test engine: one each for Exams 70-740, 70-741, and 70-742.

How to Contact Sybex or the Authors

Sybex strives to keep you supplied with the latest tools and information you need for your work. Please check the website at www.sybex.com/go/mcsawin2016, where we'll post additional content and updates that supplement this book, should the need arise.

You can contact Will by going to his website at www.willpanek.com. You can also watch free videos on Microsoft networking at www.youtube.com/c/williampanek. If you would like to follow information about Windows Server 2016 from Will Panek, please visit Twitter @AuthorWillPanek.

Good luck on the exam. We're hoping this book helps you pass.

Chapter
1

Installing Windows Servers in Host and Compute Environments

THE FOLLOWING MCSA WINDOWS SERVER 2016 EXAM TOPICS ARE COVERED IN THIS CHAPTER:

✓ **1.1 Install, upgrade, and migrate servers and workloads**

- This objective may include but is not limited to: Determine Windows Server 2016 installation requirements; determine appropriate Windows Server 2016 editions per workloads; install Windows Server 2016; install Windows Server 2016 features and roles; install and configure Windows Server Core; manage Windows Server Core installations using Windows PowerShell, command line, and remote management capabilities; implement Windows PowerShell Desired State Configuration (DSC) to install and maintain integrity of installed environments; perform upgrades and migrations of servers and core workloads from Windows Server 2008 and Windows Server 2012 to Windows Server 2016; determine the appropriate activation model for server installation, such as Automatic Virtual Machine Activation (AVMA), Key Management Service (KMS), and Active Directory-Based Activation

✓ **1.2 Install and configure Nano Server**

- This objective may include but is not limited to: Determine appropriate usage scenarios and requirements for Nano Server; install Nano Server; implement Roles and Features on Nano Server; use Nano Server Image Builder; manage and configure Nano Server; manage Nano Server remotely using MMC, Windows PowerShell, and Server Management Tools

✓ **1.3 Create, manage, and maintain images for deploymen**

- This objective may include but is not limited to: Plan
  for Windows Server virtualization; assess virtualization
  workloads using the Microsoft Assessment and Planning
  (MAP) Toolkit; determine considerations for deploying
  workloads into virtualized environments; update images
  with patches, hotfixes, last cumulative updates, and drivers; install roles and features in offline images; manage an
  maintain Windows Server Core, Nano Server images, and
  VHDs using Windows PowerShell

1. You are the administrator for your company network and you are looking to install Windows Server 2016. You need to decide which version would best fit your environment. You maintain a small office that has only 10 users and about 20 devices. Which version of Windows Server would fit your needs?

    A. Windows Server 2016 Datacenter

    B. Windows Server 2016 Essentials

    C. Windows Server 2016 Standard

    D. Windows Server 2016 Web Server Core

2. You are the administrator for your company network and you need to figure out what installation type of Windows Server 2016 you want to use. You are looking for a server type that is designed for private clouds and datacenters that will allow you to remotely administer the server operating system. What version should you install?

    A. Windows Server 2016 (Desktop Experience)

    B. Windows Server 2016 Server Core

    C. Windows Server 2016 Nano Server

    D. Windows Server 2016 Web Server Core

3. You are the administrator for your company network. You have a Windows Server 2016 server named Server1. You want to configure Server1 as a multitenant RAS Gateway. What should you install on Server1?

    A. Network Policy and Access Services server role

    B. Remote Access server role

    C. Data Center Bridging feature

    D. Network Controller server role

4. You are the administrator for your company network. You have a Windows Server 2016 server named Server1. This server hosts a line-of-business application named App1. App1 has a memory leak that occasionally causes it to consume an excessive amount of memory. You want to log the event in the Application event log whenever this application consumes more than 4 GB of memory. What should you do?

    A. Create a system configuration information data collector.

    B. Create a performance counter data collector.

    C. Create a performance counter alert data collector.

    D. Create an event trace data collector.

5. You are the administrator for your company network. You have just finished installing Windows Server 2016 on a new server. Your colleague has informed you that it is essential that you activate Windows Server. Which of the following command-line tools can be used to activate Windows Server?

    A. `Netdom C:\windows\system32\slmgr.vbs -ato`

    B. `Netsh C:\windows\system32\slmgr.vbs -ato`

    C. `Ocsetup C:\windows\system32\slmgr.vbs -ato`

    D. `Cscript C:\windows\system32\slmgr.vbs -ato`

6. You are the administrator for your company network. You and a colleague are discussing Nano Server. You know that with Nano Server some packages are installed directly with their own Windows PowerShell switches (such as -Compute) whereas others are installed by passing package names to the -Packages parameter that can combine them in a comma-separated list. If you want to add IIS to your Nano Server, what command should you use?

  A. -Compute

  B. -Packages

  C. -Containers

  D. -Storage

7. You are the administrator for your company network. You have decided to install Windows Server 2016 by choosing the Server Core Installation option. What tools would you use if you want to install, configure, or uninstall server roles remotely?

  A. Windows PowerShell

  B. Server Manager

  C. Remote Server Administration Tools (RSAT)

  D. All of the above

8. You are the administrator for your company network. Your network contains an Active Directory domain called abc.com. You want to create a Nano Server image named Nano1 that will be used as a virtualization host. The Windows Server 2016 source files are located in drive D. What Windows PowerShell cmdlet should you run?

  A. New-NanoServerImage –Edition Datacenter –DeploymentType Host –Defender –EnableEMS –MediaPath 'D:\' –TargetPath C:\Nano1\Nano1.wim –ComputerName Nano1 –DomainName abc.com

  B. New-NanoServerImage –Edition Datacenter –DeploymentType Host –Package Microsoft-NanoServer-SCVMM-Package –MediaPath 'D:\' –TargetPath C:\ Nano1\Nano1.wim –ComputerName Nano1 –DomainName abc.com

  C. New-NanoServerImage –Edition Datacenter –DeploymentType Host –Package Microsoft-ServerCore-Compute-Package –MediaPath 'D:\' –TargetPath C:\ Nano1\Nano1.wim –ComputerName Nano1 –DomainName ABC

  D. New-NanoServerImage –Edition Datacenter –DeploymentType Host –Compute –MediaPath 'D:\' –TargetPath C:\Nano1\Nano1.wim –ComputerName Nano1 –DomainName abc.com

9. You are the administrator for your company network. You have a physical Nano Server machine that runs Windows Server 2016. You have not installed any packages on this machine. You decide to attach a new disk and then initialize the disk as a GUID Partition Table (GPT) disk. What should you do first if you need to create a ReFS-formatted volume on the new disk?

  A. From the physical server, log on to the Nano Server Recovery Console.

  B. Install the Microsoft-NanoServer-Host-Package package.

  C. Run the Format-Volume cmdlet and specify the -FileSystem switch.

  D. Install the Microsoft-NanoServer-Storage-Package package.

10. You are the administrator for your company network. You create a Nano Server image named `Nano1.vhdx` by using the `New-NanoServerImage` cmdlet and attach it to a Generation 1 virtual machine named Nano1. When you start Nano1, you get an error message that states, "Boot failure. Reboot and select proper Boot device or Insert Boot Media in selected Boot device." What should you do to successfully start the Nano Server?

   A. Attach `Nano1.vhdx` to a SCSI controller.

   B. Recreate Nano1 as a Generation 2 virtual machine.

   C. Increase the memory of Nano1 to 512 MB.

   D. Modify the BIOS settings of Nano1.

11. You are the administrator for your company network. You have a Nano Server image named `Disk1.vhdx`. You mount `Disk1.vhdx`. What tool or cmdlet should you use if you need to add a folder that contains several files to the image?

   A. `Copy-Item`

   B. `Add-WindowsImage`

   C. `Add-WindowsPackage`

   D. `Edit-NanoServerImage`

12. You are the administrator for your company network. You have a Windows Server 2016 server named Server1. You use the Basic template to create a new data collector set named CollectorSet1 on this server. What should you do before you start CollectorSet1 if you need to configure it to generate performance alerts?

   A. Modify the performance counter data collector of CollectorSet1.

   B. Add a new data collector to CollectorSet1.

   C. Modify the configuration data collector of CollectorSet1.

   D. Add a new task to CollectorSet1.

13. You are the administrator for your company network. Your network contains an Active Directory forest named ABC Company. The forest has a Distributed File System (DFS) namespace named `\\abccompany.com\namespace1`. The domain contains a file server named FS1 that runs Windows Server 2016. You create a folder named `Folder1` on FS1. Which two cmdlets should you use? (Choose two.)

   A. `New-DfsnFolderTarget`

   B. `Install-WindowsFeature`

   C. `Grant-DfsnAccess`

   D. `New-DfsnFolder`

   E. `New-SmbShare`

14. You are the administrator for your company network. You have two Windows Server 2016 servers named Server1 and Server2. There is a firewall between the two servers. Both servers run Windows Server Update Services (WSUS). Server1 downloads updates from Microsoft Update. What port should be open on the firewall if Server2 must synchronize updates from Server1?

    A. 80

    B. 443

    C. 3389

    D. 8530

15. You are the administrator for your company network. You administer a large network, and a colleague installs a new machine with Windows Server 2016 Datacenter Server Core. It is determined that it should have been Windows Server 2016 Datacenter (Desktop Experience). What should you do?

    A. On the same machine, reinstall the Windows Server 2016 Datacenter Server Core.

    B. Install Windows Server 2016 Datacenter Server Core on a new machine.

    C. Convert the current Windows Server 2016 Datacenter Server Core to the Windows Server 2016 Datacenter (Desktop Experience) version.

    D. Dual-boot the machine with both Windows Server 2016 Datacenter Server Core and Windows Server 2016 Datacenter (Desktop Experience).

16. You are the administrator for your company network. You are looking to upgrade Windows Server 2012 Standard with GUI to Windows Server 2016. If you want to maintain the GUI interface, what version of Windows Server 2016 does Microsoft recommend?

    A. Windows Server 2016 Datacenter (Desktop Experience)

    B. Windows Server 2016 Standard (Desktop Experience)

    C. Windows Server 2016 Datacenter

    D. Windows Server 2016 Standard

17. You are the administrator for your company network. You administer a network that has a Nano Server named Nano1. You want to see if the DNS Server role is installed on this machine. What cmdlet should you use?

    A. Find-NanoServerPackage

    B. Get-Package

    C. Find-Package

    D. Get-WindowsOptionalFeature

18. You are the administrator for your company network. Your network contains an Active Directory domain. There is a company policy that indicates that new servers should run Nano Server whenever possible. What server role can be deployed on Nano Server?

    A. Active Directory Domain Services

    B. DHCP Server

    C. Network Policy and Access Services

    D. Web Server (IIS)

19. You are the administrator for your company network. You are planning on creating an answer file. What should you name the answer file so that it will work with unattended installations?

   A. `Autounattend.txt`

   B. `Autounattend.xls`

   C. `Autounattend.xml`

   D. `Autounattend.docx`

20. You are the administrator for your company network. You have a Windows Server 2016 server named Server1. You create a Nano Server image named `Disk1.vhdx`. You need to start Server1 by using `Disk1.vhdx`. What three actions should you perform? (Choose three.)

   A. Restart Server1.

   B. Run the `bcdboot.exe` command.

   C. Run the `bootcfg.exe` command.

   D. Run the `Edit-NanoServerImage` cmdlet.

   E. Mark a partition as active.

   F. Mount `Disk1.vhdx`.

21. You are the administrator for your company network. You have a Windows Server 2016 server named Server1. The server has an application named App1 that writes entries to the Application event log when errors are encountered. The events have IDs of either 111 or 112. What should you do to restart the service whenever one of these events is logged?

   A. Run the `Get-SMServerEvent` cmdlet and pipe the output to the `Start-NetEvent` using Windows PowerShell.

   B. Use create task to create one task that includes triggers for both event IDs from Task Scheduler.

   C. Create a custom view that has a filter for the event IDs from Event Viewer.

   D. Run the `Write-EventLog` cmdlet and specify the `-EventID` parameter using Windows PowerShell.

22. You are the administrator for your company network. You have a server named Server1 that is an iSCSI target. You have a server named Server2 that runs Windows Server 2016. Server2 has an iSCSI disk named Disk1. Disk1 contains one volume that is assigned a drive letter of E:. What should you do if you need to increase the size of Disk1?

   A. Run the `Resize-Partition` cmdlet and specify the `-ComputerName` Server2 parameter.

   B. Run the `Resize-IscsiVirtualDisk` cmdlet and specify the `-ComputerName` Server2 parameter.

   C. Run the `Resize-IscsiVirtualDisk` cmdlet and specify the `-ComputerName` Server1 parameter.

   D. Run the `Resize-Partition` cmdlet and specify the `-ComputerName` Server1 parameter.

23. You are the administrator for your company network. You are deciding on an upgrade path. You are currently using Windows Server 2012 R2 Standard in your environment. What is the recommended upgrade path you should choose? (Choose all that apply.)

   A. Windows Server 2016 Standard

   B. Windows Server 2016 Datacenter

   C. Windows Server 2016 Essentials

   D. Windows Storage Server 2016

24. You are the administrator for your company network. You have a Windows Server 2016 server named Server1 that has Windows Defender enabled. Server1 runs an application named App1 that stores various types of files in Microsoft OneDrive and Microsoft SharePoint Online. App1 also interacts with several local services. What should you do on Server1 if you need to prevent Windows Defender from scanning any files opened by App1?

   A. In Windows Defender, modify the real-time protection settings.

   B. In Windows Defender, modify the cloud-based protection settings.

   C. Run the `New-AppLockerPolicy` cmdlet.

   D. From the Windows Defender settings, configure a process exclusion.

25. You are the administrator for your company network. You have a Windows Server 2016 server named Server1. A Microsoft Azure Backup of Server1 is created automatically every day. What cmdlet should you run if you need to view the items that are included in the backup?

   A. `Get-OBPolicyState`

   B. `Get-OBJob`

   C. `Get-OBPolicy`

   D. `Get-WBSummary`

26. You are the administrator for your company network. You have a Windows Server 2016 server named Server1. A Microsoft Azure Backup of Server1 is created automatically every day. You rename Server1 to Server2. You discover that backups are no longer being created in Azure. You need to ensure that the server is backed up to Azure. What should you do?

   A. Upload the Server2 certificate as a management certificate from the Azure Management Portal.

   B. Run the `Start-OBRegistration` cmdlet on Server2.

   C. Run the `Add-WBBackupTarget` cmdlet on Server2.

   D. Modify the configuration on the backup vault from the Azure Management Portal.

27. You are the administrator for your company network and you are planning on upgrading your Windows Server 2012 R2 Datacenter with GUI machine to Windows Server 2016. The company is planning on virtualizing 25 servers. What version of Windows Server 2016 should you upgrade to while maintaining the GUI interface?

   A. Windows Server 2016 Datacenter (Desktop Experience)

   B. Windows Server 2016 Standard (Desktop Experience)

   C. Windows Server 2016 Datacenter

   D. Windows Server 2016 Standard

28. You are the administrator for your company network. You and a colleague are discussing Windows Server 2016 Server Core. Windows Server 2016 Server Core has many benefits. Which of the following are some of the benefits of using Windows Server 2016 Server Core? (Choose all that apply.)

    A. Reduced management

    B. Minimal maintenance

    C. Smaller footprint

    D. Tighter security

29. You are the administrator for your company network and you are looking to save hard drive space on the Windows Server 2016 Datacenter machine. What feature can you use to help you save hard disk space?

    A. HDSaver.exe

    B. Features On Demand

    C. ADDS

    D. WinRM

30. You are the administrator for your company network. If physical security is a concern in an area, what type of domain controller should you install?

    A. Primary domain controller

    B. Backup domain controller

    C. Read-only domain controller

    D. Locked-down domain controller

31. You are the administrator for your company network. You have a Windows Server 2016 server named Server1. The Windows Server 2016 installation media is mounted as drive D. You copy the `NanoServerImageGenerator` folder from the `D:\NanoServer` folder to the `C:\NanoServer` folder. You create a custom Nano Server image that includes the Hyper-V server role. What two commands should you run if you want this image to be used to deploy Nano Servers to physical servers? (Choose two.)

    A. `New-NanoServerImage –Edition Standard –DeploymentType Guest –MediaPath D:\-TargetPath \NanoServerImage\NanoServer.wim -Compute`

    B. `Install-PackageProvider NanoServerPackage`

    C. `Import-PackageProvider NanoServerPackage`

    D. `New-NanoServerImage –Edition Standard –DeploymentType Host –MediaPath D:\ -TargetPath \NanoServerImage\NanoServer.wim -Compute`

    E. `Import-Module C:\NanoServer\NanoServerImageGenerator`

32. You are the administrator for your company network. You are trying to decide if you'd like to install a Windows Server 2016 Nano Server on the network. What are some good options that Nano Server would be ideal for? (Choose all that apply.)

    A. A DNS server

    B. As a storage machine for file servers

    C. A domain controller

    D. Systems Center Data Protection Manager

    E. NIC Teaming

    F. An IIS server

    G. An application server for cloud-based applications

33. You are the administrator for your company network. You have a Hyper-V host named Server1 that runs Windows Server 2016. The installation source files for Windows Server are located in D:\Source. You need to create a Nano Server image. Which cmdlets should you run? (Choose all that apply.)

    A. `Add-WindowsImage`

    B. `Import-Module`

    C. `Install-Module`

    D. `New-NanoServerImage`

    E. `New-WindowsCustomImage`

34. You are the administrator for your company network. You have a Hyper-V host named Server1 that runs Windows Server 2016. Server1 hosts a virtual machine named VM1. What should you do first if you need to provide VM1 with direct access to a graphics processing unit (GPU) on Server1?

    A. On Server1, disable the display adapter device.

    B. Add a RemoteFX 3D Video Adapter in the settings of VM1.

    C. Install the Quality Windows Audio Video Experience (qWave) feature on VM1.

    D. On Server1, dismount the display adapter.

35. You are the administrator for your company network. You are preparing an image of Windows Server 2016. You notice that the image is missing the driver for a network adapter. This is required in your environment. You need to ensure that the image contains the network adapter driver. What three cmdlets should you use? (Choose three.)

    A. `Mount-WindowsImage`

    B. `Add-WindowsDriver`

    C. `Get-WindowsImage`

    D. `Save-WindowsImage`

    E. `Add-WindowsFeature`

    F. `Dismount-WindowsImage`

    G. `Optimize-WindowsImage`

36. You are the administrator for your company network. You have a Windows Server 2016 server named Server1. You plan to use Windows Server Backup to back up all of the data on Server1. You create a new volume on Server1. You need to ensure that the new volume can be used as a backup target. The backup target must support incremental backups. Which of the following could you do? (Choose three.)

   A. Mount the volume to C:\Backup and format the volume by using NTFS.

   B. Mount the volume to C:\Backup and format the volume by using ReFS.

   C. Mount the volume to C:\Backup and format the volume by using FAT32.

   D. Mount the volume to C:\Backup and format the volume by using exFAT.

37. You are the administrator for your company network. You have Hyper-V virtual machines that run 50 web servers, 10 Microsoft SQL Server servers, 10 file servers, and 8 domain controllers. You need to implement a backup strategy that meets the following requirements:

   - Backs up all servers
   - Centralizes application-level backups
   - Performs application-level backups
   - Provides the ability to perform bare metal recovery

   What should you use?

   A. Microsoft Azure VM Backup

   B. Microsoft Azure Backup Agent

   C. Windows Server Backup

   D. Microsoft Azure Backup Server

38. You are the administrator for your company network. Your company has two main offices. One of the offices is located in Boston and the other in New York. All servers at both locations run Windows Server 2016. In the New York office, there is a Distributed File System (DFS) server named DFS1. DFS1 has a folder named Folder1 that contains large Windows image files. In the Boston office, you deploy a DFS server named DFS2, and you then replicate Folder1 to DFS2. After several days, you find out that the replication of certain files failed to complete. What should you do if you need to ensure that all of the files in Folder1 can replicate to DFS2?

   A. On the drive that contains Folder1, modify the disk quota.

   B. Run dfsutil /purgemupcache from a command prompt.

   C. Using File Server Resource Manager (FSRM), create a quota for Folder1.

   D. On Folder1, modify the size of the staging area.

39. You are the administrator for your company network. Your company has two main offices. One of the offices is located in Boston and the other in New York. All servers at both locations run Windows Server 2016. In the New York office, there is a Distributed File System (DFS) server named DFS1. DFS1 has a folder named Folder1 that contains large Windows image files. In the Boston office, you deploy a DFS server named DFS2, and you then replicate Folder1 to DFS2. Users in both offices frequently add files to Folder1. You monitor DFS Replication and discover excessive replication over the WAN link during business hours. You want to reduce the amount of bandwidth used for replication during business hours. What should you do to ensure that the users can continue to save content to Folder1?

  A. On DFS2, modify the quota settings for Folder1.

  B. Modify the properties of the replication group.

  C. On DFS2, configure the copy of Folder1 as read-only.

  D. On DFS1, modify the replicated folder properties of Folder1.

40. You are the administrator for your company network. You are looking to use the Windows Server Migration Tools. Where must this feature be installed?

  A. On the source computer only

  B. On the destination computer only

  C. On both the source and destination computers

  D. On the main administrative server

41. You deploy a Hyper-V server named Server1 in an isolated test environment. The test environment cannot access the Internet. Server1 runs Windows Server 2016 Datacenter edition. You plan to deploy the following guest virtual machines on the server.

Quantity	Operating System	Domain Member
10	Windows Server 2012 R2	Yes
4	Windows Server 2016	No
5	Windows Server 2016	Yes

For the virtual machines, which activation model should you use?

  A. Multiple Activation Key (MAK)

  B. Automatic Virtual Machine Activation (AVMA)

  C. Original Equipment Manufacturer (OEM) key

  D. Key Management Service (KMS)

42. You are the administrator for your company network. You want to install a role that allows you to build PKI and provide public key cryptography. What role do you install?

  A. Active Directory Certificate Services (AD CS)

  B. Active Directory Domain Services (AD DS)

  C. Active Directory Federation Services (AD FS)

  D. Active Directory Rights Management Services (AD RMS)

43. You are the administrator for your company network. You want to install a role that provides Internet-based clients with a secure identity access solution that works on both Windows and non-Windows operating systems. What role do you install?

    A. Active Directory Certificate Services (AD CS)

    B. Active Directory Domain Services (AD DS)

    C. Active Directory Federation Services (AD FS)

    D. Active Directory Rights Management Services (AD RMS)

44. You are the administrator for your company network. Your company purchases a laptop for an employee who travels frequently. The company wants to use BitLocker to secure the hard drive in case it is lost or stolen. While attempting to enable BitLocker, you receive an error message that states, "This device can't use a Trusted Platform Module. Your administrator must set the Allow BitLocker Without a Compatible TPM option in the Require Additional Authentication at Startup policy for OS volumes." Which of the following statements is true?

    A. A nonsupported configuration for BitLocker is possible on this laptop.

    B. A supported configuration for BitLocker is possible on this laptop.

    C. A supported configuration for BitLocker is not possible on this laptop.

    D. A nonsupported configuration for BitLocker is not possible on this laptop.

45. You are the administrator for your company network. You are planning on installing the Windows Server Migration Tools using PowerShell on a Server Core installation of a Windows Server 2016. What command should you use to install the Windows Server Migration Tools?

    A. `New-MigrationTarget`

    B. `Install-WindowsFeature`

    C. `Grant-MigrationAccess`

    D. `New-MigrationFolder`

46. You are the administrator for your company network. You are planning on setting up NIC Teaming and you'd like to also set up fault protection. What is the minimum number of Ethernet adapters you must have?

    A. One

    B. Two

    C. Three

    D. Four

47. You are the administrator for your company network. Windows Server 2016 Nano Server is a lot like Server Core, but the advantage is that it is an even smaller installation of the operating system. Nano Server has no local logon or GUI capabilities, and it will allow only ___-bit applications and utilities.

    A. 16

    B. 32

    C. 64

    D. 128

48. You are the administrator for your company network and you are planning on installing Nano Server. Nano Server is available for which two editions of Windows Server 2016? (Choose two.)

　　A. Windows Server 2016 Datacenter

　　B. Windows Server 2016 Essentials

　　C. Windows Server 2016 Standard

　　D. Windows Server 2016 Web Server Core

49. You are the administrator for your company network. You are trying to decide if installing a Nano Server will work for your organization. There are some disadvantages of using Nano Server. Which of the following are some disadvantages? (Choose all that apply.)

　　A. It cannot act as a domain controller.

　　B. Group Policy Objects (GPOs) are not supported.

　　C. It cannot be configured to use System Center Configuration Manager.

　　D. It cannot be used as a proxy server.

　　E. All of the above.

50. You are the administrator for your company network. Your network contains a single Active Directory domain that has a Key Management Service (KMS) host. You deploy Windows Server 2016 to several laptops. You need to ensure that Windows Server 2016 is activated on the laptops immediately. Which command should you run?

　　A. ospp.vbs/act

　　B. slmgr.vbs/dli

　　C. slmgr.vbs/ato

　　D. ospp.vbs/dstatus

51. You are the administrator for your company network. You are planning on using Windows Deployment Services (WDS) to install a Windows operating system without using an installation disk. What is the first step you need to do when preparing the WDS server?

　　A. Configure and start WDS.

　　B. Install WDS.

　　C. Configure the WDS server to respond to client computers.

　　D. Make sure that the server meets the requirements of running WDS.

52. You are the administrator for your company network. You are planning on using Windows Deployment Services (WDS) to install a Windows operating system without using an installation disk. There are some requirements for using WDS. One of the requirements states that at least one of the partitions must be formatted as what type of file system?

　　A. FAT

　　B. NTFS

　　C. FAT32

　　D. ReFS

53. You are the administrator for your company network. You are planning on creating a Nano Server virtual hard disk (VHD). What is one of the easiest ways to create a Nano Server VHD?

  A. Open the folder `NanoServer` found on the physical media.

  B. Use Nano Server Image Builder.

  C. Use Windows PowerShell to install Nano Server.

  D. Choose Basic Installation as the deployment type.

54. You are the administrator for your company network. You have a Key Management Service (KMS) host and an administrative workstation named Computer1. From Computer1, you need to validate the activation status on a computer named Computer2. What should you run?

  A. `Get-RDLicenseConfiguration Computer2`

  B. `slmgr.vbs computer2 /dlv`

  C. `winrs.exe -r:Computer2 netdom.exe`

  D. `ospp.vbs /tokact:computer2`

55. You are the administrator for your company network. You need to create a script to verify the activation status on 100 computers. What should you use in the script?

  A. The `slmgr.vbs` script and the `/dli` parameter

  B. The `sfc.exe` command and the `/scannow` parameter

  C. The `slmgr.vbs` script and the `/ipk` parameter

  D. The `sfc.exe` command and the `/verifyonly` parameter

56. You are the administrator for your company network. You need to run `slmgr.vbs` remotely. What else must you include in the script in order for it to run properly? (Choose all that apply.)

  A. The computer name of the target computer

  B. The username of the account that has local administrator rights on the target computer

  C. The password for the account that has local administrator rights on the target computer

  D. The username of the account that has local administrator rights on the source computer

57. You are the administrator for your company network. What tool can you use to activate computers through the domain connection?

  A. Automatic Virtual Machine Activation (AVMA)

  B. Active Directory-Based Activation (ADBA)

  C. Key Management Service (KMS)

  D. Entering Licensing Keys

58. You are the administrator for your company network. You are installing Windows Server 2016 Nano Server. What type of servicing is currently the only option available for Nano Server?

    A. Long-Term Servicing Branch (LTSB)

    B. 5+5 servicing

    C. Current Branch for Business (CBB)

    D. Lifecycle Servicing Branch (LSB)

59. You are the administrator for your company network. Your company needs to install a version of Windows Server 2016 that uses the Current Branch for Business servicing model. What version would you install?

    A. Windows Server 2016 Nano Server

    B. Windows Server 2016 Standard

    C. Windows Server 2016 Essentials

    D. Windows Server 2016 Datacenter

60. You are the administrator for your company network, and you are planning on using the WSDUTIL command-line utility to configure your Windows Deployment Services (WDS) server. What switch would you use if you wanted to initialize the configuration of the WDS server?

    A. /enable

    B. /copy-image

    C. /uninitialized-server

    D. /initialize-server

61. You are the administrator for your company network. You are planning on using Windows Deployment Services (WDS). What is one component that you must pay attention to when using WDS?

    A. The boot firmware

    B. The Preboot Execution Environment (PXE) network devices

    C. How you create the image using the imgcrt tool

    D. The type of computer data storage

62. You are the administrator for your company network. You are planning on using Windows Deployment Services (WDS). What network services must be running on the WDS server or be accessible to the WDS server from another network server? (Choose all that apply.)

    A. TCP/IP installed and configured

    B. A DHCP server

    C. A DNS server

    D. Active Directory

63. You are the administrator for your company network. You are looking to install Windows Server 2016, and you need to decide which version to install. You need to install a version of Windows that is just for logon authentication and nothing else. You are looking for the most secure option, and cost is not an issue. Which version should you install?

A. Windows Server 2016 Datacenter (Desktop Experience)

B. Windows Server 2016 Datacenter Server Core

C. Windows Server 2016 Standard (Desktop Experience)

D. Windows Server 2016 Web Server

64. You are the administrator for your company network. You have been hired to help a small organization set up their first Windows network. They have had the same small number of employees during the short time they have been open. They currently have no plans for expansion. What version of Windows Server 2016 should you recommend?

A. Windows Server 2016 Datacenter (Desktop Experience)

B. Windows Server 2016 Standard (Desktop Experience)

C. Windows Server 2016 Datacenter

D. Windows Server 2016 Essentials

65. You are the administrator for your company network. Microsoft Windows Server 2016 offers two types of containers. One of the container types provides application isolation through process and namespace isolation technology. This container shares a kernel with the container host and all containers running on the host. What container type is being described?

A. Hyper-V Container

B. Windows Server Container

C. Windows Full Container

D. Windows Limited Container

66. You are the administrator for your company network. You are looking at the Hyper-V role for Windows Server 2016. What does the Hyper-V role allow?

A. Network Load Balancing

B. The creation of Virtual Private Networks (VPNs)

C. Server virtualization

D. Updating Windows Server 2016

67. You are the administrator for your company network. You are looking at roles and features to implement for Windows Server 2016. What is described here provides the point of automation needed for continual configuration, monitoring, and diagnostics of virtual networks, physical networks, network services, network topology, address management, and so on within a datacenter.

A. Host Guardian Service

B. Network Policy and Access Services

C. MultiPoint Services

D. Network Controller

68. You are the network administrator for your company network. You have a reference computer that runs Windows Server 2016. You need to create and deploy an image of the Windows Server 2016 computer. You create an answer file and name it answer.xml. You need to make sure that the installation applies the answer file after you deploy the image. Which command should you run before you capture the image?

A. ICD.exe /append answer.xml/check

B. ICD.exe /mount answer.xml/verify

C. Sysprep.exe/reboot/audit/unattend: answer.xml

D. Sysprep.exe/generalize/oobe/unattend: answer.xml

69. You are the administrator for your company network. You have a Windows Server 2016 Windows Image (WIM) that is mounted. What should you do if you need to display information about the image?

A. Run DISM and specify the /get-ImageInfo parameter.

B. Run Driverquery.exe and use the /si parameter.

C. From Device Manager, view all hidden drivers.

D. From File Explorer, open the mount folder.

70. You are a network administrator for your company network. You need to deploy Windows Server 2016 to multiple computers. You want to automate the installation so that no user interaction is required during the installation process. Which of the following utilities could you use?

A. Image Capture Wizard

B. System Preparation Tool

C. WDSUTIL

D. Windows SIM

71. You are the administrator for your company network. You need to start a new installation of Windows Server 2016 using the command-line utility. You plan to accomplish this by using the Setup.exe command-line setup utility, and you will be using an answer file with this command. What command-line option should you use?

A. /unattend

B. /apply

C. /noreboot

D. /generalize

72. You are the administrator for your company network. You are using Sysprep.exe to prepare a system for imaging. What Sysprep option should you use if you want to restart the computer?

A. /generalize

B. /start

C. /restart

D. /reboot

73. You are the administrator for your company network. You are using `Sysprep.exe` to prepare a system for imaging. What Sysprep option should you use if you want to enable end users to customize their Windows operating systems, create user accounts, name their computers, and other tasks?

    A. `/generalize`

    B. `/oobe`

    C. `/audit`

    D. `/unattend`

74. You are the administrator for your company network. You are looking to start an unattended installation of Windows Server 2016. What command can be used to initiate the unattended installation?

    A. `setup.exe /answerfile:unattend`

    B. `answerfile:unattend setup.exe`

    C. `unattend: answerfile setup.exe`

    D. `setup.exe /unattend:answerfile`

75. You are the administrator for your company network. You run a classroom that needs the same software installed from scratch on the classroom computers each week. You decide to use Image Capture Wizard to deploy disk images. What Windows Server 2016 utility can you use along with Image Capture Wizard to create these disk images?

    A. UAF

    B. System Preparation Tool

    C. Answer Manager

    D. Setup Manager

76. You are the administrator for your company network. You are trying to decide whether you'd like to use WDS as a method of installing Windows Server 2016. Which of the following options is not an advantage to using a WDS automated installation?

    A. Security is retained when you restart the computer.

    B. The installation media does not need to be deployed to each computer.

    C. Unique information is stripped out of the installation image so that it can be copied to other computers.

    D. You can quickly recover the operating system in the event of a system failure.

77. You are the administrator for your company network. You are planning on deploying a new Windows Server 2016 image to a large number of client computers that are all similarly configured. You plan on using the Windows SIM tool to create an answer file that will be used to automate the installation. You want each computer to contain two partitions, one for the system partition and one as a data partition. What component of the answer file do you need to modify to support this configuration?

    A. Windows PE

    B. oobeSystem

    C. auditSystem

    D. specialize

78. You are the administrator for your company network. You need to install a group of 25 computers by using disk images created in conjunction with the System Preparation Tool. You want to create an image from a reference computer first and then copy the image to the rest of the computers. What `Sysprep.exe` command-line option should you use if you do not want to create a SID on the destination computer when you use the image?

   A. `/specialize`

   B. `/generalize`

   C. `/oobe`

   D. `/quiet`

79. You are the administrator for your company network. You and a colleague are discussing the Microsoft Assessment and Planning (MAP) Toolkit. MAP is a utility that will locate computers on a network and then perform a thorough inventory of these computers. MAP uses which of the following utilities to obtain this inventory? (Choose all that apply.)

   A. Windows Management Instrumentation (WMI)

   B. Remote Registry Service

   C. Active Directory Domain Services (AD DS)

   D. Simple Network Management Protocol (SNMP)

80. You are the administrator for your company network. When the Microsoft Assessment and Planning (MAP) Toolkit generates a report, what file format will the report be generated in? (Choose all that apply.)

   A. A Microsoft Word document

   B. A Microsoft Excel document

   C. A Microsoft OneNote document

   D. A Microsoft PowerPoint document

81. You are the administrator for your company network. You are planning on using the Sysprep utility to create images. Where can you find the `Sysprep.exe` file?

   A. `\Windows\Setup\Sysprep`

   B. `\Windows\Boot\Sysprep`

   C. `\Windows\System\Sysprep`

   D. `\Windows\System32\Sysprep`

82. You are the administrator for your company network and you have a computer named Computer1 that has a virtual hard disk (VHD) named `Disk1.vhdx`. You are going to configure Computer1 for dual boot using `Disk1.vhdx`. You need to install Windows Server 2016 on `Disk1.vhdx` by using `dism.exe`. What should you run before you install Windows Server 2016?

   A. `Add-Windows Image`

   B. `bcdboot.exe`

   C. `bcdedit.exe`

   D. `bootcfg.exe`

E. bootim.exe

F. bootsect.exe

G. diskpart.exe

H. Expand-Windows Image

83. You are the administrator for your company network. You are using the Deployment Image Servicing and Management (DISM) tool to manipulate an image. What DISM option should you use if you want to display information about images?

A. /Capture-Image

B. /List-Image

C. /Get-ImageInfo

D. /Apply-Image

84. You are the administrator for your company network. You are planning on performing an unattended installation for a large number of computers. What are some of the advantages of using an unattended installation? (Choose all that apply.)

A. It saves time and money.

B. It can be configured to provide automated responses.

C. It can be used to install clean copies or upgrade existing operating systems.

D. It can be expanded to include installation instructions.

E. The physical media does not need to be distributed to all the computers.

F. All of the above.

85. You are the administrator for your company network. You are planning on using Sysprep to set up images. You remember that the Windows activation clock starts to decrease as soon as Windows starts for the first time, but you can restart the clock. How many times are you allowed to restart the activation clock using Sysprep?

A. One

B. Two

C. Three

D. Four

E.   bootim.exe

F.   bootsec.exe

G.   dcapart.exe

H.   Custom Windows Image

63.   You are the administrator for your company's network. You are named the Deployment Administrator and Maintenance (DSM) tool to manage your images. What DSM option should you use with to display information in an image?

A.   Capture-Image

B.   Wim-Image

C.   Start-ImageInfo

D.   Apply-Image

64.   You are the administrator for your company's network. You are planning on changing an image that is installed on one type of hardware computer. What are some of the advantages of using an unattended installation? Choose all that apply.

A.   It saves time and money.

B.   It can be configured to provide an automatic response.

C.   It can be used to install of a separate application system on the system.

D.   It can be applied to individual and identical computers.

E.   Deployment can be done automatically to install all the computers.

F.   All of the above.

65.   You are the administrator for your company's network. You are planning on installing Sysprep on a computer. You run it. After that, the Windows 10 computer will start to the user interface in Windows automatically. But, upon an error on the clock. How can ensure that you should not reset the automatical clocking system.

A.   One

B.   Two

C.   Three

D.   Four

Chapter

2

Implement Storage Solutions

THE FOLLOWING MCSA WINDOWS SERVER 2016 EXAM TOPICS ARE COVERED IN THIS CHAPTER:

✓ **2.1 Implement server storage**

- This objective may include but is not limited to: Configure storage pools; implement simple, mirror, and parity storage layout options for disks or enclosures; expand storage pools; configure Tiered Storage; configure iSCSI target and initiator; configure iSNS; configure Data Center Bridging (DCB); configure Multipath I/O (MPIO); determine usage scenarios for Storage Replica: implement Storage Replica for server-to-server, cluster-to-cluster, and stretch cluster scenarios

✓ **2.2 Implement Data Deduplication**

- This objective may include but is not limited to: Implement and configure Deduplication; determine appropriate usage scenarios for Deduplication; monitor Deduplication: implement a backup and restore solution with Deduplication

1. You are the administrator for your company network. You have a Windows Server 2016 server named Server1. The server contains a storage pool named Pool1. Pool1 contains five physical disks named Disk1, Disk2, Disk3, Disk4, and Disk5. A virtual disk named VD1 is stored in Pool1. VD1 uses the parity storage layout. Which two commands should you run if you need to remove Disk3 after it fails from Pool1? (Choose two.)

    A. `Remove-PhysicalDisk-FriendlyName Disk3`

    B. `Update-StoragePool-FriendlyName Pool1`

    C. `Reset-PhysicalDisk-FriendlyName Disk3`

    D. `Set-PhysicalDisk-FriendlyName Disk3-Usage Retired`

    E. `Set-ResiliencySetting-StoragePool Pool1-PhysicalDiskRedundancyDefault 4`

2. You are the administrator for your company network. You have been asked to configure the company's Windows Server 2016 domain controller. Company policy requires that all new computer accounts be placed in the General OU whenever computers join the domain. What command should you use to accomplish this?

    A. Dsmove

    B. Netdom

    C. Redircmp

    D. None of these

3. You are the administrator for your company network. You have two Windows Server 2016 servers named Server1 and Server2. Server1 contains a volume named Volume1. You decide to implement a Storage Replica that replicates the contents of Volume1 from Server1 and Server2. One day, Server1 fails. You need to ensure that you can access the contents of Volume1. What command/cmdlet should you run from Server2?

    A. `Set-SRPartnership`

    B. `Update-StoragePool`

    C. `vssadmin revert shadow`

    D. `Clear-FileStorageTier`

4. You are the administrator for your company network. You and a colleague are discussing Windows Server 2016 platforms. The Windows Server 2016 platform can support two main filesystems. What are they? (Choose two.)

    A. File Allocation Table (FAT)

    B. File Allocation Table 32 (FAT32)

    C. Windows NT File System (NTFS)

    D. Resilient File System (ReFS)

5. You are the administrator for your company network. You have a Windows Server 2016 server named Server1. Server1 has four SCSI disks and a storage pool named Pool1 that contains three disks. You create a virtual disk named VDisk1 that uses a mirrored layout.

You create a partition named Partition1 that uses all of the available space on VDisk1. You want to extend Partition1. What should you do first?

A. Run the `Expand-IscsiVirtualDisk` cmdlet from Windows PowerShell.

B. Run the `Resize-VirtualDisk` cmdlet from Windows PowerShell.

C. Extend the volume from Disk Management.

D. Modify the properties of Partition1 from Disk Management.

6. You are the administrator for your company network. You have two Windows Server 2016 servers named Server1 and Server2. You plan to implement Storage Replica to replicate the contents of volumes on Server1 to Server2. What cmdlet should you run if you need to ensure that the replication traffic between the servers is limited to a maximum of 100 Mbps?

A. `Set-NetUDPSetting`

B. `New-StorageQosPolicy`

C. `Set-SmbBandwidthLimit`

D. `Set-NetTCPSetting`

7. You are the administrator for your company network. You have a server and you want to provision a new volume that will be used to create large, fixed-size VHDX files. You want to minimize the amount of time required to create the VHDX files. What type of filesystem should you use on the new volume?

A. ReFS

B. NTFS

C. CVFS

D. exFAT

8. You are the administrator for your company network. The network contains an Active Directory domain. The domain contains a new file server named Server1 that runs a Server Core installation of Windows Server 2016. Server1 has an ReFS-formatted volume D: and NTFS-formatted volume E:. The volumes do not contain any data. You install the Data Deduplication role service on Server1. You want to implement Data Deduplication for volumes on D: and E:. What should you do?

A. From Windows PowerShell, run `Format-Volume D: -FileSystem EXFat` and `Enable-DeDupVolume -Volume D:,E:`

B. From Windows PowerShell, run `Format-Volume E: -FileSystem ReFS` and `Enable-DeDupVolume -Volume D:,E:`

C. From Windows PowerShell, run `Enable-DeDupVolume-Volume D:,E:`

D. From Windows PowerShell, run `Enable-DeDupVolume-Volume E: D:`

9. You are the administrator for your company network. You are planning to install Active Directory. What filesystem must you use in order to install Active Directory?

A. ReFS

B. exFAT

C. FAT

D. NTFS

10. You are the administrator for your company network. The network contains an Active Directory domain. The domain contains two servers named Server1 and Server2. Both servers have the same hardware configuration. What should you do if you need to asynchronously replicate volume F: from Server1 to Server2?

A. Run `New-SRPartnership` and specify the `-ReplicationMode` parameter.

B. Install the Failover Clustering feature and create a new cluster resource group.

C. Install the Failover Clustering feature and use Cluster Shared Volumes (CSV).

D. Run `Set-DfsrServiceConfiguration` and specify the `-RPCPort` parameter.

11. You are the administrator for your company network. You and a colleague are discussing the Master Boot Record (MBR). On the disk drive, a MBR has a partition table that indicates where the partitions are located. How big are volumes that are supported by a MBR?

A. 1 TB (1,024 GB)

B. 2 TB (2,048 GB)

C. 3 TB (3,072 GB)

D. 4 TB (4,096 GB)

12. You are the administrator for your company network and you have a Windows Server 2016 server. You install three additional physical disks named Disk1, Disk2, and Disk3. You want to use these physical disks to store data. You plan to create a volume to store data. What actions should you perform if you need to prevent data loss in the event of a single disk failure? (Choose three.)

A. Create a virtual disk.

B. Create a storage pool.

C. Create a new storage tier.

D. Create a volume.

E. Assign a single tier to a virtual disk.

F. Create a virtual disk clone.

13. You are the administrator for your company network. You have client computers that run Windows Server 2016. Each computer has two hard drives. Which kind of dynamic volume should you create if you need to create a dynamic volume on each computer that will maximize write performance and provide data fault tolerance?

A. Striped volume

B. RAID-5 volume

C. Spanned volume

D. Mirrored volume

14. You are the administrator for your company network. You have a Windows Server 2016 server named Server1. The disks on Server1 are configured as shown in the following table:

Volume	Type	Filesystem	Capability
C:	Attached Locally	NTFS	150 GB
D:	Attached Locally	exFAT	100 GB
E:	Attached Locally	NTFS	20 GB
F:	Attached Locally	ReFS	1 TB
G:	iSCSI LUN	NTFS	2 TB

Windows Server 2016 is installed in `C:\Windows`. You want to enable data deduplication. Which two volumes can you use for data deduplication? (Choose two.)

A. C:

B. D:

C. E:

D. F:

E. G:

15. You are the administrator for your company network. You and a colleague are discussing using the `convert` command. What does the command `convert d: /fs:ntfs` do?

A. Formats drive D to FAT.

B. Converts drive D from NTFS to FAT.

C. Converts drive D from FAT to NTFS.

D. Scans drive D for errors.

16. You are the administrator for your company network. You want to remove the host from the iSNS server. What command should you use?

A. `iscsicli addisnsserver <`*server_name*`>`

B. `iscsicli removeisnsserver <`*server_name*`>`

C. `iscsicli refreshisnsserver <`*server_name*`>`

D. `iscsicli listisnsservers <`*server_name*`>`

17. You are the administrator for your company network. You want to register the iSCSI initiator manually to an iSNS server. What command should you use?

A. `iscsicli addisnsserver <`*server_name*`>`

B. `iscsicli removeisnsserver <`*server_name*`>`

C. `iscsicli refreshisnsserver <`*server_name*`>`

D. `iscsicli listisnsservers <`*server_name*`>`

18. You are the administrator for your company network. You are looking at using shared folder permissions. Which of the following are true regarding shared folder permissions? (Choose all that apply.)

   A. Apply to files

   B. Apply to folders

   C. Apply locally to the data

   D. Apply remotely to the data

19. You are the administrator for your company network. You are trying to determine what the default TCP port for iSCSI is. Which one is it?

   A. 21

   B. 1433

   C. 3260

   D. 3389

20. You are the administrator for your company network. Matt is a member of both the Human Resources and Marketing departments. There is a shared folder called Apps that everyone uses. Here are the current permissions on the Apps shared folder:

Group/User	NTFS	Shared
Sales	Read	Deny
Marketing	Modify	Full Control
R&D	Read	Read
HR	Full Control	Deny
Admin	Full Control	Change

What will Matt's local and remote permissions be when he logs into the Apps folder?

   A. Local = Full Control and Remote = Deny

   B. Local = Deny and Remote = Deny

   C. Local = Full Control and Remote = Change

   D. Local = Change and Remote = Read

21. You are the administrator for your company network. You have a Windows Server 2016 computer that has a shared folder named C:\Sales. The shared folder is on an NTFS volume. The current NTFS and share permissions are configured as follows: User1 is a member of both the Everyone group and the Sales group. User1 must access C:\Sales from across the network. What permission should you set if you need to identify the effective permissions of User1 to the C:\Sales folder?

   A. Full Control

   B. Read and Execute

   C. Read

   D. Modify

22. You are the administrator for your company network. You have a computer named Server1 that runs Windows Server 2016. You add a 1 TB hard drive and create a new volume that has the drive letter D. You format the drive by using NTFS. You need to limit the amount of space that each user can consume on D: to 200 GB. Members of the Administrators group should have no limit. What actions should you perform? (Choose three.)

A. Set a default quota limit.

B. Run `convert D: /FS:NTFS`.

C. Run `fsutil quota violations D:`.

D. Enable the Deny disk space to users exceeding quota limit setting.

E. Add a quota entry.

23. You are the administrator for your company network. You have a computer that runs Windows Server 2016. You add three new 3 TB disks and you want to create a new 9 TB volume. What two actions should you perform? (Choose two.)

A. Create a new spanned volume using Disk Management.

B. Convert all of the 3 TB disks to GPT using Disk Management.

C. Run the `New-VirtualDisk` cmdlet using PowerShell.

D. Bring all the disks offline using Disk Management.

E. Run the `convert MBR` command using Diskpart.

F. Run the `Add-PhysicalDisk` cmdlet using PowerShell.

24. You are the administrator for your company network. Your network contains a single Active Directory domain. The domain contains two computers named Server1 and Server2. A user named User1 is a member of the local Administrators group on Server1 and Server2. User1 fails to remotely manage the devices on Server2 by using Device Manager on Server1. User1 can connect to Server2 remotely by using Computer Management. What do you need to do to ensure that User1 can disable a device on Server2 remotely?

A. On Server2, modify the Windows Firewall settings.

B. Enable Remote Desktop on Server2 and instruct User1 to use Remote Desktop.

C. On Server2, start the Plug and Play and Remote Registry services.

D. On Server2, enable the Allow remote access to the Plug and Play interface Group Policy setting.

25. You are the administrator for your company network. You have a computer that runs Windows Server 2016. You install a second hard disk drive on the computer and create a new volume named E. What tool can you use to set up the new hard drive and volume?

A. The `wbadmin` command

B. The Settings app

C. Computer Management

D. The `Set-Volume` cmdlet

26. You are the administrator for your company network. You have a computer named Computer1 that has a 1 TB volume named E. What tool should you use if you want to receive a notification when volume F has less than 100 GB of free space?

    A. Performance Monitor

    B. Disk Cleanup

    C. System Configuration

    D. Resource Monitor

    E. Event Viewer

27. You are the administrator for your company network. You have a computer named Computer1 that runs Windows Server 2016. Computer1 has two volumes named C and D. Volume C is formatted NTFS and volume D is formatted exFAT. What should you use if you need to ensure that you can recover files stored in D:\Data?

    A. System Restore points

    B. File History

    C. wbadmin.exe

    D. Backup and Restore

28. You are the administrator for your company network. You have two computers named Computer1 and Computer2 that run Windows Server 2016. You create a provisioning package named Package1 on Computer1. What file must be applied to Computer2 if you plan to apply the provisioning package to Computer2?

    A. Package1.icdproj.xml

    B. Customizations.xml

    C. Package1.ppkg

    D. Package1.cat

29. You are the administrator for your company network. You have a computer named Computer1 that has a virtual hard disk (VHD) named Disk1.vhdx. You plan to configure Computer1 for dual boot from Disk1.vhdx. You need to install Windows on Disk1.vhdx by using dism.exe. What should you run before you install Windows Server 2016?

    A. Add-Windows Image

    B. bcdboot.exe

    C. bcdedit.exe

    D. bootcfg.exe

    E. bootim.exe

    F. bootsect.exe

    G. diskpart.exe

    H. Expand-Windows Image

30. You are the administrator for your company network. You have a computer named Computer1. Computer1 has a virtual hard disk (VHD) named `Disk1.vhdx`. Windows is installed on `Disk1.vhdx`. In File Explorer, `Disk1.vhdx` is visible as drive E. You need to configure Computer1 to start from VHDX. Hardware virtualization must not be available when Computer1 starts from VHDX. What should you run?

  A. `Add-Windows Image`

  B. `bcdboot.exe`

  C. `bcdedit.exe`

  D. `bootcfg.exe`

  E. `bootim.exe`

  F. `bootsect.exe`

  G. `diskpart.exe`

  H. `Expand-Windows Image`

31. You are the administrator for your company network. You have a computer that runs Windows Server 2012 R2. You create a system image backup on the computer and then you upgrade to Windows Server 2016. You need to access a file from the backup. The solution must use the least amount of administrative effort. What should you do?

  A. Add a drive from the Backup section of the Settings app.

  B. Add a drive from the File History section of the Settings app.

  C. Attach a VHD from the Computer Management console.

  D. Restore the personal files from the File History Control Panel item.

32. You are the administrator for your company network. You are looking at the NTFS filesystem. What are some of the advantages to using NTFS?

  A. Compression

  B. Encryption

  C. Quotas

  D. Security

  E. All of the above

33. You are the administrator for your company network. You want to turn your FAT32 partition into an NTFS partition. What command-line utility should you use?

  A. `upgrade`

  B. `convert`

  C. `change part`

  D. `Ntfsutil`

34. You are the administrator for your company network. You have a virtual machine named VM1. VM1 uses a fixed size virtual hard disk (VHD) named `Disk1.vhd`. `Disk1.vhd` is 200 GB. You shut down VM1. What action should you use from the Edit Virtual Hard Disk Wizard if you need to reduce the size of `Disk1.vhd`?

    A. Merge

    B. Compact

    C. Shrink

    D. Convert

35. You are the administrator for your company network. You create a new virtual disk in a storage pool by using the New Virtual Disk Wizard. You discover that the new virtual disk has a write-back cache of 1 GB. What should you do if you need to ensure that the virtual disk has a write-back cache of 5 GB?

    A. Detach the virtual disk and then run the `Resize-VirtualDisk` cmdlet.

    B. Detach the virtual disk and then run the `Set-VirtualDisk` cmdlet.

    C. Delete the virtual disk and then run the `New-StorageSubSystemVirtualDisk` cmdlet.

    D. Delete the virtual disk and then run the `New-VirtualDisk` cmdlet.

36. You are the administrator for your company network. You decide to purchase a new desktop computer that has four external USB hard drives. You want to create a single volume by using the four USB drives. You want the volume to be expandable, portable, and resilient in the event of failure of an individual USB hard drive. What should you do so you can create the required volume?

    A. Create a new Storage Space across the four USB hard drives. Set the resiliency type to a three-way mirror.

    B. Create a new spanned volume.

    C. Create a new Storage Space across the four USB hard drives. Set the resiliency type to parity.

    D. Create a new striped volume.

37. You are the administrator of your company network. The network contains three servers named ServerA, ServerB, and ServerC. All servers run Windows Server 2016. What should you do on ServerA so that it can provide iSCSI storage for the other two servers?

    A. Start the Microsoft iSCSI Initiator Service and configure the iSCSI Initiator Properties.

    B. Install the iSNS Server service feature and create a discovery domain.

    C. Install the Multipath I/O (MPIO) feature and configure the MPIO Properties.

    D. Install the iSCSI Target Server role service and configure iSCSI targets.

38. You are the administrator for your company network. You are trying to determine the default TCP port for RDP. Which one is it?

    A. 21

    B. 1433

    C. 3260

    D. 3389

39. You are the administrator for your company network. Lisa is a member of both the Sales and R&D departments. There is a shared folder called Apps that everyone uses. Here are the current permissions on the Apps shared folder:

Group/User	NTFS	Shared
Sales	Read	Deny
Marketing	Modify	Full Control
R&D	Read	Read
HR	Full Control	Deny
Admin	Full Control	Change

What will Lisa's local and remote permissions be when she logs into the Apps folder?

A. Local = Read and Remote = Read

B. Local = Read and Remote = Deny

C. Local = Deny and Remote = Read

D. Local = Deny and Remote = Deny

40. You are the administrator for your company network. You are debating the benefits of the various filesystems available. Which filesystem was designed specifically with the issues of scalability and performance in mind?

A. FAT

B. exFAT

C. NTFS

D. ReFS

41. You are the administrator for your company network. You are debating the benefits of the NTFS filesystem. You are thinking about establishing disk quotas. By default, Windows Server 2016 supports disk quota restrictions. At which level is the default?

A. Folder level

B. Drive level

C. Volume level

D. Partition level

42. You are the administrator for your company network. You are discussing the benefits of using the NTFS filesystem with a colleague. One of the benefits allows you to move infrequently used files to external hard drives. What benefit are you discussing?

A. Mounted drives

B. Self-healing NTFS

C. Dynamic volumes

D. Remote storage

43. You are the administrator for your company network. You are planning on installing Active Directory. You remember that the NTFS filesystem is required. But you also know that a mandatory number of partition(s) are needed to run Active Directory. How many partitions are required to run Active Directory?

　　A. One

　　B. Two

　　C. Three

　　D. Four

44. You are the administrator for your company network. You and a colleague are discussing disk configurations. Microsoft Windows Server 2016 supports two types of disk configurations. What are they? (Choose two.)

　　A. Basic

　　B. Primary

　　C. Dynamic

　　D. Effective

45. You are the administrator for your company network. Your network contains an Active Directory domain that contains two Windows Server 2016 servers named Server1 and Server2. Each server has an operating system disk and four data disks. All of the disks are locally attached SATA disks. Each disk is a basic disk, is initialized as a MBR disk, and has a single NTFS volume. You plan to implement Redundant Array of Independent Disks (RAID) by using the data disks on Server1 and Server2. What should you do if you need to prepare the data disks for the implementation?

　　A. Initialize the data disks as GPT disks and create a ReFS volume on each disk.

　　B. Format the volumes on the data disks as exFAT.

　　C. Delete the volumes from the data disks.

　　D. Convert the data disks to dynamic disks.

46. You are the network administrator for your company network. You are discussing managing volumes with a colleague. When talking about volume sets, you are discussing a volume set that is a simple volume that spans multiple disks. What type of volume are you discussing?

　　A. Simple volume

　　B. Spanned volume

　　C. Striped volume

　　D. Mirrored volume

　　E. RAID-5 volume

47. You are the network administrator for your company network. You are discussing managing volumes with a colleague. When talking about volume sets, you are discussing a volume set that duplicates data across two disks. What type of volume are you discussing?

   A. Simple volume

   B. Spanned volume

   C. Striped volume

   D. Mirrored volume

   E. RAID-5 volume

48. You are the network administrator for your company network. You are discussing managing volumes with a colleague. When talking about volume sets, you are discussing a volume set that stores data in stripes across three or more disks. What type of volume are you discussing?

   A. Simple volume

   B. Spanned volume

   C. Striped volume

   D. Mirrored volume

   E. RAID-5 volume

49. You are the network administrator for your company network. You are discussing Redundant Array of Independent Disks (RAID) with a colleague. Microsoft Windows Server 2016 supports three types of RAID. What are they? (Choose three.)

   A. RAID-0

   B. RAID-1

   C. RAID-2

   D. RAID-3

   E. RAID-4

   F. RAID-5

50. You are the network administrator for your company network. You are discussing Redundant Array of Independent Disks (RAID) with a colleague. Of the three types of RAID supported by Windows Server 2016, one is not fault tolerant. Which one is it?

   A. RAID-0

   B. RAID-1

   C. RAID-2

   D. RAID-3

   E. RAID-4

   F. RAID-5

59. You are the network administrator for your company network. You are using the Diskpart command-line utility. You want to use the switch that will allow you to reduce the physical size of the file. What switch command do you use?

A. Diskpart /assign

B. Diskpart /compact

C. Diskpart /convert

D. Diskpart /reduce

60. You are the administrator for your company network. You are planning on installing Data Center Bridging (DCB). DCB can be installed using Server Manager or using PowerShell. You have opted for using PowerShell. What command must you run to install DCB?

A. Install-WindowsFeature -name data-center-bridging

B. Install-WindowsFeature -name dcb

C. Install-WindowsFeature -name data center bridging

D. Install-WindowsFeature -name DCB

61. You are the administrator for your company network. You are working with Windows PowerShell and Server Message Block (SMB), which is a network-sharing protocol that allows Windows machines that are running applications to read and write data to files. What PowerShell command would you use if you wanted to retrieve the connections established from the SMB client to the SMB servers?

A. Get-SmbDelegation

B. Get-SmbServerConfiguration

C. Get-SmbSharedAccess

D. Get-SmbConnection

62. You are the administrator for your company network. You are working with Windows PowerShell and Server Message Block (SMB), which is a network-sharing protocol that allows Windows machines that are running applications to read and write data to files. What PowerShell command would you use if you wanted to modify the properties of the SMB share?

A. Set-SmbClientConfiguration

B. Set-SmbShare

C. Set-SmbServerConfiguration

D. Set-SmbShareAccess

63. You are the administrator for your company network. You and a colleague are discussing Server Message Block (SMB). SMB is a network-sharing protocol that allows Windows machines (either client- or server-based operating systems) that are running applications to read and write data to files. It also allows systems to request services or resources that are running on remote servers. What is one advantage to using SMB?

A. SMB allows for the use of any network protocol, running on top of the protocol being used.

B. SMB allows for the use of any network protocol, running underneath the protocol being used.

C. SMB does not allow for the use of any network protocol, running on top of the protocol being used.

D. SMB does not allow for the use of any network protocol, running underneath the protocol being used.

64. You are the administrator for your company network. An employee leaves unexpectedly and has encrypted files using EFS. There are two ways for you to unencrypt the files. What are two ways that an administrator can unencrypt the files? (Choose two.)

A. Log in using the user's account and unencrypt the files.

B. Become a recovery agent and manually unencrypt the files.

C. Become a restore agent and manually unencrypt the files.

D. Log in as the administrator and unencrypt the files.

65. You are the administrator for your company network. You have decided to take advantage of the security provided by the NTFS filesystem. The default security permissions for Users is _____ on new folders and shares. (Fill in the blank.)

A. Read

B. Write

C. Full Control

D. Change

66. You are the administrator for your company network. Matt is a member of both the Sales and R&D departments. There is a shared folder called Apps that everyone uses. Here are the current permissions on the Apps shared folder:

Group/User	NTFS	Shared
Sales	Full Control	Read
Marketing	Modify	Full Control
R&D	Modify	Change
HR	Full Control	Deny
IT	Full Control	Read

Matt is trying to make changes to a document in the Apps folder. He cannot make the changes necessary. What permission will need to change in order for him to make the necessary changes?

A. Sales folder shared permission needs to be changed to Change.

B. Sales folder shared permission needs to be changed to Modify.

C. R&D folder NTFS permission needs to be changed to Change.

D. Nothing. The Sales folder shared permission meets his requirements.

67. You are the administrator for your company network. Matt is a member of the Sales, R&D, and HR departments. There is a folder called Apps on the server. Here are the current permissions on the Apps folder:

Group/User	NTFS
Sales	Read
Marketing	Modify
R&D	Modify
HR	Full Control
IT	Full Control

What is Matt's effective NTFS permission?

A. Read

B. Modify

C. Full Control

D. Deny

68. You are the administrator for your company network. Lisa is a member of the Sales, R&D, and HR departments. There is a folder called Apps on the server. Here are the current permissions on the Apps folder:

Group/User	NTFS
Sales	Read
Marketing	Modify
R&D	Modify
HR	Deny
IT	Full Control

What is Lisa's effective NTFS permission?

A. Read

B. Modify

C. Full Control

D. Deny

69. You are the administrator for your company network. You have decided to take advantage of the security provided by shared permissions. The default shared permission for Administrators is _____ on new folders. (Fill in the blank).

   A. Read

   B. Write

   C. Full Control

   D. Change

70. You are the administrator for your company network. Company policy states that you must set up disk quotas to limit how much storage space a user can use on the hard drive. What filesystem must you use in order to take advantage of disk quotas?

   A. FAT

   B. FAT32

   C. NTFS

   D. exFAT

71. You are the administrator for your company network. You are discussing disk quotas with a colleague. You know that there are a few options available when setting up disk quotas. Which of the following types of quota is a predefined way to set up quotas?

   A. Quotas by volume

   B. Quotas by user

   C. Specifying quota entries

   D. Quota templates

72. You are the administrator for your company network. You are discussing storage options with a colleague. You are discussing a feature in Windows Server 2016 that gives administrators the ability to use both solid-state drives (SSDs) and conventional hard disk drives (HDDs) within the same storage pool. What type of storage is being discussed?

   A. Tiered storage

   B. Basic storage

   C. Storage spaces direct

   D. Local storage

73. You are the administrator for your company network. You are discussing the Boot Configuration Data (BCD) store with a colleague. What utility do you use to edit the boot options in the BCD store?

   A. bcdboot utility

   B. bcdedit utility

   C. bootcfg utility

   D. bootsect utility

74. You are the administrator for your company network. You and a colleague are discussing a way of finding and removing duplicate data within the company network without compromising the integrity. What should you use?

    A. Data chunking

    B. Data redundancy

    C. Data deduplication

    D. Data replication

75. You are the administrator for your company network. You are thinking of enabling data deduplication. Where do you enable deduplication?

    A. On files

    B. On folders

    C. On volumes

    D. On partitions

76. You are the administrator for your company network. You have enabled data deduplication. Once you have enabled deduplication, the volume will contain which of the following? (Choose all that apply.)

    A. Optimized files

    B. Unoptimized files

    C. Chunk store

    D. Free space

77. You are the network administrator for your company network. You have a computer that runs Windows Server 2016 and is used by 10 users. The computer is joined to an Active Directory domain. All of the users are members of the Administrators group. Each user has an Active Directory account. You have a Microsoft Word document that contains confidential information. What should you configure if you need to ensure that you are the only user who can open the document?

    A. Account policies

    B. NTFS permissions

    C. Share permissions

    D. Encrypting File System (EFS) settings

78. You are the administrator for your company network. You are trying to determine what the default TCP port for FTP is. Which one is it?

    A. 21

    B. 1433

    C. 3260

    D. 3389

79. You are the administrator for your company network. Matt is a member of both the R&D and Marketing departments. There is a shared folder called Apps that everyone uses. Here are the current permissions on the Apps shared folder:

Group/User	NTFS	Shared
Sales	Read	Deny
Marketing	Modify	Full Control
R&D	Read	Read
HR	Full Control	Deny
Admin	Full Control	Change

What will Matt's local and remote permissions be when he logs into the Apps folder?

- **A.** Local = Full Control and Remote = Deny
- **B.** Local = Read and Remote = Deny
- **C.** Local = Modify and Remote = Full Control
- **D.** Local = Read and Remote = Change

80. You are the network administrator for your company network. You are discussing managing volumes with a colleague. When talking about volume sets, you are discussing a volume set that uses only one disk or a portion of a disk. What type of volume are you discussing?

- **A.** Simple volume
- **B.** Spanned volume
- **C.** Striped volume
- **D.** Mirrored volume
- **E.** RAID-5 volume

81. You are the administrator of your company network. You are discussing Microsoft Multipath I/O (MPIO) with a colleague. Of all the supported load balancing policies that Windows Server 2016 supports, which one designates a preferred path that will handle all process requests until it fails, after which the standby path will become active until the primary reestablishes a connection and automatically regains control?

- **A.** Failover
- **B.** Failback
- **C.** Round robin
- **D.** Round robin with a subset of paths
- **E.** Dynamic least queue depth
- **F.** Weighted path

82. You are the administrator of your company network. You are discussing the benefits of NTFS with a colleague. One of the benefits allows an administrator to map a local disk drive to an NTFS directory name. What is being discussed?

    A. Dynamic volumes

    B. Remote storage

    C. Mounted drives

    D. Disk quotas

83. You are the administrator of your company network. You want to see the logical and physical disks that are currently configured on your system. What tool should you use?

    A. Disk Management

    B. Device Manager

    C. Task Manager

    D. File Explorer

84. You are the administrator of your company network. You are discussing adding disk drives to a server partition. Once you have physically installed the disk drive, it must be initialized. There are two different types of partition styles that are used to initialize disks. What are they? (Choose two.)

    A. Master Boot Record (MBR)

    B. Hard Disk Drive (HDD)

    C. Solid State Drive (SSD)

    D. GUID Partition Table (GPT)

85. You are the administrator of your company network. You are talking to a colleague about establishing a RAID-5 volume. What type of disk configuration should you use if you want to implement RAID?

    A. Basic

    B. Standard

    C. Dynamic

    D. Duplex

Chapter

3

Implement Hyper-V

THE FOLLOWING MCSA WINDOWS SERVER 2016 EXAM TOPICS ARE COVERED IN THIS CHAPTER:

✓ **3.1 Install and configure Hyper-V**

- This objective may include but is not limited to: Determine hardware and compatibility requirements for installing Hyper-V; install Hyper-V; install management tools: upgrade from existing versions of Hyper-V; delegate virtual machine management; perform remote management of Hyper-V hosts; use Windows PowerShell Direct; implement nested virtualization

✓ **3.2 Configure virtual machine (VM) settings**

- This objective may include but is not limited to: Add or remove memory in a running VM; configure dynamic memory; configure Non-Uniform Memory Access (NUMA) support; configure smart paging; configure Resource Metering; manage Integration Services; create and configure Generation 1 and 2 VMs and determine appropriate usage scenarios; implement enhanced session mode; create Linux and FreeBSD VMs; install and configure Linux Integration Services (LIS); install and configure FreeBSD Integration Services (BIS); implement Secure Boot for Windows and Linux environments; move and convert VMs from previous versions of Hyper-V to Windows Server 2016 Hyper-V; export and import VMs; implement Discrete Device Assignment (DDA); troubleshoot VM configuration versions

✓ **3.3 Configure Hyper-V storage**

- This objective may include but is not limited to: Create VHDs and VHDX files using Hyper-V Manager; create shared VHDX files; configure differencing disks; modify virtual hard disks; configure pass-through disks; resize a virtual hard disk; manage checkpoints; implement production checkpoints; implement a virtual Fibre Channel adapter; configure storage Quality of Service (QoS)

✓ 3.4 Configure Hyper-V networking

- This objective may include but is not limited to: Add and remove virtual network interface cards (vNICs); configure Hyper-V virtual switches; optimize network performance; configure MAC addresses; configure network isolation; configure synthetic and legacy virtual network adapter; configure NIC teaming in VMs; configure virtual machine queue (VMQ); enable Remote Direct Memory Access (RDMA) on network adapters bound to a Hyper-V virtual switch using Switch Embedded Teaming (SET); configure Bandwidth Management

1. You are the administrator for your company network. You have a Windows Server 2016 Hyper-V host named Server1. Server1 has a dynamically expanding virtual hard disk (VHD) file that is 950 GB. The VHD currently contains about 450 GB of free space. What command/cmdlet should you use if you want to reduce the amount of disk space used by the VHD?

   A. Mount-VHD cmdlet

   B. DiskPart command

   C. Set-VHD cmdlet

   D. Optimize-VHD cmdlet

2. You are the administrator for your company network. You have a Windows Server 2016 Hyper-V host named Server1. Server1 contains a virtual machine named VM1. What should you run on Server1 if you need to make sure that you can use nested virtualization on VM1?

   A. Mount-VHD cmdlet

   B. DiskPart command

   C. Set-VMProcessor cmdlet

   D. Set-VM cmdlet

3. You are the administrator for your company network. You have a Windows Server 2016 Hyper-V host named Server1. Server1 contains two virtual machines named VM1 and VM2. You need to ensure that VM1 and VM2 can communicate with each other only. What cmdlet should you use to prevent VM1 and VM2 from communicating with Server1?

   A. Set-NetNeighbor

   B. Remove-VMSwitchTeamMember

   C. Set-VMSwitch

   D. Enable-VMSwitchExtension

4. You are the administrator for your company network. You have a Windows Server 2016 Hyper-V host named Server1. Server1 contains a virtual machine named VM1. You want to deploy several shielded virtual machines on VM1. You deploy a Host Guardian on a new server. What should you run if you want to view the process of the shielded virtual machines installation?

   A. Get-ShieldedVMProvisioningStatus cmdlet

   B. Diskpart command

   C. Set-VHD cmdlet

   D. Set-VM cmdlet

5. You are the administrator for your company network. You have a Windows Server 2016 Hyper-V host named Server1. The host contains a virtual machine named VM1. VM1 has resource metering enabled. What cmdlet should you run if you need to use resource metering to track the amount of network traffic that VM1 sends to the 10.10.16.0/20 network?

   A. Add-VMNetworkAdapter

   B. Set-VMNetworkAdapter

   C. New-VMResourcePool

   D. Set-VMNetworkAdapterRoutingDomainMapping

6. You are the administrator for your company network. You have a Windows Server 2016 server named Server1, which has the Hyper-V Server role installed. You want to create a virtual machine named VM1 on Server1. You need to make sure that you can start VM1 from the network. What are two possible ways to do this? (Choose two.)

    A. Create a Generation 2 virtual machine.

    B. Create a Generation 1 virtual machine and run the `Enable-NetAdapterPackageDirect` cmdlet.

    C. Create a Generation 1 virtual machine that has a legacy network adapter.

    D. Create a Generation 1 virtual machine and configure a Single Root I/O Virtualization (SR-IOV) interface for the network adapter.

7. You are the administrator for your company network. You have a Windows Server 2016 Hyper-V host named Server1. Server1 contains a virtual machine named VM1. What should you run on Server1 if you need to ensure that you can use nested virtualization on VM1?

    A. `Mount-VHD` cmdlet

    B. `Diskpart` command

    C. `Set-VHD` cmdlet

    D. `Set-VM` cmdlet

    E. `Set-VMHost` cmdlet

    F. `Set-VMProcessor` cmdlet

    G. `Install-WindowsFeature` cmdlet

    H. `Optimize-VHD` cmdlet

8. You are the administrator for your company network. You have a Windows Server 2016 Hyper-V host named Server1. You plan to deploy several shielded virtual machines on Server1 and deploy a Host Guardian on the server. What should you run first if you need to ensure that Server1 can host shielded virtual machines?

    A. `Mount-VHD` cmdlet

    B. `Diskpart` command

    C. `Set-VHD` cmdlet

    D. `Set-VM` cmdlet

    E. `Set-VMHost` cmdlet

    F. `Set-VMProcessor` cmdlet

    G. `Install-WindowsFeature` cmdlet

    H. `Optimize-VHD` cmdlet

9. You are the administrator for your company network. You have a Windows Server 2016 Hyper-V host named Server1. Server1 has a virtual machine that uses a VHD named Disk1.vhdx. You receive a warning message from Event Viewer stating that "One or more virtual hard disks have a physical sector size that is smaller than the physical sector size of the storage on which the virtual hard disk file is located." What should you run if you need to resolve the problem that causes the warning message?

    A. Mount-VHD cmdlet

    B. Diskpart command

    C. Set-VHD cmdlet

    D. Set-VM cmdlet

    E. Set-VMHost cmdlet

    F. Set-VMProcessor cmdlet

    G. Install-WindowsFeature cmdlet

    H. Optimize-VHD cmdlet

10. You are the administrator for your company network. You have a Windows Server 2016 Hyper-V host named Server1. Server1 has a virtual machine named VM1 that uses a single VHDX file. VM1 is configured as shown in the following table.

Configuration	Details
Virtual Machine Generation	V2
Operating System	Windows 8
Filesystem	NTFS
Number of Partitions	1
Disk Type	Basic
Unallocated Disk Space	100 GB

You plan to use VM1 as a virtual machine template to deploy shielded virtual machines. What should you run if you need to ensure that VM1 can be used to deploy shielded virtual machines?

    A. Mount-VHD cmdlet

    B. Diskpart command

    C. Set-VHD cmdlet

    D. Set-VM cmdlet

    E. Set-VMHost cmdlet

    F. Set-VMProcessor cmdlet

    G. Install-WindowsFeature cmdlet

    H. Optimize-VHD cmdlet

11. You are the administrator for your company network. Your network contains an Active Directory forest. You install Windows Server 2016 on 10 virtual machines. You need to deploy the Web Server (IIS) server role identically to the virtual machines. What should you do?

A. Use PowerShell Desired State Configuration (DSC) to create a default configuration and then apply the configuration to the virtual machines.

B. Create a software installation package and then publish the package to the virtual machines by using a Group Policy Object (GPO).

C. From a Group Policy Object (GPO), create an application control policy and then apply the policy to the virtual machines.

D. From Windows System Image Manager, create an answer file, copy the file to C:\Sysprep on each virtual machine, and then run the Apply-Image cmdlet.

12. You are the administrator for your company network. You have a Windows Server 2016 Hyper-V host named Server1. Server1 contains four virtual machines. VM1 is a shielded virtual machine that runs Windows Server 2012 R2. VM2 is a shielded virtual machine that runs Windows Server 2016. VM3 is a virtual machine that runs Windows Server 2012 R2 and has Secure Boot enabled. VM4 is a virtual machine that runs Windows Server 2016 and has all of its drives protected by using BitLocker Drive Encryption (BitLocker). Using the Virtual Machine Connection tool from Hyper-V Manager, what machine or machines can you connect to?

A. VM1, VM2, VM3, and VM4

B. VM4 only

C. VM1 and VM2 only

D. VM3 and VM4 only

E. VM2 only

13. You are the administrator for your company network. You have decided to delete a virtual machine using Hyper-V Manager. What else must you do?

A. The only way you can do this is by using PowerShell.

B. Manually delete any virtual disks that were part of the virtual machine to free up disk space after the virtual machine has been deleted using Hyper-V Manager.

C. You must first delete the virtual machine's files on the hard drive before deleting the virtual machine using Hyper-V Manager.

D. Nothing; everything will be deleted when you use Hyper-V Manager.

14. You are the administrator for your company network. You are planning on deploying virtual machines. Which of the following statements is true regarding virtual machines?

A. Virtual machines each run in their own child partitions. Child partitions have direct access to hardware resources.

B. Virtual machines each run in their own child partitions. Child partitions do not have direct access to hardware resources.

C. Virtual machines run in another server's child partitions. Child partitions have direct access to hardware resources.

D. Virtual machines run in another server's child partitions. Child partitions do not have direct access to hardware resources.

15. You are the network administrator for your company network. You are looking at the different types of hard disks available with Hyper-V. One type of disk starts with a small VHD file and expands it on demand once an installation takes place. What type of hard disk is being described?

A. Dynamically expanding

B. Fixed size

C. Differencing

D. Physical (or pass-through) disk

16. You are the network administrator for your company network. You have a Windows Server 2016 Hyper-V host named Server1 and a two-node scale-out file server cluster named Cluster1. A virtual machine named VM1 runs on Server1. What tool should you use if you need to migrate the storage on VM1 to Cluster1?

A. The `clussvc.exe` command

B. The `cluster.exe` command

C. The Computer Management console

D. The `configurehyperv.exe` command

E. The Disk Management console

F. The Failover Cluster Manager console

G. The Hyper-V Manager console

H. Server Manager

17. You are the network administrator for your company network. You have three Windows Server 2016 servers named Server1, Server2, and Server3. Server1 and Server2 have the Hyper-V server role installed. Server3 has the iSCSI Target Server role installed. What tool should you use first if you need to create a Hyper-V cluster?

A. The `clussvc.exe` command

B. The `cluster.exe` command

C. The Computer Management console

D. The `configurehyperv.exe` command

E. The Disk Management console

F. The Failover Cluster Manager console

G. The Hyper-V Manager console

H. Server Manager

18. You are the administrator for your company network. You are planning the configuration of a virtual network switch for your Hyper-V network. It will contain the following Hyper-V hosts. Server1 will have 10 virtual machines that must be able to communicate with each other. The virtual machines must be prevented from communicating with Server1 and all other servers on the corporate network. The Hyper-V network will also have a two-node failover cluster named Cluster1 that will have 20 virtual machines. The virtual machines will run on both nodes. Hyper-V hosts on the corporate network must be able to connect to the virtual machines. What type of virtual switch should you select for the 10 virtual machines on Server1?

    A. External

    B. Internal

    C. Private

    D. Public

19. You are the administrator for your company network. You are planning the configuration of a virtual network switch for your Hyper-V network. It will contain the following Hyper-V hosts. Server1 will have 10 virtual machines that must be able to communicate with each other. The virtual machines must be prevented from communicating with Server1 and all other servers on the corporate network. The Hyper-V network will also have a two-node failover cluster named Cluster1 that will have 20 virtual machines. The virtual machines will run on both nodes. Hyper-V hosts on the corporate network must be able to connect to the virtual machines. What type of virtual switch should you select for the 20 virtual machines on Cluster1?

    A. External

    B. Internal

    C. Private

    D. Public

20. You are the administrator for your company network. You have an application named App1. App1 is distributed to multiple Hyper-V virtual machines in a multitenant environment. What should you include in the environment if you need to ensure that the traffic is distributed evenly among the virtual machines that host App1?

    A. A network controller and Windows Server Network Load Balancing (NLB) nodes

    B. A network controller and Windows Server Software Load Balancing (SLB) nodes

    C. A RAS Gateway and Windows Server Network Load Balancing (NLB) nodes

    D. A RAS Gateway and Windows Server Software Load Balancing (SLB) nodes

21. You are the administrator for your company network. You have a Windows Server 2016 Hyper-V host named Server1. What counter should you use from Performance Monitor if you need to identify the amount of processor resources consumed by Hyper-V and virtual machines?

    A. `\Hyper-V Hypervisor\Logical Processors`

    B. `\Hyper-V Hypervisor Virtual Processor(_Total)\% Hypervisor Run Time`

    C. `\Hyper-V Hypervisor Logical Processor(_Total)\% Total Run Time`

    D. `\Hyper-V Hypervisor Root Virtual Processor(_Total)\% Guest Run Time`

22. You are the administrator for your company network. You have a Windows Server 2016 server named Server1. Server1 also has the Hyper-V role installed. Virtual machines on Server1 are connected to an external switch named Switch1. You create a virtual machine named VM1 on Server1 by running the following cmdlets:

    ```
    Add-VM VM1
    Add-VMHardDiskDrive –VMName VM1 –ControllerType IDE –Path C:\VMs\Disk1.vhd
    Add-VMNetworkAdapter –VMName VM1
    ```

    What should you do if you need to ensure that you can install the operating system on VM1 by using Windows Deployment Services?
    A. Add a SCSI controller to VM1.
    B. Modify the `DefaultFlowMinimumBandwidthWeight` parameter of Switch1.
    C. Modify the `SwitchType` parameter of Switch1.
    D. Add a legacy network adapter to VM1.

23. You are the administrator for your company network. You have a four-node Hyper-V cluster named Cluster1. A virtual machine named VM1 runs on Cluster1. VM1 has a network adapter that connects to a virtual machine named Network1. What command should you run if you need to prevent a network disconnection on VM1 from causing VM1 to move to another cluster node?
    A. `Remove-ClusterVMMonitoredItem –VirtualMachine VM1`
    B. `Set-VM –VMName VM1`
    C. `Set-VMNetworkAdapter –VMName VM1`
    D. `Set-VMSwitch –Name Network1`

24. You are the administrator for your company network. You have a Windows Server 2016 Hyper-V host named Server1. Server1 hosts a virtual machine named VM1. You install the Hyper-V server role on VM1. What should you do if you need to ensure that the virtual machines hosted on VM1 can communicate with the virtual machines hosted on Server1?
    A. Run the `Set-VMNetworkAdapterIsolation` cmdlet and specify the `MultiTenantStack Off` parameter on Server1.
    B. Run the `Set-VMNetworkAdapter` cmdlet and specify the `MacAddressSpoofing Off` parameter on VM1.
    C. Run the `Set-VMNetworkAdapterIsolation` cmdlet and specify the `MultiTenantStack On` parameter on VM1.
    D. Run the `Set-VMNetworkAdapter` cmdlet and specify the `MacAddressSpoofing On` parameter on Server1.

25. You are the administrator for your company network. You have two Windows Server 2016 Hyper-V hosts named Server1 and Server2. Server1 and Server2 are connected on the same network. You create an external network switch named Switch1 on Server1 and Server2. You have the virtual machines shown in the following table.

Virtual Machine Name	IP Address	Subnet Mask	Hyper-V Host
VM1	192.168.1.16	255.255.255.0	Server1
VM2	192.168.1.32	255.255.255.0	Server2
VM3	192.168.1.48	255.255.255.0	Server2

All three virtual machines are connected to Switch1. You need to prevent applications in VM3 from being able to capture network traffic from VM1 or VM2. What should you do to ensure that VM1 retains network connectivity?

A. Configure network virtualization for VM1 and VM2.

B. Modify the subnet mask of VM1 and VM2.

C. Configure the VLAN ID setting of Switch1 on Server2.

D. Create an external switch and connect VM3 to the switch on Server2.

26. You are the administrator for your company network. Your network contains an Active Directory domain. The domain contains a Windows Server 2016 Hyper-V host named Server1. Server1 hosts four machines that are members of the domain. The virtual machines are configured as shown:

Virtual Machine Name	Operating System	Virtual Machine Generation	Type of VHD File
VM1	Windows 10	2	VHD
VM2	Windows Server 2016	2	VHD
VM3	Windows Server 2012 R2	2	VHDX
VM4	Windows Server 2016	1	VHDX

What virtual machines can you manage by using PowerShell Direct?

A. Only VM2

B. VM1, VM2, and VM4

C. Only VM4

D. VM1, VM2, and VM3

27. You are the administrator for your company network. You need to implement network virtualization. On what item should you configure the Virtual Subnet ID?

   A. Virtual switch

   B. Hyper-V Server

   C. Virtual machine

   D. Virtual network adapter

28. You are the administrator for your company network. You have a Windows Server 2016 virtual machine named VM1. VM1 hosts a service that requires high network throughput. VM1 has a virtual network adapter that connects to a Hyper-V switch named Switch1, which has one network adapter. The network adapter supports Remote Direct Memory Access (RDMA), the Single Root I/O Virtualization (SR-IOV) interface, Quality of Service (QoS), and Receive Side Scaling (RSS). You need to ensure that the traffic from VM1 can be processed by multiple networking processors. What PowerShell command should you run on the host of VM1?

   A. `Set-NetAdapterRss`

   B. `Set-NetAdapterRdma`

   C. `Set-NetAdapterQos`

   D. `Set-NetAdapterSriov`

29. You are the administrator for your company network. The network contains one Active Directory domain. The domain contains two Windows Server 2016 Hyper-V hosts named Host1 and Host2. Host1 contains a virtual machine named VM1. You plan to move VM1 to Host2. What cmdlet should you use if you need to generate a report that lists any configuration issues on Host2 that will prevent VM1 from being moved successfully?

   A. `Move-VM`

   B. `Test-VHD`

   C. `Debug-VM`

   D. `Compare-VM`

30. You are the administrator for your company network. You have a Windows Server 2016 server named Host1. You configure Host1 as a virtualization host and create 20 new virtual machines on Host1. You need to ensure that all of the virtual machines can connect to the Internet through Host1. What three actions should you perform? (Choose three.)

   A. Install the Remote Access server role on a virtual machine.

   B. Enable virtual LAN identification from the properties of each virtual machine.

   C. Connect to the virtual machine switch from the properties of each virtual machine.

   D. Configure the network address translation (NAT) network on Host1.

   E. Create an internal virtual machine switch and specify an IP address for the switch on Host1.

31. You are the administrator for your company network. You have a Windows Server 2016 Hyper-V host named Server1. The network adapters on Server1 have Single Root I/O Virtualization (SR-IOV) enabled. Server1 hosts a Windows Server 2016 virtual machine named VM1. What should you do if you need to identify whether SR-IOV is used by VM1?

   A. Open Hyper-V Manager and view the Integration Services settings of VM1 on Server1.

   B. Open Device Manager and view the properties of the network adapters.

   C. Sign in to VM1. View the properties of the network connections.

   D. Open Hyper-V Manager and view the properties of the network adapters.

32. You are the administrator for your company network. You want to capture the state, data, and hardware configuration of a running virtual machine. What checkpoint can be useful if you need to recreate a specific state or condition of a running virtual machine so that you can troubleshoot a problem?

   A. Production

   B. Standard

   C. Fabrication

   D. Customary

33. You are the administrator for your company network. You know that Virtual Network Manager offers three types of virtual networks that you can use to define various networking topologies for virtual machines and the virtualization server. Which type of virtual network is isolated from all external network traffic on the virtualization server, as well as any network traffic between the management operating system and the external network?

   A. Private virtual network

   B. Internal virtual network

   C. Public virtual network

   D. External virtual network

34. You are the administrator for your company network. Your company has a Windows Server 2016 Hyper-V environment configured as shown:

Hyper-V Host Name	Configuration	Virtual Switch Name
Host1	Uses an Intel processor Is a member of a SAN named SAN1	Switch1
Host2	Uses an AMD processor Has local storage only	Switch2

Hyper-V Host Name	Configuration	Virtual Switch Name
Host3	Uses an Intel processor Is a member of a SAN named SAN1	Switch1
Host4	Uses an Intel processor Has local storage only	Switch2

All of the virtual switches are the external type. What should you do if you need to ensure that you can move virtual machines between the hosts without causing the virtual machines to disconnect from the network?

A. Implement a Hyper-V replica between Host2 and Host4.

B. Implement Live Migration by using Host3 and Host4.

C. Implement Live Migration by using Host1 and Host2.

D. Implement Live Migration by using Host1 and Host3.

35. You are the administrator for your company network. You have a Windows Server 2016 server named Server1. Server1 is a Hyper-V host that hosts a virtual machine named VM1. Server1 has three network adapter cards that are connected to virtual switches named vSwitch1, vSwitch2, and vSwitch3. You configure NIC Teaming on VM1. The team name is VM1 NIC Team. Added to the team are Ethernet2 (10 Gbps) and Ethernet3 (10 Gbps). The teaming mode is Switch Independent. What should you do if you need to ensure that VM1 will retain access to the network if a physical adapter card fails on Server1?

A. Run the `Set-VMNetworkAdapterTeamMapping` cmdlet using PowerShell on VM1.

B. Modify the settings on VM1 from Hyper-V Manager on Server1.

C. Run the `Set-VMNetworkAdapterFailoverConfiguration` cmdlet from PowerShell on Server1.

D. Add the adapter named Ethernet to the NIC Team from the properties of the NIC Team on VM1.

36. You are the administrator for your company network. You have two Windows Server 2016 Hyper-V hosts named Server1 and Server2. Server1 and Server2 are connected to the same network. You create an external network switch named Switch1 on Server1 and Server2. You have the virtual machines shown in the following table:

Virtual Machine Name	IP Address	Subnet Mask	Hyper-V Host
VM1	192.168.1.16	255.255.255.0	Server1
VM2	192.168.1.32	255.255.255.0	Server2
VM3	192.168.1.48	255.255.255.0	Server2

All three virtual machines are connected to Switch1. On VM3, you need to prevent applications from being able to capture network traffic from VM1 or VM2. The solution must ensure that VM1 retains network connectivity. What should you do?

A. Configure the VLAN ID setting of Switch1 on Server2.

B. Create an external switch and connect VM3 to the switch on Server2.

C. Modify the subnet mask of VM1 and VM2.

D. Configure network virtualization for VM1 and VM2.

37. You are the administrator for your company network. You have a Windows Server 2016 Hyper-V host named Server1. Server1 has a virtual disk file named Disk1.vhdx that contains an installation to Windows Server 2016. You create a virtual disk file named Disk2.vhdx that is configured as shown:

PS c:\ Get-VHD Path C:\folder1\Disk2.vhdx

ComputerName   : SERVER1

Path   : c:\folder1\disk2.vhdx

VHDFormat   : VHDX

What command should you run if you want to move Disk1.vhdx to a new folder called C:\Folder2 and be able to use Disk2.vhdx only after you run this command?

A. Merge-VHD

B. Optimize-VHD

C. Optimize-VHDSet

D. Set-VHD

E. Test-VHD

38. You are the administrator for your company network. You have a Windows Server 2016 Hyper-V host named Server1. Server1 has a virtual disk file named Disk1.vhdx that contains an installation to Windows Server 2016. You create a virtual disk file named Disk2.vhdx that is configured as shown:

PS c:\ Get-VHD Path C:\folder1\Disk2.vhdx

ComputerName   : SERVER1

Path   : c:\folder1\disk2.vhdx

VHDFormat   : VHDX

What command should you run before you can copy the files directly into Disk2.vhdx?

A. Merge-VHD

B. Optimize-VHD

C. Optimize-VHDSet

D. Set-VHD

E. Test-VHD

47. You are the administrator for your company network. You have a computer named Computer1 that has the Hyper-V feature enabled. You have two virtual machines named VM1 and VM2 hosted on Computer1. VM1 can communicate with VM2 and Computer1. VM1 fails to connect to the Internet; however, Computer1 can still connect to the Internet. What should you do if you need to ensure that VM1 can connect to the Internet?

   A. On Computer1, modify the network settings.

   B. Enable port mirroring on VM1.

   C. Create an external virtual switch and configure VM1 to use the switch.

   D. On VM1, select Enable Virtual LAN Identification.

48. You are the administrator for your company network. You have a Windows Server 2016 Hyper-V host that contains a virtual machine named VM1 that has Resource Metering enabled. What cmdlet should you run if you need to use Resource Metering to track the amount of network traffic that VM1 sends to the 10.0.0.0/8 network?

   A. Add-VMNetworkAdapter

   B. Set-VMNetworkAdapter

   C. New-VMResourcePool

   D. Set-VMNetworkAdapterRoutingDomainMapping

49. You are the administrator for your company network. What statement is true when you use Hyper-V Manager to delete a virtual machine?

   A. You will delete the virtual machine configuration file and all related virtual disks.

   B. You will delete the virtual machine configuration file and the primary virtual disk.

   C. You will delete only the virtual machine configuration file.

   D. The virtual machine will only be removed from the Hyper-V Manager; the virtual machine configuration file will still exist in the filesystem.

50. You are the administrator for your company network. What are the minimum CPU requirements in order to run Hyper-V on a machine? (Choose all that apply.)

   A. Hardware Data Execution Prevention (DEP), specifically Intel XD bit (execute disable bit) or AMD NX bit (no execute bit), must be available and enabled.

   B. An x64-compatible processor with Intel VT or AMD-V technology must be enabled.

   C. Hardware Data Execution Protection (DEP) must be disabled.

   D. You must have a minimum of 1.4 GHz.

51. You are the administrator for your company network. How do you move one virtual machine from one Hyper-V server to another machine?

   A. You move the virtual machine configuration file and all related files like virtual disks to the other machine and use the Import function on the target machine.

   B. You use the Export function in Hyper-V Manager, then make the export path available on the target machine and use Import on the target machine.

   C. You use the Export function in Hyper-V Manager, then make the export path available on the target machine and use Open Virtual Machine on the target machine.

   D. You move the virtual machine configuration file and all related files like virtual disks to the other machine and use Open Virtual Machine on the target machine.

52. You are the administrator for your company network. You plan to utilize Hyper-V. Hyper-V allows your organization to do which of the following?

   A. Hyper-V gives a small company the ability to run a single server on multiple boxes and compete with a company of any size.

   B. Hyper-V gives a small company the ability to run multiple servers on a single box and compete with a company of any size.

   C. Hyper-V gives a small company the ability to run a single server on a single box and compete with a company of any size.

   D. Hyper-V gives a small company the ability to run multiple servers on multiple boxes and compete with a company of any size.

53. You are the administrator for your company network. You are looking at the benefits of using Hyper-V. Different forms of virtualization are available. Name the type of virtualization being described here: applications run on a different computer, and only the screen information is transferred to your computer.

   A. Server virtualization

   B. Presentation virtualization

   C. Desktop virtualization

   D. Application virtualization

54. You are the administrator for your company network. You are looking at the benefits of using Hyper-V. Different forms of virtualization are available. Name the type of virtualization being described here: enables multiple servers to run on the same physical server and is a tool that allows you to move physical machines to virtual machines and manage them on a few physical servers.

   A. Server virtualization

   B. Presentation virtualization

   C. Desktop virtualization

   D. Application virtualization

55. You are the administrator of your company network. You are planning on running Hyper-V, but you are not sure what guest operating system versions (32- or 64-bit) it supports. What guest operating system versions can Hyper-V run?

   A. 32-bit only

   B. 64-bit only

   C. 128-bit only

   D. Both 32-bit and 64-bit

56. You are the administrator of your company network. You are planning on running Hyper-V Server. You know that Hyper-V allows for support for symmetric multiprocessors. What is the maximum number of processors that Hyper-V Server can use in a virtual machine environment?

A. 28

B. 36

C. 64

D. 128

57. You are the administrator for your company network. You are planning on installing Hyper-V, and one of its key features allows you to install virtual machines on a properly activated Windows Server 2016 system without the need to manage individual product keys for each virtual machine. What key feature is being described?

A. Automatic Virtual Machine Activation (AVMA)

B. Discrete Device Assignment (DDA)

C. Virtual Machine Queue (VMQ)

D. Non-Uniform Memory Access (NUMA)

58. You are the administrator for your company network. You are planning on installing Hyper-V. You understand that certain hardware requirements must be met. What is Microsoft's recommended minimum amount of RAM needed to run Hyper-V?

A. 2 GB

B. 4 GB

C. 6 GB

D. 8 GB

59. You are the administrator for your company network. You are planning on installing Hyper-V. You understand that certain software requirements must be met. There are three editions of Windows Server that Hyper-V can run on. What are they? (Choose three.)

A. Windows Server 2016 Standard Edition

B. Windows Server 2016 Datacenter Edition

C. Windows Server 2016 Nano Server Edition

D. Microsoft Hyper-V Server 2012 R2 Edition

60. You are the administrator for your company network. You are managing your virtual networks using Virtual Switch Manager, which allows you to create, manage, and delete virtual switches. Virtual Switch Manager allows you to define the type of network. Name the network type described here: this option allows virtual machines to communicate with each other and with the host system, but not with the physical network.

A. External

B. Private

C. Internal

D. Public

61. You are the administrator for your company network. You know that Hyper-V offers various types of hard disks to use. Name the one described here: this type of disk is associated in a parent-child relationship with another disk.

   A. Dynamically expanding

   B. Fixed size

   C. Differencing

   D. Physical (pass-through)

62. You are the administrator for your company network. You know that Hyper-V offers various types of hard disks to use. Name the one described here: this type provides the highest performance of all disk types and thus should be used for production servers where performance is the top priority.

   A. Dynamically expanding

   B. Fixed size

   C. Differencing

   D. Physical (pass-through)

63. You are the administrator for your company network. You want to boot a Linux operating system with the Secure Boot option enabled in a virtual machine. What must you do if this will be the first time you boot the OS?

   A. Set `-BootOrder` to `HardDiskDrive`.

   B. Configure the virtual machine to use the Microsoft UEFI Certificate Authority.

   C. You can't enable Secure Boot with Linux.

   D. Set `-EnableSecureBoot` without specifying a template.

64. You are the administrator for your company network. You are creating a Nano server image named `Nano1.vhdx` by using the `New-NanoServerImage` cmdlet. You attach `Nano1.vhdx` to a Generation 1 virtual machine named Nano1. When you start Nano1, you get the following error message: "Boot failure. Reboot and select proper Boot device or Insert Boot Media in selected Boot device." What should you do if you need to successfully start Nano server?

   A. Attach `Nano1.vhdx` to a SCSI controller.

   B. Recreate Nano1 as a Generation 2 virtual machine.

   C. Increase the memory of Nano1 to 512 MB.

   D. Modify the BIOS settings of Nano1.

65. You are the administrator for your company network. You plan on using NIC Teaming when setting up your virtualization as a way to have load balancing with Hyper-V. What is the maximum number of network adapters that you can include in a NIC Team?

   A. 16

   B. 32

   C. 64

   D. 128

66. You are the administrator for your company network. You plan on using NIC Teaming. As an administrator, you can configure NIC Teaming in different configuration models. Those models include which of the following? (Choose all that apply.)

A. Switch Separated

B. Switch Subordinate

C. Switch Independent

D. Switch Dependent

67. You are the administrator for your company network. You plan on setting up Storage Quality of Service (QoS). You can use Storage QoS in Windows Server 2016 to accomplish which of the following? (Choose all that apply.)

A. Relieve problem neighbor issues.

B. Monitor end-to-end storage performance.

C. Manage Storage I/O per workload needs.

D. Allow the guest operating system to communicate with host devices.

68. You are the administrator for your company network. You have a Windows Server 2016 Hyper-V host named Server1. Server1 hosts a virtual machine named VM1. VM1 is in a workgroup. VM1 is currently in a running state. You need to create 10 copies of VM1 on Server1 in the least amount of time possible. What cmdlets should you use?

A. Stop-VM and then Import-VM

B. Export-VM and then Import-VM

C. Checkpoint-VM and then New-VM

D. Copy-VMFile and then New-VM

69. You are the administrator for your company network. Your network contains two Hyper-V servers named Server1 and Server2. Server1 has Windows Server 2012 R2 installed and Server2 has Windows Server 2016 installed. You perform a live migration of a virtual machine named VM1 from Server1 to Server2. What three PowerShell cmdlets should you run if you need to create a production checkpoint for VM1 on Server2? (Choose three.)

A. Set-VM

B. Update-VMVersion

C. Checkpoint-VM

D. Set-VMHost

E. Stop-VM

70. You are the administrator for your company network. You would like to use PowerShell to configure features of the virtual network adapter in a virtual machine or the management operating system. What PowerShell cmdlet should you use?

A. Set-VMNetworkAdapter

B. New-VMNetworkAdapter

C. Get-VMNetworkAdapter

D. Add-VMNetworkAdapter

71. You are the administrator for your company network. You are planning on using Switch Embedded Teaming (SET). SET allows an administrator to combine a group of physical adapters into software-based virtual adapters. What is the maximum number of adapters that can be part of a SET?

A. 4

B. 8

C. 12

D. 16

72. You are the administrator for your company network. You are planning on using Switch Embedded Teaming (SET). Which of the following is true when setting up SET?

A. All network adapters that are members of the SET group can be different adapters.

B. All network adapters that are members of the SET group must be from different manufacturers.

C. There are no requirements when it comes to the adapter types.

D. All network adapters that are members of the SET group must be identical adapters.

73. You are the administrator for your company network. You have a Windows Server 2016 Hyper-V host named Server1. You have two network adapter cards on Server1 that are Remote Direct Memory Access (RDMA)-capable. You need to combine the bandwidth of the network adapter cards for a virtual machine on Server1. You must ensure that the virtual machine can use the RDMA capabilities of the network adapter cards. What PowerShell command should you run first?

A. `Add-NetLbfoTeamNic`

B. `Add-VMNetworkAdapter`

C. `New-NetLbfoTeam`

D. `New-VMSwitch`

74. You are the administrator for your company network. You have a Hyper-V server that is running a Generation 1 Windows Server 2016 virtual machine. You need to add another hard drive to the virtual machine. The Hyper-V server has 1 TB of available free space for another hard drive. When you try to add the hard drive to the virtual machine, the options are grayed out. What do you need to do to add the hard drive to the virtual machine?

A. Go to the virtual machine settings and use the New Hard Drive Wizard.

B. On the Hyper-V host, add the hard drive to the virtual machine by using Disk Management.

C. Shut down the virtual machine, then go into the virtual machine settings and use the New Hard Drive Wizard to add the drive.

D. You cannot add another hard drive to an existing virtual machine.

75. You are the administrator for your company network. You manage a computer that runs Windows Server 2016 and has Hyper-V enabled. You create two virtual machines that can communicate with each other and with the host operating system. The virtual machines are not able to connect to the Internet. What should you do if you need to ensure that the virtual machines can connect to the Internet?

    A. Create an external virtual switch.

    B. Configure the MAC Address Range.

    C. Configure NUMA Spanning.

    D. Configure Enhanced Session Mode.

76. You are the administrator for your company network. You are planning on installing Hyper-V, and one of the key features allows a processor to access its local memory more quickly than memory located on another processor. It allows a system to access memory quickly by providing separate memory on each processor. What key feature is being described?

    A. Automatic Virtual Machine Activation (AVMA)

    B. Discrete Device Assignment (DDA)

    C. Virtual Machine Queue (VMQ)

    D. Non-Uniform Memory Access (NUMA)

77. You are the administrator for your company network. You are planning on installing Hyper-V. You know that Hyper-V provides a virtualization layer that runs directly on the system hardware. What is this layer of the microkernel architecture called?

    A. Hypervisor

    B. Hyper Virtual Machine Assistant

    C. Hyper Virtual Assistant

    D. Virtual Assistant

78. You are the administrator for your company network. You are planning on installing Hyper-V, and one of the key features is Enhanced Session Mode, which enhances the interactive session of the Virtual Machine Connection for Hyper-V administrators who want to connect to their virtual machines. Enhanced Session Mode gives administrators benefits for _____ . (Fill in the blank.)

    A. Remote resource redirection

    B. Remote device redirection

    C. Local resource redirection

    D. Local device redirection

79. You are the administrator for your company network. You are planning on installing Hyper-V, and you have heard of a new feature of Hyper-V in Windows Server 2016 that allows you to run a virtual machine within a virtual machine. What is this new feature called?

    A. Virtual machine queue

    B. Hyper-V nesting

    C. Network isolation

    D. Shared virtual hard disk

80. You are the administrator for your company network. You have a Windows Server 2016 Hyper-V host named Server1. Server1 connects to your corporate network. The corporate network uses the 10.10.0.0/16 address space. Server1 hosts a virtual machine named VM1; VM1 is configured to have an IP address of 172.16.1.54/16. You need to ensure that VM1 can access the resources on the corporate network. What should you connect VM1 to?

    A. An external virtual switch

    B. An internal virtual switch

    C. A private virtual switch

    D. A public virtual switch

81. You are the administrator for your company network. You have a Windows Server 2016 Hyper-V host named Server1. Server1 connects to your corporate network. The corporate network uses the 10.10.0.0/16 address space. Server1 hosts a virtual machine named VM1, which is configured to have an IP address of 172.16.1.54/16. You need to ensure that VM1 can access the resources on the corporate network. What should you run on Server1?

    A. Add-VMNetworkAdapterRoutingDomainMapping

    B. Get-VMNetworkAdapterRoutingDomainMapping

    C. Netsh.exe

    D. Route.exe

82. You are the administrator for your company network. You have a Windows Server 2016 Hyper-V host named Server1. Server 1 hosts a virtual machine named VM1 that runs Windows Server 2016. Server1 has a USB 3.0 device attached to a PCI Express (PCIe) bus. What three actions should you perform if you need to provide VM1 with pass-through access to the USB 3.0 device? (Choose three.)

    A. Run the Dismount-VMHostAssignableDevice cmdlet on Server1.

    B. Run the Add-VMAssignableDevice cmdlet on Server1.

    C. Run the Disable-PnPDevice cmdlet on Server1.

    D. Run the Enable-PnPDevice cmdlet on VM1.

    E. Run the Mount-VMHostAssignableDevice cmdlet on VM1.

83. You are the administrator for your company network. You have two Windows Server 2016 Hyper-V hosts named Server1 and Server2. Server1 hosts a virtual machine named VM1 that is in a Running state. On Server1, you export VM1 and then you import VM1 on Server2. On Server2, what is the current state of VM1?

    A. Off

    B. Saved

    C. Running

    D. Paused

84. You are the administrator for your company network. Hyper-V provides two tools that allow you to manage virtual hard disks. These tools can be found on the Action pane in Hyper-V Manager. What are these two tools? (Choose two.)

    A. Examine Disk

    B. Inspect Disk

    C. Edit Disk

    D. Manage Disk

85. You are the administrator for your company network. Windows Server 2016 Hyper-V has a feature that is used to bridge the memory gap between minimum memory and startup memory. This allows your virtual machines to restart properly. What is the name of this feature?

    A. Smart Paging

    B. Checkpoints

    C. Memory

    D. Integration Services

Chapter

4

Implement Windows Containers

THE FOLLOWING MCSA WINDOWS SERVER 2016 EXAM TOPICS ARE COVERED IN THIS CHAPTER:

✓ **4.1 Deploy Windows containers**

- This objective may include but is not limited to: Determine installation requirements and appropriate scenarios for Windows Containers; install and configure Windows Server container host in physical or virtualized environments; install and configure Windows Server container host to Windows Server Core or Nano Server in a physical or virtualized environment; install Docker on Windows Server and Nano Server; configure Docker startup options; install PowerShell for Docker; install a base container image; tag an image; remove a container; create Windows Server containers; create Hyper-V Containers

✓ **4.2 Manage Windows containers**

- This objective may include but is not limited to: Manage Windows containers by using Docker CLI and PowerShell for Docker; manage container networking; manage container data volumes; manage Resource Control; create new container images using Dockerfile; manage container images using Docker Hub repository for public and private scenarios; manage container images using Microsoft Azure

1. You are the administrator for your company network. You have a Windows Server 2016 Hyper-V server named Server1. Server1 has an IP address of 192.168.1.78 and has a container named Container1 that hosts a web application on port 84. Container1 has an IP address of 172.16.5.6 and a port mapping from port 80 on Server1 to port 84 on Container1. You have a server named Server2 that has an IP address of 192.168.1.79. To what IP address and port should you connect if you need to connect to the web application from Server2?

    A. 192.168.1.78:84

    B. 192.168.1.78:80

    C. 172.16.5.6:80

    D. 172.16.5.6:84

2. You are the administrator for your company network. You have a Windows Server 2016 Hyper-V host named Server1. Server1 has a virtual machine named VM1 that is configured to run the Docker daemon. On VM1 you have a container network that uses transparent mode. What should you do if you need to ensure that containers that run on VM1 can obtain IP addresses from DHCP?

    A. Run `docker network connect` on Server1.

    B. Run `docker network connect` on VM1.

    C. Run `Get-VMNetworkAdapter-VMName VM1| Set-VMNetworkAdapter-MacAddressSpoofing On` on VM1.

    D. Run `Get-VMNetworkAdapter-VMName VM1| Set-VMNetworkAdapter-MacAddressSpoofing On` on Server1.

3. You are the administrator for your company network. You have a Windows Server 2016 server named Server1 and you install the Docker daemon. What should you do if you need to configure the Docker daemon to accept connections only on TCP port 64500?

    A. Edit the `daemon.json` file.

    B. Edit the configuration JSON file.

    C. Run the `New-NetFirewallRule` cmdlet.

    D. Run the `Set-Service` cmdlet.

4. You are the administrator for your company network. You have a Windows Server 2016 server named Server1. You plan to deploy Internet Information Services (IIS) in a Windows container. What three actions should you perform if you need to prepare Server1 for the planned deployment? (Choose three.)

    A. Install the Hyper-V Server role.

    B. Install the Base Container images.

    C. Install the Container feature.

    D. Install the Web Server role.

    E. Install Docker.

5. You are the administrator for your company network. You are discussing container types with a colleague. Which container type provides application isolation through process and namespace isolation technology and shares a kernel with the container host and all containers running on the host?

   A. Hyper-V Container

   B. Windows Server Container

   C. Docker Container

   D. Docker Daemon Container

6. You are the administrator for your company network. You have a Windows Server 2016 server named Server1 that runs the Docker daemon. What should you do if you need to ensure that members of a security group named Docker Administrators can administer Docker?

   A. Run the `sc privs` command.

   B. Edit the `daemon.json` file.

   C. Add Docker Administrators to the local Administrators group.

   D. Edit the `configuration.json` file.

7. You are the administrator for your company network. You have a Windows Server 2016 container host named Server1. What parameter should you use with the `docker run` command if you need to start a Hyper-V Container on Server1?

   A. `--entrypoint`

   B. `--expose`

   C. `--runtime`

   D. `--isolation`

   E. `--privileged`

8. You are the administrator for your company network. You have a Windows Server 2016 container host named Server1. On Server1, you create a container named Container1. What should you run if you need to mount `C:\ContainerFiles` from Server1 to Container1?

   A. `dockerd --storage-opt dm.mountopt=ContainerFiles Container1`

   B. `docker run -it -vC:\ContainerFiles:c:\ContainerFiles Container1`

   C. `dockerd --storage-opt dm.datadev=/c/ContainerFiles Container1`

   D. `docker run -it -v c:\ContainerFiles Container1`

9. You are the administrator for your company network. You have a Windows Server 2016 server named Server1 that has the Containers feature installed. You create a text file that contains the commands that will be used to automate the creation of new containers. What should you name the file if you need to ensure that the commands in the text file are used when you create new containers?

   A. `Bootstrap.ini`

   B. `Config.ini`

   C. Dockerfile

   D. `Unattend.txt`

10. You are the administrator for your company network. You have a Windows Server 2016 Nano Server named Nano1. You deploy several containers to Nano1 that use an image named Image1. What should you run if you need to deploy a new container to Nano1 that uses Image1?

   A. The `docker run` command

   B. The `docker load` command

   C. `Install-NanoServerPackage` cmdlet

   D. `Install-WindowsFeature` cmdlet

11. You are the administrator for your company network. You are having a discussion with a colleague regarding the use of Docker and Windows Containers. Which of the following statements is true?

   A. The Docker application does not need to be installed to work with Windows Containers.

   B. The Docker application does need to be installed to work with Windows Containers.

   C. Neither needs to be installed; they are both already installed by default.

   D. Each operates separately and they do not work together.

12. You are the administrator for your company network. You are discussing the Docker Restart Policy with a colleague. What is the default setting for a container when working with the Docker Restart Policy?

   A. `always`

   B. `on-failure[:max-retries]`

   C. `no`

   D. `unless-stopped`

13. You are the administrator for your company network. One of the advantages of using Docker is that you can go to Docker's website to look at the different images that are available. There are images for operating systems, applications, and software. But what happens if you can't find an image that meets your needs?

   A. You must find the image template that best matches your needs.

   B. Just create your own Dockerfile.

   C. Just pick the image template that most closely resembles what you are looking for.

   D. There is nothing you can do.

14. You are the administrator for your company network. You and a colleague are discussing how Windows Containers differ from Hyper-V Containers. Which statement is true?

   A. There are no differences.

   B. Windows Containers utilize their own instance of the Windows kernel and Hyper-V Containers share the system's kernel between all containers and the host.

   C. Windows Containers utilize their own instance of the Windows kernel and Hyper-V Containers utilize the system's kernel on just the host.

   D. Windows Containers share the system's kernel between all containers and the host and Hyper-V Containers utilize their own instance of the Windows kernel.

15. You are the administrator for your company network. You have just installed Docker. When you install Docker, how many networks are created automatically?

  A. 1

  B. 2

  C. 3

  D. 4

16. You are the administrator for your company network. You and a colleague are discussing the Azure Container Service and what it can be used for. Which statement is true?

  A. The Azure Container Service uses proprietary scheduling and management tools.

  B. The Azure Container Service uses open source scheduling and management tools.

  C. The Azure Container Service uses commercial scheduling and management tools.

  D. The Azure Container Service uses registered scheduling and management tools.

17. You are the administrator for your company network. You want to view the information about containers. What PowerShell cmdlet will allow you to view that information?

  A. Get-ContainerHost

  B. Get-ContainerNetworkAdapter

  C. Get-ContainerImage

  D. Get-Container

18. You are the administrator for your company network. You are discussing Dockerfile commands with a colleague. What Dockerfile command allows you to create a mount point and externally mounted volumes from host systems or other containers?

  A. Volume

  B. Onbuild

  C. Expose

  D. Run

19. You are the network administrator for your company network. The company has decided to start using containers. What command would you use to create a new container?

  A. docker build container

  B. docker create

  C. docker new

  D. docker build

20. You are the network administrator for your company network. The company has decided to start using containers. You have created some images. Now you'd like to see the images you created. What command allows you to see your images?

  A. docker see

  B. docker images

  C. docker info

  D. docker view

21. You are the network administrator for your company network. The company has decided to start using containers. You need to build and use a Dockerfile. What command would you use if you need to compile and create an image using the Dockerfile?

    A. docker build

    B. docker run

    C. docker compile

    D. docker rm

22. You are the network administrator for your company network. The company has decided to start using containers. You need to build and use a Dockerfile. What command would you use if you need to execute commands within the Dockerfile?

    A. docker build

    B. docker run

    C. docker compile

    D. docker rm

23. You are the network administrator for your company network. The company has decided to start using containers. You need to build and use a Dockerfile. What command would you use if you need to delete a container?

    A. docker delete

    B. docker kill container

    C. delete-docker-Container

    D. remove-container

24. You are the network administrator for your company network. The company has decided to start using containers. You need to build a new image using Windows Server Core. What command would you use to get a Windows Server Core image?

    A. docker get microsoft/windowsservercore

    B. docker run microsoft/windowsservercore

    C. docker pull microsoft/windowsservercore

    D. docker build microsoft/windowsservercore

25. You are the administrator for your company network. The company has decided to start using containers. Your supervisor wants to know which client operating systems can host containers. Which of the following client operating systems do you tell him? (Choose all that apply.)

    A. Windows 7 Professional

    B. Windows 8.1 Enterprise

    C. Windows 10 Home

    D. Windows 10 Enterprise (Anniversary Update)

    E. Windows Server 2016

26. You are the administrator for your company network. The network contains an Active Directory domain. The domain contains a Windows Server 2016 server named Server1. Server1 allows inbound connectivity from all computers in the domain. Server1 has an IP address of 192.168.0.10 and hosts a Windows container named Container1. Container1 hosts a website that is accessible on port 80. You need to ensure that you can use the Docker client to manage Container1 from any computer in the domain. What four cmdlets should you run? (Choose four.)

   A. `Restart-Service docker`

   B. `New-ContainerNetwork- Name nat1 -Mode NAT-SubnetPrefix 192.168.0.0/24 -GatewayAddress 192.168.0.10`

   C. `Add-Content 'c:\programdata\docker\config\daemon.json' '{"hosts": ["tcp://127.0.0.1:80", "npipe://"]}'`

   D. `Add-Content 'c"\programdata\docker\config\daemon.json' '{"hosts": [tcp://0.0.0.0:2375", npipe://" ] }']`

   E. `New-Item-Type File c:\programData\docker\config\daemon.json`

27. You are the administrator for your company network. The network has a main office and three branch offices and consists of an Active Directory domain. The main office contains three domain controllers and each branch office has one domain controller. You discover that the new settings in the Default Domain Policy are not applied in one of the branch offices, but all other Group Policy Objects (GPOs) are applied. What should you do from a domain controller in the main office if you need to check the replication of the Default Domain Policy for the branch office?

   A. From Group Policy Management, click Default Domain Policy and then open the Details tab.

   B. From Group Policy Management, click Default Domain Policy and then open the Scope tab.

   C. Run `repadmin.exe` from a command prompt.

   D. Run `dcdiag.exe` from a command prompt.

28. You are the administrator for your company network. You and a colleague are discussing Windows Containers. Which of the following statements is true regarding Windows Containers?

   A. They are independent and isolated environments that run an operating system.

   B. They are independent and isolated environments that support user Home Folders.

   C. They are dependent and non-isolated environments that run an operating system.

   D. They are dependent and non-isolated environments that support user Home Folders.

29. You are the administrator for your company network. You are discussing container types with a colleague. Which container type runs within a virtual machine, and the container host's kernel is not shared between the other containers?

   A. Hyper-V Container

   B. Windows Server Container

   C. Docker Container

   D. Docker Daemon Container

30. You are the administrator for your company network. You are discussing Container components with a colleague. Which component can be on a physical or virtual machine, and is configured with the Windows Container feature?

A. Container Image

B. Container Host

C. Container OS Image

D. Container Registry

31. You are the administrator for your company network. You are discussing Container components with a colleague. Which component contains all of the layers of the container?

A. Container Image

B. Container Host

C. Container OS Image

D. Container Registry

32. You are the administrator for your company network. You are discussing Container components with a colleague. Your colleague is telling you about the component that runs the Docker application. What is this component called?

A. Container Registry

B. Docker daemon

C. Dockerfile

D. Docker Hub repositories

33. You are the administrator of your company network. You are planning on using containers on a virtualized network. You currently have the Hyper-V role installed on the system and have the Windows Server 2016 operating system installed. You are concerned that you might not have enough RAM. What is the minimum amount of RAM required to run containers in a virtualized network?

A. 2 GB

B. 4 GB

C. 6 GB

D. 8 GB

34. You are the administrator for your company network. The company has decided to start using containers. You want to see what version of Windows you have installed because you know that the operating system on the host machine must match the operating system of the Windows Container. What is one tool can you use to see what version of Windows is currently installed on the host machine?

A. repadmin.exe

B. dcdiag.exe

C. regedit.exe

D. perfmon.exe

35. You are the administrator for your company network. The company has decided to install Docker. Which of the following statements regarding Docker are true? (Choose all that apply.)

   A. It is a software package that allows you to create and manipulate containers and images.

   B. It is a hardware package that allows you to create and manipulate containers and images.

   C. It is a third-party application that Microsoft uses for containers.

   D. It consists of a Docker engine and a Docker client (Docker daemon).

36. You are the administrator for your company network. The company has decided to start using containers. You need to find out which version of Windows is installed on the host machine. What registry key should you search for to see the version currently installed?

   A. HKEY_LOCAL_MACHINE\Software\Microsoft\Windows 10\CurrentVersion

   B. HKEY_LOCAL_MACHINE\Software\Microsoft\Windows 2016\CurrentVersion

   C. HKEY_LOCAL_MACHINE\Software\Microsoft\Windows \CurrentVersion

   D. HKEY_LOCAL_MACHINE\Software\Microsoft\Windows NT\CurrentVersion

37. You are the administrator for your company network. You have installed Docker. There are some Docker switches that can be used. The Docker switches can be run in PowerShell or at an elevated command prompt. Which command allows an administrator to debug and build a new image?

   A. docker attack

   B. docker build

   C. docker commit

   D. docker deploy

38. You are the administrator for your company network. You have installed Docker. There are some Docker switches that can be used. The Docker switches can be run in PowerShell or at an elevated command prompt. Administrators use which command to create and modify a stack?

   A. docker attack

   B. docker build

   C. docker commit

   D. docker deploy

39. You are the administrator for your company network. You have installed Docker. You plan on using the Docker command that allows you to copy files and folders between the container and the local computer system. What command do you use?

   A. docker copy

   B. docker cp

   C. docker create

   D. docker replicate

40. You are the administrator for your company network. You have installed Docker. You plan on using the Docker command that allows you to view all of the containers. What command do you use?

A. docker ps

B. docker examine

C. docker containers

D. docker replicate

41. You are the administrator for your company network. You are discussing the Docker Restart Policy with a colleague. What Docker Restart Policy setting will try to restart the container indefinitely as well as always start on daemon startup?

A. always

B. on-failure[:max-retries]

C. no

D. unless-stopped

42. You are the network administrator for your company network. The company has decided to start using containers. You want to look to see if any containers are currently running. What command will allow you to see which containers are running?

A. docker see

B. docker images

C. docker info

D. docker view

43. You are the administrator for your company network. You have installed Docker. You plan on using the Docker command that allows you to pull an image from a registry. What command do you use?

A. docker pull

B. docker push

C. docker ps

D. docker run

44. You are the network administrator for your company network. The company has decided to start using containers. You have decided to delete an image from a container. What command would you use to delete an image from a container?

A. docker remove

B. docker delete

C. docker rmv

D. docker rm

45. You are the network administrator for your company network. The company has decided to start using containers. You have installed Docker and now want to add an image to a container. You check out what images are currently available in your repository. Now, what item do you need to turn the image into a container?

   A. Image Name

   B. Image ID

   C. Image Info

   D. Image Status

46. You are the administrator for your company network. You create a bunch of different images and you'd like to do something to the images that will allow you to access them more easily. What is one way that you can keep track of the different images on your machine?

   A. Search by name.

   B. Search by date.

   C. Name the images.

   D. Tag the images.

47. You are the administrator for your company network. You have recently installed Docker and are unable to locate an image that you want to use on the Docker website. So, you have decided to use Dockerfile to create your own image. What are some of the advantages of building your own Dockerfile? (Choose all that apply.)

   A. Administrators can store images as code.

   B. It's an easy way to store your INI files.

   C. You can have rapid re-creation of images.

   D. You can customize exactly what you want.

48. You are the administrator for your company network. You have decided to create your own image using Dockerfile. To make programming easier for future use, you have decided to add comments to the Dockerfile. What should you use for making commands?

   A. Use the underscore (_) symbol and state exactly why each line is included.

   B. Use the pound (#) symbol and state exactly why each line is included.

   C. Use the percent (%) symbol and state exactly why each line is included.

   D. Use the asterisk (*) symbol and state exactly why each line is included.

49. You are the administrator for your company network. You are creating your own image using Dockerfile. There are different Dockerfile commands that you can use. Which command will copy new files, directories, or remote file URLs from a source (<src>) location to the filesystem of the image destination <dest>?

   A. Expose

   B. Copy

   C. Add

   D. Volume

50. You are the administrator for your company network. You are creating your own image using Dockerfile. There are different Dockerfile commands that you can use. Which command tells Docker that the container is listening on the specified network ports during runtime?

    A. Expose

    B. Copy

    C. Add

    D. Volume

51. You are the administrator for your company network. You are creating your own image using Dockerfile. Different Dockerfile commands are available for your use. What command allows an administrator to create a mount point and externally mounted volumes from host systems or other containers?

    A. Expose

    B. Copy

    C. Add

    D. Volume

52. You are the administrator for your company network. You are creating your own image using Dockerfile. Different Dockerfile commands are available for your use. Which setting allows you to set a trigger that is executed when the image is used as the base for another build?

    A. Run

    B. Onbuild

    C. Workdir

    D. Label

53. You are the administrator for your company network. You have installed Docker. You notice that Docker has created three networks out of the box. Which network is described as an automatically generated network with a subnet and a gateway?

    A. Bridge

    B. Host

    C. Proxy

    D. None

54. You are the administrator for your company network. You have installed Docker. You notice that Docker has created three networks out of the box. Which network is described as a container-specific network stack that lacks a network interface?

    A. Bridge

    B. Host

    C. Proxy

    D. None

55. You are the administrator for your company network. You are discussing an advantage of using Docker with a colleague. You are discussing the public database of images that you have access to. What is this repository of images called?

   A. Docker Hub

   B. DockerCenter

   C. DockerImageCenter

   D. DockerDatabase

56. You are the administrator for your company network. You and a colleague are discussing using Docker Hub to set up a private repository. But you are not sure if this is an available option. What statement is true regarding Docker Hub and a private repository?

   A. The Docker Hub repository allows only Windows images.

   B. Once images are added to the Docker Hub, everyone will have access to the images; there is no private option.

   C. Administrators can add users and accounts to the Docker Hub to verify that only the organization's users are accessing the images.

   D. To set up a private Docker Hub repository, you must pay a monthly fee.

57. You are the administrator for your company network. You have decided to upload corporate images to Docker Hub. What is the first thing you need to do in order to create a Docker Hub account?

   A. Create a user account.

   B. Create a repository.

   C. Enter the Docker ID namespace.

   D. Go to the URL `https://cloud.docker.com/`.

58. You are the administrator for your company network. You and a colleague are discussing PowerShell for containers and Docker. Which cmdlet allows an administrator to view information about containers?

   A. `Get-ContainerHost`

   B. `Get-Container`

   C. `New-Container`

   D. `Export-ContainerImage`

59. You are the administrator for your company network. You and a colleague are discussing PowerShell commands for containers and Docker. Which cmdlet can administrators use to view local container images?

   A. `Get-ContainerHost`

   B. `Get-Container`

   C. `New-Container`

   D. `Get-ContainerImage`

60. You are the administrator for your company network. You and a colleague are discussing PowerShell commands for containers and Docker. Which cmdlet allows an administrator to add a virtual network adapter to a container?

   A. Add-VirtualNetworkAdapter

   B. Add-ContainerNetworkAdapter

   C. New-ContainerNetworkAdapter

   D. Add-ContainerAdapter

61. You are the administrator for your company network. You and a colleague are discussing Docker and Windows Containers. Which of the following statements is true in regard to working with Docker and Windows Containers?

   A. Windows Containers are required in order to work with Docker.

   B. Docker is required in order to work with Windows Containers.

   C. Windows Containers are not required in order to work with Docker.

   D. Docker is not required in order to work with Windows Containers.

62. You are the administrator for your company network. You are planning on using Windows Containers. You know that two container base images are supported. What are they? (Choose two.)

   A. Windows Server Core

   B. Windows Server 2016 Standard

   C. Windows 10 Enterprise

   D. Nano Server

63. You are the administrator for your company network. You are planning on using containers on a virtualized network. You currently have the Hyper-V role installed on the system and have the Windows Server 2016 operating system installed. How many virtual processors for the container host virtual machine are needed?

   A. 2

   B. 4

   C. 6

   D. 8

64. You are the administrator for your company network. You have installed Docker. You plan on using the Docker command that allows you to terminate running containers. What command do you use?

   A. docker terminate

   B. docker stop

   C. docker kill

   D. docker replicate

65. You are the administrator for your company network. You have installed Docker. You plan on using the Docker command that allows an administrator to view changes to files or directories in the container's filesystem. What command do you use?

A. docker diff

B. docker filesystem

C. docker files

D. docker deploy

66. You are the administrator for your company network. You have installed Docker. You plan on using the Docker command that allows you to run a new command in an existing container. What command do you use?

A. docker exist

B. docker filesystem

C. docker commit

D. docker exec

67. You are the administrator for your company network. You have installed Docker. "Swarm mode" is a Docker feature that provides built-in container capabilities, including native clustering of Docker hosts and scheduling of workloads. A group of Docker hosts form a "swarm" cluster when their Docker engines are running together in swarm mode. A swarm is composed of two types of container hosts: manager nodes and worker nodes. What is the minimum number of manager nodes needed to run in swarm mode?

A. 1

B. 2

C. 3

D. 4

68. You are the administrator for your company network. You are discussing container types with a colleague. Name the container type described here: the container host's kernel is not shared between the other containers.

A. Hyper-V Container

B. Windows Server Container

C. Docker Container

D. Docker Daemon Container

69. You are the administrator for your company network. You are discussing container components with a colleague. Your colleague is telling you about the component that is a location where all of your images are stored. What component is she talking about?

A. Container Registry

B. Docker daemon

C. Dockerfile

D. Docker Hub repositories

70. You are the administrator for your company network. You are discussing the Docker Restart Policy with a colleague. What Docker Restart Policy command will always restart the container unless the container was stopped before the restart?

   A. always

   B. on-failure[:max-retries]

   C. no

   D. unless-stopped

71. You are the administrator for your company network. You are creating your own image using Dockerfile. Different Dockerfile commands are available that you can use. What command allows you to add an environmental variable?

   A. ENV

   B. Environment

   C. EnvironmentalVariable

   D. Variable

72. You are the administrator for your company network. You are creating your own image using Dockerfile. Different Dockerfile commands are available that you can use. What command shows the location of the container image that will be used during the image creation process?

   A. User

   B. Where

   C. From

   D. Location

73. You are the administrator for your company network. You have installed Docker and plan on using the Docker Hub repository to search for images. The Docker Hub repository has images for Microsoft, Unix, Linux, and hundreds more. You want to search for what Microsoft has in the repository. How do you search Docker for Microsoft images?

   A. docker search Microsoft

   B. search docker Microsoft

   C. docker search MS

   D. search docker MS

74. You are the administrator for your company network. You have installed Docker. You plan on using the Docker command that allows you to send an image to a registry. What command do you use?

   A. docker pull

   B. docker push

   C. docker ps

   D. docker run

75. You are the administrator for your company network. You have installed Docker. You notice that Docker has created three networks out of the box. Which network adds a container on the host's network stack?

    A. Bridge

    B. Host

    C. Proxy

    D. None

76. You are the administrator for your company network. You have a Windows Server 2016 container host named Server1. What parameter should you use with the `docker run` command if you want to see a port or a range of ports?

    A. `--entrypoint`

    B. `--expose`

    C. `--runtime`

    D. `--isolation`

    E. `--privileged`

77. You are the administrator for your company network. You have a Windows Server 2016 container host named Server1. What parameter should you use with the `docker run` command if you want to set up an IPv4 address?

    A. `--ip`

    B. `--ip4`

    C. `--ip6`

    D. `--ipconfig`

78. You are the administrator for your company network. You have installed Docker and now would like to view the current list of Docker networks. What command should you use to see the list of available networks?

    A. `docker network list`

    B. `docker network`

    C. `docker network ls`

    D. `docker list`

79. You are the administrator for your company network. You have recently installed Docker. You want to create a bridge network with a specific subnet, gateway, and name. You want the network to have a subnet of 192.168.5.0/24, a gateway of 192.168.5.10, and a name of new_subnet1. What command would you run?

    A. `docker network create --driver=bridge --subnet=192.168.5.0/24 --gateway=192.168.5.10 new_subnet1`

    B. `docker network create --driver=bridge --subnet=192.168.5.10 --gateway=192.168.5.0/24 new_subnet1`

    C. `docker create network --driver=bridge --subnet=192.168.5.0/24 --gateway=192.168.5.10 new_subnet1`

    D. `docker create network --driver=bridge --subnet=192.168.5.10 --gateway=192.168.5.0/24 new_subnet1`

80. You are the administrator for your company network. You are planning on using containers on a virtualized network. You need to install the Hyper-V role while connected locally to the server. What command do you use to install Hyper-V if you're using PowerShell?

   A. `Install-Feature -Name Hyper-V -ComputerName <computer_name>`

   B. `Install-WindowsFeature -Name Hyper-V -ComputerName <computer_name>`

   C. `Install-Feature -Name Hyper-V`

   D. `Install-WindowsFeature -Name Hyper-V`

81. You are the administrator for your company network. You have installed Docker and now would like to set the metadata on a container. What command should you use?

   A. `--tag`

   B. `--label`

   C. `--name`

   D. `--label-file`

82. You are the administrator for your company network. You and a colleague are discussing the Azure Container Registry. What does the Azure Container Registry do?

   A. It stores and manages public Docker container images.

   B. It stores and manages public Docker containers.

   C. It stores and manages private Docker container images.

   D. It stores and manages private Docker containers.

83. You are the administrator for your company network. You are planning on using Windows Containers. You know that two container base images are supported. If your application will be built for the cloud and uses the .NET Core, what base image should you use?

   A. Windows Server Core

   B. Windows Server 2016 Standard

   C. Windows 10 Enterprise

   D. Nano Server

84. You are the administrator for your company network. You and a colleague are discussing PowerShell commands for containers and Docker. Which cmdlet can administrators use to install a software package on a computer?

   A. `Install-Package`

   B. `Add-Package`

   C. `Import-Package`

   D. `Install-SoftwarePackage`

85. You are the administrator for your company network. You and a colleague are discussing PowerShell cmdlets for containers and Docker. Which cmdlet can administrators use to stop a container?

   A. `Halt-Container`

   B. `Seize-Container`

   C. `Stop-Container`

   D. `End-Container`

Chapter

5

Implement High Availability

THE FOLLOWING MCSA WINDOWS SERVER 2016 EXAM TOPICS ARE COVERED IN THIS CHAPTER:

✓ **5.1 Implement high availability and disaster recovery options in Hyper-V**

- This objective may include but is not limited to: Implement Hyper-V Replica; implement Live Migration, including Shared Nothing Live Migration; configure CredSSP or Kerberos authentication protocol for Live Migration; implement storage migration

✓ **5.2 Implement failover clustering**

- This objective may include but is not limited to: Implement Workgroup, Single, and Multi-Domain clusters; configure quorum; configure cluster networking; restore single node or cluster configuration; configure cluster storage; implement Cluster-Aware Updating; implement Cluster Operating System Rolling Upgrade; configure and optimize clustered shared volumes (CSVs); configure clusters without network names; implement Scale-Out File Server (SoFS); determine different scenarios for the use of SoFS vs File Server for general use; determine usage scenarios for implementing guest clustering; implement a Clustered Storage Spaces solution using Shared SAS storage enclosures; implement Storage Replica; implement Cloud Witness; implement VM resiliency; implement shared VHDX as a storage solution for guest clusters

✓ **5.3 Implement Storage Spaces Direct**

- This objective may include but is not limited to: Determine scenario requirements for implementing Storage Spaces Direct; enable Storage Spaces Direct using Windows PowerShell; implement a disaggregated Storage Spaces Direct scenario; implement a hyper-converged Storage Spaces Direct scenario

✓ **5.4 Manage failover clustering**

- This objective may include but is not limited to: Configure role-specific settings, including continuously available shares; configure VM monitoring; configure failover and preference settings; implement stretch and site-aware failover clusters; enable and configure node fairness

✓ **5.5 Manage VM movement in clustered nodes**

- This objective may include but is not limited to: Perform Live Migration; perform quick migration; perform storage migration; import, export, and copy VMs; configure VM network health protection; configure drain on shutdown

1. You are the administrator for your company network. What cmdlet should you use if you need to create highly available storage spaces that connect directly to the attached storage on the hosts?

   A. `Enable-ClusterStorageSpacesDirect`

   B. `Set-StoragePool`

   C. `Add-ClusterDisk`

   D. `Update-ClusterVirtualMachineConfiguration`

2. You are the network administrator for your company network. You have two Windows Server 2016 servers named Server1 and Server2. Both servers have the Hyper-V Server role installed and are nodes in a failover cluster. You create a virtual machine named VM1 on Server1. What tool should you use to configure VM1 for high availability?

   A. The `clussvc.exe` command

   B. The `cluster.exe` command

   C. The Computer Management console

   D. The `configurehyperv.exe` command

   E. The Disk Management console

   F. The Failover Cluster Manager console

   G. The Hyper-V Manager console

   H. The Server Manager Desktop app

3. You are the network administrator for your company network. You have a two-node Hyper-V cluster named Cluster1 at a main office and a stand-alone Hyper-V host named Server1 at a branch office. A virtual machine named VM1 runs on Cluster1. You configure a Hyper-V Replica of VM1 to Server1. What tool should you use if you need to perform a test failover of VM1?

   A. The `clussvc.exe` command

   B. The `cluster.exe` command

   C. The Computer Management console

   D. The `configurehyperv.exe` command

   E. The Disk Management console

   F. The Failover Cluster Manager console

   G. The Hyper-V Manager console

   H. The Server Manager Desktop app

4. You are the network administrator for your company network. You have a two-node Hyper-V cluster named Cluster1. A virtual machine named VM1 runs on Cluster1. You need to configure monitoring of VM1. What tool should you use if you need to move VM1 to a different node if the Print Spooler service on VM1 stops unexpectedly?

   A. The clussvc.exe command

   B. The cluster.exe command

   C. The Computer Management console

   D. The configurehyperv.exe command

   E. The Disk Management console

   F. The Failover Cluster Manager console

   G. The Hyper-V Manager console

   H. The Server Manager Desktop app

5. You are the administrator for your company network. You have an Active Directory domain that contains two Hyper-V servers named Server1 and Server2. Server1 runs Windows Server 2016 and Server2 runs Windows Server 2012 R2. Each Hyper-V server has three network cards, and each card is connected to a different subnet. Server1 contains a dedicated migration network. Server2 contains a virtual machine named VM2. You plan to perform a Live Migration of VM2 to Server1. What command should you run if you need to ensure that Server1 uses all available networks to perform the Live Migration of VM2?

   A. The Mount-VHD cmdlet

   B. The Set-VMHost cmdlet

   C. The Diskpart command

   D. The Install-WindowsFeature cmdlet

   E. The Set-VHD cmdlet

   F. The Optimize-VHD cmdlet

   G. The Set-VM cmdlet

   H. The Set-VMProcessor cmdlet

6. You are the administrator for your company network. The company has 10 offices. Each office has a local network that contains several Windows Server 2016 Hyper-V hosts. All of the offices are connected using high-speed, low-latency WAN links. What component should you install if you need to ensure that you can use Quality of Service (QoS) policies for Live Migration traffic between the offices?

   A. The Multipath I/O feature

   B. The Routing role service

   C. The Network Controller server role

   D. The Canary Network Diagnostics feature

   E. The Data Center Bridging feature

7. You are the administrator for your company network and you have an Active Directory domain. The domain contains Windows Server 2016 servers named Server1, Server2, and Server3. Server1 and Server2 are nodes in a Hyper-V cluster named Cluster1. You add a Hyper-V Replica Broker role named Broker1 to Cluster1. Server3 is a Hyper-V server. A virtual machine named VM1 runs on Server3. Live Migration is enabled on all three servers, and they are configured to use Kerberos authentication only. What should you do if you need to ensure that you can perform the migration of VM1 to Server2?

A. For Cluster1, modify the Cluster permissions.

B. On Server1 and Server2, add the Server3 computer account to the Replicator group.

C. On the Server3 computer account, modify the Delegation settings.

D. On Server3, modify the Storage Migration settings.

8. You are the administrator for your company network and you have an Active Directory domain. The domain contains two Hyper-V hosts. You plan to perform Live Migrations between the hosts. You need to ensure that the Live Migration traffic is authenticated by using Kerberos. What should you do first?

A. From Server Manager, install the Host Guardian Service server role on a domain controller.

B. From Active Directory Users and Computers, add the computer accounts for both servers to the Cryptographic Operators group.

C. From Active Directory Users and Computers, modify the Delegation properties of the computer accounts for both servers.

D. From Server Manager, install the Host Guardian Service server role on both servers.

9. You are the administrator for your company network. The network contains two Hyper-V servers named Server1 and Server2. Server1 has Windows Server 2012 R2 installed and Server2 has Windows Server 2016 installed. You perform a Live Migration of a virtual machine named VM1 from Server1 to Server2. What PowerShell cmdlets should you run if you need to create a production checkpoint for VM1 on Server2? (Choose all that apply.)

A. Set-VM

B. Update-VMVersion

C. Checkpoint-VM

D. Set-VMHost

E. Stop-VM

10. You are the administrator for your company network. You have five Hyper-V hosts that are configured as shown here:

Hyper-V Host Name	Configuration
Server1	Windows Server 2012 R2 and an Intel Xeon E7 Processor
Server2	Windows Server 2012 R2 and an Intel i7 Processor
Server3	Windows Server 2016 and an Intel i7 Processor
Server4	Windows Server 2016 and an AMD Opteron Processor
Server5	Windows Server 2016 and an Intel Xeon E7 Processor

What are two valid Live Migration scenarios for virtual machines in your environment? (Choose two.)

A. From Server4 to Server5

B. From Server1 to Server5

C. From Server3 to Server4

D. From Server2 to Server3

11. You are the administrator for your company network. You have a computer named Computer1 that has the following four hard disk drives installed:

- Drive A: 500 GB OS volume
- Drive B: 400 GB data volume
- Drive C: 400 GB empty volume
- Drive D: 500 GB empty volume

Using Storage Spaces, you want to create a two-way mirror. Which drives should you use while minimizing data loss?

A. Drive A and Drive B

B. Drive A and Drive D

C. Drive B and Drive C

D. Drive C and Drive D

12. You are the administrator for your company network. You purchase a new desktop computer. You have six external USB hard drives and you want to create a single volume by using these USB drives. You want the volume to be expandable, portable, and resilient in the event of simultaneous failure of two USB hard drives. What should you do to create the volume?

A. From Control Panel, create a new Storage Space across six USB hard drives. Set resiliency type to three-way mirror.

B. From Control Panel, create a new Storage Space across six USB hard drives. Set resiliency type to parity.

C. From Disk Management, create a new spanned volume.

D. From Disk Management, create a new striped volume.

13. You are the administrator for your company network. You purchase a new desktop computer that has four external USB hard drives. You want to create a single volume by using the four USB drives. You want the volume to be expandable, portable, and resilient in the event of failure of an individual USB hard drive. What should you do?

  A. From the Control Panel, create a new Storage Space across four USB hard drives. Set resiliency type to three-way mirror.

  B. From the Control Panel, create a new Storage Space across four USB hard drives. Set resiliency type to parity.

  C. From Disk Management, create a new spanned volume.

  D. From Disk Management, create a new striped volume.

14. You are the administrator for your company network. You are configuring a Windows Server 2016 failover cluster in a workgroup. Before installing one of the nodes, you run the `ipconfig /all` command and receive the following output:

```
Windows IP Configuration
Host Name . . . . . . . . . . . . . . : Server1
Primary Dns Suffix . . . . . . . :
Node Type . . . . . . . . . . . . . : Hybrid
IP Routing Enabled . . . . . . . . : No
WINS Proxy Enabled . . . . . . . : No
DNS Suffix Search List. . . . . :
Ethernet Adapter Ethernet:
Connection-specific DNS Suffix. :
Description . . . . . . . . . . . . . : Microsoft Hyper-V Network Adapter
Physical Address . . . . . . . . . . : 00-15-SD-01-62-17
DHCP Enabled . . . . . . . . . . . . : Yes
Autoconfiguration Enabled . . . . : Yes
Link-local IPv6 Address . . . : fe80::75438:46d8:8ffc:d5ab%17(Preferred)
IPv4 Address . . . . . . . . . . . . . . : 192.168.1.154(Preferred)
Subnet Mask . . . . . . . . . . . . . . : 255.255.255.0
Default Gateway . . . . . . . . . . . : 192.168.1.10
DHCPv6 IAID . . . . . . . . . . . . . . : 369099429
DHCPv6 Client DUID . . . . . . . . : 00-01-00-01-1A-1D-5D-60-00-02-A5-
4E-F4-85
DNS Server . . . . . . . . . . . . . . : 192.168.1.32
NetBIOS over Tcpip . . . . . . . . . : Disabled
```

What should you do if you need to ensure that Server1 can be added as a node in the cluster?

  A. Change Node Type to Broadcast.

  B. Assign a static IP address.

  C. Enable NetBIOS over TCP/IP.

  D. Configure a primary DNS suffix.

15. You are the administrator for your company network. You have a Windows Server 2016 Hyper-V failover cluster. This cluster contains two nodes named NodeA and NodeB. On NodeA, you create a virtual machine named VM1 by using Hyper-V Manager. You need to configure VM1 to move to NodeB automatically if NodeA becomes unavailable. What should you do?

    A. Run the Configure Role actions in the Failover Cluster Manager.

    B. Click VM1 and click Enable Replication in the Hyper-V Manager.

    C. Click NodeA and modify the Hyper-V settings in the Hyper-V Manager.

    D. Run the `Enable-VMReplication` cmdlet.

16. You are the administrator for your company network. You have a Scale-Out File Server that has a share named Share1 that contains a virtual disk file named `Disk1.vhd`. You plan to create a guest failover cluster. What cmdlet should you use if you need to ensure that you can use the virtual disk as a shared virtual disk for the guest failover cluster?

    A. `Optimize-VHDSet`

    B. `Optimize-VHD`

    C. `Set-VHD`

    D. `Convert-VHD`

17. You are the administrator for your company network. You have a failover cluster named Cluster1 that runs a highly available virtual machine named VM1. A custom application named App1 runs on VM1. You need to configure monitoring of VM1. If App1 adds an error entry to the Application event log, VM1 should be automatically rebooted and moved to another cluster node. What tool should you use to accomplish this?

    A. Hyper-V Manager

    B. Failover Cluster Manager

    C. Server Manager

    D. Resource Monitor

18. You are the administrator for your company network. You have four Windows Server 2016 servers named Server1, Server2, Server3, and Server4. Each server has a single 4 TB SATA hard disk. You attach a new 4 TB SATA hard disk to each server. You need to create a new storage cluster that uses Storage Spaces Direct. The storage pool must contain all of the new disks. What command should you run before you enable Storage Spaces Direct?

    A. `Get-ClusterAvailableDisk -Cluster Cluster1 | Add-ClusterDisk`

    B. `Add-ClusterSharedVolume -Name "Disk 1" -Cluster Cluster 1`

    C. `New-Cluster -Name Cluster1 -Node 'Server1', Server2, Server3, Server4 -NoStorage`

    D. `New-ClusterStorageEnclosure -id 1 -name Cluster 1 -type jbod -ConnectionString Server1, Server2, Server3, Server4`

19. You are the administrator for your company network. A colleague previously opened Hyper-V Manager, selected a virtual machine, and used the Enable Replication Wizard. The process was completed successfully and replication occurred as expected. Several weeks later you decide you want to run a planned failover. How should you first proceed?

   A. Right-click the primary virtual machine and select Replication ➢ Planned Failover.

   B. Right-click the replica virtual machine and select Replication ➢ Planned Failover.

   C. Right-click the primary virtual machine and select Replication ➢ Extend Replication.

   D. Right-click the replica virtual machine and select Replication ➢ Test Failover.

20. You are the administrator for your company network. You have two Windows Server 2016 Hyper-V hosts named Server1 and Server2 that are nodes in a failover cluster. You have a virtual machine named VM1 that connects to a virtual switch named vSwitch1. You discover that VM1 automatically live migrates when vSwitch1 temporarily disconnects. What should you do if you need to prevent VM1 from being live migrated when vSwitch1 temporarily disconnects?

   A. Run the `Set-VMNetworkAdapter` cmdlet and set `StormLimit` to 0.

   B. From the network adapter setting of VM1, disable the Heartbeat integration service.

   C. Run the `Set-VMNetworkAdapter` cmdlet and set `IsManagementOS` to `False`.

   D. From the network adapter settings of VM1, disable the Protected network setting.

21. You are the administrator for your company network. You decide to implement Switch Embedded Teaming (SET). You and a colleague are discussing creating a new SET team. You must configure it so that you have member adapters and load balancing mode configured. Which load balancing mode ensures that outbound loads are distributed based on a hash of the TCP ports and IP addresses? This mode also re-balances loads in real time so that a given outbound flow can move back and forth between SET team members.

   A. Dynamic

   B. Hyper-V Port

   C. Dynamic Hyper-V

   D. Outbound

22. You are the administrator for your company network. You have a Windows Server 2016 Hyper-V host named Server1 that hosts two virtual machines named VM1 and VM2. On the Hyper-V host, you create two virtual disks named Disk1 and Disk2. You plan to create a test environment for Storage Spaces Direct. What should you use if you need to configure the virtual machines to connect to the virtual disks?

   A. An iSCSI target

   B. A virtual SCSI controller

   C. A virtual Fibre channel adapter

   D. A virtual IDE controller

23. You are the administrator for your company network. You have a Hyper-V failover cluster that contains three nodes. The virtual machines are distributed evenly across the cluster nodes. Which settings should you modify if you need to ensure that if a node loses connectivity from the other nodes that the virtual machines on the node will be transitioned to one of the remaining nodes after one minute?

A. `ResiliencyPeriod` and `ResiliencyLevel`

B. `SameSubnetDelay` and `CrossSubnetDelay`

C. `QuorumArbitrationTimeMax` and `RequestReplyTimeout`

D. `QuarantineDuration` and `QuarantineThreshold`

24. You are the administrator for your company network. You create a Storage Spaces Direct hyper-converged failover cluster that contains three nodes and a 1 TB Storage Spaces Direct volume. The cluster will store virtual machines. You plan to extend the volume by adding an additional 3 TB. What is the minimum amount of extra disk capacity required to accommodate extending the volume?

A. 3 TB per node

B. 4 TB per node

C. 3 TB on the coordinator node

D. 4 TB on the coordinator node

25. You are the administrator for your company network. You are going to deploy two servers that run Windows Server 2016. You install the Failover Clustering feature on both servers. What should you do if you need to create a workgroup cluster?

A. Create matching local administrative accounts on both of the servers. Assign the same primary DNS suffix to both of the servers. Run the `New-Cluster` cmdlet and specify an administrative access point of None.

B. Configure both of the servers to be in a workgroup named Workgroup. Configure the Cluster Service to log on as Network Service. Run the `New-Cluster` cmdlet and specify an administrative access point of DNS.

C. Create matching local administrative accounts on both of the servers. Assign the same primary DNS suffix to both of the servers. Run the `New-Cluster` cmdlet and specify an administrative access point of DNS.

D. Configure both of the servers to be in a workgroup named Workgroup. Configure the Cluster Service to log on as Network Service. Run the `New-Cluster` cmdlet and specify an administrative access point of None.

26. You are the administrator for your company network. You and a colleague are discussing working with cluster nodes. Once a node is created there are a few actions that are available to you. One of the options is that you can set the node to prevent resources from being failed over or moved to the node. What is this called?

A. Evict

B. Add

C. Pause

D. Stop

27. You are the administrator for your company network. One of the nodes in a cluster has become damaged beyond repair. What action must you perform to remove the node from the cluster?

A. Evict

B. Delete

C. Remove

D. Expel

28. You are the administrator for your company network. You have a Windows Server 2016 failover cluster named Cluster1 that contains three nodes named Server1, Server2, and Server3. Each node hosts several virtual machines. The virtual machines are configured to fail over to another node in Cluster1 if the hosting node fails. What setting should you configure if you need to ensure that if the Cluster service fails on one of the nodes, the virtual machine of that node will fail over immediately?

A. `FailureConditionLevel`

B. `QuarantineDuration`

C. `ResiliencyPeriod`

D. `ResiliencyLevel`

29. You are the administrator for your company network. You have two Windows Server 2016 servers that are configured as shown:

Server Name	Workgroup	DNS Suffix
Server1	Workgroup1	None
Server2	Workgroup2	abc.com

What commands should you run if you need to create a failover cluster that contains both servers? (Choose two.)

A. `New-Cluster-Name Cluster1-Node Server1,`
`Server2-AdministrativeAccessPoint ActiveDirectoryAndDns`

B. `New-Cluster-Name Cluster1-Node Server1,`
`Server2-AdministrativeAccessPoint DNS`

C. `New-Cluster-Name Cluster1-Node Server1,`
`Server2-AdministrativeAccessPoint None`

D. `wmic ComputerSystem Set Workgroup= "Workgroup2"`

E. `netdom computername Server1/MakePrimary:server1.abc.com`

30. You are the administrator for your company network. Your network contains an Active Directory domain that contains two Windows Server 2016 servers named Server1 and Server2. Each server has an operating system disk and four data disks. All of the disks are locally attached SATA disks. Each disk is a basic disk, is initialized as an MBR disk, and has a single NTFS volume. You plan to implement Storage Spaces Direct by using the data disks on Server1 and Server2. What should you do to prepare the data disks for the Storage Spaces Direct implementation?

  A. Initialize the data disks as GPT disks and create an ReFS volume on each disk.

  B. Format the volumes on the data disks as exFAT.

  C. Delete the volumes from the data disks.

  D. Convert the data disks to dynamic disks.

31. You are the administrator for your company network. You have two Windows Server 2012 R2 Hyper-V hosts named Server1 and Server2. The servers are nodes in a failover cluster named Cluster1. You perform a rolling upgrade of the cluster nodes to Windows Server 2016. What cmdlet should you use if you need to ensure that you can implement the Virtual Machine Load Balancing feature?

  A. `SetCauClusterRole`

  B. `Update-ClusterFunctionalLevel`

  C. `Update-ClusterNetworkNameResource`

  D. `Set-ClusterGroupSet`

32. You are the administrator for your company network. You have an Active Directory domain that contains several Windows Server 2016 Hyper-V hosts. What component must be installed for the planned deployment if you want to deploy network virtualization and centrally manage Data Center Firewall policies?

  A. The Routing role service

  B. The Data Center Bridging feature

  C. The Canary Network Diagnostics feature

  D. The Network Controller server role

33. You are the administrator for your company network. The network contains an Active Directory forest with a Windows Server 2016 forest functional level. You have a failover cluster named Cluster1 that has two nodes named Node1 and Node2. All the optional features in Active Directory are enabled. A colleague accidentally deletes the computer object named Cluster1. You discover that Cluster1 is offline. What should you do to restore the operation of Cluster1 as quickly as possible?

  A. Recover the deleted object from the Active Directory Recycle Bin.

  B. Run the `Enable-ADAccount` cmdlet from the PowerShell.

  C. Perform an authoritative restore by running ntdutil.exe.

  D. Perform a tombstone reanimation by running `ldp.exe`.

34. You are the administrator for your company network. Your network contains two Windows Server 2016 Web servers named Server1 and Server2. Server1 and Server2 are nodes in a Network Load Balancing (NLB) cluster that contains an application named App1 that is accessed by using the URL http://app1.abc.com. You plan to perform maintenance on Server1. What should you run to ensure that all new connections to App1 are directed to Server2 while not disconnecting the existing connections to Server1?

A. The nlb.exe stop command

B. The Suspend-NlbClusterNode cmdlet

C. The Set-NlbCluster cmdlet

D. The nlt.exe suspend command

35. You are the administrator for your company network. You need to perform maintenance against a Network Load Balancing (NLB) cluster node, but you do not want to terminate current connections. What should you use?

A. Evict

B. Drainstop

C. Stop

D. Pause

36. You are the administrator for your company network. You have two servers that run Windows Server 2016. You are planning to create a Network Load Balancing (NLB) cluster that will contain both servers. What should you do to configure the network cards on the servers for the planned NLB configuration?

A. Configure the network cards to be on the same subnet and have static IP addresses. Configure the cluster to use unicast.

B. Configure the network cards to be on different subnets and have static IP addresses. Configure the cluster to use unicast.

C. Configure the network cards to be on the same subnet and have dynamic IP addresses. Configure the cluster to use multicast.

D. Configure the network cards to be on different subnets subnet and have dynamic IP addresses. Configure the cluster to use multicast.

37. You are the administrator for your company network. You are discussing affinity settings with a colleague. You know there are several different affinity settings available. You are discussing the New Cluster Wizard. What is the default affinity setting that the New Cluster Wizard uses?

A. No affinity (none)

B. Single affinity

C. Class C affinity

D. Multiple affinity

38. You are the administrator for your company network. You and a colleague are discussing virtual machine checkpoints. When setting up virtual machine checkpoints, the virtual checkpoints can be accessed from up to _____ hours ago.

   A. 12

   B. 18

   C. 24

   D. 36

39. You are the administrator for your company network. You and a colleague are discussing Windows Server 2016 Network Load Balancing. Network Load Balancing is designed to work with which of the following?

   A. Web servers

   B. FTP servers

   C. Firewalls

   D. Proxy servers

   E. Virtual Private Networks (VPNs)

   F. All of the above

40. You are the administrator for your company network. You and a colleague are discussing Network Load Balancing (NLB). How many computers can a single cluster with NLB scalability support?

   A. 16

   B. 32

   C. 48

   D. 64

41. You are the administrator for your company network. You and a colleague are discussing port rules. You know that port rules allow you to configure which ports are going to be enabled or disabled. HTTP uses what port number?

   A. 20

   B. 25

   C. 80

   D. 443

42. You are the administrator for your company network. You and a colleague are discussing failover clustering. You know that there are network requirements that must be met for failover clustering. What is one requirement?

   A. Network adapters should be of different makes, use the same driver, and have the firmware version in each cluster node.

   B. Network adapters should be the same make, use the same driver, and have the firmware version in each cluster node.

   C. Network adapters should be the same make, use different drivers, and have the firmware version in each cluster node.

   D. Network adapters should be of different makes, use different drivers, and have the firmware version in each cluster node.

43. You are the administrator for your company network. You and a colleague are discussing the types of network connections that are available in a failover cluster. What are the two types? (Choose two.)

A. Public network

B. Internal network

C. External network

D. Private network

44. You are the administrator for your company network. Your network contains an Active Directory domain that contains two Windows Server 2016 member servers named Server1 and Server2, which both have the Failover Clustering feature installed. The servers are configured as nodes in a failover cluster named Cluster1. You add two additional nodes to the cluster. What should you configure to make sure that Cluster1 will stop running if three nodes fail?

A. Set the node to Affinity-None.

B. Set the failover settings.

C. Set the cluster quorum settings.

D. Set the node to Affinity-Single.

45. You are the administrator for your company network. You and a colleague are discussing the Virtual Machine Load Balancing feature, which is new to Windows Server 2016. This new load balancing feature helps optimize the nodes in a cluster. To set up Node Fairness, you use the PowerShell command (Get-Cluster).AutoBalancerLevel = <value>. If you want a Low setting, which setting do you choose?

A. 1

B. 2

C. 3

D. Low

46. You are the administrator for your company network. Your network contains an Active Directory domain that contains a Windows Server 2016 server named Server1 and has the DHCP Server role installed. Server1 has an IPv6 scope named Scope1. You implement an additional DHCP server named Server2 that runs Windows Server 2016. What should you do if you need to provide high availability for Scope1?

A. Create a scope on Server2.

B. Configure DHCP failover on Server1.

C. Install and configure Failover Clustering on Server1 and Server2.

D. Install and configure Network Load Balancing (NLB) on Server1 and Server2.

47. You are the administrator for your company network. The network contains an Active Directory domain. Your company has a main office and a remote office. The remote office is used for disaster recovery. The domain contains Windows Server 2016 member servers named Server1, Server2, and Server3. Server1 and Server2 are located in the main office. Server3 is located in the remote office. All servers have the Failover Clustering feature installed. The servers are configured as nodes in a failover cluster named Cluster1. Storage is replicated between the main office and the remote site. What are two possible quorum configurations if you need to ensure that Cluster1 is available if two nodes in the same office fail? (Choose two.)

   A. Majority Node

   B. No Majority: Disk Only

   C. Node and Disk Majority

   D. Node and File Share Majority

48. You are the administrator for your company network. You have a Windows Server 2016 virtual machine named VM1. VM1 hosts a service that requires high network throughput. VM1 has a virtual network adapter that connects to a Hyper-V switch named vSwitch1 that has one network adapter. The network adapter supports Remote Direct Memory Access (RMDA), the Single Root I/O Virtualization (SR-IOV) interface, Quality of Service (QoS), and Receive Side Scaling (RSS). What PowerShell command should you run on the host of VM1 if you need to ensure that the traffic from VM1 can be processed by multiple networking processors?

   A. Set-NetAdapterQoS

   B. Set-NetAdapterSriov

   C. Set-NetAdapterRdma

   D. Set-NetAdapterRss

49. You are the administrator for your company network. You have decided to set up a Network Load Balancing (NLB) cluster. What cmdlet should you use if you want to use PowerShell to set up the cluster?

   A. Set-NlbCluster

   B. Create-NlbCluster

   C. New-NlbCluster

   D. Setup-NlbCluster

50. You are the administrator for your company network. You have an application named App1. App1 is distributed in a multitenant setup across multiple Hyper-V virtual machines. What should you include in the environment if you need to ensure that the traffic is distributed evenly among the virtual machines that host App1?

   A. Network Controller and Windows Server Network Load Balancing (NLB) nodes

   B. Network Controller and Windows Server Software Load Balancing (SLB) nodes

   C. RAS Gateway and Windows Server Software Load Balancing (SLB) nodes

   D. RAS Gateway and Windows Server Network Load Balancing (NLB) nodes

51. You are the administrator for your company network. You and a colleague are discussing Network Load Balancing (NLB). Which of the following actions should be performed against an NLB cluster node if maintenance needs to be performed and all connections must be terminated immediately?

A. Evict

B. Drainstop

C. Pause

D. Stop

52. You are the administrator for your company network. You and a colleague are discussing stopping virtual machine replication. What PowerShell command would you use if you wanted to stop virtual machine replication?

A. Stop-VMReplication

B. Terminate-VMReplication

C. Kill-VMReplication

D. Drainstop-VMReplication

53. You are the administrator for your company network. You are planning on configuring Network Load Balancing (NLB). To configure an NLB cluster with unicast, what is the minimum number of network adapters required in each node?

A. One

B. Two

C. Three

D. Six

54. You are the administrator for your company network. You use Network Load Balancing (NLB). Users who are connecting to an NLB cluster have been complaining that after using the site for a few minutes they are prompted to log in using their username. What should you do to fix the problem and retain scalability?

A. Create a port rule to allow only ports 80 and 443.

B. Set the cluster affinity to None.

C. Set the filtering mode to Single Host.

D. Set the cluster affinity to Single.

55. You are the administrator for your company network. You use Network Load Balancing (NLB). Users who are connecting to an NLB cluster through the Internet are complaining that they keep connecting to different NLB nodes in different locations. What should you do if you want to keep Internet users connecting to the same NLB members each time they connect?

A. Create a port rule to allow only ports 80 and 443.

B. Set the cluster affinity to None.

C. Set the cluster affinity to Class C.

D. Set the cluster affinity to Single.

56. You are the administrator for your company network. You are planning on implementing site-aware clustering. What two PowerShell commands would you use to help you set up site-aware clustering? (Choose two.)

   A. `(Get-Cluster).CrossSiteDelay = <value>`

   B. `(Get-Cluster).CrossSiteThreshold = <value>`

   C. `(Add-Cluster).CrossSiteDelay = <value>`

   D. `(Add-Cluster).CrossSiteThreshold = <value>`

57. You are the administrator for your company network. You and a colleague are discussing failover clusters. What is the maximum number of nodes that can participate in a Windows Server 2016 failover cluster?

   A. 2

   B. 4

   C. 16

   D. 64

58. You are the administrator for your company network. You are planning on configuring storage spaces. Which PowerShell cmdlet would you use if you want to create highly available storage spaces that connect to directly attached storage on the hosts?

   A. `Enable-ClusterStorageSpacesDirect`

   B. `Set-StoragePool`

   C. `Add-ClusterDisk`

   D. `Update-ClusterVirtualMachineConfiguration`

59. You are the administrator for your company network. You and a colleague are discussing when to use the Validate a Configuration Wizard. If you have a running cluster and need to run the Validate a Configuration Wizard, which of the following tests may require cluster resources to be taken offline?

   A. Network tests

   B. Storage tests

   C. System configuration tests

   D. Inventory tests

60. You are the administrator for your company network. You and a colleague are discussing the Failover Clustering feature versus Network Load Balancing (NLB). Which of the following applications would be better suited on a failover cluster instead of a network load-balanced cluster? (Choose all that apply.)

   A. SQL Server

   B. Website

   C. Exchange Mailbox Server

   D. VPN services

61. You are the administrator for your company network. You plan to set up and test a cluster. What PowerShell cmdlet would you use to run a validation test on a cluster?

A. `Test-Cluster`

B. `Validate-Cluster`

C. `Set-Cluster`

D. `Add-Cluster`

62. You are the administrator for your company network. You and a colleague are discussing site-aware failover clusters. What is the mechanism that is used in clustering to see if a node is online or if the node is not responding?

A. Testbeat

B. Heartbeat

C. Testnode

D. Pulse

63. You are the administrator for your company network. You and a colleague are discussing cluster quorums. In a four-node cluster set to a Node and File Share Majority quorum model, how many votes can be lost before quorum is lost?

A. One

B. Two

C. Three

D. Four

64. You are the administrator for your company network. You and a colleague are discussing cluster quorums. In a three-node cluster set to a Node Majority quorum model, how many cluster nodes can be offline before quorum is lost?

A. Zero

B. One

C. Two

D. Three

65. You are the administrator for your company network. You and a colleague are discussing Network Load Balancing (NLB). Which of the following editions of Windows Server 2016 can be configured in an NLB cluster? (Choose all that apply.)

A. Windows Server 2016 Virtual Edition

B. Windows Server 2016 Standard Edition

C. Windows Server 2016 Small Business Server

D. Windows Server 2016 Datacenter Edition

66. You are the administrator for your company network. You and a colleague are discussing NIC Teaming. What is the maximum number of network adapters that can participate in a NIC Team?

A. 4

B. 16

C. 32

D. 64

67. You are the administrator for your company network. You and a colleague are discussing Network Load Balancing (NLB) versus failover clusters. Which of the following applications would be better suited on an NLB cluster instead of a failover cluster? (Choose all that apply.)

    A. SQL Server

    B. Website

    C. Database servers

    D. Terminal Services

68. You are the administrator for your company network. You have a two-node cluster and have a specific resource that fails frequently but is not crucial to the functionality. What would you do to keep the resource from causing the entire application from failing to the other node while still providing redundancy for the application when needed?

    A. Deselect the option to allow the resource to fail over the service or application.

    B. Remove one node of the possible owners from the cluster nodes.

    C. Select the option to run the resource in a separate resource monitor.

    D. Select the option to allow the resource to fail over the service or application.

69. You are the administrator for your company network. You and a colleague are discussing a high availability plan that is usually expressed in percentages of the time the application is available. What type of high availability plan is being discussed?

    A. Disaster Recovery (DR)

    B. Service Level Agreement (SLA)

    C. Recovery Point Objective (RPO)

    D. Recovery Time Objective (RTO)

70. You are the administrator for your company network. You are discussing high availability. You know that Windows Server 2016 provides two types of high availability. What are the two types? (Choose two.)

    A. Network Load Balancing (NLB)

    B. Hyper-V

    C. Failover Clustering

    D. Software Load Balancing (SLB)

71. You are the administrator for your company network. You are setting up Live Migration, and one of the settings that you can manipulate is the type of authentication you can use. You want the option that will allow an administrator to set up better security but requires constrained delegation for Live Migration. You will want the ability to sign in to the source server. What type of authentication do you choose?

    A. Kerberos

    B. Compression

    C. Credential Security Support Provider (CredSSP)

    D. Server Message Block (SMB)

72. You are the administrator for your company network. You are planning on setting up an advanced quorum configuration. You are planning on setting up a Failover Cluster quorum witness that utilizes Microsoft Azure as the intercession point. What witness type are you planning on setting up?

- **A.** Cloud witness
- **B.** File Share witness
- **C.** Disk witness
- **D.** Computer witness

73. You are the administrator for your company network. You plan on setting up your Hyper-V virtualized cluster to use a shared VHDX virtual disk. Shared virtual disks are useful in providing highly available shared storage. What types of virtualized workloads can use a shared VHDX? (Choose all that apply.)

- **A.** SQL Server
- **B.** DHCP Server
- **C.** Virtual Machine Manager
- **D.** Exchange Server

74. You are the administrator for your company network. You are planning to install Storage Spaces Direct. You and a colleague are discussing the various deployment options available. Your colleague is discussing the option where there is only one cluster for storage and compute; this option reduces the hardware costs for associated deployments. What option is being discussed?

- **A.** Converged
- **B.** Scale-Out File Server (SoFS)
- **C.** Hyper-Converged
- **D.** Network Attached Storage (NAS)

75. You are the administrator for your company network. You are planning to install Storage Spaces Direct. You and a colleague are discussing the various deployment options available. Your colleague is discussing the option in which there are separate clusters for each storage and compute, which allows for scaling computer/workloads separately from the storage cluster. What option is being discussed?

- **A.** Converged
- **B.** Scale-Out File Server (SoFS)
- **C.** Hyper-Converged
- **D.** Network Attached Storage (NAS)

76. You are the administrator for your company network. You are planning to install Storage Spaces Direct. You know you must meet minimum and maximum hardware requirements. What is the maximum number of servers that are allowed to set up Storage Spaces Direct?

- **A.** 2
- **B.** 4
- **C.** 8
- **D.** 16

77. You are the administrator for your company network. You are discussing Network Load Balancing (NLB) features with a colleague. NLB uses what networking protocol to distribute traffic?

  A. Transmission Control Protocol/Internet Protocol (TCP/IP)

  B. User Datagram Protocol (UDP)

  C. File Transfer Protocol (FTP)

  D. Hypertext Transfer Protocol (HTTP)

78. You are the administrator for your company network. You know that if the primary or secondary (extended) host server location goes offline, you can manually initiate failover and that it's not automatic. There are several types of manually initiating failover. Which one is being described if you verify that the replica virtual machine can successfully start in the secondary site?

  A. Planned Failover

  B. Unplanned Failover

  C. Test Failover

  D. Scheduled Failover

79. You are the administrator for your company network. One advantage in Windows Server 2016 is dynamic quorum management. Which statement best describes dynamic quorum management?

  A. Allows you to assign or remove quorum votes on a per-node basis

  B. Allows you to manually manage the vote assignment to nodes

  C. Allows you to remove votes from the nodes in the backup site

  D. Automatically manages the vote assignment to nodes

80. You are the administrator for your company network. Windows Server 2016 allows you to set up a cluster without using Active Directory dependencies. Administrators can create clusters in which of the following situations? (Choose all that apply.)

  A. All nodes in the cluster are part of the same domain.

  B. Nodes in the cluster are part of different domains.

  C. Nodes are member servers and part of a workgroup.

  D. It can be a single-domain, multidomain, or workgroup cluster.

81. You are the administrator for your company network. You have a failover cluster and you make a software change to the cluster. What should you do to identify if there are any issues that can cause a problem with the failover cluster?

  A. Check the Hardware Compatibility List (HCL).

  B. Run the Validate a Configuration Wizard.

  C. Restart the cluster.

  D. Run the Validate Software Wizard.

82. You are the administrator for your company network. You are planning to install Storage Spaces Direct. You know you must meet minimum and maximum hardware requirements. What is the number of NICs that are recommended to set up Storage Spaces Direct?

A. 2

B. 3

C. 4

D. 5

83. You are the administrator for your company network. You are discussing the Virtual Machine Advanced Features with a colleague. What feature allows the ability to set Network Health Detection at the virtual machine level for a Hyper-V host cluster?

A. Router Guard

B. DHCP Guard

C. MAC Addressing

D. Protected Network

84. You are the administrator for your company network. You are discussing using Switch Embedded Teaming (SET) as an alternative to using NIC Teaming. What else does SET allow you to do?

A. It allows an administrator to combine a group of physical adapters (a minimum of one adapter and a maximum of eight adapters) into hardware-based virtual adapters.

B. It allows an administrator to combine a group of physical adapters (a minimum of one adapter and a maximum of eight adapters) into software-based virtual adapters.

C. It allows an administrator to combine a group of virtual adapters (a minimum of one adapter and a maximum of eight adapters) into software-based virtual adapters.

D. It allows an administrator to combine a group of virtual adapters (a minimum of one adapter and a maximum of eight adapters) into hardware-based virtual adapters.

85. You are the administrator for your company network. You are using PowerShell to set up your Hyper-V high availability. Which cmdlet allows you to configure a host as a replica server?

A. Get-VMReplicationServer

B. Set-VMReplication

C. Set-VMReplicationServer

D. Get-VMReplication

Chapter

6

Implement Domain Name System (DNS)

THE FOLLOWING MCSA WINDOWS SERVER 2016 EXAM TOPICS ARE COVERED IN THIS CHAPTER:

✓ **6.1 Install and Configure DNS Servers**

- This objective may include but is not limited to: Determine DNS installation requirements; determine supported DNS deployment scenarios on Nano Server; install DNS; configure forwarders; configure Root Hints; configure delegation; implement DNS policies; configure DNS Server settings using Windows PowerShell; configure Domain Name System Security Extensions (DNSSEC); configure DNS Socket Pool; configure cache locking; enable Response Rate Limiting; configure DNS-based Authentication of Named Entities (DANE); configure DNS logging; configure delegated administration; configure recursion settings; implement DNS performance tuning; configure global settings

✓ **6.2 Implement and Maintain IP Address Management (IPAM)**

- This objective may include but is not limited to: Provision IPAM manually or by using Group Policy; configure server discovery; create and manage IP blocks and ranges; monitor utilization of IP address space; migrate existing workloads to IPAM; configure IPAM database storage using SQL Server; determine scenarios for using IPAM with System Center Virtual Machine Manager for physical and virtual IP address space management; manage DHCP server properties using IPAM; configure DHCP scopes and options; configure DHCP policies and failover; manage DNS server properties using IPAM; manage DNS zones and records; manage DNS and DHCP servers in multiple Active Directory forests; delegate administration for DNS and DHCP using role-based access control (RBAC); audit the changes performed on the DNS and DHCP servers; audit the IPAM address usage trail; audit DHCP lease events and user logon events

1. You are the administrator for your company network. You have a Windows Server 2016 Nano Server named Server1. You want to install the Domain Name System (DNS) Server role on Server1. What should you run?

   A. The dns.exe command

   B. The Enable-WindowsOptionalFeature cmdlet

   C. The Install-Package cmdlet

   D. The optionalfeature.exe command

2. You are the administrator for your company network. You have a Windows Server 2016 Hyper-V host. The host contains a virtual machine named VM1 that has resource metering enabled. What cmdlet should you run if you need to use resource metering to track the amount of network traffic that VM1 sends to the 10.0.0.0/8 network?

   A. New-VMResourcePool

   B. Set-VMNetworkAdapter

   C. Set-VMNetworkAdapterRoutingDomainMapping

   D. Add-VMNetworkAdapterAcl

3. You are the administrator for your company network. You have a Windows Server 2016 server named Server1 that is configured as a domain controller. You install the DNS Server role on Server1. You plan to store a DNS zone in a custom Active Directory partition. What should you use if you need to create a new Active Directory partition for the zone?

   A. dnscmd.exe

   B. Set-DnsServer

   C. dns.exe

   D. Active Directory Sites and Services

4. You are the administrator for your company network. You have an IP Address Management (IPAM) deployment that is used to manage all of the DNS servers on the network. IPAM is configured to use Group Policy provisioning. You discover that a user has added a new mail exchanger (MX) record to one of the DNS zones and you want to figure out which user added the record. You open Event Catalog on an IPAM server and discover that the most recent event occurred yesterday. What should you do if you need to ensure that the operational events in the event catalog are never older than one hour?

   A. From Task Scheduler, create a scheduled task that runs the Update-IpamServer cmdlet.

   B. From Task Scheduler, modify the Microsoft\Windows\IPAM\Audit task.

   C. From the properties on the DNS zone, modify the refresh interval.

   D. From an IPAM_DNS Group Policy Object (GPO), modify the Group Policy refresh interval.

5. You are the administrator for your company network. You are discussing Group Policy Objects (GPOs) with a colleague. If you choose the Group Policy–based provisioning method for IPAM, you must also provide a GPO name prefix in the provisioning wizard. After you provide a GPO name prefix, the wizard will display the GPO names that must be created in domains that will be managed by IPAM. In the following PowerShell command, how many GPOs would be created?

```
Invoke-IpamGpoProvisioning -Domain abc.com -GpoPrefixName
IPAM1-DelegatedGpoUser user1 -IpamServerFqdn ipam1.abc.com
```

A. 1

B. 2

C. 3

D. 4

6. You are the administrator for your company network. What should you do if you need to modify the GPO prefix by IPAM?

A. Run the `Invoke-IpamGpoProvisioning` cmdlet.

B. Run the `Set-IpamConfiguration` cmdlet.

C. Click Provision the IPAM Server in Server Manager.

D. Click Configure Server Discovery in Server Manager.

7. You are the administrator for your company network. You have a Windows Server 2016 IPAM server named IPAM1 that manages 10 DHCP servers. You need to provide a user with the ability to track which clients receive which IP addresses from DHCP. The solution must minimize administrative privileges. To which group should you add this user?

A. IPAM User

B. IPAM MSM Administrators

C. IPAM ASM Administrators

D. IPAM IP Audit Administrators

8. You are the administrator for your company network. Your network contains an Active Directory domain that has a Windows Server 2016 server named Server1, which is a member server and has the DNS Server role installed. Automatic scavenging of state records is enabled, and the scavenging period is set to 10 days. All client computers dynamically register their names in the DNS zone on Server1. You discover that the names of multiple client computers that were removed from the network several weeks ago can still be resolved. What should you do if you need to configure Server1 to automatically remove the records of the client computers that have been offline for more than 10 days?

A. Run the `dnscmd.exe` command and specify the `/AgeAllRecords` parameter for the zone.

B. Modify the Zone Aging/Scavenging properties of the zone.

C. Set the Time to Live (TTL) value of all the records in the zone.

D. Set the Expires After value of the zone.

9. You are the administrator for your company network. You have 2,000 devices, and 100 of these are mobile devices that have physical addresses beginning with 98-5F. You have a Windows Server 2016 DHCP server named Server1. What should you do if you need to ensure that the mobile devices register their host names by using a DNS suffix of mobile.abc.com?

   A. Create a new filter from IPv4.

   B. Create a reservation.

   C. Modify the Conflict Detection Attempts setting from the properties of Scope1.

   D. Run the DHCP Policy Configuration Wizard from IPv4.

   E. Configure Name Protection from the properties of Scope1.

   F. Configure the bindings from the properties of IPv4.

   G. Create an exclusion range from the properties of Scope1.

   H. Modify the properties of Ethernet from the Control Panel.

10. You are the administrator for your company network. You and a colleague are discussing client reservations. With client reservations, you can reserve an IP address for permanent use by a DHCP client. Typically, you will need to do this if the client uses an IP address that was assigned using another method for TCP/IP configuration. If you are reserving an IP address for a new client, or an address that is different from its current one, you should verify that the address has not already been leased by the DHCP server. Reserving an IP address in a scope does not automatically force a client currently using that address to stop using it. So, what ipconfig command would you use if the address is already in use?

   A. ipconfig /release

   B. ipconfig /renew

   C. ipconfig /flushdns

   D. ipconfig /registerdns

11. You are the administrator for your company network. You and a colleague are discussing Domain Name System (DNS). The DNS Server service provides several types of zones. What zone type helps to keep delegated zone information current, improve name resolution, and simplify DNS administration, but is not an alternative for enhancing redundancy and load sharing?

   A. Secondary zone

   B. Stub zone

   C. Principal zone

   D. Primary zone

12. You are the administrator for your company network. You and a colleague are discussing DNS queries. The following is an example of DNS query results that are performed from a DNS client computer using the Resolve-DnsName cmdlet:

   resolve-dnsname -name finance.secure.abc.com -type A -server dns1.abc.com

What extra parameter should you use if you want to include the DO bit in a DNS query to make sure the client is DNSSEC-aware and that it is okay for the DNS server to return DNSSEC data in a response?

A. `-DnssecCd`

B. `-DnssecOk`

C. `-DnsOnly`

D. `-LlmnrOnly`

13. You are the administrator for your company network. You and a colleague are discussing socket pools. The socket pool enables a DNS server to use source port randomization when issuing DNS queries. What command offers the greatest protection?

A. `dnscmd /config /socketpoolsize 0`

B. `dnscmd /config /socketpoolsize 1`

C. `dnscmd /config /socketpoolsize 1000`

D. `dnscmd /config /socketpoolsize 1000 /socketpoolexcludedportranges 1-65535`

14. You are the administrator for your company network. You have a Windows Server 2016 server named Server1 that has the DHCP Server and the Windows Deployment Service (WDS) server roles installed. Server1 is located on the same subnet as client computers. You need to ensure that clients can perform a PXE boot from Server1. Which IPv4 options should you configure in DHCP? (Choose two.)

A. 003 Router

B. 006 DNS Servers

C. 015 DNS Domain Name

D. 060 Option 60

E. 066 Boot Server Host Name

15. You are the administrator for your company network. You have two Windows Server 2016 DNS servers named Server1 and Server2. All client computers run Windows 10 and are configured to use Server1 for DNS name resolution. Server2 hosts a primary zone named abc.com. Your network recently experienced several DNS spoofing attacks. What should you do to prevent further attacks from succeeding on Server2? (Choose two.)

A. Configure the abc.com zone to be Active Directory integrated.

B. Sign the abc.com zone.

C. Configure DNS Cache locking.

D. Configure Response Rate Limiting (RRL).

16. You are the administrator for your company network. You have a Windows Server 2016 DHCP server named Server1 that has the following scopes configured:

Scope Name	Address Pool	Default Gateway	DNS Server
Desktops	192.168.0.0/24	192.168.0.1	192.168.0.140
Visitors	192.168.0.1/24	192.168.1.1	192.168.0.140

All other scope settings are set to the default values. There are no available address spaces for another scope to be created. Your network has 150 desktop computers that have access to the corporate network. Your company also provides visitors with Wi-Fi access to the network. There can be up to 200 visitors each day. What should you do to ensure that you have enough address spaces for Visitors?

A. Configure a superscope that contains the Visitors scope.

B. For the Visitors scope, run the DHCP Split Scope Configuration Wizard.

C. Run Set-DhcpServer4Scope –Name Mobile –LeaseDuration 0.02:00:00.

D. Run Set-DhcpServer4Scope –ActivatePolicies $True –Name Mobile –MaxBootPClients 200.

17. You are the administrator for your company network. You have a DHCP server named Server1. Server1 has an IPv4 scope that serves 75 client computers that run Windows 10. When you review the address leases in the DHCP console, you discover that there are several leases for devices that you do not recognize. What should you do if you need to ensure that only the 75 Windows 10 computers can obtain a lease from the scope?

A. Run the Add-DhcpServerv4ExclusionRange cmdlet.

B. Create a DHCP policy for the scope.

C. Create and enable a DHCP filter.

D. Run the Add-DhcpServerv4OptionDefinition cmdlet.

18. You are the administrator for your company network. You have Windows Server 2016 servers named Server1 and DHCP1. DHCP1 contains an IPv4 scope named Scope1. You have 1,000 client computers. You need to configure Server1 to lease IP addresses for Scope1. The solution must ensure that Server1 is used to respond to up to 30 percent of the DHCP client requests only. On Server1, you install the DHCP Server role. What should you do next?

A. Run the Configure Failover Wizard from the DHCP console.

B. Create a superscope from the DHCP console.

C. Install the Network Load Balancing (NLB) feature from Server Manager.

D. Install the Failover Clustering feature from Server Manager.

19. You are the administrator for your company network. You have a DHCP server named Server1 that has three network cards. Each network card is configured to use a static IP address. Each network card connects to a different network segment. Server1 has an IPv4 scope named Scope1. What should you do if you need to ensure that Server1 only uses one network card when leasing IP addresses in Scope1?

A. Create a reservation.

B. Modify the Conflict Detection Attempts setting from the properties of Scope1.

    C. Create a new filter from IPv4.

    D. Configure Name Protection from the properties of Scope1.

    E. Create an exclusion range from the properties of Scope1.

    F. Run the DHCP Policy Configuration Wizard from IPv4.

    G. Configure the bindings from the properties of IPv4.

    H. Modify the properties of Ethernet from the Control Panel.

20. You are the administrator for your company network. You have a DHCP server named Server1 that has an IPv4 scope named Scope1. Users report that when they turn on their computers it takes a long time to access the network. You validate that it takes a long time for the computers to receive an IP address from Server1. You monitor the network traffic and discover that Server1 issues five ping commands on the network before leasing an IP address. What should you do if you need to reduce the amount of time it takes for the computers to receive an IP address?

    A. Create a reservation.

    B. Modify the Conflict Detection Attempts setting from the properties of Scope1.

    C. Create a new filter from IPv4.

    D. Configure Name Protection from the properties of Scope1.

    E. Create an exclusion range from the properties of Scope1.

    F. Run the DHCP Policy Configuration Wizard from IPv4.

    G. Configure the bindings from the properties of IPv4.

    H. Modify the properties of Ethernet from the Control Panel.

21. You are the administrator for your company network. Your network contains Windows and non-Windows devices. You have a DHCP server named Server1 that has an IPv4 scope named Scope1. What should you do if you need to prevent a client computer that uses the same name as an existing registration from updating the registration?

    A. Create a reservation.

    B. Modify the Conflict Detection Attempts setting from the properties of Scope1.

    C. Create a new filter from IPv4.

    D. Configure Name Protection from the properties of Scope1.

    E. Create an exclusion range from the properties of Scope1.

    F. Run the DHCP Policy Configuration Wizard from IPv4.

    G. Configure the bindings from the properties of IPv4.

    H. Modify the properties of Ethernet from the Control Panel.

22. You are the administrator for your company network. You have an Active Directory forest that contains 30 servers and 6,000 client computers. You deploy a new DHCP server that runs Windows Server 2016. What command should you run if you need to retrieve the list of the authorized DHCP servers?

    A. `Get-DhcpServerDatabase`

    B. `Netstat -p IP -s -a`

    C. `Get-DhcpServerInDC`

    D. `Show-ADAuthenticationPolicyExpression-AllowedToAuthenticateTo`

23. You are the administrator for your company network. You have a DHCP server named Server1. Server1 has an IPv4 scope that contains 100 addresses for a subnet named Subnet1. Subnet1 provides guest access to the Internet. There are never more than 20 client computers on Subnet1 simultaneously; however, the computers that connect to Subnet1 are rarely the same computers. You discover that some client computers are unable to access the network. The computers that are having connection issues have IP addresses in the range of 169.254.0.0/16. What should you do if you need to ensure that all of the computers can connect successfully to the network and access the Internet?

   A. Modify the lease duration.

   B. Configure Network Access Protection (NAP) integration on the existing scope.

   C. Create a new scope that uses IP addresses in the range of 169.254.0.0/16.

   D. Modify the scope options.

24. You are the administrator for your company network. Your network contains an Active Directory domain. The domain contains a Windows Server 2016 server named Server1 that has IPAM installed. IPAM is configured to use the Group Policy–based provisioning method. The prefix for the IPAM Group Policy Objects (GPOs) is IP. From Group Policy Management, you manually rename the IPAM GPOs to have a prefix of IPAM. What should you do if you need to modify the GPO prefix used by IPAM?

   A. Run the `Invoke-IpamGpoProvisioning` cmdlet.

   B. Click Configure Server Discovery in Server Manager.

   C. Click Provision the IPAM Server in Server Manager.

   D. Run the `Set-IpamConfiguration` cmdlet.

25. You are the administrator for your company network. Your network contains one Active Directory domain named abc.com that contains an IPAM server named Server1. Server1 manages several DHCP and DNS servers. From Server Manager on Server1, you create a custom role for IPAM. What should you do if you need to assign the role to a group named IP_Admins?

   A. Run the `Add-Member` cmdlet using PowerShell.

   B. Run the `Set-IpamConfiguration` cmdlet using PowerShell.

   C. Create an access policy using Server Manager.

   D. Create an access scope using Server Manager.

26. You are the administrator for your company network. Your network contains an Active Directory domain that contains a Windows Server 2016 DNS server named Server1. All domain computers use Server1 for DNS. You sign the domain by using DNSSEC. What should you configure in Group Policy if you need to configure the domain computers to validate DNS responses for records?

   A. Name Resolution Policy Table (NRPT)

   B. Network List Manager Policies

   C. Network Access Protection (NAP)

   D. Public Key Policy

27. You are the administrator for your company network. Your network contains an Active Directory forest. Users frequently access the website of an external partner company. The URL of the website is `http://partners.abc.com`. The partner company informs you that it will perform maintenance on its web server and that the IP address of the web server will change. After the change is complete, the users on your internal network report that they fail to access the website. However, some users who work from home report that they are able to access the website. You need to ensure that your DNS servers can resolve `partners.abc.com` to the correct IP address immediately. What should you do?

A. Run dnscmd and specify the `CacheLockingPercent` parameter.

B. Run `Set-DnsServerGlobalQueryLockList`.

C. Run `ipconfig` and specify the `Renew` parameter.

D. Run `Set-DnsServerCache`.

28. You are the administrator for your company network. What should you run if you need to verify whether a DNS response from a DNS server is signed by DNSSEC?

A. `dnscmd.exe`

B. `nslookup.exe`

C. `Get-NetIPAddress`

D. `Resolve-DnsName`

29. You are the administrator for your company network. You have a Windows Server 2016 DNS server named Server1. You need to disable recursion on Server1. What are three possible ways to achieve this goal? (Choose three.)

A. Create a reverse lookup zone named 0.in-addr.arpa.

B. Create a forward lookup zone named GlobalNames.

C. From DNS Manager, modify the advanced properties of Server1.

D. From DNS Manager, modify the forwarders properties of Server1.

E. Create a forward lookup zone named "".

F. Run `dnscmd.exe` and specify the `/config` parameter.

30. You are the administrator for your company network. You have a Windows Server 2016 DHCP server named Server1. You have a single IP subnet. Server1 has an IPv4 scope named Scope1. Scope1 has an IP address range of 10.0.1.10 to 10.0.1.200 and a length of 24 bits. What should you do if you need to create a second logical IP network on the subnet? The subnet will use an IP address range of 10.0.2.10 to 10.0.2.200 and a length of 24 bits.

A. Create a second scope and then run the DHCP Split-Scope Configuration Wizard.

B. Create a superscope and then configure an exclusion range in Scope1.

C. Create a new scope and then modify the IPv4 bindings.

D. Create a second scope and then create a superscope.

31. You are the administrator for your company network. You are implementing a new network. The network contains a Windows Server 2016 DHCP server named DHCP1 that contains a scope named Scope1 for the 192.168.0/24 subnet. Your company has the following policies:

- All server addresses must be excluded from DHCP scopes.

- All client computers must receive IP addresses from Scope1.

- All Windows servers must have IP addresses in the range of 192.168.0.200 to 192.168.0.240.

- All other network devices must have IP addresses in the range of 192.168.0.180 to 192.168.0.199.

You deploy a print device named Print1. What command should you run if you need to ensure that Print1 adheres to the policies for allocating IP addresses?

A. Add-DhcpServerv4Reservation

B. Add-DhcpServerv4Lease

C. Add-DhcpServerv4ExclusionRange

D. Add-DhcpServerv4Filter

32. You are the administrator for your company network. Your network contains an Active Directory domain named abc.com. The domain contains two Windows Server 2016 servers named Server1 and Server2. Server1 has IPAM installed. Server2 has Microsoft System Center 2016 Virtual Machine Manager (VMM) installed. You need to integrate IPAM and VMM. What type of object should you create on Server1?

A. Access Policy

B. Network Service

C. User Role

D. Service Template

33. You are the administrator for your company network. You and a colleague are discussing the use of network IDs. Because the network ID bits must always be chosen in a contiguous fashion from the high-order bits, a shorthand way of expressing a subnet mask is to denote the number of bits that define the network ID as a network prefix using the network prefix notation: /<# of bits>. What is the network prefix for Class B?

A. /8

B. /16

C. /24

D. /64

34. You are the administrator for your company network. You and a colleague are discussing private IP address ranges as specified by the Internet Request for Comments (RFC) 1918. Which of the following is *not* a recognized private IP address range as specified by RFC 1918?

A. 10.0.0.0–10.255.255.255

B. 128.24.0.0–128.24.255.255

C. 172.16.0.0–172.31.255.255

D. 192.168.0.0–192.168.255.255

35. You are the administrator for your company network. You and a colleague are discussing network IDs. What is the network ID of the IP node 129.56.189.41 with a subnet mask of 255.255.240.0?

    A. 129.56.176.0

    B. 129.56.176.1

    C. 129.56.189.0

    D. 129.56.189.1

36. You are the administrator for your company network. You are deploying a network that has 30 client computers. The network uses the 192.168.1.0/24 address space. All of the computers obtain their IP configurations from a DHCP server named Server1. You install a server named Server2 that runs Windows Server 2016. Server2 has two network adapters named Internal and Internet. Internet connects to an Internet Service Provider (ISP) and obtains the 131.107.0.10 IP address. Internal connects to the internal network and is configured to use the 192.168.1.250 IP address. What should you do if you need to provide Internet connectivity for the client computers?

    A. Select the Internet and Internal network adapters and bridge the connections on Server2. On Server1, using the DHCP console, authorize Server2.

    B. Stop the DHCP server on Server1. On Server2, on the Internal network adapter, enable Internet Connection Sharing (ICS).

    C. Run the `New-NetNat Name NAT1 -InternalIPInterfaceAddressPrefix 192.168.1.0/24` cmdlet on Server2. Configure Server1 to provide the 003 Router option of 131.107.0.10.

    D. Install the Routing role service on Server2 and configure the NAT routing protocol. Configure Server1 to provide the 003 Router option of 192.168.1.250.

37. You are the administrator for your company network. You have a Windows Server 2016 server named Server1 that has two network cards. One network card connects to your internal network and the other network card connects to the Internet. You plan to use Server1 to provide Internet connectivity for client computers on the internal network. What server role or role service should you install on Server1 first if you need to configure Server1 as a network address translation (NAT) server?

    A. DirectAccess and VPN

    B. Network Controller

    C. Routing and Remote Access

    D. Web Application Proxy

38. You are the administrator for your company network. Your network contains three subnets:

- Production Servers: A production network
- Development Servers: A development network
- Client Computers: A client network

The development network is used to test applications and reproduces servers that are located on the production network. The development network and the production network use the same IP address range. A user, User1, has a client computer on the client network. User1 reports that when he attempts to connect to the IP address 10.10.1.6 from his computer, he connects to a server on the production network. What should you run if you need to ensure that when User1 connects to 10.10.1.6, he connects to a server on the development network?

A. New-NetNeighbor

B. New-NetRoute

C. Set-NetNeighbor

D. Set-NetTcpSetting

39. You are the administrator for your company network. You have a Windows Server 2016 server named Server1 that has a Server Core installation. Server1 is configured to obtain an IP address automatically. What should you run if you need to configure the IPv4 address, subnet mask, and default gateway manually for a network interface named Ethernet on Server1?

A. Set-NetIPv4Protocol

B. New-NetIPAddress

C. Set-NetAdapter

D. Set-NetNat

40. You are the administrator for your company network. Your network contains an Active Directory domain. The domain contains a Windows Server 2016 DNS server named Server1 that you want to have Response Rate Limiting (RRL). What cmdlet should you run to enable RRL?

A. Add-DnsServerClientSubnet

B. Enable-DnsServerPolicy

C. Set-DnsServerResponseRateLimiting

D. Set-DnsServerResponeRateLimitingExceptionlist

41. You are the administrator for your company network. You have a Windows Server 2016 server named Server1. You promote Server1 to a domain controller. What should you do on Server1 if you need to view the service location (SRV) records that Server1 registers in DNS?

A. Open the netlogon.dns file.

B. Open the srv.sys file.

C. Run Get-DnsServerDiagnostics.

D. Run ipconfig /displaydns.

42. You are the administrator for your company network. Your network contains a Windows Server 2016 DNS server named Server1. The network also contains a Windows Server 2012 R2 server named Server2. You change the IP address of Server2. A few hours later several users report that they cannot connect to Server2. On the users' client computers, you flush the DNS client resolver cache and the users can successfully connect to Server2. What value should you modify in the Start of Authority (SOA) record if you need to reduce the amount of time that the client computers cache DNS records?

A. Expires After

B. Minimum (Default) TTL

C. Refresh Interval

D. Retry Interval

43. You are the administrator for your company network. Your network contains an Active Directory domain. The domain contains a domain controller named Server1 that has the DNS Server role installed. Server1 hosts a primary zone for the domain. The domain contains a member server named Server2 that is configured to use Server1 as its primary DNS server. From Server2, you run `nslookup.exe`. The DNS request times out, showing the default server as unknown. What should you do if you need to ensure that when you run Nslookup that the correct name of the default server is displayed?

A. Create a reverse lookup zone on Server1.

B. Modify the security settings of the primary zone on Server1.

C. Add the primary zone to the DNS suffix list from Advanced TCP/IP Settings on Server1.

D. Add the primary zone to the DNS suffix list from Advanced TCP/IP Settings on Server2.

44. You are the administrator for your company network. The network consists of a single Active Directory domain named abc.com. You have a server named Server1 that runs a custom network application. Server1 has the following IP addresses:

- 192.168.15.10

- 192.168.15.11

What should you do if you need to ensure that a client computer resolves Server1.abc.com to only the 192.168.15.11 IP address?

A. Edit the LMHOSTS file.

B. Run `ipconfig.exe /flushdns`.

C. Edit the HOSTS file.

D. Run `netsh interface ipv4 reset`.

45. You are the administrator for your company network. Your network contains an Active Directory domain named abc.com. You currently have an intranet website that is hosted by two Windows Server 2016 web servers named Web1 and Web2. Users use the name intranet.abc.com to request the website and use DNS round robin. You plan to implement the NLB feature on Web1 and Web2. What should you do if you need to make changes to the DNS records for the planned implementation?

  A. Create two resource records for intranet.abc.com. Point one record to Web1 and point one record to Web2.

  B. Create a new host (A) record named Intranet. Remove both host (A) records for Web1 and Web2.

  C. Delete both host (A) records named Intranet. Create a pointer (PTR) record for each web server.

  D. Delete one of the host (A) records named Intranet. Modify the remaining host (A) record named Intranet.

46. You are the administrator for your company network. Your company has a single Active Directory domain. All servers run Windows Server 2016. You install an additional DNS server. What should you do if you need to delete the pointer record for the IP address 10.3.2.127?

  A. From the command prompt, run the dnscmd /ZoneDelete 127.in-addr.arpa command.

  B. Use DNS Manager to delete the 127.in-addr.arpa zone.

  C. From the command prompt, run the dnscmd /RecordDelete 10.in-addr.arpa. 127.2.3 PTR command.

  D. From the command prompt, run the dnscmd /RecordDelete 10.3.2.127 command.

47. You are the administrator for your company network. Your network contains two Windows Server 2016 servers named Server1 and Server2. Both servers have the DNS Server role installed. You create a standard primary zone named abc.com on Server1. What should you do from Server1 if you need to ensure that Server2 can host a secondary zone?

  A. Convert the primary zone to an Active Directory integrated zone.

  B. Create a zone delegation that points to Server2.

  C. Create a trust anchor named Server2.

  D. Create a new secondary zone for Server2.

48. You are the administrator for your company network. You have a Windows Server 2016 DHCP server that fails. You restore the server from backup. What should you do if you need to prevent the DHCP server from issuing any IP addresses that are already being used on the network?

  A. Set the Conflict Detection value to 0.

  B. Set the Conflict Detection value to 2.

  C. Set the Duplicate Address option on the DHCP scope.

  D. Set the Duplicate Address option on the DHCP server.

49. You are the administrator for your company network. The Windows Server 2016 network uses DHCP. You notice that your DHCP database is getting too large and you want to reduce the size of the database. What should you do to the folder that contains the DHCP database?

   A. Run jetpack.exe dhcp.mdb temp.

   B. Run shrinkpack.exe dhcp.mdb temp.

   C. Run jetshrink.exe dhcp.mdb temp.

   D. Run shrinkjet.exe dhcp.mdb temp.

50. You are the administrator for your company network. You administer a server that assigns IP addresses via DHCP. You want to make sure that a particular client always receives the same IP address from the DHCP server. You create an exclusion for that address, but you find that the computer isn't being properly configured at bootup. What could be causing the problem?

   A. You excluded the wrong IP address.

   B. You need to create a superscope for the address.

   C. You need to make a reservation for the client that ties the IP address to the computer's MAC address and then delete the exclusion.

   D. You must configure the client manually. You cannot assign the address via the DHCP server.

51. You are the administrator for your company network. In the middle of the day, your DHCP server crashes. You reboot the server and get it back up and running within 5 minutes. However, nobody but yourself seems to notice that it had gone down. What additional steps must you take?

   A. None. If there were no lease-renewal requests during the 5-minute period in which the DHCP server was down, none of the clients will ever know that it went down.

   B. You need to renew all the leases manually.

   C. None. The DHCP server automatically assigned new addresses to all the clients on the network transparently.

   D. You must reboot all of the client machines.

52. You are the administrator for your company network. You are going to modify the IP configuration on your network to take advantage of DHCP. You are explaining how DHCP works to a colleague. You want your colleague to understand how a client obtains an address from the DHCP server. What are the steps that occur in the initial DHCP lease process? (Choose all that apply.)

   A. Search

   B. Offer

   C. Acknowledgment

   D. Announce

   E. Request

   F. Discovery

   G. Selection

53. You are the administrator for your company network. You assign two DNS server addresses as part of the options for a scope. Later you find that a client workstation isn't using those addresses that you set up for DNS. What is most likely the cause of the problem?

    A. The client didn't receive the option information as part of its lease.

    B. The client has been manually configured with a different set of DNS servers.

    C. The client has a reserved IP address in the address pool.

    D. There's a glitch in the DHCP server service.

54. You are the administrator for your company network. You are working on a client machine that obtains its IP configuration from a DHCP server. You notice that the client received different configuration information the last few times its lease was renewed. What is most likely causing this to occur?

    A. The DHCP server is not working properly.

    B. Another computer on the network has taken over your machine's configuration information since the last renewal.

    C. When clients renew their leases, they receive all of their configuration information. An administrator is changing the configuration information between lease renewals.

    D. The client is receiving only the information that has changed since the last renewal. An administrator is changing the configuration information between lease renewals.

55. You are the administrator for your company network. You have a single Active Directory forest and your DNS servers are configured as Active Directory Integrated zones. When you look at the DNS records in Active Directory, you notice that there are many records for computers that do not exist on your domain. You want to make sure only domain computers register with your DNS servers. What should you do to resolve this issue?

    A. Set dynamic updates to Nonsecure and Secure.

    B. Set dynamic updates to Domain Users Only.

    C. Set dynamic updates to None.

    D. Set dynamic updates to Secure Only.

56. You are the administrator for your company network. Your company consists of a single Active Directory forest. You have a Windows Server 2016 domain controller named Server1 that also has the DNS role installed. You also have a Unix-based DNS server at the same location. What should you do if you need to configure your Windows DNS server to allow zone transfers to the Unix-based DNS server?

    A. Enable BIND secondaries.

    B. Convert the DNS server to Active Directory Integrated.

    C. Configure the Unix server as a stub zone.

    D. Configure the Microsoft DNS server to forward all requests to the Unix DNS server.

57. You are the administrator for your company network. The network has one main site and one branch office. Your company has a single Active Directory forest named abc.com. You have a single domain controller named Server1 that is located in the main office and has the DNS role installed. Server1 is configured as a primary DNS zone. You have decided to place a domain controller named Server2 in the branch office and implement the DNS role on that server. How should you configure the DNS servers so that if the WAN link fails, users in both sites can still update records and resolve any DNS queries?

   A. Configure Server2 as a stub zone.

   B. Configure Server2 as a secondary DNS server. Set replication to occur every 5 minutes.

   C. Convert Server1 to an Active Directory Integrated zone and configure Server2 as a secondary zone.

   D. Configure Server2 as an Active Directory Integrated zone and convert Server1 to an Active Directory Integrated zone.

58. You are the administrator for your company network. A new company policy states that all inbound DNS queries need to be recorded. What can you do to verify that the IT department is compliant with this new policy?

   A. Enable Server Auditing—Object Access.

   B. Enable DNS debug logging.

   C. Enable DNS Auditing—Object Access.

   D. Enable server database query logging.

59. You are the administrator for your company network. You are responsible for the DNS server. When you look at the DNS database, you see a large number of older records on the server. These records are no longer valid. What should you do?

   A. Manually delete all the old records.

   B. Set Dynamic Updates to None.

   C. Enable Zone Aging and Scavenging in the zone properties.

   D. Enable Zone Aging and Scavenging in the server properties.

60. You are the administrator for your company network. Your IT team has been informed by the Compliance team that they need copies of the DNS Active Directory Integrated zones for security reasons. What should you run if you need to give the Compliance team a copy of the DNS zone?

   A. Run dnscmd /zonecopy.

   B. Run dnscmd /zoneexport.

   C. Run dnscmd /zonefile.

   D. Run dnscmd /zoneinfo.

61. You are the administrator for your company network. Your network is running Windows Server 2016. You have multiple remote locations connected to your main office by slow satellite links. You want to install DNS into these offices so that clients can locate authoritative DNS servers in the main location. What type of DNS servers should be installed in the remote locations?

    A. Primary DNS zones

    B. Secondary DNS zones

    C. Active Directory Integrated zones

    D. Stub zones

62. You are the administrator for your company network. You have an IPv6 prefix of 2001:DB8:BBCC:0000::/53 and you need to set up your network so that your IPv6 addressing scheme can handle 1,000 more subnets. Which network mask would you use?

    A. /60

    B. /61

    C. /62

    D. /63

    E. /64

63. You are the administrator for your company network. You have a Windows Server 2016 machine that needs to be able to communicate with all computers on the internal network. The company decides to add 15 new segments to its IPv6 network. How should you configure the IPv6 address so that the server can communicate with all of the segments?

    A. Configure the address as fd00::2b0:e0ff:dee9:4143/8.

    B. Configure the address as fe80::2b0:e0ff:dee9:4143/32.

    C. Configure the address as ff80::2b0:e0ff:dee9:4143/64.

    D. Configure the address as fe80::2b0:e0ff:dee9:4143/64.

64. You are the administrator for your company network. The network is using the address 137.25.0.0; it is composed of 20 subnets, with a maximum of 300 hosts on each subnet. The company continues on a merger-and-acquisitions spree, and your manager has told you to prepare for an increase to 50 subnets with some containing more than 600 hosts. Using the existing network address, which of the following subnet masks would work for this requirement?

    A. 255.255.240.0

    B. 255.255.248.0

    C. 255.255.252.0

    D. 255.255.254.0

65. You are the administrator for your company network. You are speaking to a colleague regarding using Classless Inter-Domain Routing (CIDR). Which of the following subnet masks are represented with the CIDR of /27?

    A. 255.255.255.224

    B. 255.255.255.240

    C. 255.255.255.248

    D. 255.255.255.254

66. You are the administrator for your company network. You have 1,600 client computers on a single subnet. You need to select a subnet mask that will support all the client computers. You have to minimize the number of unused addresses. Which subnet mask should you choose?

  A. 255.255.240.0

  B. 255.255.248.0

  C. 255.255.252.0

  D. 255.255.254.0

67. You are the administrator for your company network. You ask one of your technicians to get the IPv6 address off a new Windows Server 2016 machine. The technician comes back and hands you a note with FE80::0203:FFFF:FE11:2CD written on it. What can you tell from this address? (Choose two.)

  A. That it is a globally unique IPv6 address.

  B. That it is a link-local IPv6 address.

  C. That it is a multicast IPv6 address.

  D. In EUI-64 format, you can see the MAC address of the node.

  E. In EUI-64 format, you can see the IPv4 address of the node.

68. You are the administrator for your company network. Your company has a single subnet with 600 client computers. You need choose a subnet mask that will support the client computers and minimize the number of unused addresses. What subnet mask should you choose?

  A. 255.255.252.0

  B. 255.255.254.0

  C. 255.255.255.0

  D. 255.255.255.128

69. You are the administrator for your company network. You have 3,500 client computers on a single subnet. You need to select a subnet mask that will support all the client computers. You have to minimize the number of unused addresses. Which subnet mask should you choose?

  A. 255.255.240.0

  B. 255.255.248.0

  C. 255.255.252.0

  D. 255.255.254.0

70. You are the administrator for your company network. You are speaking with a colleague regarding IPv6 address types. Which of the following are valid IPv6 address types? (Choose three.)

  A. Anycast

  B. Broadcast

  C. Multicast

  D. Simulcast

  E. Staticast

  F. Unicast

71. You are the administrator for your company network. You are troubleshooting an error where a client computer seems to not be able to communicate on the network. What command should you use to see all of your TCP/IP settings along with other network settings?

A. `ipconfig /cleardns`

B. `nslookup /flushdns`

C. `dns /register`

D. `ipconfig /all`

72. You are the administrator for your company network. Your company is migrating to IPv6. You have been testing an IPv6 pilot network within the company and want to access resources in the IPv6 Internet. You are currently using the 10.0.0.0 IPv4 address space internally and have Internet connectivity through a pool of public addresses made available from your ISP. Which of the following mechanisms would be appropriate to test your pilot network implementation? (Choose two.)

A. IPv6-only stack on your host machines

B. IPv4-only stack on your host machines

C. IPv4/IPv6 dual stack on your host machines

D. Teredo available on your host machines

E. 6to4 available on your host machines

F. PAT with Traversal on your host machines

73. You are the administrator for your company network. You are discussing IPv6 with a colleague. If given the IPv6 address 2001:0DB8:0000:0000:0000:BEE0:0000:1234, what would be the appropriate condensed IPv6 address displayed if it's entered as an interface address on Windows Server 2016?

A. 2001:DB8::BEE0:0:1234

B. 2001:0DB8::BEE:0:1234

C. 2001:DB8::BEE:0:1234

D. 2::1:DB8:0:0:0:BEE0:1234

E. 2001:DB8::BEE0::1234

74. You are the administrator for your company network. You have a single Active Directory forest and you have a requirement to implement DHCP for the organization. You need to ensure that your DHCP deployment configuration is both fault-tolerant and redundant. Out of the options provided, which is the most reliable DHCP configuration that you could implement?

A. DHCP multicast scope

B. DHCP split scope

C. DHCP super scope

D. DHCP failover

75. You are the administrator for your company network. You need to configure the settings of an existing IPv4 scope. What PowerShell cmdlet would you use?

   A. `Set-DhcpServerScope`

   B. `Set-Serverv4Scope`

   C. `Set-DhcpServerv4Scope`

   D. `Set-DhcpScope`

76. You are the administrator for your company network. You have decided to split the DHCP scope between two DHCP servers. What is the recommended split that Microsoft states that you should use?

   A. 50/50

   B. 60/40

   C. 70/30

   D. 80/20

77. You are the administrator for your company network. You have two Windows Server 2016 servers named Server1 and Server2. Server2 is a DHCP server. You want Server1 to help lease addresses for Server2. You add the DHCP role to Server1. What should you do next?

   A. Run the Configure Failover Wizard in the DHCP console.

   B. Run the Configure Zone Wizard in the DHCP console.

   C. Set the DHCP role to Enabled on Server2.

   D. Start the Share Zone Information Wizard on Server1.

78. You are the administrator for your company network. You have been asked to set up the default gateway setting using DHCP. What option would you configure?

   A. 003 Router

   B. 006 DNS

   C. 015 DNS Domain Name

   D. 028 Broadcast Address

79. You are the administrator for your company network. You have been asked to set up the DNS setting of all your clients using DHCP. Which option would you configure?

   A. 003 Router

   B. 006 DNS

   C. 015 DNS Domain Name

   D. 028 Broadcast Address

80. You are the administrator for your company network. Your network contains an Active Directory domain. The domain contains a Windows Server 2016 member server named Server1 and is a DHCP server. The network contains 75 client computers and 75 IP phones. The computers and the IP phones are from the same vendor. You create an IPv4 scope that contains addresses from 172.32.0.1 to 172.32.1.254. You need to make sure that the IP phones receive addresses in the range of 172.32.1.150 to 172.32.1.254. What should you set up to accomplish this goal while minimizing the administrative effort?

A. Exclusions

B. Reservations

C. Scope level policies

D. Server level policies

81. You are the administrator for your company network. Your DHCP infrastructure includes the use of DNS dynamic updates. You need to ensure that DNS host A records are not overwritten by new DNS devices with the same host name during DNS dynamic updates. Which DHCP configuration option would fulfill this requirement?

A. Configure DNS Registration

B. Configure DHCP Name Protection

C. Configure DHCP High Availability

D. Implement a DHCPv6 Scope

82. You are the administrator for your company network. The company has two Windows Server 2016 DNS servers named DNS1 and DNS2. Both DNS servers reside on domain controllers. DNS1 is set up as a standard primary zone and DNS2 is set up as a secondary zone. A new security policy states that all DNS zone transfers must be encrypted. How can you implement the new security policy?

A. Enable the Secure Only setting on DNS1.

B. Enable the Secure Only setting on DNS2.

C. Configure Secure Only on the Zone Transfers tab for both servers.

D. Delete the secondary zone on DNS2. Convert both DNS servers to use Active Directory Integrated zones.

83. You are the administrator for your company network. Your network contains an Active Directory domain named abc.com. The domain contains a Windows Server 2016 member server named Server1. You install IP Address Management (IPAM) on Server1. You select the automatic provisioning method and then you specify a prefix of IPAM1. You need to configure the environment for automatic IPAM provisioning. Which cmdlet should you run?

A. `Add-IpamDiscoveryDomain -Domain "abc.com" -AssetTag "IPAM1"`

B. `Invoke-IpamGpoProvisioning -Domain "abc.com" -GpoPrefixName "IPAM1"`

C. `Set-IpamConfiguration -Domain "abc.com" -AssetTag "IPAM1"`

D. `Enable-IpamCapability -Domain "abc.com" -ProvisioningMethod "IPAM1"`

84. You are the administrator for your company network. Your network contains an Active Directory domain named abc.com. The domain contains a DNS server named Server1. Server1 is configured to use a forwarder named server2.abc.com that has an IP address of 10.0.0.10. What command should you run if you need to prevent Server1 from using root hints if the forwarder is unavailable?

   A. Suspend-DnsServerZone -Name "." -PassThru

   B. Set-DnsServer -IPAddress 10.0.0.10

   C. Set-DnsServerRootHint -NameServer server2.abc.com

   D. Set-DnsServerForwarder -UseRootHint $false

85. You are the administrator for your company network. Your network contains an Active Directory domain named abc.com. The domain contains a Windows Server 2016 server named Server1. You install IP Address Management (IPAM) on Server1. You need to manually start discovery of the servers that IPAM can manage in abc.com. Which cmdlets should you run? (Choose three.)

   A. Add-IpamAddress

   B. Add-IpamDiscoveryDomain

   C. Add-IpamSubnet

   D. Update-IpamServer

   E. Invoke-IpamServerProvisioning

   F. Start-ScheduledTask

Chapter

7

Implement Network Connectivity and Remote Access Solutions

THE FOLLOWING MCSA WINDOWS SERVER 2016 EXAM TOPICS ARE COVERED IN THIS CHAPTER:

✓ **7.1 Implement virtual private network (VPN) and DirectAccess solutions**

   ▪ This objective may include but is not limited to: Implement remote access and site-to-site (S2S) VPN solutions using remote access gateway; configure different VPN protocol options; configure authentication options; configure VPN reconnect; create and configure connection profiles; determine when to use remote access VPN and site-to-site VPN and configure appropriate protocols; install and configure DirectAccess; implement server requirements; implement client configuration; troubleshoot DirectAccess

1. You are the administrator for your company network. You have a Windows Server 2016 server named Server1 that will be used as a virtual private network (VPN) server. What VPN protocol should you use if you need to configure Server1 to support VPN Reconnect?

    A. Internet Key Exchange Protocol Version 2 (IKEv2)

    B. Layer 2 Tunneling Protocol (L2TP)

    C. Point-to-Point Tunneling Protocol (PPTP)

    D. Secure Socket Tunneling Protocol (SSTP)

2. You are the administrator for your company network. You have a Windows Server 2016 server named Server1 that is located on the perimeter network and only uses inbound TCP port 443 to connect from the Internet. You install the Remote Access server role on Server1. You need to configure Server1 to accept VPN connections over port 443. Which VPN protocol should you use?

    A. Internet Key Exchange Protocol Version 2 (IKEv2)

    B. Layer 2 Tunneling Protocol (L2TP)

    C. Point-to-Point Tunneling Protocol (PPTP)

    D. Secure Socket Tunneling Protocol (SSTP)

3. You are the administrator for your company network. You create a VPN connection that has the VPN type set to Automatic. What VPN protocol will be used first when attempting to establish a VPN connection?

    A. Internet Key Exchange Protocol Version 2 (IKEv2)

    B. Layer 2 Tunneling Protocol (L2TP)

    C. Point-to-Point Tunneling Protocol (PPTP)

    D. Secure Socket Tunneling Protocol (SSTP)

4. You are the administrator for your company network. You have an Active Directory domain. The domain contains Windows Server 2016 servers named Server1 and Server2. On Server1, you install the Remote Access server role. On Server2, you install the Network Policy and Access Services server role. What should you do if you need to configure Server1 to use Server2 as a Remote Authentication Dial-In User Service (RADIUS) server?

    A. Configure the authentication provider from Routing and Remote Access.

    B. Create a Connection Manager profile from the Connection Manager Administration Kit.

    C. Create an Access Policy from Server Manager.

    D. Modify the Delegation settings of the Server1 computer account from Active Directory Users and Computers.

5. You are the administrator for your company network. The network contains one Active Directory domain named abc.com. You deploy DirectAccess on the network. During the deployment, you enable DirectAccess only for a group called ABC\Test Computers. What should you do if you need to enable DirectAccess for all the client computers in the domain after the initial installation?

    A. Modify the membership of the Windows Authorization Access Group from Active Directory Users and Computers.

    B. Modify the security filtering of an object named DirectAccess Client Setting Group Policy from Group Policy Management.

    C. Run the Set-DAClient cmdlet using PowerShell.

    D. Run the Set-DirectAccess cmdlet using PowerShell.

6. You are the administrator for your company network. Your network contains an Active Directory forest. The forest contains two domains named abc.com and xyz.com. The company recently deployed DirectAccess for the members of a group named DA_Computers. All client computers are members of DA_Computers. You discover that DirectAccess clients can access the resources located in the abc.com domain only. The clients can access the resources in the xyz.com domain by using an L2TP VPN connection to the network. What should you do if you need to ensure that the DirectAccess clients can access the resources in the xyz.com domain?

    A. Configure the Delegation settings from the properties of the servers in xyz.com.

    B. Create a zone delegation for xyz.com on an external DNS server.

    C. Modify the Name Resolution Policy Table (NRPT) from a Group Policy Object (GPO).

    D. Add the servers in xyz.com to the RAS and IAS Servers group.

7. You are the administrator for your company network. You have a Windows Server 2016 Remote Access server named Server1 that has DirectAccess enabled. You have a proxy server named Server2. All computers on the internal network connect to the Internet by using the proxy. You run the cmdlet Set-DAClient -forceTunnel Enabled on Server1. Which cmdlet should you run on Server1 if you need to ensure that when a DirectAccess client connects to the network the client accesses all the Internet resources through the proxy?

    A. Set-DAEntryPoint

    B. Set-DnsClientGlobalSetting

    C. Set-DnsClientNrptGlobal

    D. Set-DnsClientNrptRule

8. You are the administrator for your company network. You are discussing Remote Access Service (RAS) Gateway modes with a colleague. Which mode are you describing here? Deploy the RAS Gateway as an edge VPN server, an edge DirectAccess server, or both simultaneously. In this configuration, RAS Gateway provides remote employees with connectivity to your network by using either VPN or DirectAccess connections.

    A. Multitenant mode

    B. Single tenant mode

    C. Unattached tenant mode

    D. Remote tenant mode

9. You are the administrator for your company network. Your company has a main office and has 1,000 users who are located in other countries. You plan to deploy a large Remote Access solution for the company. The main office has three Windows Server 2016 servers named Server1, Server2, and Server3. You plan to use Server1 as a VPN server, Server2 as a RADIUS proxy, and Server3 as a RADIUS server. What actions should you perform on Server2 if you need to configure Server2 to support the planned deployment? (Choose three.)

A. Add a RADIUS client.

B. Create a connection request policy.

C. Create a network policy.

D. Create a remote RADIUS server group.

E. Deploy a Windows container.

10. You are the administrator for your company network. Your network contains an Active Directory forest that has a functional level of Windows Server 2012. The forest contains five domain controllers and five VPN servers that run Windows Server 2016. The VPN server has 500 users who connect daily. What should you do first if you need to configure a new RADIUS server named Server1?

A. Deploy the Remote Access server role on Server1.

B. Set the forest functional level to Windows Server 2016 on a domain controller.

C. Deploy the Network Policy and Access Services role on Server1.

D. Run the `New-NpsRadiusClient` cmdlet on each VPN server.

11. You are the administrator for your company network. Your company has 5,000 remote users. You have 40 VPN servers that host the remote connections. You plan to deploy a RADIUS solution that contains five RADIUS servers. What should you do if you need to ensure that client authentication requests are distributed evenly among the RADIUS servers?

A. Install the Network Load Balancing (NLB) role service on all of the RADIUS servers and configure all of the RADIUS clients to connect to a virtual IP address.

B. Deploy a RADIUS proxy to a new server and configure all of the RADIUS clients to connect to the RADIUS proxy.

C. Deploy a RAS Gateway to a new server and configure all of the RADIUS clients to connect to the RAS Gateway.

D. Install the Failover Clustering role service on all of the RADIUS servers and configure all of the RADIUS clients to connect to the IP address of the cluster.

12. You are the administrator for your company network. You have multiple servers that run Windows Server 2016 and are configured as VPN servers. You deploy a Network Policy Server (NPS) server named NPS1. What should you configure on NPS1 so that it will accept authentication requests from the VPN servers?

A. Add a connection request policy from Policies.

B. Add a remote RADIUS server group from RADIUS Clients and Servers.

C. Add RADIUS clients from RADIUS Clients and Servers.

D. Add a network policy from Policies.

13. You are the administrator for your company network. Your company has a Sales department. The network contains an Active Directory domain. The domain contains two top-level organizational units (OUs) named Sales_Computers, which contains the computer accounts, and Sales_Users, which contains the user accounts. You link a new Group Policy Object (GPO) named GPO1 to Sales_Computers. You need to deploy a VPN connection to all of the users who sign in to the Sales department computers. The users must be placed where?

   A. Computer Configuration/Policies/Administrative Templates/Network/Network Connections

   B. Computer Configuration/Preferences/Control Panel Settings/Network Options

   C. User Configuration/Preferences/Control Panel Settings/Network Options

   D. User Configuration/Policies/Administrative Templates/Network/Network Connections

14. You are the administrator for your company network. The company has employees who work remotely by using a VPN connection from their computers. These employees use an application to access the company intranet database servers. The company recently decided to distribute the latest version of the application using a public cloud. Some users report that every time they try to download the application by using Internet Explorer they receive a warning message that indicates the application could harm their computer. What should you do if you need to recommend a solution that prevents this warning message from appearing, without compromising the security protection of the computers?

   A. Use the intranet website to publish the application.

   B. Use the Windows Store to publish the application.

   C. Use a public File Transfer Protocol (FTP) site to publish the application.

   D. Using the Internet Explorer settings, instruct the employees to disable the SmartScreen Filter.

15. You are the administrator for your company network. Which Control Panel application should you use if you need to change the password used for an L2TP VPN connection?

   A. Credential Manager

   B. System

   C. Network and Sharing Center

   D. Phone and Modem

   E. Power Options

   F. RemoteApp and Desktop Connections

   G. Sync Center

   H. Work Folders

16. You are the administrator for your company network. Your company has 100 client computers. The client computers are connected to a corporate private network. You deploy a Remote Desktop Gateway, DirectAccess, and a VPN server at the main office. Users are currently unable to connect from their home computers to their work computers by using Remote Desktop. You need to ensure that users can remotely connect to their office computers by using Remote Desktop. What should you configure if the users must not be able to access any other corporate network resource from their home computers?

A. A VPN connection

B. The Remote Desktop Gateway IP address in the advanced Remote Desktop Connection settings on each client

C. The local resource settings of the Remote Desktop connection

D. A DirectAccess connection

17. You are the administrator for your company network. Your network contains a single Active Directory domain. The domain contains a VPN server that supports all of the VPN protocols. A user named Sue works from home and has a desktop computer. She has an application named App1 that requires access to a server on the corporate network. She creates a VPN connection on the computer. What should you do if you need to ensure that, when Sue opens App1, she can access the required data?

A. Click Turn on Password Protected Sharing.

B. Disable Network Discovery.

C. Modify the Profile settings of an incoming firewall rule.

D. Run the `Add-VpnConnectionTriggerApplication` cmdlet.

E. Run the `New-NetFirewallRule` cmdlet and specify the `-Direction Outbound` parameter.

F. Run the `New-VpnConnection` cmdlet.

G. Run the `Set-NetConnectionProfile` cmdlet.

H. Run the `Set-VpnConnection` cmdlet.

18. You are the administrator for your company network. Your network contains a single Active Directory domain. The domain contains a VPN server that supports all of the VPN protocols. A user named User1 creates an SSTP VPN connection to a network named VPN1. User1 successfully connects to the VPN server. When the user roams between different Wi-Fi access points, the user loses the connection to the corporate network and must manually reestablish the VPN connection. What should you do if you need to ensure that VPN1 automatically maintains the connection while the user roams between Wi-Fi access points?

A. Click Turn on Password Protected Sharing.

B. Disable Network Discovery.

C. Modify the Profile settings of an incoming firewall rule.

D. Run the `Add-VpnConnection Trigger Application` cmdlet.

E. Run the `New-NetFirewallRule` cmdlet and specify the `-Direction Outbound` parameter.

F. Run the `New-VpnConnection` cmdlet.

G. Run the `Set-NetConnectionProfile` cmdlet.

H. Run the `Set-VpnConnection` cmdlet.

19. You are the administrator for your company network. Your network contains a single Active Directory domain. The domain contains a VPN server that supports all of the VPN protocols. You have mobile devices and have a VPN connection to the VPN server. What should you do if you need to ensure that when users work remotely they can connect to the VPN, and that only traffic for the corporate network is sent through the VPN server?

A. Click Turn on Password Protected Sharing.

B. Disable Network Discovery.

C. Modify the Profile settings of an incoming firewall rule.

D. Run the `Add-VpnConnection Trigger Application` cmdlet.

E. Run the `New-NetFirewallRule` cmdlet and specify the `-Direction Outbound` parameter.

F. Run the `New-VpnConnection` cmdlet.

G. Run the `Set-NetConnectionProfile` cmdlet.

H. Run the `Set-VpnConnection` cmdlet.

20. You are the administrator for your company network. A user connects to a wireless network and receives the following message: "Do you want to allow your PC to be discoverable by other PCs and devices on this network?" The user clicks No. The user is unable to browse to the shared folders of other computers on the network by using File Explorer. What should you do if you need to ensure that the user can browse to the other computers?

A. Click Turn on Password Protected Sharing.

B. Disable Network Discovery.

C. Modify the Profile settings of an incoming firewall rule.

D. Run the `Add-VpnConnection Trigger Application` cmdlet.

E. Run the `New-NetFirewallRule` cmdlet and specify the `-Direction Outbound` parameter.

F. Run the `New-VpnConnection` cmdlet.

G. Run the `Set-NetConnectionProfile` cmdlet.

H. Run the `Set-VpnConnection` cmdlet.

21. You are the administrator for your company network. Your network contains a single Active Directory domain. What should you do if you need to prevent computers from connecting to hosts on subnet 131.107.0.0/24?

   A. Click Turn on Password Protected Sharing.

   B. Disable Network Discovery.

   C. Modify the Profile settings of an incoming firewall rule.

   D. Run the `Add-VpnConnection Trigger Application` cmdlet.

   E. Run the `New-NetFirewallRule` cmdlet and specify the `-Direction Outbound` parameter.

   F. Run the `New-VpnConnection` cmdlet.

   G. Run the `Set-NetConnectionProfile` cmdlet.

   H. Run the `Set-VpnConnection` cmdlet.

22. You are the administrator for your company network. You have a Windows Server 2016 server named Server1. What should you install on Server1 if you need to configure Server1 as a multitenant RAS Gateway?

   A. The Network Controller server role

   B. The Network Policy and Access Services server role

   C. The Data Center Bridging feature

   D. The Remote Access server role

23. You are the administrator for your company network. You are planning to implement a VPN. You currently have the following servers:

   ▪ DC1 – Domain Controller and DNS Server

   ▪ FS1 – DHCP Server and File Server

   ▪ RA1 – Remote Access Server

   ▪ RS1 – Network Policy Server (NPS) Server

   ▪ RP1 – Network Policy Server (NPS) Server

   RA1 will use the RADIUS proxy for authentication. You need to ensure that VPN clients can be authenticated and can access internal resources. What actions should you perform if you need to ensure that RS1 is used as a RADIUS server and RP1 is used as a RADIUS proxy? (Choose two.)

   A. On RS1, create a connection request policy.

   B. On RP1, create a connection request policy.

   C. On FS1, create a network policy.

   D. On RS1, delete the default connection request policy.

   E. On RP1, create a network policy.

24. You are the administrator for your company network. You support desktop computers and tablets that run an older version of Windows. All of the computers are able to connect to your company network from the Internet by using DirectAccess. Your company wants to deploy a new application to the tablets. The deployment solution must meet the following requirements:

- The application is isolated from other applications.

- The application uses the least amount of disk space on the tablet.

- The application can access files stored on an internal Solid State Drive (SSD) on the tablets.

What should you do if you need to deploy the new application to the tablets?

A. Install the application in a Windows To Go workspace.

B. Install Hyper-V on a tablet and then install the application on a virtual machine.

C. Deploy the application as an Application Virtualization (App-V) package and install the App-V 4.6 client on the tablets.

D. Install the application on a local drive on the tablets.

E. Publish the application to Windows Store.

F. Install the application within a separate installation in a virtual hard disk (VHD) file and then configure the tablets with dual boot.

G. Deploy the application as a published application on the Remote Desktop server and create a Remote Desktop connection on the tablets.

H. Install the application within a separate installation in a VHDX file and then configure tablets with dual boot.

25. You are the administrator for your company network. You have a Windows Server 2016 server named Server1 that is configured as a VPN server. Server1 is configured to allow domain users to establish VPN connections from 6:00 a.m. to 6:00 p.m. every day of the week. What should you do if you need to ensure that domain users can establish VPN connections Monday through Friday only?

A. Configure the Properties of Server1 from Routing and Remote Access.

B. Modify the Access Policies on Server1 from Server Manager.

C. Modify the Dial-in Properties of the computer accounts from Active Directory Users and Computers.

D. Modify the Network Policy on Server1 from Network Policy Server.

26. You are the administrator for your company network. You have a DirectAccess server that is accessible by using the name `directaccess.abc.com`. On the DirectAccess server you install a new server certificate that has the same subject name. You then configure the DNS records for `directaccess.abc.com`. What cmdlet should you run if you need to change the endpoint name for DirectAccess to `directaccess.abc.com`?

A. `Set-DaServer -ConnectToAddress directaccess.abc.com`

B. `Set-DaEntryPoint -EntrypointName directaccess.abc.com`

C. `Set-DaEntryPoint -ComputerName directaccess.abc.com`

D. `Set-DaClient -ComputerName directaccess.abc.com`

27. You are the administrator for your company network. You are deploying DirectAccess to a server named DirectAccess1. DirectAccess1 will be located behind a firewall and will have a single network adapter. The network will be IPv4. To support DirectAccess, what protocol and port would you assign to Teredo traffic?

A. Internet Protocol (IP) ID 1

B. Internet Protocol (IP) ID 41

C. Transmission Control Protocol (TCP) 443

D. User Datagram Protocol (UDP) 3544

28. You are the administrator for your company network. You are deploying DirectAccess to a server named DirectAccess1. DirectAccess1 will be located behind a firewall and will have a single network adapter. The network will be IPv4. To support DirectAccess, what protocol and port would you assign to 6to4 traffic?

A. Internet Protocol (IP) ID 1

B. Internet Protocol (IP) ID 41

C. Transmission Control Protocol (TCP) 443

D. User Datagram Protocol (UDP) 3544

29. You are the administrator for your company network. You are deploying DirectAccess to a server named DirectAccess1. DirectAccess1 will be located behind a firewall and will have a single network adapter. The network will be IPv4. To support DirectAccess, what protocol and port would you assign to IP-HTTPS traffic?

A. Internet Protocol (IP) ID 1

B. Internet Protocol (IP) ID 41

C. Transmission Control Protocol (TCP) 443

D. User Datagram Protocol (UDP) 3544

30. You are the administrator for your company network. Your network contains an Active Directory domain. The functional level of the domain is Windows Server 2012. The network uses an address space of 192.168.0.0/16 and contains multiple subnets. The network is not connected to the Internet. The domain contains three servers:

- Server1—Domain Controller and DNS Server
- Server2—Member Server
- Server3—DHCP Server

Client computers obtain their TCP/IP settings from Server3. You add a second network adapter to Server2. You connect the new network adapter to the Internet. You install the Routing role service on Server2. Server1 has four DNS zones configured:

DNS Zone Name	Type	Zone Filename
abc.com	Active-Directory Integrated	None
xyz.com	Primary	xyz.com.dns
lmn.com	Primary	lmn.com.dns
168.192.in-addr.arpa	Primary	168.192.in-addr.arpa.dns

You want to enable Server2 as a NAT server. What should you do?

A. Run the `Install-WindowsFeature` cmdlet.

B. Run the `New-RoutingGroupConnector` cmdlet.

C. Add an interface from Routing and Remote Access.

D. Add a routing protocol from Routing and Remote Access.

31. You are the administrator for your company network. You are configuring the network for a small branch office. Currently, the branch office does not connect directly to the Internet. You deploy a new server named Server1, in the branch office, that has a Server Core installation of Windows Server 2016. Server1 has two network adapters configured as:

Network Adapter Name	IP Address	Connects To
NIC1	192.168.1.1/24	The branch office network
NIC2	131.107.10.1/29	The Internet

You plan to use Server1 to provide Internet connectivity for the branch office. Routing and Remote Access Service (RRAS) is installed and configured for VPN remote access on Server1. What command or cmdlet should you use first if you need to configure RRAS on Server1 to provide Network Address Translation (NAT)?

A. `New-NetNat NAT1 –ExternalIPInterfaceAddressPrefix 131.107.10.1/29`

B. `Route.exe add 192.168.1.1 255.255.255.0 131.107.10.1 metric 1`

C. `Enable-NetNatTransitionConfiguration`

D. `Netsh.exe routing ip nat install`

32. You are the administrator for your company network. You have an internal network that contains multiple subnets. You have a Microsoft Azure subscription that contains multiple virtual networks. You need to deploy a hybrid routing solution between the network and the Azure subscription. The solution must ensure that the computers on all of the networks can connect to each other. You install RAS Gateway and enable Border Gateway Protocol (BGP) routing on the network and in Azure. What three actions should you perform next?

   A. Create a new route for each network.

   B. Deploy a site-to-site VPN.

   C. Advertise all of the routes on all of the BGP routers.

   D. Deploy a point-to-site VPN.

   E. Install the Routing Information Protocol (RIP).

   F. Configure BGP Peering.

33. You are the administrator for your company network. Your client computers use DirectAccess. What should you implement on the client computers if you need to ensure that the client computers can communicate to IPv4 resources by name?

   A. AAAA (Quad A) resource records

   B. Intra-Site Automatic Tunnel Addressing Protocol (ISATAP)

   C. NAT64/DNS64

   D. Teredo relays

   E. Teredo tunnels

34. You are the administrator for your company network. You and a colleague are discussing Border Gateway Protocol (BGP). What PowerShell cmdlet would you use to see the configuration information for your BGP routers?

   A. Add-BgpClient

   B. Get-BgpRouter

   C. Get-Router

   D. Set-RouterClient

35. You are the administrator for your company network. What PowerShell cmdlet would you use if you need to see a list of client security groups that are a part of the DirectAccess deployment?

   A. Get-Client

   B. Get-DAClient

   C. Get-VpnClient

   D. Get-RASClient

36. You are the administrator for your company network. Your network contains an Active Directory domain. Network Access Protection (NAP) is deployed to the domain. What should you run if you need to create NAP event trace log files on a client computer?

A. Logman

B. Register-EngineEvent

C. Register-ObjectEvent

D. Tracert

37. You are the administrator for your company network. You and a colleague are discussing DirectAccess and VPN servers. What PowerShell cmdlet would you use to view the configuration of a DirectAccess or VPN server?

A. Get-RASAccess

B. Get-RemoteAccess

C. Get-Server

D. View-Server

38. You are the administrator for your company network. Your network contains four NPS servers named Server1, Server2, Server3, and Server4. Server1 is configured as a RADIUS proxy that forwards connection requests to a remote RADIUS server group named Group1. You need to ensure that Server2 and Server3 receive connection requests. Server4 should receive connection requests only if Server2 and Server3 are both unavailable. How should you configure Group1?

A. Change the weight of Server2 and Server3 to 10.

B. Change the weight of Server4 to 10.

C. Change the priority of Server2 and Server3 to 10.

D. Change the priority of Server4 to 10.

39. You are the administrator for your company network. You and a colleague are discussing DirectAccess. What PowerShell cmdlet would you use if you need to set the properties of your DirectAccess server?

A. Set-DirectAccessServer

B. Set-DAServer

C. Set-DirectServer

D. Set-RASServer

40. You are the administrator for your company network. You and a colleague are discussing implementing a VPN server. You want to use PowerShell to implement the VPN server. You want to set the authentication type. What cmdlet do you use?

A. Set-AuthType

B. Set-VpnAuth

C. Set-VpnAuthType

D. Set-VpnType

41. You are the administrator for your company network. Your network contains an Active Directory domain where all servers run Windows Server 2016. The domain contains a server named Server1 that has the NPS server role and the Remote Access server role installed. The domain contains a server named Server2 that is configured as a RADIUS server. Server1 provides VPN access to external users. What should you run if you need to ensure that all of the VPN connections to Server1 are logged to the RADIUS server on Server2?

A. `Add-RemoteAccessRadius -ServerNameServer1`
`- AccountingOnOffMsg Enabled -SharedSecret "Secret" -Purpose Accounting`

B. `Add-RemoteAccessRadius -ServerName Server2`
`-AccountingOnOffMsg Enabled -SharedSecret "Secret" -Purpose Accounting`

C. `Set-RemoteAccessAccounting -AccountingOnOffMsg Enabled`
`-AccountingOnOffMsg Enabled`

D. `Set-RemoteAccessAccounting -EnableAccountingType Inbox`
`-AccountingOnOffMsg Enabled`

42. You are the administrator for your company network. What PowerShell cmdlet would you use if you needed to add a new external RADIUS server for VPN connectivity?

A. `Add-RASServer`

B. `Add-RemoteAccess`

C. `Add-RemoteAccessRadius`

D. `Add-RemoteAccessServer`

43. You are the administrator for your company network. You and a colleague are discussing different protocols. What protocol handles the details of establishing and configuring the lowest-level Point-to-Point Protocol (PPP) link?

A. Challenge Handshake Authentication Protocol (CHAP)

B. Compression Control Protocol (CCP)

C. IP Control Protocol (IPCP)

D. Link Control Protocol (LCP)

44. You are the administrator for your company network. Your network contains an Active Directory domain. The domain contains a server named Server1 that has the Remote Access server role installed. By using the default configuration, DirectAccess is implemented on Server1. You discover that DirectAccess clients do not use DirectAccess when accessing websites on the Internet. What should you do if you need to ensure that DirectAccess clients access all Internet websites by using their DirectAccess connection?

A. Configure DirectAccess to enable force tunneling.

B. Configure a DNS suffix search list on the DirectAccess clients.

C. Disable the DirectAccess Passive Mode policy setting in the DirectAccess Client Settings GPO.

D. Enable the Route All Traffic Through The Internal Network policy setting in the DirectAccess Server Settings GPO.

45. You are the administrator for your company network. You and a colleague are discussing protocols. Which of the following is a more secure protocol between Point-to-Point Tunneling Protocol (PPTP) and Layer 2 Tunneling Protocol (L2TP)?

   A. PPTP and L2TP. Both of them define the same security standard.

   B. PPTP is more secure than L2TP.

   C. PPTP and L2TP. Both of them are used to provide the database connection.

   D. L2TP is more secure than PPTP.

46. You are the administrator for your company network. You have a Windows Server 2016 server named Server1 that has the Remote Access server role installed. What should you modify if you need to configure the ports on Server1 to ensure that client computers can establish VPN connections to Server1 by using TCP port 443?

   A. WAN Miniport (IKEv2)

   B. WAN Miniport (L2TP)

   C. WAN Miniport (PPTP)

   D. WAN Miniport (PPPOE)

   E. WAN Miniport (SSTP)

47. You are the administrator for your company network. You and a colleague are discussing Server Logging properties. By default, where are the log files stored?

   A. systemroot\system\Logs

   B. systemroot\system\LogFiles

   C. systemroot\system32\Logs

   D. systemroot\system32\LogFiles

48. You are the administrator for your company network. You and a colleague are discussing setting VPN options. On which tab of the Connection Properties dialog box do you set the VPN options?

   A. The General tab

   B. The Networking tab

   C. The Options tab

   D. The Security tab

49. You are the administrator for your company network. Your network contains an Active Directory domain. The domain contains a Windows Server 2016 RADIUS server named Server1. You add a VPN server named Server2 to the network. On Server1, you create several network policies. Which tool should you use on Server1 if you need to configure Server1 to accept authentication requests from Server2?

   A. Connection Manager Administration Kit (CMAK)

   B. Network Policy Server (NPS)

   C. Routing and Remote Access

   D. Set-RemoteAccessRadius

50. You are the administrator for your company network. You are discussing RAS Gateway modes with a colleague. Which RAS Gateway mode is being described if you deploy a RAS Gateway server between your Cloud Service Providers (CSPs) and Enterprise networks?

  A. Multitenant mode

  B. Single tenant mode

  C. Unattached tenant mode

  D. Remote tenant mode

51. You are the administrator for your company network. You have a VPN server setup. Users are connecting to the VPN but are not disconnecting. What PowerShell cmdlet will allow you to disconnect a user from the VPN?

  A. `Disconnect-User`

  B. `Disconnect-VpnUser`

  C. `Remove-User`

  D. `Remove-VpnUser`

52. You are the administrator for your company network. Your network contains an Active Directory domain. The domain contains a Windows Server 2016 server named Server1 that has the NPS role service installed. You plan to configure Server1 as a NAP health policy server for VPN enforcement by using the Configure NAP Wizard. You need to ensure that you can configure the VPN enforcement method on Server1 successfully. What should you install on Server1 before you run the Configure NAP Wizard?

  A. A computer certificate

  B. A system health validator (SHV)

  C. Host Credential Authorization Protocol (HCAP)

  D. The Remote Access server role

53. You are the administrator for your company network. Your company has offices in five locations around the country. Most of the users' activity is local to their own networks. Sometimes, some of the users in one location need to send confidential information to one of the other locations or retrieve information from one of them. The communication between the remote locations is periodic and intermittent, so you have configured RRAS to use demand-dial lines to set up the connections. You want this communication to be appropriately secured. Which of the following steps should you take to ensure that this communication is appropriately secure? (Choose two.)

  A. Configure Challenge Handshake Authentication Protocol (CHAP) on all the RRAS servers.

  B. Configure Password Authentication Protocol (PAP) on all the RRAS servers.

  C. Configure Microsoft Point-to-Point Encryption (MPPE) on all the RRAS servers.

  D. Configure Layer 2 Tunneling Protocol (L2TP) on all the RRAS servers.

  E. Configure Microsoft Challenge-Handshake Authentication Protocol v2 (MS-CHAPv2) on all the RRAS servers.

54. You are the administrator for your company network. Your network contains an Active Directory domain. The domain contains a Windows Server 2016 server named Server1 that has the Network Policy and Access Services server role installed. You plan to deploy 802.1X authentication to secure the wireless network. You need to identify which NPS authentication method supports certificate-based mutual authentication for the 802.1X deployment. Which authentication method should you identify?

    A. Extensible Authentication Protocol (EAP) Transport Layer Security (TLS)—EAP-TLS

    B. Microsoft Challenge-Handshake Authentication Protocol (MS-CHAP)

    C. Microsoft Challenge-Handshake Authentication Protocol v2 (MS-CHAPv2)

    D. Protected Extensible Authentication Protocol (PEAP) - Microsoft Challenge-Handshake Authentication Protocol v2 (MS-CHAPv2)—PEAP-MS-CHAPv2

55. You are the administrator for your company network. Your network contains an Active Directory domain. The domain contains a Windows Server 2016 server named Server1 that has the Network Policy and Access Services server role installed. Company policy requires that certificate-based authentication be used by some network services. You need to identify which NPS authentication methods comply with the security policy. Which authentication methods should you identify? (Choose two.)

    A. Challenge-Handshake Authentication Protocol (CHAP)

    B. Microsoft Challenge-Handshake Authentication Protocol (MS-CHAP)

    C. Microsoft Challenge-Handshake Authentication Protocol v2 (MS-CHAPv2)

    D. Extensible Authentication Protocol (EAP) Transport Layer Security (TLS) - EAP-TLS

    E. Protected Extensible Authentication Protocol (PEAP) Microsoft Challenge-Handshake Authentication Protocol v2 (MS-CHAPv2)—PEAP-MS-CHAPv2

56. You are the administrator for your company network. All servers run Windows Server 2016. You want to set up an accounting system so each department is responsible for their cost of using network services. Your network contains a NPS server named Server1. The network contains a server named Database1 that has Microsoft SQL Server installed. You configure NPS on Server1 to log accounting data to a database on Database1. What should you do if you need to ensure that the accounting data is captured if Database1 fails, while minimizing cost?

    A. Implement database mirroring.

    B. Implement failover clustering.

    C. Modify the SQL Server Logging properties.

    D. Run the Accounting Configuration wizard.

57. You are the administrator for your company network. Your network contains an Active Directory domain. The domain contains a Windows Server 2016 server named Server1 that has Network Policy Server, DirectAccess, and VPN (RRAS) installed. Remote users have client computers that run legacy Windows operating systems. You need to ensure that only the client computers that run Windows 7 or Windows 10 can establish VPN connections to Server1. What should you configure on Server1?

A. A condition of a NPS connection request policy

B. A condition of a NPS network policy

C. A constraint of a NPS network policy

D. A vendor-specific RADIUS attribute of a NPS connection request policy

58. You are the administrator for your company network. You and a colleague are discussing Point-to-Point Protocol (PPP) and the protocols that run on top of it. Which protocol allows the client to authenticate itself to the server and functions much like a regular network logon in that once the client presents its logon credentials, the server can figure out what access to grant?

A. Link Control Protocol (LCP)

B. Callback Control Protocol (CBCP)

C. Challenge Handshake Authentication Protocol (CHAP)

D. Compression Control Protocol (CCP)

59. You are the administrator for your company network. You and a colleague are discussing a process that allows the client to take a packet with private content, wrap it inside an IP datagram, and send it to the server. The server, in turn, processes the IP datagram, routing real datagrams normally and handling any packets with the appropriate protocol. What is this process called?

A. Multilink

B. Encrypted tunnel

C. Primer

D. Encapsulation

60. You are the administrator for your company network. Your company network includes two branch offices. Users at the company access internal virtual machines (VMs). You want to ensure secure communications between the branch offices and the internal VMs and network. You want to create a site-to-site VPN connection. What are two possible ways to achieve this goal?

A. Using a private IPv4 IP address and a compatible VPN device

B. Using a private IPv4 IP address and an RRAS running on Windows Server 2016

C. Using a public-facing IPv4 IP address and a compatible VPN device

D. Using a public-facing IPv4 IP address and an RRAS running on Windows Server 2016

61. You are the administrator for your company network. You and a colleague are discussing the benefits of using VPNs. Which of the following is a benefit of using VPN support?

   A. Can have unlimited simultaneous connections

   B. Can set up account lockout policies for dial-up and VPN users

   C. VPNs will automatically connect when the client machine sees an Internet connection.

   D. Clients need to be using Windows 10 only.

62. You are the administrator for your company network. You and a colleague are discussing the VPN connection process and how it works. Once the client establishes a connection to the Internet, what is the next phase?

   A. The client authenticates itself to the server.

   B. The client and server negotiate parameters for the VPN session.

   C. The client and server go through the PPP negotiation process.

   D. The client sends a VPN connection request to the server.

63. You are the administrator for your company network. You and a colleague are discussing how encapsulation works. Which of the following describes how encapsulation works?

   A. Software at each level of the OSI model has to see header information to figure out where a packet is coming from and where it's going.

   B. Hardware at each level of the OSI model has to see header information to figure out where a packet is coming from and where it's going.

   C. Software at each level of the OSI model has to see trailer information to figure out where a packet is coming from and where it's going.

   D. Hardware at each level of the OSI model has to see trailer information to figure out where a packet is coming from and where it's going.

64. You are the administrator for your company network. You and a colleague are discussing the Point-to-Point Tunneling Protocol (PPTP) tunneling process. When the client and server have successfully established a PPTP tunnel, the authorization process begins. This process is an exchange of credentials that allows the server to decide whether the client is permitted to connect. Once the server sends a challenge message to the client, what is the next phase of the process?

   A. The server checks the response to see whether the answer is right. The challenge-response process allows the server to determine which account is trying to make a connection.

   B. The client answers with an encrypted response.

   C. The server determines whether the user account is authorized to make a connection.

   D. If the account is authorized, the server accepts the inbound connection.

65. You are the administrator for your company network. You and a colleague are discussing Secure Sockets Tunneling Protocol (SSTP) as a secure way to make a VPN connection using the Secure Sockets Layer v.3 (SSL) using port 443. Once the client connects to the server through the Internet using port 443, what is the next step?

A. During the SSL authentication phase, the client machine receives the server certificate.

B. The client machine will send HTTPS requests on top of the encrypted SSL session.

C. During the TCP session, SSL negotiation takes place.

D. The client machine will then also send SSTP control packets on top of the HTTPS session.

66. You are the administrator for your company network. You want to configure the Point-to-Point Protocol options that are available to clients. Where do you modify these properties?

A. In the PPP tab of the RRAS server's Properties dialog box

B. In the Security tab of the RRAS server's Properties dialog box

C. In the General tab of the RRAS server's Properties dialog box

D. In the Logging tab of the RRAS server's Properties dialog box

67. You are the administrator for your company network. You want to configure the Point-to-Point Protocol options that are available to clients. The properties tab has four check boxes. Which box is checked by default?

A. Dynamic Bandwidth Control Using BAP Or BACP check box

B. Link Control Protocol (LCP) Extensions check box

C. Software Compression check box

D. Multilink Connections check box

68. You are the administrator for your company network. You and a colleague are discussing VPNs. When setting up a VPN, where does it sit?

A. A VPN sits between your external network and the Internet, accepting connections from clients in the outside world.

B. A VPN sits between your internal network and the Internet, accepting connections from clients in the outside world.

C. A VPN sits behind the firewall on your internal network and the Internet, rejecting connections from clients in the outside world.

D. A VPN sits behind the firewall on your external network and the Internet, rejecting connections from clients in the outside world.

69. You are the administrator for your company network. You want to enable your RRAS server to act as a VPN. Where do you modify the properties to specify whether your RRAS server is a router, a Remote Access server, or both?

    A. In the PPP tab of the server's Properties dialog box

    B. In the Security tab of the server's Properties dialog box

    C. In the General tab of the server's Properties dialog box

    D. In the Logging tab of the server's Properties dialog box

70. You are the administrator for your company network. You and a colleague are discussing the three controls that are pertinent to a VPN configuration. What check box must be activated in order to accept VPN connections?

    A. Remote Access Connections (Inbound Only) check box

    B. Demand-Dial Routing Connections (Inbound and Outbound) check box

    C. Maximum Ports check box

    D. Remote Access Connections (Outbound Only) check box

71. You are the administrator for your company network. When you install RRAS, by default what is the number of inbound connections that are supported for PPTP?

    A. 2

    B. 5

    C. 100

    D. 250

72. You are the administrator for your company network. You and a colleague are discussing troubleshooting a VPN. What is the first thing you should check when troubleshooting a VPN connection?

    A. That the VPN protocol used by the client is enabled on the server

    B. That the username and password are correct

    C. That your clients can make the underlying connection to their Internet service provider (ISP)

    D. That the authentication settings in the server's policies (if any) match the supported set of authentication protocols

73. You are the administrator for your company network. You and a colleague are discussing RAS. A standard RRAS installation will always log some data locally. You can manage logging through which folder?

    A. `Remote Logging/Local File`

    B. `Remote Access Logging/Local File`

    C. `Remote Logging/Remote File`

    D. `Remote Access Logging/Remote File`

74. You are the administrator for your company network. You and a colleague are discussing setting server logging properties at the server level. If you use the Logging tab and want to instruct the server to log errors and nothing else, what radio button should you select?

   A. Log Errors Only radio button

   B. Log Errors and Warnings radio button

   C. Log All Events radio button

   D. Do Not Log Any Events radio button

75. You are the administrator for your company network. You and a colleague are discussing Network Address Translation (NAT). What is a huge advantage of using NAT?

   A. The ability for you to share multiple public IP addresses and a single Internet connection between multiple locations using private IP addressing schemes

   B. The ability for you to share a single public IP address and multiple Internet connections between multiple locations using private IP addressing schemes

   C. The ability for you to share multiple public IP addresses and multiple Internet connections between multiple locations using private IP addressing schemes

   D. The ability for you to share a single public IP address and a single Internet connection between multiple locations using private IP addressing schemes

76. You are the administrator for your company network. You and a colleague are discussing how to program the route on your Microsoft-based network. What command should you use?

   A. Path

   B. Route

   C. RouteConfig

   D. Router

77. You are the administrator for your company network. You and a colleague are discussing a way to automatically program routes in your large company network. What can you use to automatically program routes on your Microsoft-based network?

   A. Routing Information Protocol (RIP)

   B. Open Shortest Path First (OSPF)

   C. Enhanced Interior Gateway Routing Protocol (EIGRP)

   D. Intermediate System to Intermediate System (IS-IS)

78. You are the administrator for your company network. You and a colleague are discussing configuring a VPN client. Which tab of the Connection Properties dialog box is where you would want to enter the VPN server address or host name?

   A. The Security tab

   B. The General tab

   C. The Options tab

   D. The Networking tab

79. You are the administrator for your company network. You and a colleague are discussing Web Application Proxies (WAPs). What does the Web Application Proxy feature allow?

  A. Allows applications running on servers outside the corporate network to be accessed by any device inside the corporate network

  B. Allows applications running on servers inside the corporate network to be accessed by any device inside the corporate network

  C. Allows applications running on servers outside the corporate network to be accessed by any device outside the corporate network

  D. Allows applications running on servers inside the corporate network to be accessed by any device outside the corporate network

80. You are the administrator for your company network. You are setting up a Web Application Proxy (WAP) so that your users can access applications, but you must also have some kind of security or anyone with a device would be able to access and use your applications. What must always be deployed with WAP?

  A. Active Directory Domain Services (AD DS)

  B. Active Directory Federation Services (AD FS)

  C. Active Directory Lightweight Directory Services (AD LDS)

  D. Active Directory Certificate Services (AD CS)

81. You are the administrator for your company network. You and a colleague are discussing DirectAccess. To establish a connection, which of the following does DirectAccess use?

  A. Internet Protocol (IP) and IPv6

  B. Internet Protocol Security (IPsec) and IPv4

  C. Internet Protocol Security (IPsec) and IPv6

  D. Internet Protocol (IP) and IPv4

82. You are the administrator for your company network. You and a colleague are discussing DirectAccess prerequisites on the server side. Which of the following is a DirectAccess server with Advanced Settings prerequisite?

  A. A public key infrastructure must be deployed.

  B. A private key infrastructure must be deployed.

  C. A private trust license must be deployed.

  D. A public trust license must be deployed.

83. You are the administrator for your company network. You and a colleague are discussing configuring wireless access. When you install Windows Server 2016, it provides built-in support for 802.11 wireless LAN networking. There are two operating modes you can use. Which one is being described here? By using this mode, wireless network computers connect directly to each other without the use of an access point (AP) or bridge.

    A. Infrastructure mode

    B. Ad Hoc mode

    C. Wired Equivalent Privacy

    D. Wi-Fi Protected Access

84. You are the administrator for your company network. You and a colleague are discussing the authentication protocols that Windows Server 2016 supports. Which protocol is being described here? It is the simplest authentication protocol. It transmits all authentication information in clear text with no encryption, which makes it vulnerable to snooping if attackers can put themselves between the modem bank and the Remote Access server.

    A. Extensible Authentication Protocol (EAP)

    B. Transport Layer Security/Secure Sockets Layer (TLS/SSL) (Schannel)

    C. Kerberos

    D. Password Authentication Protocol (PAP)

85. You are the administrator for your company network. You and a colleague are discussing using PowerShell for remote access. What cmdlet allows an administrator to add a new application server security group to DirectAccess?

    A. Add-DAClient

    B. Add-DirectAccessServer

    C. Add-DAAppServer

    D. Add-DirectAccessApp

Chapter

8

Implement an Advanced Network Infrastructure

THE FOLLOWING MCSA WINDOWS SERVER 2016 EXAM TOPICS ARE COVERED IN THIS CHAPTER:

✓ **8.1 Implement high performance network solutions**

- This objective may include but is not limited to: Implement NIC Teaming or the Switch Embedded Teaming (SET) solution and identify when to use each; enable and configure Receive Side Scaling (RSS); enable and configure network Quality of Service (QoS) with Data Center Bridging (DCB); enable and configure SMB Direct on Remote Direct Memory Access (RDMA)–enabled network adapters; configure SMB Multichannel; enable and configure virtual Receive Side Scaling (vRSS) on a Virtual Machine Queue (VMQ)–capable network adapter; enable and configure Virtual Machine Multi-Queue (VMMQ); enable and configure Single-Root I/O Virtualization (SR-IOV) on a supported network adapter

✓ **8.2 Determine scenarios and requirements for implementing Software Defined Networking (SDN)**

- This objective may include but is not limited to: Determine deployment scenarios and network requirements for deploying SDN; determine requirements and scenarios for implementing Hyper-V Network Virtualization (HNV) using Network Virtualization Generic Route Encapsulation (NVGRE) or Virtual Extensible LAN (VXLAN) encapsulation; determine scenarios for implementation of Software Load Balancer (SLB) for North-South and East-West load balancing; determine implementation scenarios for various types of Windows Server Gateways, including L3, GRE, and S2S, and their use; determine requirements and scenarios for Datacenter firewall policies and network security groups

1. You are the administrator for your company network. You and a colleague are discussing Software Defined Networking (SDN). You know that SDN provides a method to centrally configure and manage physical and virtual network devices such as routers, switches, and gateways in your datacenter. Virtual network elements such as Hyper-V Virtual Switch, Hyper-V Network Virtualization, and RAS Gateway are designed to be integral elements of your SDN infrastructure. Software-defined networking provides which of the following capabilities?

   A. The ability to centrally define and control policies that govern both physical and virtual networks, including traffic flow between these two network types

   B. The ability to implement network policies in a consistent manner at scale, even as you deploy new workloads or move workloads across virtual or physical networks

   C. The ability to abstract your applications and workloads from the underlying physical network, which is accomplished by virtualizing the network

   D. All of these

2. You are the administrator for your company network. You plan to deploy several Windows Server 2016 Hyper-V hosts. The deployment will use Software Defined Networking (SDN) and Virtual Extensible LAN (VXLAN). What server role should you install on the network to support the planned deployment?

   A. Host Guardian Service

   B. Remote Access

   C. Network Controller

   D. Network Policy and Access Services

3. You are the administrator for your company network. By using the Network Controller server role, you implement Software Defined Networking (SDN). You have a virtual network named VN1 that contains servers. What should you configure if you need to ensure that only devices from the 192.168.0.0/24 subnet can access the virtual machine in VN1?

   A. Dynamic Access Control

   B. Role-Based Access Control

   C. Network Security Group (NSG)

   D. Universal Security Group

4. You are the administrator for your company network. You and a colleague are discussing NIC Teaming. Which of the following is *true* with regards to NIC Teaming? (Choose all that apply.)

   A. It allows for traffic failover to prevent connectivity loss if a network component fails.

   B. It prevents bandwidth aggregation.

   C. It supports a maximum of five NICs in a team.

   D. It supports a maximum of 32 NICs in a team.

5. You are the administrator for your company network. You have an Active Directory domain that contains several Windows Server 2016 Hyper-V hosts. You plan to deploy network virtualization and to centrally manage Datacenter Firewall policies. What component must you install for the planned deployment?

    A. The Canary Network Diagnostics feature

    B. The Data Center Bridging (DCB) feature

    C. The Network Controller server role

    D. The Routing role service

6. You are the administrator for your company network. You have a Windows Server 2016 server named Server1. What should you install if you need to configure Server1 as a multitenant RAS Gateway?

    A. The Data Center Bridging feature

    B. The Network Controller server role

    C. The Network Policy and Access Services server role

    D. The Remote Access server role

7. You are the administrator for your company network. You create an application named App1. App1 is going to be distributed to multiple Hyper-V virtual machines in a multitenant environment for both virtual and non-virtual networks. What should you include in the environment if you need to ensure that the traffic is distributed evenly among the virtual machines that host App1?

    A. Network Controller and Windows Server Network Load Balancing (NLB) nodes

    B. Network Controller and Windows Server Software Load Balancing (SLB) nodes

    C. A RAS Gateway and Windows Server Network Load Balancing (NLB) nodes

    D. A RAS Gateway and Windows Server Software Load Balancing (SLB) nodes

8. You are the administrator for your company network. You and a colleague are planning to set up NIC Teaming. You want to provide fault protection. What is the minimum number of Ethernet adapters you must have to take advantage of fault protection in NIC Teaming?

    A. 1

    B. 2

    C. 3

    D. 4

9. You are the administrator for your company network. You want to deploy the RAS Gateway as an Edge VPN server, an Edge DirectAccess server, or both simultaneously. The RAS Gateway will provide remote employees with connectivity to your network by using either VPN or DirectAccess connections. What RAS Gateway Mode type will you be setting up?

    A. Dual tenant mode

    B. Lone tenant mode

    C. Multitenant mode

    D. Single tenant mode

10. You are the administrator for your company network. You have a Windows Server 2016 virtual machine named VM1 that hosts a service that requires high network throughput. VM1 has a virtual network adapter that connects to a Hyper-V switch named vSwitch1. vSwitch1 has one network adapter. The network adapter supports Remote Direct Memory Access (RMDA), the Single Root I/O Virtualization (SR-IOV) interface, Quality of Service (QoS), and Receive Side Scaling (RSS). You need to ensure that the traffic from VM1 can be processed by multiple networking processors. What Windows PowerShell cmdlet should you run in the host of VM1?

    A. `Set-NetAdapterRss`

    B. `Set-NetAdapterRdma`

    C. `Set-NetAdapterSriov`

    D. `Set-NetAdapterQoS`

11. You are the administrator for your company network. You have a test environment that includes two Windows Server 2016 servers named Server1 and Server2. What feature should the servers support if you need to ensure that you can implement SMB Direct between the servers?

    A. Multipath I/O (MPIO)

    B. Remote Direct Memory Access (RDMA)

    C. Single Root I/O Virtualization (SR-IOV)

    D. Virtual Machine Queue (VMQ)

12. You are the administrator for your company network. You have a Windows Server 2016 server named Server1. You install the Hyper-V server role on Server1, and it has eight network adapters that are dedicated to virtual machines. The network adapters are RDMA-enabled. You plan to use SDN. You will host the virtual machines for multiple tenants on the Hyper-V host. What should you implement if you need to ensure that the network connections for the virtual machines are resilient if one or more physical network adapters fail?

    A. Single Root I/O Virtualization (SR-IOV)

    B. Switch Embedded Teaming (SET)

    C. NIC Teaming on the Hyper-V host

    D. Virtual Receive Side Scaling (vRSS)

13. You are the administrator for your company network. You have a Windows Server 2016 Hyper-V host named Server1 that has two network adapters that are RDMA-enabled. What cmdlet should you use if you need to verify whether SET is enabled?

    A. `Get-NetworkSwitchFeature`

    B. `Get-VMNetworkAdapter`

    C. `Get-VMNetworkAdapterFailoverConfiguration`

    D. `Get-VMSwitch`

14. You are the administrator for your company network. You have a Windows Server 2016 server named Hyperv1, which is a Hyper-V host that hosts a virtual machine named VM1. Hyperv1 has three network adapter cards that are connected to virtual switches named Ethernet1, Ethernet2, and Ethernet3. NIC Teaming on VM1 is currently configured as follows:

    Team Name: VM1 NIC Team

    Member Adapters: Ethernet2   10 Gbps

    Ethernet3   10 Gbps

    Teaming Mode: Switch Independent

    Load Balancing Mode: Address Hash

    Standby Adapter: None (all adapters Active)

    Primary Team Interface: VM1 NIC Team; Default VLAN

    What should you do if you need to ensure that VM1 will retain access to the network if a physical network adapter card fails on Hyperv1?

    A. From the properties of the NIC team on VM1, add the adapter named Ethernet1 to the NIC team.

    B. From Hyper-V Manager on Hyperv1, modify the settings on VM1.

    C. From PowerShell on VM1, run the `Set-VmNetworkAdapterTeamMapping` cmdlet.

    D. From PowerShell on Hyperv1, run the `Set-VmNetworkAdapterFailoverConfiguration` cmdlet.

15. You are the administrator for your company network. You can use Policy-based QoS to control bandwidth costs, manage traffic, or negotiate service levels with bandwidth providers or business departments. QoS policies can define priority through a Differentiated Services Code Point (DSCP) value. The DSCP applies a value (0–63) within the Type of Service (TOS) field in an IPv4 packet's header and within the Traffic Class field in IPv6. This value provides classification at the Internet Protocol (IP) level, which routers can use to decide queuing behavior. You can also limit an application's outbound network traffic by specifying a throttle rate. The Wi-Fi Alliance has established a certification for Wireless Multimedia (WMM) that defines four access categories (WMM_AC) for prioritizing network traffic transmitted on a wireless network. Which group should have the highest DSCP value?

    A. Background (BK)

    B. Best effort (BE)

    C. Video (VI)

    D. Voice (VO)

16. You are the administrator for your company network. Your company has 10 offices. Each office has a local network that contains several Windows Server 2016 Hyper-V hosts. All of the offices are connected by high speed, low latency WAN links. What component should you install if you need to ensure that you can use QoS policies for Live Migration traffic between the offices?

A. The Canary Network Diagnostics feature

B. The Data Center Bridging feature

C. The Multipath I/O feature

D. The Network Controller server role

E. The Routing role service

17. You are the administrator for your company network. You have a Windows Server 2016 server named Server1 that is a Hyper-V host. You have two network adapter cards on Server1 that are RDMA-capable. You need to aggregate the bandwidth of the network adapter cards for a virtual machine on Server1. You must ensure that the virtual machine can use the RDMA capabilities of the network adapter cards. What command should you run?

A. `Add-NetLbfoTeamNic -Name Production -NetAdapterName "NIC1", "NIC2" -EnableEmbeddedTeaming`

B. `Add-VmNetworkAdapter -Name Production -NetAdapterName "NIC1", "NIC2" -EnableIov`

C. `New-NetLbfoTeam -Name Production -NetAdapterName "NIC1", "NIC2" -EnablePacketDirect`

D. `New-VmSwitch -Name Production -NetAdapterName "NIC1", "NIC2" -EnableEmbeddedTeaming`

18. You are the administrator for your company network. You have decided to start using network controllers. What PowerShell cmdlet allows you to create a new network controller?

A. `New-NetworkController`

B. `New-NetworkControllerObject`

C. `New-NetworkControllerNodeObject`

D. `New-NetworkControllerServerObject`

19. You are the administrator for your company network. You want to create a virtual disk that clones a local drive available on your host machine. Using Hyper-V Manager, what types of disks can you use to copy a physical disk to a virtual disk? (Choose all that apply.)

A. Differencing

B. Dynamically expanding

C. Fixed size

D. Physical or pass-through

20. You are the administrator for your company network. You and a colleague are planning to set up NIC Teaming. What is the maximum number of Ethernet adapters that you can set up in a NIC Team?

  A. 12

  B. 24

  C. 32

  D. 56

21. You are the administrator for your company network. You and a colleague are discussing how to move virtual machines between host machines. How do you accomplish this?

  A. Create a snapshot of the virtual machine and apply it to a different machine.

  B. In Hyper-V, use the Export and Import Virtual Machine command.

  C. In Hyper-V, use the Save command.

  D. Move the virtual machine files to the target host and add them to Hyper-V.

22. You are the administrator for your company network. You are planning to add a hard disk drive to a virtual machine using PowerShell. What cmdlet should you run?

  A. Add-VMDvdDrive

  B. Add-VMHardDrive

  C. Add-VMHardDiskDrive

  D. Add-VMDrive

23. You are the administrator for your company network. You and a colleague are discussing NIC Teaming. You know that NIC Teaming gives an administrator the ability to allow multiple network adapters on a system to be placed into a team. What is another name for NIC Teaming?

  A. Network Load Balancing (NLB)

  B. Load Balancing and Failover (LBFO)

  C. Software Load Balancing (SLB)

  D. High-Performance Networking (HPN)

24. You are the administrator for your company network. If you have a running cluster and need to run the Validate a Configuration Wizard, which of the following tests may require cluster resources to be taken offline?

  A. Inventory tests

  B. Network tests

  C. Storage tests

  D. System configuration tests

25. You are the administrator for your company network. You have two Windows Server 2016 servers named Server1 and Server2. You plan to implement Storage Replica to replicate the contents of volumes on Server1 to Server2. What cmdlet should you run if you need to ensure that the replication traffic between the servers is limited to a maximum of 100 Mbps?

   A. `New-StorageQosPolicy`

   B. `Set-NetTCPSetting`

   C. `Set-NetUDPSetting`

   D. `Set-SmbBandwidthLimit`

26. You are the administrator for your company network. You and a colleague are discussing SLB. Which of the following processes inbound network traffic and maps Virtual IPs (VIPs) to Dynamic IPs (DIPs), then forwards the traffic to the correct DIP?

   A. Host Agent

   B. Northbound Application Program Interfaces (API)

   C. System Center Virtual Machine Manager (SCVMM)

   D. SLB Multiplexer (MUX)

27. You are the administrator for your company network. You have an Active Directory domain. The domain contains Windows Server 2016 Hyper-V hosts named Server1 and Server2. The Hyper-V hosts are configured to use Network Virtualization Generic Route Encapsulation (NVGRE) for network virtualization. You have six virtual machines that are connected to an external switch. The virtual machines are configured as shown here.

Virtual Machine Name	Hyper-V Host	IP Address	Netmask	GRE Key
VM1	Server1	192.168.1.16	255.255.255.0	16
VM2	Server2	192.168.1.232	255.255.255.0	32
VM3	Server3	192.168.1.32	255.255.255.0	32
VM4	Server4	192.168.1.25	255.255.255.0	25
VM5	Server5	192.168.1.116	255.255.255.0	16
VM6	Server6	192.168.1.132	255.255.255.0	32

What virtual machine or virtual machines can VM1 and VM3 connect to?

   A. VM1 can connect to VM5 only and VM3 can connect to VM2 and VM6 only.

   B. VM1 can connect to VM2 only and VM3 can connect to VM6 only.

   C. VM1 can connect to VM2, VM3, VM5, and VM6 only and VM3 can connect to VM4, VM5, and VM6 only.

   D. VM1 can connect to VM1, VM2, VM4, VM5, and VM6 only and VM3 can connect to VM6 only.

28. You are the administrator for your company network. You are planning to install Hyper-V. One benefit with Windows Server 2016 Hyper-V is that it now includes _____, which allows one computer to directly access memory from the memory of another computer without the need of interfacing with either one's operating system.

   A. NIC Teaming

   B. Switch Embedded Teaming (SET)

   C. Remote Direct Memory Access (RDMA)

   D. High-Performance Networking (HPN)

29. You are the administrator for your company network. You have a Windows Server 2016 Hyper-V host named Server1 that has the following virtual switches:

Virtual Switch Name	Virtual Switch Type	Physical Network Adapter Name
vSwitch1	External	NIC1
vSwitch2	External	NIC2

You create a virtual machine named VM1. VM1 has two network adapters. One network adapter connects to vSwitch1. The other network adapter connects to vSwitch2. You configure NIC Teaming on VM1. What should you run if you need to ensure that if a physical NIC fails on Server1, VM1 remains connected to the network?

   A. Add a new network adapter to VM1.

   B. Create a new virtual switch on Server1.

   C. Modify the properties of vSwitch1 and vSwitch2.

   D. Run the `Set-VmNetworkAdapter` cmdlet.

30. You are the administrator for your company network. You have a Windows Server 2016 Hyper-V host named Server1 that hosts several virtual machines. Each virtual machine has two network adapters. Server1 also contains several virtual switches. On Server1, you create a NIC Team that has two network adapters. You discover that the NIC Team is set to Static Teaming mode. What cmdlet should you use if you need to modify the NIC Teaming mode to Switch Independent?

   A. `Set-NetLbfoTeam`

   B. `Set-NetLbfoTeamNic`

   C. `Set-VMNetworkAdapter`

   D. `Set-VMSwitch`

31. You are the administrator for your company network. You and a colleague are discussing Switch Embedded Teaming (SET). You know that there are requirements when adding members to a SET group. What is a requirement of SET?

   A. All members of the SET group can be different adapter types from the same manufacturer.

   B. All members of the SET group can be different adapter types from different manufacturers.

   C. All members of the SET group must be identical adapter types from the same manufacturer.

   D. There are no requirements to becoming a member of a SET group.

32. You are the administrator for your company network. You have a Windows Server 2016 failover cluster that contains four nodes. Each node has four network adapters. The network adapters on each node are configured as shown in the following table:

Network Adapter Name	Cluster Network Name	Link Speed
NIC1	ClusterNetwork1	1 Gbps
NIC2	ClusterNetwork2	1 Gbps
NIC3	ClusterNetwork3	1 Gbps
NIC4	ClusterNetwork4	10 Gbps

NIC4 supports Remote Direct Memory Access (RDMA) and Receive Side Scaling (RSS). The cluster networks are configured as shown in the following table:

Cluster Network Name	Metric	Role
ClusterNetwork1	39984	1
ClusterNetwork2	39983	1
ClusterNetwork3	79984	3
ClusterNetwork4	79840	3

What should you do if you need to ensure that ClusterNetwork4 is used for Cluster Shared Volumes (CSVs) redirected traffic?

A. Set the metric of ClusterNetwork4 to 30,000 and disable SMB Multichannel.

B. Set the metric of ClusterNetwork4 to 90,000 and disable SMB Multichannel.

C. On each server, replace NIC4 with a 1 Gbps network adapter.

D. On each server, enable RDMA on NIC4.

33. You are the administrator for your company network. You and a colleague are discussing NIC Teaming. You know that you can set up NIC Teaming by using Server Manager or PowerShell and that different configuration models are available. If you want all the NIC adapters to be connected to the same switch, what is this configuration called?

A. Switch Dependent

B. Switch Reliant

C. Switch Independent

D. Switch Autonomous

34. You are the administrator for your company network. Your network contains an Active Directory domain. The domain contains a Windows Server 2016 server named Server1 that has the Hyper-V server role installed. Server1 has a virtual switch named Switch1. You replace all of the network adapters on Server1 with new network adapters that support SR-IOV. What actions should you perform if you need to enable SR-IOV for all of the virtual machines on Server1? (Choose two.)

A. Delete and then re-create the Switch1 virtual switch.

B. Modify the Advanced Features settings of the network adapter on each virtual machine.

C. Modify the BIOS settings on each virtual machine.

D. Modify the Hardware Acceleration settings of the network adapter on each virtual machine.

E. Modify the settings of the Switch1 virtual switch.

35. You are the administrator for your company network. You have 10 Windows Server 2016 Hyper-V hosts. Each Hyper-V host has eight virtual machines that run a distributed web application named App1. You plan to implement a Software Load Balancing (SLB) solution for client access to App1. You deploy two new virtual machines named SLB-VM1 and SLB-VM2. What components should you install if you need to install the required components on the Hyper-V hosts and the new servers for the planned implementation? (Choose two.)

A. Install SLB Host Agent on SLB-VM1 and SLB-VM2.

B. Install Network Load Balancing (NLB) on SLB-VM1 and SLB-VM2.

C. Install SLB Multiplexer (MUX) on SLB-VM1 and SLB-VM2.

D. Install SLB Host Agent on each Hyper-V host.

E. Install SLB Multiplexer (MUX) on each Hyper-V host.

F. Install Host Guardian Service server role on each Hyper-V host.

36. You are the administrator for your company network. You and a colleague are discussing NIC Teaming. You know that you can set up NIC Teaming by using Server Manager or PowerShell and that different configuration models are available. If you want each NIC adapter connected into a different switch, what is this configuration called?

A. Switch Dependent

B. Switch Reliant

C. Switch Independent

D. Switch Autonomous

37. You are the administrator for your company network. You have a Windows Server 2106 virtual machine named Server1 that you plan to use as part of a Software Defined Networking (SDN) solution. What should you install if you need to implement the Border Gateway Protocol (BGP) on Server1?

A. Peer Name Resolution Protocol (PNRP) feature

B. Network Device Enrollment Service role service

C. Network Policy and Access Services server role

D. Routing Role service

38. You are the administrator for your company network. You have a Windows Server 2016 Hyper-V host named Server1 that has two network adaptors named NIC1 and NIC2. Server2 has two virtual switches named vSwitch1 and vSwitch2. N1C1 connects to vSwitch1. NIC2 connects to vSwitch2. Server1 hosts a virtual machine named VM1. VM1 has two network adapters named vmNIC1 and vmNIC2. vmNIC1 connects to vSwitch1 and vmNIC2 connects to vSwitch2. What should you run on VM1 if you need to create a NIC Team on VM1?

   A. `$var1 = "LACP" $var2 = "Dynamic"`

   B. `$var1 = "Static" $var2 = "HyperVPort"`

   C. `$var1 = "SwitchIndependent" $var2 = "TransportPorts"`

   D. `$var1 = "SwitchIndependent" $var2 = "HyperVPort"`

39. You are the administrator for your company network. You and a colleague are discussing enabling and configuring network QoS with DCB using PowerShell. What command will obtain the DCB Exchange settings?

   A. `Set-NetQosDcbxSetting`

   B. `Get-NetQosDcbxSetting`

   C. `Get-NetQosDcbxControl`

   D. `Set-NetQosDcbxControl`

40. You are the administrator for your company network. You decide to implement Switch Embedded Teaming (SET). You and a colleague are discussing creating a new SET team. You must configure it so that you have member adapters and load balancing mode configured. Which load balancing mode ensures that outbound loads are distributed based on a hash of the TCP ports and IP addresses while also rebalancing loads in real time so that a given outbound flow can move back and forth between SET team members?

   A. Dynamic

   B. Dynamic Hyper-V

   C. Hyper-V Port

   D. Outbound

41. You are the administrator for your company network. You are discussing using Switch Embedded Teaming (SET) as an alternative to NIC Teaming. What else does SET allow you to do?

   A. Allows an administrator to combine a group of physical adapters (minimum of one adapter and a maximum of eight adapters) into hardware-based virtual adapters

   B. Allows an administrator to combine a group of physical adapters (minimum of one adapter and a maximum of eight adapters) into software-based virtual adapters

   C. Allows an administrator to combine a group of virtual adapters (minimum of one adapter and a maximum of eight adapters) into software-based virtual adapters

   D. Allows an administrator to combine a group of virtual adapters (minimum of one adapter and a maximum of eight adapters) into hardware-based virtual adapters

42. You are the administrator for your company network. You have two Windows Server 2016 Hyper-V servers named Server1 and Server2. You want a dedicated area created on the physical network adapter for each virtual network adapter to use. What is this feature called?

    A. Remote Direct Memory Access (RDMA)

    B. Multipath I/O (MPIO)

    C. Virtual Machine Queue (VMQ)

    D. Single root I/O virtualization (SR-IOV)

43. You are the administrator for your company network. You and a colleague are discussing a feature that allows a system's network adapter to spread the network processing between multiple processor cores in systems that have a multicore processor. What is this called?

    A. Receive Side Scaling (RSS)

    B. Remote Direct Memory Access (RDMA)

    C. Switch Embedded Teaming (SET)

    D. Virtual Machine Queue (VMQ)

44. You are the administrator for your company network. You and a colleague are discussing virtual Receive Side Scaling (vRSS). vRSS is a Windows Server 2016 feature that allows virtual network adapters to distribute the load across multiple virtual processors in a virtual machine. vRSS can work with many different types of technologies, including which of the following?

    A. IPv4 and IPv6

    B. Transmission Control Protocol (TCP) and User Datagram Protocol (UDP)

    C. Live Migration

    D. Network Virtualization using Generic Routing Encapsulation (NVGRE)

    E. All of the above

45. You are the administrator for your company network. You and a colleague are discussing Receive Side Scaling (RSS). You know that it allows a system's network adapter to spread the network processing between multiple processors. RSS has the ability to work with systems that have more than how many processors?

    A. 12

    B. 24

    C. 36

    D. 64

46. You are the administrator for your company network. You are planning to enable virtual Receive Side Scaling (vRSS). What two PowerShell commands can you run to enable vRSS?

    A. `Enable-NetAdapterRSS -Name "AdapterName"` or

       `Set-NetAdapterRSS -Name "AdapterName" -Enabled $False`

    B. `Enable-NetAdapterRSS -Name "AdapterName"` or

       `Set-NetAdapterRSS -Name "AdapterName" -Enabled $True`

    C. `Enable-NetAdapterVRSS -Name "AdapterName"` or
       `Set-NetAdapterRSS -Name "AdapterName" -Enabled $False`

    D. `Enable-NetAdapterVRSS -Name "AdapterName"` or

       `Set-NetAdapterRSS -Name "AdapterName" -Enabled $True`

47. You are the administrator for your company network. You are planning to disable virtual Receive Side Scaling (vRSS). What two PowerShell commands can you run to disable vRSS?

    A. `Disable-NetAdapterRSS -Name "AdapterName"` or

       `Set-NetAdapterRSS -Name "AdapterName" -Enabled $False`

    B. `Disable-NetAdapterRSS -Name "AdapterName"` or
       `Set-NetAdapterRSS -Name "AdapterName" -Enabled $True`

    C. `Disable-NetAdapterVRSS -Name "AdapterName"` or
       `Set-NetAdapterRSS -Name "AdapterName" -Enabled $False`

    D. `Disable-NetAdapterVRSS -Name "AdapterName"` or
       `Set-NetAdapterRSS -Name "AdapterName" -Enabled $True`

48. You are the administrator for your company network. You and a colleague are discussing a feature that allocates multiple queues to a single virtual machine, and each queue has its own affinity settings to a core. What is this new Windows Server 2016 feature called?

    A. Receive Side Scaling (RSS)

    B. Remote Direct Memory Access (RDMA)

    C. Switch Embedded Teaming (SET)

    D. Virtual Machine Multi-Queue (VMMQ)

49. You are the administrator for your company network. You have a Windows Server 2016 Hyper-V machine and you want to control the traffic that is generated by the virtual machine. What is the name of the Hyper-V feature that allows you to do this?

    A. Switch Embedded Teaming (SET)

    B. Virtual Receive Side Scaling (vRSS)

    C. Virtual Machine Quality of Service (vmQoS)

    D. Virtual Machine Multi-Queue (VMMQ)

50. You are the administrator for your company network. You and a colleague are discussing Data Center Bridging (DCB). You plan to install DCB using PowerShell. What PowerShell cmdlet do you use to enable DCB, including the management tools?

A. `Install-WindowsFeature -Name Data Center Bridging -IncludeManagementTools`

B. `Install-WindowsFeature -Name Data-Center-Bridging -IncludeManagementTools`

C. `Install-WindowsFeature -Name DCB -IncludeManagementTools`

D. `Install-Feature -Name Data Center Bridging -IncludeManagementTools`

51. You are the administrator for your company network. You manage a Windows Server 2016 Software Defined Network (SDN). The network controller is installed on a three-node, domain-joined cluster of virtual machines. You need to add a new Access Control List (ACL) for the network controller to the network interface on a tenant virtual machine. The ACL will have only one rule that prevents only outbound traffic from the 10.10.10.0/24 subnet. You will run the following Windows PowerShell commands:

```
$ruleproperties = new-object
Microsoft.Windows.NetworkController.AclRuleProperties
$ruleproperties.SourcePortRange = "0-65535"
$ruleproperties.DestinationPortRange = "0-65535"
$ruleproperties.Action = "Deny"
$ruleproperties.Priority = "100"
$ruleproperties.Type = "Outbound"
$ruleproperties.Logging = "Enabled"
```

What remaining properties should you add to the rule? (Choose three.)

A. `$ruleproperties.DestinationAddressPrefix = "10.10.10.0/24"`

B. `$ruleproperties.SourceAddressPrefix = "10.10.10.0/24"`

C. `$ruleproperties.Protocol = "ALL"`

D. `$ruleproperties.Protocol = "TCP"`

E. `$ruleproperties.DestinationAddressPrefix = "*"`

F. `$ruleproperties.SourceAddressPrefix = "*"`

52. You are the administrator for your company network. You and a colleague are discussing Software Defined Network (SDN) and how SDN can use Software Load Balancing (SLB) to evenly distribute network traffic between virtual network resources. There are a few terms that refer to the way that your application traffic patterns go in context of your datacenter. If applications have a pattern that sends data to other applications within the same datacenter or between datacenters, it is said to be what kind of pattern?

A. An East-West traffic pattern

B. An East-South traffic pattern

C. A North-South traffic pattern

D. A North-West traffic pattern

53. You are the administrator for your company network. Your datacenter contains 10 Hyper-V hosts that host 100 virtual machines. You plan to secure access to the virtual machines by using the Datacenter Firewall service. You have four servers available for the Datacenter Firewall service and they are configured as shown:

Server Name	Platform	Windows Server 2016 Edition
Server1	Physical	Standard
Server2	Physical	Standard
Server3	Virtual	Datacenter
Server4	Virtual	Datacenter

You need to install the required server roles for the planned deployment. What server role should you deploy to Server3 and Server4?

A. Multipoint Services

B. Network Controller

C. Network Policy and Access Services

D. Quality of Service

54. You are the administrator for your company network. You and a colleague are discussing Datacenter Firewalls, which is a new Windows Server 2016 network layer, stateful, multi-tenant firewall. Datacenter Firewalls provide several benefits. Which one of the following is a true Datacenter Firewall benefit?

A. Administrators have the ability to define firewall rules to protect data between virtual machines on the same Layer 2 (L2) or different Layer 2 (L2) virtual subnets.

B. Administrators have the ability to define firewall rules to protect data between virtual machines on different Layer 2 (L2) virtual subnets.

C. Administrators have the ability to define firewall rules to protect data between virtual machines on the same Layer 5 (L5) or different Layer 5 (L5) virtual subnets.

D. Administrators have the ability to define firewall rules to protect data between virtual machines on the same Layer 3 (L3) or different Layer 3 (L3) virtual subnets.

55. You are the administrator for your company network. You have an internal network that contains multiple subnets. You have a Microsoft Azure subscription that contains multiple virtual networks. You need to deploy a hybrid routing solution between the network and the Azure subscription. You must ensure that the computers on all the networks can connect to each other. You install Remote Access Service (RAS) Gateway and enable Border Gateway Protocol (BGP) routing on the network and in Azure. What actions should you perform next? (Choose three.)

A. Advertise all the routes on all the Border Gateway Protocol (BGP) routers.

B. Create a new route for each network.

   C. Configure Border Gateway Protocol (BGP) peering.

   D. Deploy a Site-to-Site (S2S) VPN.

   E. Deploy a Point-to-Site (P2S) VPN.

   F. Install the Routing Information Protocol (RIP).

56. You are the administrator for your company network. You and a colleague are discussing Software Defined Network (SDN) and how SDN can use Software Load Balancing (SLB) to evenly distribute network traffic between virtual network resources. There are a few terms that refer to the way that your application traffic patterns go in context of your datacenter. If your organization has an older datacenter where clients simply request data from a single server, it is likely your datacenter has which type of pattern?

   A. An East-West traffic pattern

   B. An East-South traffic pattern

   C. A North-South traffic pattern

   D. A North-West traffic pattern

57. You are the administrator for your company network. You and a colleague are discussing RAS Gateway features in Windows Server 2016. One feature:

- Enables connectivity between tenant virtual networks and external networks
- Is lightweight, and support is available on most network devices
- Becomes an ideal choice for tunneling where encryption of data is not required
- Supports Site-to-Site (S2S) tunnels, which solves the problem of forwarding between tenant virtual networks and tenant external networks using a multitenant gateway

Which feature of RAS Gateway is being discussed?

   A. Generic Routing Encapsulation (GRE)

   B. Dynamic Routing with Border Gateway Protocol (BGP)

   C. Point-to-Site (P2S) VPN

   D. Site-to-Site (S2S) VPN

58. You are the administrator for your company network. You and a colleague are discussing routing traffic across networks of a Software Defined Network (SDN) infrastructure. You want to enable connectivity between the physical infrastructure in the datacenter and the virtualized infrastructure in the Hyper-V network virtualization cloud. What should you configure?

   A. Configure Generic Routing Encapsulation (GRE).

   B. Configure Internet Protocol Security (IPSec) connection.

   C. Configure Layer 3 (L3) forwarding.

   D. Configure Site-to-Site (S2S) VPN.

59. You are the administrator for your company network. You and a colleague are discussing Switch Embedded Teaming (SET). By using virtual adapters with SET, what are you accomplishing?

    A. You get better performance and less fault tolerance in the event of a network adapter failure.

    B. You get less performance and greater fault tolerance in the event of a network adapter failure.

    C. You get less performance and less fault tolerance in the event of a network adapter failure.

    D. You get better performance and greater fault tolerance in the event of a network adapter failure.

60. You are the administrator for your company network. You have set up Switch Embedded Teaming (SET) on your network, but now you want to remove a virtual switch named VSwitch1. What PowerShell cmdlet do you use to remove the virtual switch?

    A. `Remove-VM "VSwitch1"`

    B. `Remove-VMSwitch "VSwitch1"`

    D. `Delete-VM "VSwitch1"`

    C. `Delete-VMSwitch "VSwitch1"`

61. You are the administrator for your company network. You and a colleague are discussing Storage Quality of Service (QoS). Storage QoS allows a Hyper-V administrator to manage how virtual machines access storage throughput for Virtual Hard Disks (VHDs). Storage QoS gives an administrator the ability to guarantee which of the following?

    A. That the storage throughput of a single VHD cannot adversely affect the performance of another VHD on the same host

    B. That the storage throughput of a single VHD cannot adversely affect the performance of another VHD on a different host

    C. That the storage throughput of multiple VHDs cannot adversely affect the performance of another VHD on the same host

    D. That the storage throughput of multiple VHDs cannot adversely affect the performance of another VHD on the different hosts

62. You are the administrator for your company network. You have a Windows Server 2016 Hyper-V host server that contains production and test virtual machines (VMs). You plan to optimize the performance of the VMs. The following settings must be applied to the VMs:

    ▪ You must set a maximum value for the input/output operations per second (IOPS) on the test VMs.

    ▪ You must set a minimum value for the IOPS on the production VMs.

    How should you configure the environment?

    A. Create a shared virtual hard disk (VHD).

    B. Enable Network Quality of Service (QoS) on all virtual machines.

    C. Enable Resource Metering on the Hyper-V host server.

    D. Enable Storage Quality of Service (QoS) on all virtual machines.

63. You are the administrator for your company network. You and a colleague are discussing Software Defined Networking (SDN), which allows an administrator to control which of the following?

A. To centrally manage and control all virtual and physical network devices

B. To manage datacenter switches, routers, and gateways

C. To manage virtual elements like Hyper-V virtual switches and gateways

D. All of the above

64. You are the administrator for your company network. You and a colleague are discussing network controllers for Windows Server 2016. Network controllers use different Application Programming Interface (API) languages to control all of the different hardware on your network. Which API allows network controllers to communicate with the network?

A. Northbound API

B. Southbound API

C. Eastbound API

D. Westbound API

65. You are the administrator for your company network. You have recently installed the Network Controller feature and you now want to set up a network controller by using PowerShell. Which cmdlet should you use?

A. New-NetworkControllerNode

B. New-NetworkController

C. New-NetworkControllerCluster

D. New-NetworkControllerNodeObject

66. You are the administrator for your company network. You and a colleague are discussing RAS Gateways. You are discussing the modes used with RAS. Which mode is used for Cloud Service Providers (CSPs) or enterprise networks to allow datacenter or cloud network traffic routing between virtual and physical networks (including traffic that goes over the Internet)?

A. Dual tenant mode

B. Lone tenant mode

C. Multitenant mode

D. Single tenant mode

67. You are the administrator for your company network. You and a colleague are discussing deploying Network Controller. If the computers or virtual machines for Network Controller and the management client are domain-joined, then you will want to configure _____ for Kerberos authentication. (Fill in the blank.)

A. A security group

B. A distribution group

C. A global group

D. A universal group

68. You are the administrator for your company network. You have a Windows Server 2106 virtual machine named Server1 that you plan to use as part of a Software Defined Networking (SDN) solution. Many technologies work together to create an SDN solution. One such technology provides the ability to manage the routing of network traffic between your tenants' virtual machine networks and their remote sites. What technology is this?

   A. Border Gateway Protocol (BGP)

   B. Network Controller

   C. Internal DNS Service (iDNS) for SDN

   D. Datacenter Firewall

69. You are the administrator for your company network. You have a Windows Server 2106 virtual machine named Server1 that you plan to use as part of a Software Defined Networking (SDN) solution. Many technologies work together to create a SDN solution. One such technology is a lightweight operating system virtualization method used to separate applications or services from other services that are running on the same container host. What technology is this?

   A. Datacenter Firewall

   B. Network Controller

   C. System Center

   D. Windows Containers

70. You are the administrator for your company network. You and a colleague are discussing setting up Network Address Translation (NAT) for traffic forwarding in Software Defined Network (SDN) infrastructure. You know that NAT supports two types. Which type forwards the external traffic to a specific virtual machine in a virtual network?

   A. Internal NAT

   B. Inbound NAT

   C. Outbound NAT

   D. External NAT

71. You are the administrator for your company network. You and a colleague are discussing NIC Teaming. You know that NIC Teaming is a common practice when setting up virtualization. This is one way that you can have load balancing with Hyper-V. NIC Teaming gives an administrator the ability to do which of the following?

   A. To allow a virtual machine to use routers in Hyper-V

   B. To allow a virtual machine to use physical network switches in Hyper-V

   C. To allow a virtual machine to use virtual network adapters in Hyper-V

   D. To allow a virtual machine to use firewall software in Hyper-V

72. You are the administrator for your company network. You and a colleague are discussing NIC Teaming. You know that you can configure NIC Teaming using PowerShell, but what other tool allows you to configure NIC Teaming?

   A. Server Manager

   B. Hyper-V Manager

   C. Remote Server Administration Tools (RSAT)

   D. Active Directory

73. You are the administrator for your company network. You and a colleague are discussing technologies for a Software Defined Network (SDN) infrastructure. One such technology is defined as a network layer, 5-tuple (protocol, source and destination port numbers, source and destination IP addresses), stateful, multitenant firewall. What is being discussed?

   A. Network Controller

   B. Software Load Balancer (SLB)

   C. Internal DNS Service (iDNS)

   D. Datacenter Firewall

74. You are the administrator for your company network. You and a colleague are discussing installing a Remote Access Service (RAS) Gateway for your Software Defined Network (SDN) infrastructure. What is it called when you have the ability of a cloud infrastructure to support the virtual machine workloads of multiple tenants, yet isolate them from each other, while all of the workloads run on the same infrastructure?

   A. Single Tenant mode

   B. Multitenant mode

   C. Multiple Tenant mode

   D. Specific Tenant mode

75. You are the administrator for your company network. You are planning to deploy a Remote Access Service (RAS) Gateway in multitenant mode for use in your Software Defined Network (SDN) infrastructure. What tool must you use in order to install this?

   A. Server Manager

   B. RAS Gateway Management tool

   C. Windows PowerShell

   D. Virtual Machine Manager (VMM)

76. You are the administrator for your company network. You are planning to install Remote Access Service (RAS) Gateway with multitenant mode and Border Gateway Protocol (BGP) to your Software Defined Network (SDN) infrastructure. How do you install the Remote-Access Windows feature?

   A. `Add-WindowsFeature -Name RemoteAccess`
      `-IncludeAllSubFeature -IncludeManagementTools`

   B. `Add-WindowsFeature -Name RemoteAccessGateway`
      `-IncludeAllSubFeature -IncludeManagementTools`

   C. `Add WindowsFeature -Name RemoteAccess`
      `-IncludeAllSubFeature -IncludeManagementTools`

   D. `Add-WindowsFeature -Name RemoteGateway`
      `-IncludeAllSubFeature -IncludeManagementTools`

77. You are the administrator for your company network. You and a colleague are discussing network controllers for Windows Server 2016. Network controllers use different Application Programming Interface (API) languages to control the different hardware on your network. Which API allows the network to communicate with the network controller?

    A. Northbound API

    B. Southbound API

    C. Eastbound API

    D. Westbound API

78. You are the administrator for your company network. You and a colleague are discussing deploying the Network Controller server role on your Software Defined Network (SDN) infrastructure. Where should you deploy the Network Controller server role?

    A. On the physical hosts

    B. On a Hyper-V virtual machine on the Hyper-V host

    C. On the target machine

    D. On a Hyper-V virtual machine on the Hyper-V target machine

79. You are the administrator for your company network. You have a Windows Server 2106 virtual machine named Server1 that you plan to use as part of a Software Defined Networking (SDN) solution. Many technologies work together to create an SDN solution. One such technology hosts virtual machines (VMs) and applications require DNS to communicate within their own networks and with external resources on the Internet. You can provide tenants with DNS name resolution services for their isolated, local name space and for Internet resources. What technology is being discussed?

    A. Border Gateway Protocol (BGP)

    B. Network Controller

    C. Internal DNS Service (iDNS) for SDN

    D. Datacenter Firewall

80. You are the administrator for your company network. You and a colleague are discussing installing Network Controller for your Software Defined Network (SDN) infrastructure. You know there are installation requirements that must be met. For Windows Server 2016 deployments, you can deploy Network Controller on one or more computers, one or more VMs, or a combination of computers and VMs. All VMs and computers planned as network controller nodes must be running which edition of Windows Server 2016?

    A. Windows Server 2016 Standard edition

    B. Windows Server 2016 Nano Server

    C. Windows Server 2016 Datacenter edition

    D. Windows Server 2016 Server Core

81. You are the administrator for your company network. You have recently installed Network Controller and you now want to set up a network controller cluster by using PowerShell. Which cmdlet should you use?

   A. `Install-NetworkControllerNode`

   B. `Install-NetworkController`

   C. `Install-NetworkControllerCluster`

   D. `Install-NetworkControllerNodeObject`

82. You are the administrator for your company network. You and a colleague are discussing virtual Receive Side Scaling (vRSS). You know that vRSS is enabled by default, but you can disable it by using PowerShell. What PowerShell cmdlet can disable vRSS for a virtual machine on the Hyper-V Virtual Switch port by using the PowerShell on the Hyper-V host?

   A. `Set-VMNetworkAdapter -VrssEnabled $TRUE`

   B. `Set VMNetworkAdapter -VrssEnabled $TRUE`

   C. `Set VMNetworkAdapter -VrssEnabled $FALSE`

   D. `Set-VMNetworkAdapter -VrssEnabled $FALSE`

83. You are the administrator for your company network. You and a colleague are discussing Network Controllers. You can use the Network Controller feature to manage network infrastructure components. What are some of the network infrastructure components that network controllers might include?

   A. Physical switches

   B. Physical routers

   C. Hyper-V switches

   D. Datacenter Firewalls

   E. VPN Gateways

   F. All of the above

84. You are the administrator for your company network. You and a colleague are discussing Internal DNS Service (iDNS) for your Software Defined Network (SDN) infrastructure. Which of the following is a key feature of iDNS?

   A. Provides private Domain Name System (DNS) name resolution services for tenant workloads

   B. Provides shared Domain Name System (DNS) name resolution services for tenant workloads

   C. Provides private Domain Name System (DNS) name resolution services for host workloads

   D. Provides shared Domain Name System (DNS) name resolution services for host workloads

85. You are the administrator for your company network. You and a colleague are discussing technologies for a Software Defined Network (SDN) infrastructure. One such technology allows an administrator to set up multiple servers that can host the same workload. This gives an organization the ability to have high availability and scalability between the server's workload. What is being discussed?

   A. Network Controller

   B. Software Load Balancer (SLB)

   C. Internal DNS Service (iDNS)

   D. Datacenter Firewall

Chapter

9

Install and Configure Active Directory Domain Services (AD DS)

THE FOLLOWING MCSA WINDOWS SERVER 2016 EXAM TOPICS ARE COVERED IN THIS CHAPTER:

✓ **9.1   Install and configure Active Directory Domain Services (AD DS)**

- This objective may include but is not limited to: Install a new forest; add or remove a domain controller from a domain; upgrade a domain controller; install AD DS on a Server Core installation; install a domain controller from Install from Media (IFM); resolve DNS SRV record registration issues; configure a global catalog server; transfer and seize operations master roles; install and configure a read-only domain controller (RODC); configure domain controller cloning

1. You are the administrator for your company network. Your company has one Active Directory Domain Services (AD DS) forest that contains two domains. All servers run Windows Server 2016. The company uses iSCSI storage and Fibre Channel storage. You plan to deploy a single Hyper-V failover cluster that uses Cluster Shared Volumes (CSV). The cluster must include virtual machines from both domains. What should you do if you need to ensure that you can deploy a failover cluster?

    A. Deploy clustered storage spaces.

    B. Deploy Serial Attached SCSI (SAS).

    C. Join each Hyper-V host server to the same AD DS domain.

    D. Join each Hyper-V host server to different AD DS domains.

2. You are the administrator for your company network. Your network contains an Active Directory domain. The domain contains a Read-Only Domain Controller (RODC) named RODC1. What should you run if you need to retrieve a list of accounts that have their passwords cached on RODC1?

    A. `dcdiag.exe`

    B. `netdom.exe`

    C. `ntdsutil.exe`

    D. `repadmin.exe`

3. You are the administrator for your company network. Your network contains an Active Directory domain. All users are in an organizational unit (OU) named CorpUsers. You plan to modify the description of all the users who have a string of 603 in their mobile phone numbers. What PowerShell cmdlet should you run if you need to view a list of the users who will be modified?

    A. `Get-ADUser-Filter "MobilePhone-like '*603*'"`

    B. `Get-ADOrganizationalUnit-Filter "MobilePhone-like '*603* "'`

    C. `Get-ADUser-LDAPFilter "(MobilePhone='*603*)"`

    D. `Get-ADOrganizationalUnit-LDAPFilter "(MobilePhone='*603*')"`

4. You are the administrator for your company network. Your company is always changing, with new employees coming and going. One of your common tasks requires the deletion of user accounts for employees who are no longer with the company. What command can you use to delete user accounts?

    A. `dsmod`

    B. `dspromo`

    C. LDIFDE

    D. `netsh`

5. You are the administrator for your company network. Your network contains an Active Directory forest. What should you do if you need to identify which server is the schema master?

   A. Run `Get-ADDomainController -Discover -Service` using PowerShell.

   B. Run `netdom query fsmo` using an elevated command prompt.

   C. Open Active Directory Users and Computers, right-click the forest in the console tree, and click Operations Master.

   D. Open Active Directory Users and Computers, right-click the forest in the console tree, and click RID Master.

6. You are the administrator for your company network. You have the Active Directory Recycle Bin enabled. You discover that a colleague accidentally removed 100 users from an Active Directory group named Group1 an hour ago. What should you do if you need to restore the membership of Group1?

   A. Perform tombstone reanimation.

   B. Export and import data by using Dsamain.

   C. Perform a nonauthoritative restore.

   D. Recover the items by using Active Directory Recycle Bin.

7. You are the administrator for your company network. You have recently implemented Windows Server 2016. You have a few remote sites that are not very secure. You have decided to implement Read-Only Domain Controllers (RODCs). To do the installation of the RODCs, what forest and functional levels does the network need? (Choose all that apply.)

   A. Windows Server 2016

   B. Windows Server 2008 R2

   C. Windows Server 2012 R2

   D. Windows Server 2008

8. You are the administrator for your company network. What is the maximum number of domains that a Windows Server 2016 computer configured as a domain controller may participate in at one time?

   A. Zero

   B. One

   C. Two

   D. Any number of domains

9. You are the administrator for your company network. Your network contains a single Active Directory domain. The domain contains five Windows Server 2008 R2 domain controllers. What should you perform if you plan to install a new Windows Server 2016 domain controller? (Choose two.)

   A. Run adprep.exe /rodcprep at the command line.

   B. Run adprep.exe /forestprep at the command line.

   C. Run adprep.exe /domainprep at the command line.

   D. Raise the functional level of the domain from Active Directory Domains and Trusts.

   E. Prestage the RODC computer account from Active Directory Users and Computers.

10. You are the administrator for your company network. Your network has a single Active Directory domain. A user who has left the company returns after eight weeks. The user tries to log on to her old computer and receives an error stating that authentication has failed. The user's account has been enabled. What should you do if you need to ensure that the user is able to log on to the domain using that computer?

    A. Re-create the user account and then reconnect the user account to the computer account.

    B. Reset the computer account in Active Directory. Disjoin the computer from the domain and then rejoin the computer to the domain.

    C. Rejoin the computer account by running the Adadd command.

    D. Run the MMC utility on the user's computer and add the Domain Computers snap-in.

11. You are the administrator for your company network. Your network contains an Active Directory domain that includes 1,000 desktop computers and 500 laptops. An organizational unit (OU) named OU1 contains the computer accounts for the desktop computers and the laptops. You create a PowerShell script named Script1.ps1 that removes temporary files and cookies. You create a Group Policy Object (GPO) named GPO1 and link GPO1 to OU1. What should you do if you need to run the script once a week on the laptops only?

    A. Add Script1.ps1 as a startup script and attach a WMI filter to GPO1.

    B. Create a File preference that uses item-level targeting in GPO1.

    C. Create a Scheduled Tasks preference that uses item-level targeting in GPO1.

    D. Configure the File System security policy and attach a WMI filter to GPO1.

12. You are the administrator for your company network. Your network contains an Active Directory forest. The forest contains a domain named abc.com. The domain contains three domain controllers. A domain controller named DC1 fails and you are unable to repair it. What should you do if you need to prevent the other domain controllers from attempting to replicate to DC1?

    A. Remove the object of DC1 from Active Directory Sites and Services.

    B. Remove the computer account of DC1 from Active Directory Users and Computers.

    C. Transfer the operations master roles from DC1 from Active Directory Domains and Trusts.

    D. Perform a metadata cleanup using ntdsutil.exe.

13. You are the administrator for your company network. You have an offline root certification authority (CA) named CA1. CA1 is hosted on a virtual machine. You only turn on CA1 when the CA must be patched or when you must generate a key for subordinate CAs. You start CA1, and you discover that the filesystem is corrupted. You resolve the filesystem corruption and discover that you must reload the CA root from a backup. When you attempt to run the `Restore-CARoleService` cmdlet, you receive the following error message: "The process cannot access the file because it is being used by another process." What should you do first to resolve the issue?

   A. Stop the Active Directory Domain Services (AD DS) service.

   B. Stop the Active Directory Certificate Services (AD CS) service.

   C. Run the `Restore-CARoleService` cmdlet and specify the path to a valid CA key.

   D. Run the `Restore-CARoleService` cmdlet and specify the `Force` parameter.

14. You are the administrator for your company network. Your network contains an Active Directory domain. What tool should you use if you need to limit the number of Active Directory Domain Services (AD DS) objects that a user can create in the domain?

   A. Active Directory Administrative Center

   B. Active Directory Users and Computers

   C. Dsacls

   D. dsadd_quota

   E. Dsamain

   F. Dsmod

   G. Group Policy Management Console

   H. Ntdsutil

15. You are the administrator for your company network. Your network contains an Active Directory domain. You have an organizational unit (OU) named OU1 that contains the computer accounts of two servers and the user account of a user named User1. A Group Policy Object (GPO) named GPO1 is linked to OU1. You have an application named App1 that installs by using an application installer named `App1.exe`. What should you do if you need to publish App1 to OU1 by using Group Policy?

   A. Create a `Config.zap` file and add a file to the File System node to the Computer Configuration node of GPO1.

   B. Create a `Config.xml` file and add a software installation package to the User Configuration node of GPO1.

   C. Create a `Config.zap` file and add a software installation package to the User Configuration node of GPO1.

   D. Create a `Config.xml` file and add a software installation package to the Computer Configuration node of GPO1.

16. You are the administrator for your company network. Your network contains an Active Directory forest named abc.com. The forest contains three domains named abc.com, corp.abc.com, and office.abc.com. The forest contains three Active Directory sites named Site1, Site2, and Site3. You have the three administrators as described in the following table:

Administrator Name	Group Membership	Domain
Admin1	Domain Admins	abc.com
Admin2	Domain Admins	corp.abc.com
Admin3	Enterprise Admins	abc.com

You create a Group Policy Object (GPO) named GPO1. Who can link GPO1 to Site2?

   A. Admin1 and Admin2 only

   B. Admin1 and Admin3 only

   C. Admin1, Admin2, and Admin3

   D. Admin3 only

17. You are the administrator for your company network. Your network contains an Active Directory domain that has 5,000 user accounts. You have a Group Policy Object (GPO) named DomainPolicy that is linked to the domain and a GPO named DCPolicy that is linked to the Domain Controllers organizational unit (OU). What should you do if you need to use the application control policy settings to prevent several applications from running on the network?

   A. Modify Administrative Templates from the Computer Configuration node of DomainPolicy.

   B. Modify Administrative Templates from the User Configuration node of DomainPolicy.

   C. Modify Folder Redirection from the User Configuration node of DomainPolicy.

   D. Modify Security Settings from the Computer Configuration node of DCPolicy.

   E. Modify Security Settings from the Computer Configuration node of DomainPolicy.

   F. Modify Security Settings from the User Configuration node of DCPolicy.

   G. Modify Windows Settings from Preferences in the User Configuration node of DomainPolicy.

   H. Modify Windows Settings from Preferences in the Computer Configuration node of DomainPolicy.

18. You are the administrator for your company network. Your network contains an Active Directory forest and the functional level is Windows Server 2016. What tool should you use if you need to ensure that a domain administrator can recover a deleted Active Directory object quickly?

   A. Active Directory Administrative Center

   B. Active Directory Users and Computers

   C. Dsacls

   D. dsadd_quota

   E. Dsamain

   F. Dsmod

   G. Group Policy Management Console

   H. Ntdsutil

19. You are the administrator for your company network. Your network contains an Active Directory domain. You recently deleted 5,000 objects from the Active Directory database. You need to reduce the amount of disk space used to store the Active Directory database on a domain controller. What tool should you use?

   A. Active Directory Administrative Center

   B. Active Directory Users and Computers

   C. Dsacls

   D. dsadd_quota

   E. Dsamain

   F. Dsmod

   G. Group Policy Management Console

   H. Ntdsutil

20. You are the administrator for your company network. Your network contains an Active Directory domain. The domain functional level is Windows Server 2016. Your company hires a new security administrator to manage sensitive user data. You create a user account named Security1 for the security administrator. What tool should you use if you need to ensure that the password for Security1 has at least 12 characters and is modified every 10 days and the solution must apply to Security1 only?

   A. Active Directory Administrative Center

   B. Active Directory Users and Computers

   C. Dsacls

   D. dsadd_quota

   E. Dsamain

   F. Dsmod

   G. Group Policy Management Console

   H. Ntdsutil

21. You are the administrator for your company network. You are trying to determine which filesystem to use for a server that will become a Windows Server 2016 file server and domain controller. The company has the following requirements:

- The filesystem must allow for file-level security from within Windows 2016 Server.
- The filesystem must make efficient use of space on large partitions.
- The domain controller Sysvol must be stored on the partition.

Which of the following filesystems meets these requirements?

A. File Allocation Table (FAT)

B. File Allocation Table 32 (FAT32)

C. High Performance File System (HPFS)

D. New Technology File System (NTFS)

22. You are the administrator for your company network. You deploy a new Active Directory forest. You need to ensure that you can create a Group Managed Service Account (gMSA) for multiple member servers. What should you do?

A. Configure Kerberos constrained delegation on the computer account of each member server.

B. Configure Kerberos constrained delegation on the computer account of each domain controller.

C. Run the `Set-KdsConfiguration` PowerShell cmdlet on a domain controller.

D. Run the `Add-KdsRootKey` PowerShell cmdlet on a domain controller.

23. You are the administrator for your company network. You think you may have an issue with name resolution, and you need to verify that you are using the correct host name. You want to test DNS on the local system and see whether the host name Server1 resolves to the IP address 10.1.1.1. Which of the following provides a solution to the problem?

A. Add an A record to the local WINS server.

B. Add a DNS server to the local subnet.

C. Add the mapping for the host name Server1 to the IP address 10.1.1.1 in the local system's HOSTS file.

D. Add an MX record to the local DNS server.

24. You are the administrator for your company network. You have one Active Directory forest in your organization that contains one domain named abc.com. You have two domain controllers configured with the DNS role installed. There are two Active Directory integrated zones named abc.com and abcAD.com. One of your colleagues, who is not an administrator, needs to be able to modify the abc.com DNS server, but you need to prevent this user from modifying the abcAD.com SOA record. What should you do?

A. Modify the permissions of the abc.com zone from the DNS Manager snap-in.

B. Modify the permissions of the abcAD.com zone from the DNS Manager snap-in.

C. Run the Delegation Of Control Wizard in Active Directory.

D. Run the Delegation Of Control Wizard in the DNS snap-in.

25. You are the administrator for your company network. You and a colleague are discussing Active Directory protocols and services. Which of the following protocols and services are required in order to support Active Directory? (Choose two.)

A. DHCP

B. DNS

C. IPX/SPX

D. NetBEUI

E. TCP/IP

26. You are the administrator for your company network. The network contains an Active Directory forest. The forest contains three domain controllers configured as shown:

Server Name	Active Directory Site
Server1	Boston
Server2	Boston
Server3	New York

The company physically relocates Server2 from the Boston office to the New York office. You discover that both Server1 and Server2 authenticate users who sign in to the client computers in the Boston office. Only Server3 authenticates users who sign in to the computers in the New York office. What should you do if you need to ensure that Server2 authenticates the users in the New York office during normal network operations?

A. Modify the Internet Protocol Version 4 (TCP/IPv4) configuration from Network Connections on Server2.

B. Modify the Location Property of Server2 from Active Directory Users and Computers.

C. Run the `Move-ADDirectoryServer` cmdlet.

D. Run the `Set-ADReplicationSite` cmdlet.

27. You are the administrator for your company network. Your network contains an Active Directory domain. The domain contains a web application that uses Kerberos authentication. You change the domain name of the web application. What tool should you use if you need to ensure that the Service Principal Name (SPN) for the application is registered?

A. Active Directory Users and Computers

B. dnscmd

C. LDIFDE

D. rdspnf

28. You are the administrator for your company network. Your network contains an Active Directory domain. What should you use if you need to create a Central Store for Group Policy administrator templates?

    A. dcgpofix.exe

    B. File Explorer

    C. Group Policy Management Console (GPMC)

    D. Server Manager

29. You are the administrator for your company network. Your network contains an Active Directory domain. What should you use if you need to create a Central Store for Group Policy administrator templates?

    A. Copy-GPO

    B. Copy-Item

    C. dcgpofix.exe

    D. Group Policy Management Console (GPMC)

30. You are the administrator for a large hospital. You have dozens of doctors who are affiliated with the hospital but do not have offices within the hospital. You have been asked to install a domain controller in a small doctor's office that is offsite. The doctor's office does not have a secure server room. What is the best way to complete this task?

    A. Do not install a domain controller at their location. Install a Windows Server 2016 Server Core server and enable Universal Group Membership Caching on that server.

    B. Install a domain controller at their office and enable certificates.

    C. Make the new server a Windows Server 2016 Server Core system and install the domain controller as a Read-Only Domain Controller (RODC) server.

    D. All of the above.

31. You are the administrator for your company network. You and a colleague are discussing changing an existing partition's filesystem to another filesystem. What command-line utility should you use?

    A. CHANGE

    B. CONVERT

    C. REVERT

    D. TRANSFORM

32. You are the administrator for your company network. Your network contains an Active Directory domain. All the accounts of the users in the Marketing department are in an organizational unit (OU) named MarketingOU. An application named App1 is deployed to the user accounts in MarketingOU by using a Group Policy Object (GPO) named MarketingGPO. What should you do if you need to set the registry value of \HKEY_CURRENT_USER\Software\App1\Collaboration to 0? (Choose all that apply.)

    A. Add a user preference that has an Update action.

    B. Add a user preference that has a Replace action.

    C. Add a user preference that has a Create action.

    D. Add a user preference that has a Delete action.

33. You are the administrator for your company network. You and a colleague are discussing installing additional domain controllers by using the Install from Media (IFM) installation method. What is the name of the utility that allows you to create installation media for the creation of an additional domain controller in the domain?

    A. `dcdiag.exe`

    B. `netdom.exe`

    C. `ntdsutil.exe`

    D. `repadmin.exe`

34. You are the administrator for your company network. You and a colleague are discussing trusts. What kind of trust is set up between one domain and another domain in the same forest?

    A. Domain trust

    B. External trust

    C. Forest trust

    D. Shortcut trust

35. You are the administrator for your company network. Your network contains an Active Directory domain. You create a domain security group named Group1 and add several users to it. What should you do if you need to force all of the users in Group1 to change their passwords every 35 days while not affecting any other users?

    A. Create a Password Settings Object (PSO) from Active Directory Administrative Center.

    B. Create a forms authentication provider and then set the forms authentication credentials.

    C. Run the `Set-ADDomain` cmdlet and then run the `Set-ADAccountPassword` cmdlet using PowerShell.

    D. Modify the Password Policy settings in a Group Policy Object (GPO) that is linked to the domain and then filter the GPO to Group1 only.

36. You are the administrator for your company network. A technician named Tech1 is assigned the task of joining the laptops to the domain. The computer accounts of each laptop must be in an organizational unit (OU) that is associated with the department of the user who will use that laptop. The laptop names must start with four characters, indicating the department followed by a four-digit number. Tech1 is a member of only the Domain Users group. Tech1 has the administrator logon credentials for all the laptops. You need Tech1 to join the laptops to the domain. The solution must ensure that the laptops are named correctly and that the computer accounts of the laptops are in the correct OUs. What should you do? (Choose all that apply.)

    A. Script the creation of files for an offline domain join and then give the files to Tech1. Instruct Tech1 to sign in to each laptop and then to run `djoin.exe`.

    B. Pre-create the computer account of each laptop in Active Directory Users and Computers. Instruct Tech1 to sign in to each laptop and then to run `djoin.exe`.

    C. Instruct Tech1 to sign in to each laptop, rename each laptop by using System in Control Panel, and then to join each laptop to the domain by using the `netdom join` command.

    D. Pre-create the computer account of each laptop in Active Directory Users and Computers. Instruct Tech1 to sign in to each laptop, rename each laptop, and then to join each laptop to the domain by using System in Control Panel.

37. You are the administrator for your company network. Your network contains an Active Directory domain that has 5,000 user accounts. You have a Group Policy Object (GPO) named DomainPolicy that is linked to the domain and a GPO named DCPolicy that is linked to the domain controllers organizational unit (OU). What should you do if you need to ensure that all the client computers on the network automatically download and install Windows Updates?

   A. Modify Administrative Templates from the Computer Configuration node of DomainPolicy.

   B. Modify Administrative Templates from the User Configuration node of DomainPolicy.

   C. Modify Folder Redirection from the User Configuration node of DomainPolicy.

   D. Modify Security Settings from the Computer Configuration node of DCPolicy.

   E. Modify Security Settings from the Computer Configuration node of DomainPolicy.

   F. Modify Security Settings from the User Configuration node of DCPolicy.

   G. Modify Windows Settings from Preferences in the User Configuration node of DomainPolicy.

   H. Modify Windows Settings from Preferences in the Computer Configuration node of DomainPolicy.

38. You are the administrator for your company network. You and a colleague are discussing useful Windows Server 2016 command-line utilities. One allows you to back up and restore the operating system, volumes, files, folders, and applications while using the command prompt. Which utility are we discussing?

   A. `adsiedit.msc`

   B. `ntdsutil.exe`

   C. `repadmin.exe`

   D. `wbadmin`

39. You are the administrator for your company network. You have multiple Windows Server 2016 servers. You have a server named Server1 that is configured as a domain controller and a DNS server. What should you run if you need to create an Active Directory–integrated zone on Server1?

   A. `dism.exe`

   B. `dns.exe`

   C. `dnscmd.exe`

   D. `netsh.exe`

   E. `Set-DhcpServerDatabase`

   F. `Set-DhcpServerv4DnsSetting`

   G. `Set-DhcpServerv6DnsSetting`

   H. `Set-DNSServerSetting`

40. You are the administrator for your company network. You and a colleague are discussing the multiple ways in which you can install Active Directory. What are some of the ways? (Choose all that apply.)

A. Add/Remove Programs

B. Install from Media (IFM)

C. Server Manager

D. Windows PowerShell

41. You are the administrator for your company network. The network contains an Active Directory domain and has multiple offices. An Active Directory site exists for each of the offices. All of the sites connect to each other by using DEFAULTIPSITELINK. The company plans to open a new office. The new office will have a domain controller and 100 client computers. You install Windows Server 2016 on a member server in the new office, which will become a domain controller. You need to deploy the domain controller to the new office. You must ensure that the client computers in the new office will authenticate by using the local domain controller. What should you perform next in sequence? (Choose all that apply.)

A. Create a new connection object.

B. Create a new site object.

C. Create a new subnet object.

D. Move the server object of the domain controller.

E. Promote a member server to a domain controller.

42. You are the administrator for your company network. Your company recently deployed a new child domain to an Active Directory forest. You discover that a user modified the Default Domain Policy to configure several Windows components in the child domain. Company policy states that the Default Domain Policy must be used only to configure domain-wide security settings. You create a new Group Policy Object (GPO) and configure the settings for the Windows components in the new GPO. What should you do if you need to restore the Default Domain Policy to the default settings from when the domain was first installed?

A. Click Starter GPOs and then click Manage Backups from Group Policy Management.

B. Run the Copy-GPO cmdlet using PowerShell.

C. Run the dcgpofix.exe command from a command prompt.

D. Run ntdsutil.exe to perform a metadata cleanup and a semantic database analysis.

43. You are the administrator for your company network. Your network has a single Windows Server 2016 Active Directory domain. The domain has OUs for Sales, Marketing, Admin, R&D, and Finance. You need the users in the Finance OU only to get Microsoft Office 2016 installed automatically onto their computers. You create a GPO named OfficeApp. What is the next step in getting all the Finance users Office 2016?

    A. Edit the GPO and assign the Office application to the user's account. Link the GPO to the Finance OU.

    B. Edit the GPO and assign the Office application to the user's account. Link the GPO to the domain.

    C. Edit the GPO and assign the Office application to the computer account. Link the GPO to the domain.

    D. Edit the GPO and assign the Office application to the computer account. Link the GPO to the Finance OU.

44. You are the administrator for your company network. You are working on creating a new GPO for the Sales OU. You want the GPO to take effect immediately and you need to use PowerShell. What PowerShell cmdlet would you use?

    A. `Invoke-GPExecute`

    B. `Invoke-GPForce`

    C. `Invoke-GPResult`

    D. `Invoke-GPUpdate`

45. You are the administrator for your company network. You want to run `adprep /forestprep` to add the first Windows Server 2016 domain controller to an existing forest. In order to do so, you must be a member of what administrator group? (Choose all that apply.)

    A. Administrators group

    B. Domain Admins group

    C. Enterprise Admins group

    D. Schema Admins group

46. You are the administrator for your company network. You and a colleague are discussing DNS SRV records. DNS must have service records for which of the following? (Choose all that apply.)

    A. Domain Controllers

    B. Network Controllers

    C. Global Catalogs

    D. PDC Emulator

    E. Kerberos KDC

    F. Information Service

47. You are the administrator for your company network. You need to enable three of your domain controllers as Global Catalog servers. Where would you configure the domain controllers as Global Catalogs?

    A. Forest, NTDS settings

    B. Domain, NTDS settings

    C. Site, NTDS settings

    D. Server, NTDS settings

48. You are the administrator for your company network. Your network contains an Active Directory forest. The forest contains two Windows Server 2016 domain controllers named DC1 and DC2. DC1 holds all of the operations master roles. DC1 experiences a hardware failure. You plan to use an automated process that will create 1,000 user accounts. You need to ensure that the automated process can complete successfully. What PowerShell cmdlet should you run?

    A. `Move-ADDirectoryServerOperationMasterRole -identity "DC2" -OperationMasterRole PDCEmulator -Force`

    B. `ntdsutil -identity "DC2" -OperationMasterRole PDC Emulator Seize PDC`

    C. `ntdsutil -identity "DC2" -OperationMasterRole SchemaMaster -Force`

    D. `Move-ADDirectoryServerOperationMasterRole -identity "DC2" -OperationMasterRole PDCEmulator Seize pdc`

49. You are the administrator for your company network. You and a colleague are discussing domain controller cloning. What is the tool that you can use to clone domain controllers?

    A. sysprep.exe

    B. Windows PowerShell

    C. ntdsutil.exe

    D. Active Directory Users and Computers

50. You are the administrator for your company network. Recently, you have been asked to make changes to some of the permissions related to OUs within the domain. To restrict security for the Texas OU further, you remove some permissions at that level. Later, a junior system administrator mentions that she is no longer able to make changes to objects within the Austin OU (which is located within the Texas OU). Assuming that no other changes have been made to Active Directory permissions, which of the following characteristics of OUs might have caused the change in permissions?

    A. Delegation

    B. Group Policy

    C. Inheritance

    D. Object properties

51. You are the administrator for your company network. A user complains that she continues to have desktop wallpaper that she did not choose. You determine that a former employee created 20 Group Policy Objects (GPOs) and junior technicians have not been able to figure out which GPO is changing the user's desktop wallpaper. How can you resolve this issue?

A. Run the RSoP utility against all forest computer accounts.

B. Run the RSoP utility against the user's computer account.

C. Run the RSoP utility against the user's user account.

D. Run the RSoP utility against all domain computer accounts.

52. You are the administrator for your company network. Your network contains an Active Directory domain. The domain contains 20 domain controllers. You find that some Group Policy Objects (GPOs) are not being applied by all the domain controllers. What should you do if you need to verify whether GPOs replicate successfully to all the domain controllers?

A. From Group Policy Management, view the Status tab for the domain.

B. Run repadmin.exe for each GPO.

C. Set BurFlags in the registry and then restart the File Replication Service (FRS). Run dcdiag.exe for each domain controller.

D. Set BurFlags in the registry and then restart the File Replication Service (FRS). View the Directory Service event log.

53. You are the administrator for your company network. The network contains an Active Directory domain. The domain contains a Windows Server 2016 domain controller named DC1. You start DC1 in Directory Services Restore Mode (DSRM). You need to compact the Active Directory database on DC1. What three actions should you perform? (Choose three.)

A. Run ntdsutil.exe.

B. Run activate instance ntds.

C. From the Metadata Cleanup context, select an operation target.

D. Run dsamain.exe.

E. From the Files context, run compact.

F. From the Semantic Database Analysis context, run go fixup.

54. You are the administrator for your company network. You have a server named Server1. A Microsoft Azure Backup of Server1 is created automatically every day. You rename Server1 to Server2. Then you discover that backups are no longer being created in Azure. What should you do if you need to back up the server to Azure?

A. Upload the Server2 certificate as a management certificate from the Azure Management Portal.

B. Run the Start-OBRegistration cmdlet on Server2.

C. Run the Add-WBBackupTarget cmdlet on Server2.

D. Modify the configuration on the backup vault from the Azure Management Portal.

55. You are the administrator for your company network. You have a server named Server1 in a workgroup. What should you do if you need to configure a Group Policy setting on Server1 that will apply to only nonadministrative users?

A. Open Local Group Policy Editor; then from the File menu, modify the Options settings.

C. Open Local Group Policy Editor from the View menu and modify the Customize settings.

D. Open Local Users and Groups and create a new group by running the Run New-GPO cmdlet.

B. Run mmc.exe and add the Group Policy Object Editor snap-in and then change the Group Policy Object (GPO).

56. You are the administrator for your company network. Your network contains an Active Directory domain. Users do not have administrative privileges to their client computer. You modify a computer setting in a Group Policy Object (GPO). What should you do if you need to ensure that the setting is applied to client computers as soon as possible?

A. Run the gpudate.exe command and specify the -Force parameter from a domain controller.

B. Run the gpresult.exe command and specify the /r parameter from each client computer.

C. Run the Get-Gpo cmdlet and specify the -alt parameter from each client computer.

D. Run the Invoke-GPUpdate cmdlet from a domain controller.

57. You are the administrator for your company network. Your network contains an Active Directory domain. A Group Policy Object (GPO) named GPO1 is linked to the domain. GPO1 has computer configuration polices, user configuration policies, and user preferences configured. You need to ensure that the user preferences in GPO1 apply only to users who sign in to computers that run Windows Server 2016. All the other settings in GPO1 must be applied, regardless of the computer to which the user signs in. What should you configure?

A. Item-level targeting

B. Security filtering

C. Security settings

D. WMI filtering

58. You are the administrator for your company network. Your network contains an Active Directory domain. You have three top-level organizational units (OUs) named OU1, OU2, and OU3. OU1 contains the user accounts. OU2 contains the computer accounts for shared public computers. OU3 contains the computer accounts for laptops. You have two Group Policy Objects (GPOs) named GPO1 and GPO2. GPO1 is linked to OU1. GPO2 is linked to OU2. You need to prevent the user settings in GPO1 from being applied when a user signs in to a shared public computer. What should you configure if a user signs in to a laptop and you want the user settings in GPO1 to be applied?

A. GPO link enforcement

B. Inheritance blocking

C. Loopback processing

D. Security filtering

59. You are the administrator for your company network. The company has multiple branch offices. The network contains an Active Directory domain. In one of the branch offices, a colleague is asked to add computers to the domain. After successfully joining multiple computers to the domain, she fails to join any more computers to the domain. What should you do if you need to ensure that your colleague can join an unlimited number of computers to the domain?

A. Modify the Security settings of your colleague's user account.

B. Modify the Security settings of the Computers container.

C. Configure your colleague's user account as a managed service account.

D. Run the `redircmp.exe` command.

60. You are the administrator for your company network. Your company has a single Active Directory domain. One of the executives tries to log on to a machine and receives the error "This user account has expired. Ask your administrator to reactivate your account." What should you do if you need to make sure that this doesn't happen again to this user?

A. Configure the domain policy to disable account lockouts.

B. Configure the password policy to extend the maximum password age to 0.

C. Modify the user's properties to set the Account Never Expires setting.

D. Modify the user's properties to extend the maximum password age to 0.

61. You are the administrator for your company network. A colleague, Sue, has created a new Active Directory domain in an environment that already contains two trees. During the promotion of the domain controller, she chose to create a new Active Directory forest. Sue is a member of the Enterprise Administrators group and has full permissions over all domains. During the organization's migration to Active Directory, many updates were made to the information stored within the domains. Recently, users and other system administrators have complained about not being able to find specific Active Directory objects in one or more domains (although the objects exist in others). To investigate the problem, Sue wants to check for any objects that have not been properly replicated among domain controllers. If possible, she would like to restore these objects to their proper place within the relevant Active Directory domains. Which of the following actions should she perform to be able to view the relevant information? (Choose two.)

A. Change Active Directory permissions to allow object information to be viewed in all domains.

B. Examine the contents of the `LostAndFound` folder using the Active Directory Users and Computers tool.

C. Promote a member server in each domain to a domain controller.

D. Rebuild all domain controllers from the latest backups.

E. Select the Advanced Features item in the View menu.

62. You are the administrator for your company network. Your network contains an Active Directory forest named abc.com. A partner company has a forest named xyz.com. Each forest contains one domain. You need to provide access for a group named Sales in xyz.com to resources in abc.com. What should you do so that the solution uses the least amount of administrative privilege?

    A. Create an external trust from xyz.com to abc.com. Enable Active Directory split permissions in xyz.com.

    B. Create an external trust from abc.com to xyz.com. Enable Active Directory split permissions in abc.com.

    C. Create a one-way forest trust from abc.com to xyz.com that uses selective authentication.

    D. Create a one-way forest trust from xyz.com to abc.com that uses selective authentication.

63. You are the administrator for your company network. Your network contains an Active Directory forest named abc.com. You need to add a new domain named xyz.com to the forest. What command should you run?

    A. `Install-ADDSForest -DomainType TreeDomain`
    `- InstallDNS:$true -NewDomainName xyz.com -ParentDomainName abc.com`

    B. `Install-ADDSForest -DomainType ChildDomain`
    `- InstallDNS:$true -NewDomainName xyz.com -ParentDomainName abc.com`

    C. `Install-ADDSDomain -DomainType TreeDomain`
    `-InstallDNS:$true -NewDomainName xyz.com -ParentDomainName abc.com`

    D. `Install-ADDSDomain -DomainType ChildDomain`
    `-InstallDNS:$true -NewDomainName xyz.com -ParentDomainName abc.com`

64. You are the administrator for your company network. Your network contains an Active Directory domain. You need to view a list of all the domain user accounts that are enabled. What command should you run to see those users who have not signed in over the last 30 days?

    A. `Get-LocalUser AccountExpiring -TimeSpan 30`
    `-UsersOnly | Format-Table Name, UserPrincipalName`

    B. `Net User AccountAccountInactive -TimeSpan 30`
    `-UsersOnly | Format-Table Name, UserPrincipalName`

    C. `ldp.exe PasswordExpired -TimeSpan 30`
    `-UsersOnly | Format-Table Name, UserPrincipalName`

    D. `Search-ADAccount AccountDisabled -TimeSpan 30`
    `-UsersOnly | Format-Table Name, UserPrincipalName`

65. You are the administrator for your company network. Your network contains one Active Directory forest named abc.com. The forest contains two child domains and six domain controllers. The domain controllers are configured as shown:

Name	Domain	Site
DC1	abc.com	Main Office
DC2	abc.com	Main Office
DC3	abc.com	Europe Office
DC4	abc.com	Asia Office
DC5	sales.abc.com	Main Office
DC6	manufacturing.abc.com	Main Office

What should you use if you need to prevent administrators from accidentally deleting any of the sites in the forest?

A. Netdom

B. Set-ADDomain

C. Set-ADForest

D. Set-ADGroup

E. Set-ADReplicationSite

F. Set-ADReplicationSiteLink

G. Set-ADSite

66. You are the administrator for your company network. Your network contains one Active Directory domain named abc.com. The domain contains three users named User1, User2, and User3. You need to ensure that the users can log on to the domain by using the User Principal Names (UPNs) shown.

User	User Principal Name (UPN)
User1	User1@cde.com
User2	User2@lmn.com
User3	User3@xyz.com

What should you use?

A. The Add-DNSServerSecondaryZone cmdlet

B. The Set-ADDomain cmdlet

C. The Set-ADUser cmdlet

D. The Setspn command

67. You are the administrator for your company network. You are evaluating your organization's Active Directory domain. The domain contains more than 200,000 objects and hundreds of OUs. You begin examining the objects in the domain, but you find that the loading of the contents of a specific OU is taking a long time. Additionally, the list of objects can be large. You want to do the following:

- Use the built-in Active Directory administrative tools and avoid the use of third-party tools or utilities.
- Limit the list of objects within an OU to only the type of objects that you're examining (for example, only Computer objects).
- Prevent any changes to the Active Directory domain or any of the objects in it.

Which of the following actions meets these requirements?

A. Edit the domain Group Policy settings to allow yourself to view only the objects of interest.

B. Implement a new naming convention for objects within an OU and then sort the results using this new naming convention.

C. Use the Active Directory Domains and Trusts tool to view information from only selected domain controllers.

D. Use the Delegation of Control Wizard to give yourself permissions over only a certain type of object.

E. Use the Filter option in the Active Directory Users and Computers tool to restrict the display of objects.

68. You are the administrator for your company network. Your role is the primary system administrator for your large Active Directory domain. Recently, you hired another system administrator to whom you will be passing on some of your current responsibilities. This system administrator will be responsible for handling the help desk calls and for basic user account management. You want to allow the new employee to have permissions to reset passwords for all users within a specific OU. However, for security reasons, it's important that the user not be able to make permissions changes for objects within other OUs in the domain. What is the best way to do this?

A. Create a special administration account within the OU and grant it full permissions for all objects within Active Directory.

B. Move the user's login account into the OU that the new employee is to administer.

C. Move the user's login account to an OU that contains the OU (that is, the parent OU of the one that the new employee is to administer).

D. Use the Delegation of Control Wizard to assign the necessary permissions on the OU that the new employee is to administer.

69. You are the administrator for your company network. Your network has a single domain forest. Your company has one main office and two branch locations. All locations are configured as Active Directory sites, and all the sites are connected with the DEFAULTIPSITELINK object. Your connections are running slower than the company policy allows. What should you do if you want to decrease the replication latency between all domain controllers in the various sites?

A. Decrease the replication interval for the DEFAULTIPSITELINK object.

B. Decrease the replication interval for the site.

C. Decrease the replication schedule for the site.

D. Decrease the replication schedule for all domain controllers.

70. You are the administrator for your company network. You are responsible for managing Active Directory replication traffic for your single Active Directory domain. Currently, the environment is configured with two sites and the default settings for replication. Each site consists of 15 domain controllers. Recently, a few junior administrators have complained that Active Directory traffic has been using a large amount of available network bandwidth between the two sites. You have been asked to meet the following requirements:

- Reduce the amount of network traffic between the domain controllers in the two sites.

- Minimize the amount of change to the current site topology.

- Require no changes to the existing physical network infrastructure.

You decide that it would be most efficient to configure specific domain controllers in each site that will receive the majority of the replication traffic from the other site. Which of the following best meets your needs?

A. Create additional sites that are designed only for replication traffic and move the existing domain controllers to those sites.

B. Create multiple site links between the two sites.

C. Create a site link bridge between the two sites.

D. Configure one server at each site to act as a preferred bridgehead server.

71. You are the administrator for your company network. The network contains an Active Directory forest. The forest contains a member server named Server1. Server1 has several line-of-business applications. Each application runs as a service that uses the Network Service account. What should you do if you need to configure the line-of-business applications to run by using a virtual account?

A. Create a shim from the Microsoft Application Compatibility Toolkit (ACT).

B. Modify the Log On properties of the services from the Services console.

C. Run the Install-ADServiceAccount cmdlet from PowerShell.

D. Run the New-ADServiccAccount cmdlet from PowerShell.

72. You are the administrator for your company network. Your network contains an Active Directory forest. The company is planning to hire 300 temporary employees for a project that will last 90 days. You create a new user account for each employee. An organizational unit (OU) named TempEmployees contains the user accounts for these temporary employees. What should you do if you need to prevent the new users from accessing any of the resources in the domain after 90 days?

   A. Create a group that contains all of the users in the Temp Employees OU. Create a Password Setting Object (PSO) for the new group.

   B. Create a Group Policy Object (GPO) and link the GPO to the TempEmployees OU. Modify the Password Policy settings of the GPO.

   C. Run the `Get-ADOrganizationalUnit` cmdlet and pipe the output to the `Set-Date` cmdlet.

   D. Run the `Get-ADUser` cmdlet and pipe the output to the `Set-ADUser` cmdlet.

73. You are the administrator for your company network. You and a colleague are discussing configuring DNS SRV records. If for some reason the server is not registering with DNS, you may need to manually create a SRV record. To manually configure the SRV record, you go into the DNS under Administrative Tools and then you need to expand which of the following to see your zone name?

   A. Reverse Lookup Zone

   B. Forward Lookup Zone

   C. Secondary Zone

   D. Stub Zone

74. You are the administrator for your company network. You and a colleague are discussing creating a new user account using the command prompt. What command would you use?

   A. dsadd

   B. dscreate

   C. dsmodify

   D. dsnew

75. You are the administrator for your company network. You and a colleague are discussing the different Active Directory Administrative Tools. What Active Directory Administrative Tool is used to view and change information related to the various domains in an Active Directory environment?

   A. Active Directory Administrative Center

   B. Active Directory Domains and Trusts

   C. Active Directory Sites and Services

   D. Active Directory Users and Computers

76. You are the administrator for your company network. Your network contains an Active Directory forest. The forest contains two domains named abc.com and xyz.com. The xyz.com domain contains two domains controllers named BOS-DC1 and BOS-DC2. The domain controllers are located in a site named Boston that is associated to a subnet of 192.168.10.0/24. You discover that BOS-DC2 is not a Global Catalog server. What should you do if you need to configure BOS-DC2 as a Global Catalog server?

   A. Modify the NTDS Settings object of BOS-DC2 from Active Directory Sites and Services.

   B. Modify the properties of the 192.168.10.0/24 IP subnet from Active Directory Sites and Services.

   C. Run the Set-NetNatGlobal cmdlet from PowerShell.

   D. Run the Enable-ADOptionalFeature cmdlet from PowerShell.

77. You are the administrator for your company network. Your network contains an Active Directory forest. The forest contains two sites named Site1 and Site2. Site1 contains 10 domain controllers. Site1 and Site2 connect to each other by using a WAN link. You run the Active Directory Domain Services Configuration Wizard and it shows:

   Delegated administrator account: ABC\Site2 Admins

   Accounts that are allowed to replicate passwords to the RODC:
   ABC\Allowed RODC Password Replication Group

   Accounts that are denied from replicating passwords to the RODC:
   BUILTIN\Administrators

   BUILTIN\Server Operators

   BUILTIN\Backup Operators

Server3 is the only server in Site2. What will members of the Site2 Admins group be able to do given the current settings?

   A. Make updates to SYSVOL content.

   B. Manage the password replication policy.

   C. Stop and start the Active Directory Domain Services (AD DS).

   D. Log on with reduced security rights.

78. You are the administrator for your company network. Sue is a user who belongs to the Marketing distribution global group. She is unable to access the laser printer that is shared on the network. The Marketing global group has full access to the laser printer. How do you resolve the issue?

   A. Add the Marketing global group to the Administrators group.

   B. Add the Marketing global group to the Printer Operators group.

   C. Change the group type to a security group.

   D. Change the Marketing group to a local group.

79. You are the administrator for your company network. Your network contains an Active Directory forest. The forest contains one domain. The domain contains two domain controllers named DC1 and DC2. DC1 holds all of the operations master roles. During normal network operations, you run the following commands on DC2:

```
Move-ADDirectoryServerOperationMasterRole -Identity "DC2"
-OperationMasterRole PDCEmulator
Move- ADDirectoryServerOperationMasterRole -Identity "DC2"
-OperationMasterRole RIDMaster
```

DC1 fails. You remove DC1 from the network, and then you run the following command:

```
Move-ADDirectoryServerOperationMasterRole -Identity "DC2"
-OperationMasterRole SchemaMaster
```

Which of the following statements is true?

A. DC2 holds the schema master operations role.

B. DC2 holds the PDC emulator master operations role.

C. Currently you can add additional domains to the forest.

D. DC2 holds the RID master operations role.

80. You are the administrator for your company network. The company has a main office and three branch offices. The network contains an Active Directory domain named abc.com. The main office contains three domain controllers. Each branch office contains one domain controller. You discover that new settings in the Default Domain Policy are not applied in one of the branch offices, but all other Group Policy Objects (GPOs) are applied. What should you do from a domain controller in the main office if you need to check the replication of the Default Domain Policy for the branch office?

A. Run dcdiag.exe from a command prompt.

B. From Group Policy Management, click Default Domain Policy under abc.com, and then open the Details tab.

C. From Group Policy Management, click Default Domain Policy under abc.com, and then open the Scope tab.

D. Run repadmin.exe from a command prompt.

81. You are the administrator for your company network. You and a colleague are discussing replication. Which of the following does not need to be created manually when you are setting up a replication scenario involving three domains and three sites?

A. Connection objects

B. Sites

C. Site links

D. Subnets

82. You are the administrator for your company network. Your network contains an Active Directory forest. The forest contains two domains named abc.com and xyz.com. You have a global group named Group1 in the abc.com domain. Group1 contains the user accounts in abc.com. You need to ensure that you can add the user accounts in the xyz.com domain to Group1. What should you do?

  A. Assign the Domain Controllers group in xyz.com permissions to Group1.

  B. Change Group1 to a distribution group.

  C. Modify the scope of Group1 to Domain local.

  D. Run the Set-LocalGroup cmdlet.

83. You are the administrator for your company network. You and a colleague are discussing replication. Which of the following services of Active Directory is responsible for maintaining the replication topology?

  A. File Replication Service

  B. Knowledge Consistency Checker

  C. Windows Internet Name Service

  D. Domain Name System

84. You are the administrator for your company network. Your Active Directory environment consists of three sites. You want to configure site links to be transitive. Which of the following Active Directory objects are responsible for representing a transitive relationship between sites?

  A. Additional sites

  B. Additional site links

  C. Bridgehead servers

  D. Site link bridges

85. You are the administrator for your company network. You have configured your Active Directory environment with multiple sites and have placed the appropriate resources in each of the sites. You are now trying to choose a protocol for the transfer of replication information between two sites. The connection between the two sites has the following characteristics:

  ▪ The link is generally unavailable during certain parts of the day because of an unreliable network provider.

  ▪ The replication transmission must be attempted whether or not the link is available. If the link was unavailable during a scheduled replication, the information should automatically be received after the link becomes available again.

  ▪ Replication traffic must be able to travel over a standard Internet connection.

  Which of the following protocols meets these requirements?

  A. Dynamic Host Configuration Protocol (DHCP)

  B. Static Host Configuration Protocol (SHCP)

  C. Complex Mail Transfer Protocol (CMTP)

  D. Simple Mail Transfer Protocol (SMTP)

Chapter
10

Implement Identity Federation and Access Solutions

THE FOLLOWING MCSA WINDOWS SERVER 2016 EXAM TOPICS ARE COVERED IN THIS CHAPTER:

✓ **10.1 Install and Configure Active Directory Federation Services (AD FS)**

- This objective may include but is not limited to: Upgrade and migrate previous AD FS workloads to Windows Server 2016; implement claims-based authentication, including Relying Party Trusts; configure authentication policies; configure multi-factor authentication; implement and configure device registration; integrate AD FS with Microsoft Passport; configure for use with Microsoft Azure and Office 365; configure AD FS to enable authentication of users stored in LDAP directories

✓ **10.2 Implement Web Application Proxy (WAP)**

- This objective may include but is not limited to: Install and configure WAP; implement WAP in pass-through mode; implement WAP as AD FS proxy; integrate WAP with AD FS; configure AD FS requirements; publish web apps via WAP; publish Remote Desktop Gateway applications; configure HTTP to HTTPS redirects; configure internal and external Fully Qualified Domain Names (FQDNs)

✓ **10.3 Install and Configure Active Directory Rights Management Services (AD RMS)**

- This objective may include but is not limited to: Install a licensor certificate AD RMS server; manage AD RMS Service Connection Point (SCP); manage AD RMS templates; configure Exclusion Policies; back up and restore AD RMS

1. You are the administrator for your company network. Your network contains an Active Directory domain. The domain contains a domain controller named Server1. You recently restored a backup of the Active Directory database from Server1 to an alternate location. The restore operation did not interrupt the Active Directory services on Server1. What tool should you use if you need to make the Active Directory data in the backup accessible by using Lightweight Directory Access Protocol (LDAP)?

   A. Active Directory Administrative Center

   B. Active Directory Users and Computers

   C. Dsacls

   D. Dsadd quota

   E. Dsamain

   F. Dsmod

   G. Group Policy Management Console

   H. Ntdsutil

2. You are the administrator for your company network. You and a colleague are discussing the Federation Proxy services. The Federation Proxy services are installed through which of the following?

   A. A separate Active Directory Federation Proxy install download

   B. Server Manager ➢ Remote Access ➢ Web Proxy

   C. Server Manager ➢ Active Directory Federation Services ➢ Active Directory Proxy services

   D. PowerShell ➢ Install-Windows-Feature Web Proxy

3. You are the administrator for your company network. You and a colleague are discussing different authentication capabilities offered when using Active Directory Federation Services (AD FS) authentication. One of the features offered with AD FS is the ability to allow users to enter their credentials only once but then be authenticated to all supported published applications. What is this feature called?

   A. Multi-Factor Authentication (MFA)

   B. Multi-Factor Access Control

   C. Single Sign-On

   D. Workplace Join

4. You are the administrator for your company network. You and a colleague are discussing the Certification Authority role. What should you consider if you want the configuration modifications of the Certification Authority role service to be logged? (Choose all that apply.)

   A. Enabling auditing of system events

   B. Enabling logging

   C. Enabling auditing of object access

   D. Enabling auditing of privilege use

   E. Enabling auditing of process tracking

5. You are the administrator for your company network. Company management asks you to implement a new Windows Server 2016 system. Which of the following will you need to implement if you want to use federated identity management?

   A. Active Directory DNS Services

   B. Active Directory Federation Services

   C. Active Directory IAS Services

   D. Active Directory IIS Services

6. You are the administrator for your company network. You have a Windows Server 2016 server named Server1 that has the Windows Application Proxy role service installed. You need to publish Microsoft Exchange ActiveSync services by using the Publish New Application Wizard. The ActiveSync services must use preauthentication. How should you configure Server1's preauthentication method and preauthentication type?

   A. Configure the Active Directory Federation Services (AD FS) preauthentication method and the Oath2 preauthentication type.

   B. Configure the pass-through preauthentication method and the Web/MS-OFBA preauthentication type.

   C. Configure the pass-through preauthentication method and the HTTP Basic preauthentication type.

   D. Configure the Active Directory Federation Services (AD FS) preauthentication method and the HTTP Basic preauthentication type.

7. You are the administrator for your company network. Your network contains an Active Directory forest, which contains a member server named Server1 that runs Windows Server 2016. Server1 is located in the perimeter network. You install the Active Directory Federation Services (AD FS) server role on Server1. You create an AD FS farm by using a certificate that has a subject name of `adfs.abc.com`. What inbound TCP ports should you open on the firewall if you need to enable certificate authentication from the Internet on Server1? (Choose two.)

   A. 389

   B. 443

   C. 3389

   D. 8531

   E. 49443

8. You are the administrator for your company network. You have a Windows Server 2016 server named Server1 that has the Web Application Proxy (WAP) role service installed. You publish an application named App1 by using the WAP. What cmdlet should you run if you need to change the URL that users use to connect to App1 when they work remotely?

    A. `Set-WebApplicationProxyConfiguration`
       `-ID 874A4543-77A3-1E6D-1163E7419AC1 -ADFSUrl https://abc.com/`

    B. `Set-WebApplicationProxySslCertificate`
       `-ID 874A4543-77A3-1E6D-1163E7419AC1 -BackendServerUrl https://abc.com/`

    C. `Set-WebApplicationProxyApplication`
       `-ID 874A4543-77A3-1E6D-1163E7419AC1 -ExternalUrl https://abc.com/`

    D. `Set-WebApplicationProxy -ID 874A4543-77A3-1E6D-1163E7419AC1`
       `-InternalUrl https://abc.com/`

9. You are the administrator for your company network. Your network contains an Active Directory domain. What should you use if you need to create a Central Store for Group Policy Administrative Template files?

    A. Server Manager

    B. File Explorer

    C. `dcgpofix.exe`

    D. Group Policy Management Console (GPMC)

10. You are the administrator for your company network. You have a Windows Server 2016 server named Server1. You need to configure Server1 as a Web Application Proxy (WAP). Which server role or role service should you install on Server1?

    A. Active Directory Federation Services

    B. DirectAccess and VPN (RAS)

    C. Remote Access

    D. Web Server (IIS)

11. You are the administrator for your company network. Your network contains an Active Directory domain. You plan to deploy a Windows 2016 Active Directory Federation Services (AD FS) farm that will contain eight federation servers. You need to identify which technology or technologies must be deployed on the network before you install the federation servers. Which technology or technologies should you identify?

    A. Microsoft Forefront Identity Manager 2010

    B. Microsoft SQL Server 2016

    C. Network Load Balancing (NLB)

    D. Windows Internal Database feature

    E. The Windows Identity Foundation 3.5 feature

12. You are the administrator for your company network. Your network contains an Active Directory forest. Your company has a custom application named CustomApp1. CustomApp1 uses an Active Directory Lightweight Directory Services (AD LDS) server named Server1 to authenticate users. You have a Windows Server 2016 member server named Server2. You install the Active Directory Federation Services (AD FS) server role on Server2 and create an AD FS farm. What two cmdlets should you run if you need to configure AD FS to authenticate users from the AD LDS server? (Choose two.)

   A. You should run the `Add-AdfsRelyingPartyTrust` and `Set-AdfsEndpoint` cmdlets.

   B. You should run the `New-AdfsLdapServerConnection` and `Add-AdfsLocalClaimsProviderTrust` cmdlets.

   C. You should run the `Set-AdfsEndpoint` and `Enable-AdfsRelyingPartyTrust` cmdlets.

   D. You should run the `Enable-AdfsRelyingPartyTrust` and `New-AdfsLdapServerConnection` cmdlets.

13. You are the administrator for your company network. You are deploying a web application named WebApp1 to your internal network. WebApp1 is hosted on a Windows Server 2016 server named Web1. You deploy an Active Directory Federation Services (AD FS) infrastructure and a Web Application Proxy (WAP) to provide access to WebApp1 for remote users. What should you do if you need to ensure that Web1 can authenticate the remote users?

   A. Publish WebApp1 by using pass-through preauthentication.

   B. Publish WebApp1 by using AD FS preauthentication.

   C. Publish WebApp1 by using client certificate preauthentication.

   D. Publish WebApp1 as a Remote Desktop Gateway (RD Gateway) application in the Web Application Proxy.

14. You are the administrator for your company network. The network contains an Active Directory domain. The domain contains an Active Directory Federation Services (AD FS) server named Server1. On a stand-alone server named Server2, you install and configure the Web Application Proxy (WAP). You have an internal web application named WebApp1. AD FS has a relying party trust for WebApp1. You need to provide external users with access to WebApp1. What tool should you use to publish WebApp1 if authentication to WebApp1 must use AD FS preauthentication?

   A. On Server1, use AD FS Management.

   B. On Server1, use Remote Access Management.

   C. On Server1, use Routing and Remote Access.

   D. On Server2, use AD FS Management.

   E. On Server2, use Remote Access Management.

15. You are the administrator for your company network. You and a colleague are discussing certificates for AD FS. You store AD FS servers in an OU named Federation Servers. You want to auto-enroll the certificates used for AD FS. Which certificates should you add to the GPO?

- **A.** The Certificate Authorities (CA) certificate of the forest
- **B.** The SSL certificate assigned to the AD FS servers
- **C.** The third-party (VeriSign, Entrust) Certificate Authorities (CA) certificate
- **D.** The Token Signing certificate assigned to the AD FS servers

16. You are the administrator for your company network. You have an internal web server that hosts websites. The websites use HTTP and HTTPS. You deploy a Web Application Proxy (WAP) to your perimeter network. You need to ensure that users from the Internet can access the websites by using HTTPS only. What actions should you perform if you want Internet access to the websites to use the WAP? (Choose two.)

- **A.** Publish the websites from the Remote Access Management console. Configure pass-through authentication and select Enable HTTP to HTTPS redirection.
- **B.** Using Oauth2, configure the WAP to perform preauthentication.
- **C.** Create DNS entries that point to the private IP address of the web server on the external DNS name servers.
- **D.** Enable HTTP Redirect on the WAP server from the web server.
- **E.** Create DNS entries that point to the public IP address of the WAP on the external DNS name servers.

17. You are the administrator for your company network. You use Application Request Routing (ARR) to make internal web applications available to the Internet by using NTLM authentication. What server role should you deploy first if you need to replace ARR by using Web Application Proxy (WAP)?

- **A.** Active Directory Lightweight Directory Services (AD LDS)
- **B.** Active Directory Rights Management Services (AD RMS)
- **C.** Active Directory Federation Services (AD FS)
- **D.** Active Directory Certificate Services (AD CS)

18. You are the administrator for your company network. Your network contains an Active Directory domain. The domain contains an Active Directory Federation Services (AD FS) server named ADFS1, a Web Application Proxy (WAP) server named WAP1, and a web server named Web1. You need to publish a website on Web1 by using the WAP. Users will authenticate by using OAuth2 preauthentication. What should you do first?

- **A.** Add site bindings on Web1.
- **B.** Add a claims provider trust on ADFS1.
- **C.** Add handler mappings on Web1.
- **D.** Enable an endpoint on ADFS1.

19. You are the administrator for your company network. Your network contains an Active Directory forest. You have an Active Directory Federation Services (AD FS) farm. The farm contains a Windows Server 2012 R2 server named Server1. You add a Windows Server 2016 server named Server2 to the farm. You remove Server1 from the farm. What cmdlet should you run if you need to ensure that you can use role separation to manage the farm?

A. `Invoke-AdfsFarmBehaviorLevelRaise`

B. `Set-AdfsProperties`

C. `Set-AdfsFarmInformation`

D. `Update-AdfsRelyingPartyTrust`

20. You are the administrator for your company network. Your network contains an Active Directory forest that contains an Active Directory Federation Services (AD FS) deployment. The AD FS deployment contains the following:

- You create a Microsoft Office 365 tenant named `abc.onmicrosoft.com`.

- You use Microsoft Azure Active Directory Connect (AD Connect) to synchronize all of the users and the UPNs from the `contoso.com` forest to Office 365.

You need to configure federation between Office 365 and the on-premises deployment of Active Directory. Which commands should you run from Server1? (Choose all that apply.)

A. `Connect-MsolService`

B. `Convert-MsolDomainToFederated -DomainName abc.com`

C. `Convert_MsolDomainToFederated -DomainName adfs.abc.com`

D. `Enter-PSSession -Name Office365`

E. `Set-MsolADFSContext -Computer server1.abc.com`

F. `Set-MsolADFSContext -Computer abc.com`

21. You are the administrator for your company network. You need to see all of the location sets for the CRL Distribution Point (CDP). What PowerShell cmdlet would you use?

A. `Add-CACrlDistributionPoint`

B. `Get-CACrlDistributionPoint`

C. `See-CACrlDistributionPoint`

D. `View-CACrlDistributionPoint`

22. You are the administrator for your company network. The network contains an Active Directory domain. A previous administrator implemented a Proof of Concept installation of Active Directory Rights Management Services (AD RMS) on a server named Server1. After the Proof of Concept was complete, the AD RMS server role was removed. You attempt to deploy AD RMS. During the configuration you receive an error message indicating that an existing AD RMS Service Connection Point (SCP) was found. What should you do if you need to ensure that clients will only attempt to establish connections to the new AD RMS deployment?

A. Increase the priority of the DNS records for the new deployment of AD RMS from DNS.

B. Remove the computer object for Server1 from Active Directory.

C. Remove the records for Server1 from DNS.

D. Remove the SCP from Active Directory.

23. You are the administrator for your company network. The network contains an Active Directory domain. The domain contains an Active Directory Rights Management Services (AD RMS) cluster and a certification authority (CA). What should you do if you need to ensure that all the documents that are protected by using AD RMS can be decrypted if the account used to encrypt the documents is deleted?

    A. Configure super users in the AD RMS deployment.

    B. Manually configure the AD RMS cluster key password.

    C. On the CA, configure key archival.

    D. Using Windows Server Backup, back up the AD RMS–protected files.

24. You are the administrator for your company network. You deploy a new Enterprise Certification Authority (CA) named CA1. You plan to issue certificates based on the User certificate template. What should you do first if you need to ensure that the issued certificates are valid for two years and support auto-enrollment?

    A. Add a new certificate template for CA1 to issue.

    B. Duplicate the User certificate template.

    C. Modify the Request Handling settings for the CA.

    D. Run the `certutil.exe` command and specify the `resubmit` parameter.

25. You are the administrator for your company network. You need to ensure that clients check at least every 30 minutes as to whether a certificate has been revoked. Which of the following should you configure to accomplish this goal?

    A. Certificate templates

    B. CRL publication interval

    C. Delta CRL publication interval

    D. Key recovery agent

26. You are the administrator for your company network. You install and configure four Windows Server 2016 servers as an AD FS server farm. The AD FS configuration database is stored in a Microsoft SQL Server database. You need to ensure that AD FS will continue to function in the event of an AD FS server failure. You also need to ensure that all four servers in the AD FS farm will actively perform AD FS functions. What should you include in your solution?

    A. Network Load Balancing

    B. Windows Failover Clustering

    C. Windows Identity Foundation 3.5

    D. Web Proxy Server

27. You are the administrator for your company network. Which of the following CA types would you deploy if you wanted to deploy a CA at the top of a hierarchy that could issue signing certificates to other CAs and then would be taken offline if not issuing, renewing, or revoking signing certificates?

    A. Enterprise root

    B. Enterprise subordinate

    C. Stand-alone root

    D. Stand-alone subordinate

28. You are the administrator for your company network. Your network contains an Active Directory domain. Domain users use smartcards to sign in to their client computers. Several users report that it takes a long time to sign in to their computers and that the logon attempt times out, so they must restart the sign-in process. You discover that the issue is with checking the Certificate Revocation List (CRL) of the smartcard certificates. What should you do if you need to resolve the issue without reducing the security of the smartcard logons?

    A. Implement an Online Certification Status Protocol (OCSP) responder.

    B. Modify the Request Handling settings from the properties of the smartcard's certificate template.

    C. Modify the Issuance Requirements settings from the properties of the smartcard's certificate template.

    D. On the computers, deactivate certificate revocation checks.

29. You are the administrator for your company network. You and a colleague are discussing Active Directory Rights Management Services (AD RMS). How many AD RMS root clusters can you have per Active Directory forest?

    A. 1

    B. 2

    C. 5

    D. Unlimited

30. You are the administrator for your company network. You have an Enterprise Certification Authority (CA) named CA1. Recovery agents are configured for CA1. You duplicate the User certificate template and name it Temp_User. You plan to issue the certificates based on Temp_User to provide users with the ability to encrypt email messages and files. What should you use if you need to ensure that the recovery agents can access any user-encrypted files and email messages if the users lose their certificates?

    A. Configure the Key Recovery Agent template as a certificate template to issue on CA1.

    B. Issue a certificate based on a Key Recovery Agent certificate.

    C. Modify the Recovery Agents settings for CA1.

    D. Modify the Request Handling settings for Temp_User.

31. You are the administrator for your company network. You have a server that is configured as a hosted BranchCache server. You discover that a Service Connection Point (SCP) is missing for the BranchCache server. What should you run to register the SCP?

  A. `Enable-BCHostedServer`

  B. `ntdsutil.exe`

  C. `Reset-BC`

  D. `setspn.exe`

32. You are the administrator for your company network. Your network contains an Active Directory forest. The forest contains an Active Directory Federation Services (AD FS) farm. You install Windows Server 2016 on a server named Server2. What cmdlets should you run if you need to configure Server2 as a node in the federation server farm?

  A. `Install-AdfsFarm` and `New-AdfsOrganization`

  B. `Install-WindowsFeature` and `Install-AdfsFarm`

  C. `Install-Package` and `Set-AdfsFarmInformation`

  D. `Install-AdfsFarm` and `Set-AdfsProperties`

33. You are the administrator for your company network. You and a colleague are discussing Active Directory Certificate Services (AD CS). AD CS role provides six role services to issue and manage public key certificates in an enterprise environment. Which one retrieves revocation status requests for specific certificates and the status of these certificates, and then returns a signed response with the requested certificate status information?

  A. Certificate Authority (CA)

  B. Certificate Enrollment Web Services (CES)

  C. Online Responder

  D. Web Enrollment

34. You are the administrator for your company network. You have an Enterprise Certification Authority (CA) named CA1 that has a certificate template named CertTemplate that is based on a User certificate template. Domain users are configured to auto-enroll CertTemplate. A user named User1 has an email address defined in Active Directory and a user named User2 does not. You discover that User1 was issued a certificate based on the template automatically. A request by User2 for a certificate based on the template fails. You need to ensure that all users can auto-enroll for certificates based on the template. What setting should you configure from the properties on the CertTemplate certificate template?

  A. Cryptography

  B. Issuance Requirements

  C. Request Handling

  D. Subject Name

35. You are the administrator for your company network. You are looking at installing Active Directory Certificate Services (AD CS). To install AD CS using PowerShell, which command would you use?

   A. `Get-WindowsFeature adcs-cert-authority –IncludeManagementTools`

   B. `Get-WindowsFeature ad rms-cert-authority IncludeManagementTools`

   C. `Install-WindowsFeature adcs-cert-authority –IncludeManagementTools`

   D. `Install-WindowsFeature ad rms-cert-authority IncludeManagementTools`

36. You are the administrator for your company network. You plan to implement Active Directory Rights Management Services (AD RMS) across the enterprise. You need to plan the AD RMS cluster installations for the forest. Users in all domains will access AD RMS–protected documents. You need to minimize the number of AD RMS clusters. How many AD RMS root clusters do you require?

   A. At least one AD RMS root cluster for the enterprise

   B. At least one AD RMS root cluster per forest

   C. At least one AD RMS root cluster per domain

   D. At least one AD RMS root cluster per Active Directory site

   E. An AD RMS root cluster is not required

37. You are the administrator for your company network. You and a colleague are discussing Active Directory Federation Services (AD FS). What server should you deploy on a perimeter network if you want to configure AD FS?

   A. Claims-provider server

   B. Federation server

   C. Relying Party server

   D. Web application proxy

38. You are the administrator for your company network. You have a RADIUS server named RADIUS1. RADIUS1 is configured to use an IP address of 172.23.100.101. You want to add a Wireless Access Point (WAP) named WAP-Secure to your network that uses an IP address of 10.0.100.101. What command should you run if you need to ensure that WAP-Secure can authenticate to RADIUS1 by using a shared secret key?

   A. `Import-NpsConfiguration -address 10.0.100.101 -name WAP-Secure -SharedSecret "001001001001"`

   B. `New-NpsRadiusClient -address 10.0.100.101 -name WAP-Secure -SharedSecret "001001001001"`

   C. `Import-NpsConfiguration -address 172.23.100.101 -enabled $true -SharedSecret "001001001001"`

   D. `New-NpsRadiusClient -address 172.21.100.101 -name WAP-Secure -SharedSecret "001001001001"`

39. You are the administrator for your company network. The network contains two Active Directory forests named abc.com and xyz.com. Each forest contains two sites. Each site contains two domain controllers. What snap-in should you use if you need to configure all the domain controllers in both of the forests as global catalog servers?

    A. Active Directory Domains and Trusts

    B. Active Directory Federation Services

    C. Active Directory Sites and Services

    D. Active Directory Users and Computers

40. You are the administrator for your company network. You have users who access web applications by using HTTPS. The web applications are located on the servers in your perimeter network. The servers use certificates obtained from an enterprise root Certification Authority (CA). The certificates are generated by using a custom template named WebApps. The Certificate Revocation List (CRL) is published to Active Directory. When users attempt to access the web applications from the Internet, they report that they receive a revocation warning message in their web browsers. The users do not receive the message when they access the web applications from the intranet. What should you do if you need to ensure that the warning message is not generated when the users attempt to access the web applications from the Internet?

    A. On a server in the perimeter network, install the Certificate Enrollment Web Service role service.

    B. On a server in the perimeter network, install the Web Application Proxy role service, then create a publishing point for the CA.

    C. Modify the CRL distribution point and then reissue the certificates used by the web application servers.

    D. Modify the WebApps certificate template and then issue the certificates used by the web application servers.

41. You are the administrator for your company network. You have an Active Directory Rights Management Services (AD RMS) server named Server1 that protects multiple documents. Server1 fails and cannot be recovered. You install the AD RMS server role on a new server named Server2. You restore the AD RMS database from Server1 to Server2. Users report that they fail to open the protected documents and to protect new documents. What should you do if you need to ensure that the users can access the protected content?

    A. Create an alias (CNAME) record for Server2 from DNS.

    B. Modify the Service Location Record (SRV) for Server1 from DNS.

    C. Register a Service Principal Name (SPN) in Active Directory from Server2.

    D. Update the Service Connection Point (SCP) for Server1 from Active Directory Rights Management.

42. You are the administrator for your company network. Your network contains an Active Directory forest, abc.com, which contains an Active Directory Rights Management Services (AD RMS) deployment. Your company merges with another company. The new company network contains an Active Directory forest named xyz.com and an AD RMS deployment. What should you do if you need to ensure that users in abc.com can access rights-protected documents sent by the users in xyz.com?

   A. From AD RMS in xyz.com, configure abc.com as a trusted publisher domain.

   B. From AD RMS in abc.com, configure xyz.com as a trusted user domain.

   C. From AD RMS in xyz.com, configure abc.com as a trusted user domain.

   D. From AD RMS in abc.com, configure xyz.com as a trusted publisher domain.

43. You are the administrator for your company network. You and a colleague are discussing Workplace Join. For Workplace Join to work, a(n) _____ is placed on the mobile device. AD FS challenges the device as a claims-based authentication to applications or other resources without requiring administrative control of the device. What is being discussed?

   A. Application

   B. Certificate

   C. Module

   D. Service

44. You are the administrator for your company network. The network contains an Active Directory domain. You plan to deploy a new Active Directory Rights Management Services (AD RMS) cluster on a server named Server1. The solution must use the principle of least amount of privilege. What should you do if you need to create the AD RMS service account?

   A. In the domain, create a domain user account and add the account to the Account Operators group.

   B. On Server1, create a local user account and add the account to the Administrators group.

   C. In the domain, create a domain user account and add the account to the Domain Users group.

   D. On Server1, create a domain user account and add the account to the Administrators group.

45. You are the administrator for your company network. You and a colleague are discussing Active Directory Rights Management Services (AD RMS). What are the three database servers that AD RMS uses? (Choose all that apply.)

   A. Configuration Database

   B. Directory Services Database

   C. Logging Database

   D. Remote Database

46. You are the administrator for your company network. Your network contains an enterprise root Certification Authority (CA) named CA1. Multiple computers on the network successfully enroll for certificates that will expire in one year. The certificates are based on a template named CertificateTemplate. The template uses schema version 2. What should you do if you need to ensure that new certificates based on CertificateTemplate are valid for three years?

   A. Instruct users to request certificates by running the `certreq.exe` utility.

   B. Instruct users to request certificates by using the Certificates console.

   C. Modify the Validity period for the certificate template.

   D. Modify the Validity period for the root CA certificate.

47. You are the administrator for your company network. Your network contains an Active Directory domain. The domain contains an enterprise Certification Authority (CA) named CA1. You duplicate the Computer Certificate template and you name the template CA_Computers. What should you do if you need to ensure that all of the certificates issued based on CA_Computers have a key size of 4,096 bits?

   A. Modify the Security settings from the properties of CA1.

   B. Modify the Request Handling settings from the properties of CA1.

   C. Modify the Key Attestation settings from the properties of the Computer template.

   D. Modify the Cryptography settings from the properties of Cert_Computers.

48. You are the administrator for your company network. You and a colleague are discussing Active Directory Federation Services (AD FS). You want to start the AD FS Management console. You know that there are multiple methods for configuring AD FS. What are two methods? (Choose two.)

   A. Select Start ➢ Run and type `ADFSConfigWizard.exe`.

   B. Select Start ➢ Run and type `FsConfigWizard.exe`.

   C. Click the `ADFSConfigWizard.exe` file located in the `C:\windows\adfs` folder.

   D. Click the `FsConfigWizard.exe` file located in the `C:\windows\adfs` folder.

49. You are the administrator for your company network. You and a colleague are discussing the key archive store. The key archive stores which of the following information?

   A. The public key only

   B. The public key and private key only

   C. The public key, private key, and supported cryptographic algorithms only

   D. The subject name, public key, private key, and supported cryptographic algorithms

50. You are the administrator for your company network. Your network contains an Active Directory domain. The domain contains a member server named Server1 that has the Active Directory Federation Services (AD FS) server role installed. All servers run Windows Server 2016. You complete the AD FS Configuration Wizard on Server1. Which two actions should you perform on Server1 if you need to ensure that client devices on the internal network can use Workplace Join?

    A. Edit the multifactor authentication global authentication policy settings.

    B. Edit the primary authentication global authentication policy settings.

    C. Run `Enable-AdfsDeviceRegistration`.

    D. Run `Enable-AdfsDeviceRegistration -PrepareActiveDirectory`.

    E. Run `Set-AdfsProxyProperties HttpPort 80`.

51. You are the administrator for your company network. You and a colleague are discussing Windows Server 2016 Active Directory. Which one of the following allows users to set up a key-based authentication that allows them to authenticate by using more than just their password using biometrics or PIN numbers?

    A. Adprep

    B. Azure Active Directory Join

    C. Microsoft Passport

    D. Privileged Access Management (IPAM)

52. You are the administrator for your company network. Your company hosts a web RMS-aware application that the `abc.com` forest and `xyz.com` forest users need to access. You deploy a single AD FS server in the `abc.com` forest. Which of the following are true statements about the AD FS implementation? (Choose all that apply.)

    A. You will configure a relying party server on the `abc.com` AD FS server.

    B. The AD FS server in the `xyz.com` forest functions as the claims provider.

    C. The AD FS server in the `xyz.com` forest functions as the relying party server.

    D. You will configure a claims provider trust on the `abc.com` AD FS server.

53. You are the administrator for your company network. You have a Windows Server 2016 server named Server1. A Microsoft Azure Backup of Server1 is created automatically every day. You rename Server1 to Server2. You discover that backups are no longer created in Azure. What should you do if you need to back up the server to Azure?

    A. Run the `Add-WBBackupTarget` cmdlet on Server2.

    B. Run the `Start-OBRegistration` cmdlet on Server2.

    C. Upload the Server2 certificate as a management certificate from the Azure Management Portal.

    D. Modify the configuration on the backup vault from the Azure Management Portal.

54. You are the administrator for your company network. You have a Windows Server 2016 server named Server1. A Microsoft Azure Backup of Server1 is created automatically every day. What cmdlet should you run if you need to view the items that are included in the backup?

    A. `Get-OBJob`

    B. `Get-OBPolicy`

    C. `Get-OBPolicyState`

    D. `Get-WBSummary`

55. You are the administrator for your company network. You and a colleague are discussing Azure Active Directory (Azure AD). Under Azure AD you know that there are a couple of options for controlling devices. Which if the following provides you with all the benefits of registering a device and also changes the local state of a device? (Changing the local state enables your users to sign in to a device using an organizational work or school account instead of a personal account.)

    A. Attaching

    B. Disclosing

    C. Joining

    D. Registering

56. You are the administrator for your company network. You deploy a new Certification Authority (CA) to a Windows Server 2016 server. What should you do if you need to configure the CA to support recovery of certificates?

    A. Assign the Request Certificates permission to the user account that will be responsible for recovering certificates.

    B. Configure the Key Recovery Agent template as a certificate template to issue.

    C. Modify the extensions of the OCSP Response Signing template.

    D. Modify the Recovery Agents settings from the properties of the CA.

57. You are the administrator for your company network. Your network contains an Active Directory forest named abc.com. The forest contains an Active Directory Rights Management Services (AD RMS) cluster. A partner company has an Active Directory forest named xyz.com. The partner company does not have AD RMS deployed. You need to ensure that users in xyz.com can consume rights-protected content from abc.com. Which type of trust policy should you create?

    A. A federated trust

    B. A trusted publishing domain

    C. A trusted user domain

    D. Windows Live ID

58. You are the administrator for your company network. The network contains an Active Directory domain. You deploy a stand-alone root Certification Authority (CA) named CA1. What should you do first if you need to auto-enroll domain computers for certificates by using a custom certificate template?

    A. Modify the Policy Module for CA1.

    B. Modify the Exit Module for CA1.

    C. Install a stand-alone subordinate CA.

    D. Install an enterprise subordinate CA.

59. You are the administrator for your company network. The network contains an Active Directory forest. The forest contains three domain controllers. They are configured as shown:

Server Name	Active Directory Site
Server1	Boston
Server2	Boston
Server3	Portland

The company physically relocates Server2 from the Boston office to the Portland office. You discover that both Server1 and Server2 authenticate users who sign in to the client computers in the Boston office. Only Server3 authenticates users who sign in to the computers in the Portland office. What should you do if you need to ensure that Server2 authenticates the users in the Portland office during normal network operations?

    A. Modify the Location Property of Server2 from Active Directory Users and Computers.

    B. Modify the Internet Protocol Version 4 (TCP/IPv4) configuration from Network Connections on Server2.

    C. Run the `Move-ADDirectoryServer` cmdlet using PowerShell.

    D. Run the `Set-ADReplicationSite` cmdlet using PowerShell.

60. You are the administrator for your company network. You and a colleague are discussing Active Directory Federation Services (AD FS). What PowerShell cmdlet would you use if you wanted to add a computer to an existing federation server farm?

    A. `Add-AdfsClient`

    B. `Add-AdfsCertificate`

    C. `Add-AdfsFarmNode`

    D. `Add-AdfsNativeClientApplication`

61. You are the administrator for your company network. Your network contains an Active Directory domain. The domain contains a Windows Server 2016 server named Server1 that has the Active Directory Certificate Services (AD CS) server role installed and is configured to support key archival and recovery. You create a new Active Directory group named Group1. Which permissions should you assign to Group1 if you need to ensure that the members of Group1 can request a Key Recovery Agent (KRA) certificate? (Choose all that apply.)

    A. Auto-Enroll

    B. Enroll

    C. Full Control

    D. Read

    E. Write

62. You are the administrator for your company network. You and a colleague are discussing the different Active Directory support tools available with Windows Server 2016. You are discussing a tool that allows an administrator to migrate users, groups, and computers from a previous version of the server to a current version of the server. What tool are you discussing?

    A. Active Directory Migration Tool (ADMT)

    B. Active Directory Managed Service Accounts

    C. Active Directory Rights Management Services (AD RMS)

    D. Active Directory Users and Computers

63. You are the administrator for your company network. You and a colleague are discussing Active Directory Rights Management Services (AD RMS) and the ability to set up exclusion policies to deny certain entities the ability to acquire certificate and license requests. Which of the following are ways to exclude these entities? (Choose all that apply.)

    A. By application

    B. By lockbox version

    C. By MAC address

    D. By user

64. You are the administrator for your company network. Your network contains an Active Directory domain. The domain contains a Windows Server 2016 server named CA1 that has the Active Directory Certificate Services (AD CS) server role installed and is configured to support key archival and recovery. You need to ensure that a user named User1 can decrypt private keys archived in the AD CS database. What should you do to prevent User1 from retrieving the private keys from the AD CS database?

    A. Assign User1 the Manage Certificate Authority (CA) permission to CA1.

    B. Assign User1 the Read and Write permissions to all certificate templates.

    C. Provide User1 with access to a Key Recovery Agent certificate and a private key.

    D. Assign User1 the Issue and Manage Certificates permission to CA1.

65. You are the administrator for your company network. The network contains an Active Directory domain. The domain has an Enterprise Certification Authority (CA). You duplicate the Basic EFS template and you name the template Template1. You configure the CA to use Template1. Users are configured to obtain a new certificate automatically when they sign in to a computer in the domain. What should you modify if you need to enable the users to automatically obtain a certificate based on Template1?

A. For Template1, modify the Security settings within the CA.

B. For the CA, modify the Request Handling properties.

C. For the CA, modify the Publication Settings.

D. For Template1, modify the Request Handling properties.

66. You are the administrator for your company network. The network contains an Active Directory domain. The domain contains a Windows Server 2016 enterprise root Certification Authority (CA). What actions should you perform if you need to configure the CA to support Online Certificate Status Protocol (OCSP) responders? (Choose two.)

A. Add a new certificate template to issue.

B. Configure an enrollment agent.

C. Install a stand-alone subordinate CA.

D. Modify the Authority Information Access (AIA) of the CA.

E. Modify the CRL distribution point (CDP) of the CA.

67. You are the administrator for your company network. Your network contains an Active Directory domain. The domain contains an enterprise Certification Authority (CA) named CA1. You have a test environment that is isolated from the corporate network and the Internet. You deploy a web server to the test environment. On CA1, you duplicate the Web Server template and you name the template WS_Test. What should you do first if you need to request a certificate that does not contain the revocation information of CA1 for the web server?

A. Allow certificates to be published to the filesystem from the properties of CA1.

B. Select Restrict Enrollment Agents and then add WS_Test to the restricted enrollment agent from the properties of CA1.

C. Assign the Enroll permission to the guest account from the properties of WS_Test.

D. Set the Compatibility setting of CA1 to Windows Server 2016 from the properties of WS_Test.

68. You are the administrator for your company network. Your network contains an Active Directory domain. The domain contains a Windows Server 2016 server named Server1 that has the Active Directory Rights Management Services (AD RMS) server role installed. The domain contains a domain local group named Group1. You create a rights policy template named Template1. What should you do if you need to ensure that all the members of Group1 can use Template1?

    A. Convert the scope of Group1 to Universal and assign Group1 the rights to Template1.

    B. Convert the scope of Group1 to Global and configure the Email Address attribute of Group1.

    C. Configure the Email Address attribute of Group1 and configure the Email Address attribute of all the users who are members of Group1.

    D. Configure the email address of all the users who are members of Group1 and assign Group1 the rights to Template1.

69. You are the administrator for your company network. You have a stand-alone root Certification Authority (CA). You have a new security policy requirement stating that any changes to the CA configuration must be logged. What should you do if you need to ensure that the CA meets the new security requirement? (Choose two.)

    A. Configure auditing for policy change from the Local Group Policy Editor.

    B. Configure auditing for object access from the Local Group Policy Editor.

    C. Modify the Security settings for the CA from the Certification Authority console.

    D. Modify the Auditing settings for the CA from the Certification Authority console.

    E. Modify the Certificate Managers settings for the CA from the Certification Authority console.

70. You are the administrator for your company network. You and a colleague are discussing adding a certificate template to the Certificate Authority (CA). What PowerShell cmdlet would you use if you need to add a certificate template to the CA?

    A. `Add-CATemplate`

    B. `Add-CSTemplate`

    C. `Get-CSTemplate`

    D. `New-Template`

71. You are the administrator for your company network. You and a colleague are discussing Certificate Revocation Lists (CRLs). The CRL polling begins to consume bandwidth. What steps should you consider to reduce network traffic?

    A. Publishing more CRLs

    B. Implementing an online issuing CA and a root CA

    C. Implementing the Certificate Enrollment Policy Web Server role and Certificate Enrollment Web Services role

    D. Implementing an online responder

72. You are the administrator for your company network. You and a colleague are discussing how to view the installation state of Active Directory Federation Services (AD FS). What PowerShell cmdlet should you run to view the installation state?

    A. `Get-WindowsFeature "adfs*","*fed*"`

    B. `Get-WindowsFeature "refs*","*red*"`

    C. `Set-WindowsFeature "adfs*","*fed*"`

    D. `Run-WindowsFeature "adfs*","*fed*"`

73. You are the administrator for your company network. You and a colleague are discussing Active Directory Federation Services (AD FS). Which of the following is a federation server that receives security tokens from a trusted federation partner claims provider and then issues a new security token that is consumed locally?

    A. Attribute store

    B. Claims provider

    C. Endpoints

    D. Relying party

74. You are the administrator for your company network. You and a colleague are discussing Active Directory Federation Services (AD FS). Which of the following provides access to the federation server functionality of AD FS, such as token issuance, information card issuance, and the publishing of federation metadata? Based on the type, you can enable, disable, or control whether it is published to AD FS proxies.

    A. Attribute store

    B. Claims provider

    C. Endpoints

    D. Relying party

75. You are the administrator for your company network. You and a colleague are discussing Active Directory Federation Services (AD FS) security modes. Which security mode is described here? The client credentials are included in the header of a Simple Object Access Protocol (SOAP) message. Confidentiality is preserved by encryption inside the SOAP message.

    A. Attribute

    B. Message

    C. Mixed

    D. Transport

76. You are the administrator for your company network. You and a colleague are discussing installing the Federation Service Proxy role using PowerShell. What command would you use if you wanted to install this role?

    A. `GetFeature Federation-Proxy -IncludeManagementTools`

    B. `GetFeature Web-Application-Proxy -IncludeManagementTools`

    C. `Install-WindowsFeature Federation-Proxy -IncludeManagementTools`

    D. `Install-WindowsFeature Web-Application-Proxy -IncludeManagementTools`

77. You are the administrator for your company network. You and a colleague are discussing the Device Registration Service (DRS) that is included with the Active Directory Federation Services (AD FS) role in Windows Server 2016. DRS requires at least which one of the following?

    A. At least one global catalog server in the forest root domain

    B. At least two global catalog servers in the forest root domain

    C. At least one global catalog server in the child domain

    D. At least two global catalog servers in the child domain

78. You are the administrator for your company network. You have a Windows Server 2016 server named Server1 that has the Windows Application Proxy (WAP) role service installed. You are publishing an application using the Publish New Application Wizard. The application will be named App1, and it will use integrated Windows authentication. External users will be able to access the application. You are using the following publishing settings:

    Name: App1

    External URL: `https://server1.abc.com/publish/app1`

    External Certificate: `server1.abc.com`

    Backend Server URL: `http://server1.abc.com/publish/app1`

    Backend Server SPN:

    Before you can complete the wizard, what must you do?

    A. Change the External Certificate.

    B. Configure the Backend Server SPN.

    C. Select the Enable HTTP to HTTPS Redirection check box.

    D. Change the External URL.

79. You are the administrator for your company network. You and a colleague are discussing Active Directory Rights Management Services (AD RMS) template rights. One of the rights, if established, enables protected content to be decrypted and re-encrypted by using the same content key. Usually, when this right is established, the RMS-aware application will allow the user to change protected content and then save it to the same file. This right is effectively identical to the Save right. Which right is being discussed?

    A. Change

    B. Full Control

    C. Edit

    D. View

80. You are the administrator for your company network. You and a colleague are discussing Active Directory Rights Management Services (AD RMS) trust policies. Which trust policy is the boundary mechanism for the AD RMS root cluster to process client licensor certificates or use licenses from users whose Rights Account Certificates (RACs) were issued by another AD RMS root cluster?

  A. Trusted User Domains (TUD)

  B. Trusted Publishing Domains (TPD)

  C. Windows Live ID

  D. Federated Trust

81. You are the administrator for your company network. You and a colleague are discussing an advantage of using the Remote Access role service in Windows Server 2016 called Web Application Proxy (WAP). WAP is a feature that allows which of the following?

  A. Allows your corporate users to access applications from any device inside the network

  B. Allows all remote users to access applications from any device outside the network

  C. Allows remote users to access applications from any device inside the network

  D. Allows your corporate users to access applications from any device outside the network

82. You are the administrator for your company network. You and a colleague are discussing Web Application Proxy (WAP). What is the process of allowing an application to be available to users outside the network called?

  A. Authenticating

  B. Migrating

  C. Publishing

  D. Transferring

83. You are the administrator for your company network. You and a colleague are discussing Web Application Proxy (WAP). When an administrator publishes an application using the WAP, the method that users and devices use for authentication is known as preauthentication. Which preauthentication method is being described when users are not required to enter credentials before they are allowed to connect to published web applications?

  A. AD FS preauthentication

  B. Pass-through preauthentication

  C. Push-through preauthentication

  D. Single-Sign-On (SSO)

84. You are the administrator for your company network. The network contains an Active Directory forest. All domain controllers run Windows Server 2012 R2. You deploy a new server named Server1 that runs Windows Server 2016. A server administrator named SA01 is a member of the Domain users group. You add SA01 to the Administrators group on Server1. SA01 signs in to Server1 and successfully configures a new Active Directory Rights Management Services (AD RMS) cluster. What should you do if you need to ensure that clients can discover the AD RMS cluster by querying Active Directory?

   A. Modify the Security settings of the computer account of Server1.

   B. Register a Service Connection Point (SCP).

   C. Upgrade one domain controller to Windows Server 2016.

   D. Update the Active Directory Schema.

85. You are the administrator for your company network. You and a colleague are discussing Active Directory Federation Services (AD FS). What PowerShell cmdlet allows an administrator to add a new claims provider trust to the Federation Service?

   A. `Add-AdfsClaimsProviderTrust`

   B. `Add-AdfsClient`

   C. `Add-ClaimsProviderTrust`

   D. `Enable-AdfsApplicationGroup`

   E. `Enable-AdfsClaimsProviderTrust`

Chapter

11

Practice Exam 70-740: Installation, Storage, and Compute with Windows Server 2016

1. You are the administrator for your company network. You have a Windows Server 2016 server. What should you install if you want to configure the server as a multitenant RAS Gateway?

    A. Data Center Bridging feature

    B. Network Controller server role

    C. Network Policy and Access Services server role

    D. Remote Access server role

2. You are the administrator for your company network. You have just installed Windows Server 2016 on a new server. It is essential that you activate Windows Server. Which of the following command-line tools can be used to activate Windows Server?

    A. `Cscript C:\windows\system32\slmgr.vbs -ato`

    B. `Ocsetup C:\windows\system32\slmgr.vbs -ato`

    C. `Netdom C:\windows\system32\slmgr.vbs -ato`

    D. `Netsh C:\windows\system32\slmgr.vbs -ato`

3. You are the administrator for your company network. With Nano Server some packages are installed directly with their own PowerShell switches (such as `-Compute`), whereas others are installed by passing package names using the `-Packages` parameter that can combine in a comma-separated list. If you want to add Internet Information Services (IIS) to your Nano Server, what command should you use?

    A. `-Compute`

    B. `-Containers`

    C. `-Packages`

    D. `-Storage`

4. You are the administrator for your company network. You have a Windows Server 2016 Nano Server machine with no packages installed. You decide to attach a new disk. You also plan to initialize the disk as a GUID Partition Table (GPT) disk. First you want to create a ReFS-formatted volume on the new disk. What should you do?

    A. From the physical server, log on to the Nano Server Recovery Console.

    B. Install the `Microsoft-NanoServer-Host-Package` package.

    C. Install the `Microsoft NanoServer-Storage-Package` package.

    D. Run the `Format-Volume` cmdlet and specify the `-FileSystem` switch.

5. You are the administrator for your company network. You have two Windows Server 2016 servers named ServerA and ServerB, and there is a firewall between the two servers. Both servers run Windows Server Update Services (WSUS). ServerA downloads updates using Windows Update. What port should be open on the firewall if ServerB must synchronize updates from ServerA?

    A. 80

    B. 443

    C. 3389

    D. 8530

6. You are the administrator for your company network. Your network contains an Active Directory domain. There is a company policy in place that states that new servers should run Nano Server whenever possible. What server role can be deployed on a Nano Server?

A. Active Directory Domain Services (AD DS)

B. DHCP Server

C. Network Policy and Access Services

D. Web Server (IIS)

7. You are the administrator for your company network. You have a Windows Server 2016 server named ServerA. The server has an application named AppA, which writes entries to the Application event log when errors are encountered. The events have IDs of either 111 or 112. You want to restart the service whenever one of these events is logged. What should you do?

A. Create a custom view that has a filter for the event IDs from Event Viewer.

B. Run the `Get-SMServerEvent` cmdlet and pipe the output to the `Start-NetEvent` using PowerShell.

C. Run the `Write-Eventlog` cmdlet and specify the `-EventID` parameter using PowerShell.

D. Use Create Task to create one task that includes triggers for both event IDs from Task Scheduler.

8. You are the administrator for your company network. You have a Windows Server 2016 server named ServerA, which has Windows Defender enabled. ServerA runs an application named AppA that stores different types of files in Microsoft OneDrive and Microsoft SharePoint Online. AppA also interacts with several local services. You need to prevent Windows Defender from scanning any files opened by AppA. What should you do on ServerA?

A. Configure a process exclusion in the Windows Defender settings.

B. Modify the real-time protection settings in Windows Defender.

C. Modify the cloud-based protection settings in Windows Defender.

D. Run the `New-AppLockerPolicy` cmdlet.

9. You are the administrator for your company network. You have a Windows Server 2016 server named ServerA. The Windows Server 2016 installation media is mounted as Drive E. You copy the `NanoServerImageGenerator` folder from the `E:\NanoServer` folder to the `C:\NanoServer` folder. You create a custom Nano Server image that includes the Hyper-V server role. What two commands should you run if you want this image to be used to deploy Nano Servers to physical servers? (Choose two.)

A. `New-NanoServerImage -Edition Standard -DeploymentType Guest -MediaPath E:\-TargetPath \NanoServerImage\NanoServer.wim -Compute`

B. `Install-PackageProvider NanoServerPackage`

C. `Import-PackageProvider NanoServerPackage`

D. `New-NanoServerImage -Edition Standard -DeploymentType Host -MediaPath E:\ -TargetPath \NanoServerImage\NanoServer.wim -Compute`

E. `Import-Module C:\NanoServer\NanoServerImageGenerator`

10. You are the administrator for your company network. Your company has two main offices. One is located in Atlanta and the other in Dallas. All servers at both locations run Windows Server 2016. In the Dallas office, there is a Distributed File System (DFS) server named DFS1. DFS1 has a folder named `FolderA` that contains large Windows image files. In the Atlanta office, you deploy a DFS server named DFS2, and you then replicate `FolderA` to DFS2. After several days, you notice that the replication of certain files failed to complete. What should you do if you need to ensure that all of the files in `FolderA` can replicate to DFS2?

    A. Create a quota for `FolderA` using File Server Resource Manager (FSRM).

    B. Modify the disk quota on the drive that contains `FolderA`.

    C. Modify the size of the staging area on `FolderA`.

    D. Run `dfsutil /purgemupcache` from a command prompt.

11. You are the administrator for your company network. You have a Windows Server 2016 server named ServerA. The server contains a storage pool named PoolA. PoolA contains five physical disks named DiskA, DiskB, DiskC, DiskD, and DiskE. A virtual disk named VD1 is stored in PoolA. VD1 uses the parity storage layout. Which two commands should you run if you need to remove DiskC after it fails from PoolA? (Choose two.)

    A. `Set-PhysicalDisk-FriendlyName DiskC -Usage Retired`

    B. `Set-ResiliencySetting-StoragePool PoolA-PhysicalDiskRedundancyDefault 4`

    C. `Remove-PhysicalDisk-FriendlyName DiskC`

    D. `Update-StoragePool-FriendlyName PoolA`

    E. `Reset-PhysicalDisk-FriendlyName DiskC`

12. You are the administrator for your company network. You have two Windows Server 2016 servers named ServerA and ServerB. ServerA contains a volume named Vol1. You decide to implement a Storage Replica that replicates the content of Vol1 from ServerA and ServerB. One day, ServerA fails. You need to ensure that you can access the contents of Vol1. What should you run from ServerB?

    A. `Clear-FileStorageTier`

    B. `Set-SRPartnership`

    C. `Update-StoragePool`

    D. `vssadmin revert shadow`

13. You are the administrator for your company network. The network contains an Active Directory domain. The domain contains a new file server named ServerA that runs a Server Core installation of Windows Server 2016. ServerA has an ReFS-formatted volume D: and NTFS-formatted volume E:. The volumes do not contain any data. You install the Data Deduplication role service on ServerA. What PowerShell cmdlet should you run if you want to implement Data Deduplication for volumes on D: and E:?

    A. `Format-Volume D: -FileSystem EXFat and Enable-DeDupVolume -Volume D:,E:`

    B. `Format-Volume E: -FileSystem ReFS and Enable-DeDupVolume -Volume D:,E:`

    C. `Enable-DeDupVolume-Volume D:,E:`

    D. `Enable-DeDupVolume-Volume E: D:`

14. You are the administrator for your company network. The network contains an Active Directory domain. The domain contains two servers named ServerA and ServerB, each with the same hardware configuration. You need to asynchronously replicate volume E: from ServerA to ServerB. What should you do?

A. Install the Failover Clustering feature and create a new cluster resource group.

B. Install the Failover Clustering feature and use Cluster Shared Volumes (CSV).

C. Run `New-SRPartnership` and specify the `-ReplicationMode` parameter.

D. Run `Set-DfsrServiceConfiguration` and specify the `-RPCPort` parameter.

15. You are the administrator for your company network. You have client computers that run Windows Server 2016. Each computer has two hard drives. Which kind of volume should you create if you need to create a dynamic volume on each computer that will maximize write performance as well as provide data fault tolerance?

A. Mirrored volume

B. RAID 5 volume

C. Spanned volume

D. Striped volume

16. You are the administrator for your company network. You want to remove the host from the iSNS server. What command should you use to remove the host?

A. `iscsicli addisnsserver <server_name>`

B. `iscsicli listisnsservers <server_name>`

C. `iscsicli refreshisnsserver <server_name>`

D. `iscsicli removeisnsserver <server_name>`

17. You are the administrator for your company network. A user, Sandy, is a member of both the Human Resources and Marketing departments. There is a shared folder called App1 that everyone uses. The current permissions on the App1 shared folder are:

Group/User	NTFS	Shared
Sales	Read	Deny
Marketing	Modify	Full Control
R&D	Read	Read
Human Resources	Full Control	Deny
Admin	Full Control	Change

What will Sandy's local and remote permissions be when she logs into the App1 folder?

A. Local = Full Control and Remote = Deny

B. Local = Deny and Remote = Deny

C. Local = Full Control and Remote = Change

D. Local = Change and Remote = Read

18. You are the administrator for your company network. You have a computer that has a 1 TB volume named D. What tool should you use if you want to receive a notification when the volume has less than 100 GB of free space left?

   A. Disk Cleanup

   B. Event Viewer

   C. Performance Monitor

   D. Resource Monitor

   E. System Configuration

19. You are the administrator for your company network. You have a computer that runs Windows Server 2012 R2. You create a system image backup on the computer and then upgrade to Windows Server 2016. You need to access a file from the backup. Your solution must use the least amount of administrative effort. What should you do?

   A. From the Backup section of the Settings app, add a drive.

   B. From the File History section of the Settings app, add a drive.

   C. From the Computer Management console, attach a VHD.

   D. From the File History Control Panel item, restore the personal files.

20. You are the administrator for your company network. You decide to purchase a new computer that has four external USB hard drives. You want to create a single volume by using all the USB drives. You want the volume to be expandable, portable, and resilient in the event of failure of an individual USB hard drive. What should you do so you can create the required volume?

   A. Create a new spanned volume.

   B. Create a new striped volume.

   C. Create a new Storage Space across the four USB hard drives and set the resiliency type to three-way mirror.

   D. Create a new Storage Space across the four USB hard drives and set the resiliency type to parity.

21. You are the administrator for your company network. You have a Windows Server 2016 Hyper-V host that has a dynamically expanding virtual hard disk (VHD) file that is 950 GB. The VHD currently contains about 450 GB of free space. What cmdlet should you use if you want to reduce the amount of disk space used by the VHD?

   A. DiskPart.exe

   B. Mount-VHD

   C. Optimize-VHD

   D. Set-VHD

22. You are the administrator for your company network. Your network contains an Active Directory forest. You install Windows Server 2016 on 10 virtual machines. What should you do if you need to deploy the Web Server (IIS) server role identically to the virtual machines?

   A. Create an answer file, copy the file to `C:\Sysprep` on each virtual machine, and then run the `Apply-Image` cmdlet using Windows System Image Manager.

   B. Create an application control policy and then apply the policy to the virtual machines from a Group Policy Object (GPO).

   C. Create a default configuration and then apply the configuration to the virtual machines using PowerShell Desired State Configuration (DSC).

   D. Create a software installation package and then publish the package to the virtual machines using a Group Policy Object (GPO).

23. You are the network administrator for your company network. You are looking at the different types of hard disks that are available when using Hyper-V. One type of disk starts with a small VHD file and expands it on demand once an installation takes place. What type of hard disk is being described?

   A. Differencing disk

   B. Dynamically expanding disk

   C. Fixed-sized disk

   D. Physical (or pass-through) disk

24. You are the administrator for your company network. You are planning the configuration of a virtual network switch for your Hyper-V network that will contain several Hyper-V hosts. ServerA will have 10 virtual machines that must be able to communicate with one another. The virtual machines must be prevented from communicating with ServerA and all other servers on the corporate network. The Hyper-V network will also have a two-node failover cluster named ClusterA that will have 20 virtual machines. The virtual machines will run on both nodes. Hyper-V hosts on the corporate network must be able to connect to the virtual machines. What type of virtual switch should you select for the 20 virtual machines on ClusterA?

   A. External

   B. Internal

   C. Private

   D. Public

25. You are the administrator for your company network. You have an application that is distributed to multiple Hyper-V virtual machines in a multitenant environment. You need to ensure that the traffic is distributed evenly among the virtual machines that host the application. What should you include in the environment?

   A. A Network Controller and Windows Server Network Load Balancing (NLB) nodes

   B. A Network Controller and Windows Server Software Load Balancing (SLB) nodes

   C. A RAS Gateway and Windows Server Network Load Balancing (NLB) nodes

   D. A RAS Gateway and Windows Server Software Load Balancing (SLB) nodes

26. You are the administrator for your company network. You have a Windows Server 2016 Hyper-V host named ServerA that hosts a virtual machine named VM-1. You install the Hyper-V server role on VM-1. You need to ensure that the virtual machines hosted on VM-1 can communicate with the virtual machines hosted on ServerA. What should you do?

    A. Run the `Set-VmNetworkAdapterIsolation` cmdlet and specify the `-MultiTenantStack Off` parameter on ServerA.

    B. Run the `Set-VMNetworkAdapter` cmdlet and specify the `-MacAddressSpoofing Off` parameter on VM-1.

    C. Run the `Set-VmNetworkAdapterIsolation` cmdlet and specify the `-MultiTenantStack On` parameter on VM-1.

    D. Run the `Set-VMNetworkAdapter` cmdlet and specify the `-MacAddressSpoofing On` parameter on ServerA.

27. You are the administrator for your company network. Your network contains an Active Directory domain that contains a Windows Server 2016 Hyper-V host named ServerA. ServerA hosts four machines that are members of the domain. The virtual machines are configured as shown:

Virtual Machine Name	Operating System	Virtual Machine Generation	Type of VHD File
VM-1	Windows 10	2	VHD
VM-2	Windows Server 2016	2	VHD
VM-3	Windows Server 2012 R2	2	VHDX
VM-4	Windows Server 2016	1	VHDX

    What virtual machines can you manage by using PowerShell Direct?

    A. Only VM-2

    B. VM-1, VM-2, and VM-4

    C. Only VM-4

    D. VM-1, VM-2, and VM-3

28. You are the administrator for your company network. You have a Windows Server 2016 server named ServerA, which is a Hyper-V host that hosts a virtual machine named VM-1. ServerA has three network adapter cards that are connected to virtual switches named vSwitch-1, vSwitch-2, and vSwitch-3. You configure NIC Teaming on VM-1. The team name is VM1-NIC-Team. Added to the team are Ethernet2, which is 10 Gbps, and Ethernet3, which is 10 Gbps. The teaming mode is Switch Independent. You need to ensure that VM-1 will retain access to the network if a physical adapter card fails on ServerA. What should you do?

    A. Add the adapter named Ethernet to the NIC team from the properties of the NIC team on VM-1.

    B. Modify the settings on VM-1 from Hyper-V Manager on ServerA.

    C. Run the `Set-VmNetworkAdapterTeamMapping` cmdlet on VM-1.

    D. Run the `Set-VmNetworkAdapterFailoverConfiguration` cmdlet on ServerA.

29. You are the administrator for your company network. You have a Windows Server 2016 Hyper-V host named ServerA that has a virtual disk file named DiskA.vhdx which contains an installation to Windows Server 2016. You create a virtual disk file named DiskB.vhdx that is configured as shown:

> PS: c:\ Get-VHD Path C:\folder1\DiskB.vhdx
>
> ComputerName: SERVERA
>
> Path: c:\folder1\diskB.vhdx
>
> VhdFormat: VHDX

What command should you run if you want to move DiskA.vhdx to C:\Folder2, you will be able to use DiskB.vhdx only after you run which of the following commands

A. Merge-VHD

B. Optimize-VHD

C. Set-VHD

D. Test-VHD

30. You are the administrator for your company network. You have a Windows Server 2016 computer named ServerA that has the Hyper-V feature installed. ServerA hosts a virtual machine named VM-1. VM-1 runs Windows Server 2016 and connects to a private virtual network switch. You need to remotely execute PowerShell cmdlets on VM-1. What should you do from ServerA?

A. Run the winrm.exe command and specify the -s parameter.

B. Run the Powershell.exe command and specify the -Command parameter.

C. Run the Receive-PSSession cmdlet and specify the -Name parameter.

D. Run the Invoke-Command cmdlet and specify the -VMName parameter.

31. You are the administrator for your company network. You have a Windows Server 2016 Hyper-V server named ServerA that has an IP address of 192.168.1.78 and has a container named ContainerA that hosts a web application on port 84. ContainerA has an IP address of 172.16.5.6 and a port mapping from port 80 on ServerA to port 84 on ContainerA. You have a server named ServerB that has an IP address of 192.168.1.79. What IP address and port should you connect to if you need to connect to the web application from ServerB?

A. 172.16.5.6:80

B. 172.16.5.6:84

C. 192.168.1.78:80

D. 192.168.1.78:84

32. You are the administrator for your company network. You have a Windows Server 2016 Hyper-V host named ServerA that has a virtual machine named Server1. Server1 is configured to run the Docker daemon. On Server1 you have a container network that uses transparent mode. You need to ensure that containers that run on Server1 can obtain IP addresses from DHCP. What should you do?

    A. On ServerA, run `docker network connect`.

    B. On ServerA, run `Get-VMNetworkAdapter-VMName Server1| Set-VMNetworkAdapter-MacAddressSpoofing On`.

    C. On Server1, run `docker network connect`.

    D. On Server1, run `Get-VMNetworkAdapter-VMName Server1| Set-VMNetworkAdapter-MacAddressSpoofing On`.

33. You are the administrator for your company network. You have a Windows Server 2016 server and you install the Docker daemon. What should you do if you need to configure the Docker daemon to accept connections from TCP port 64500 only?

    A. Edit the `configuration.json` file.

    B. Edit the `daemon.json` file.

    C. Run the `New-NetFirewallRule` cmdlet.

    D. Run the `Set-Service` cmdlet.

34. You are the administrator for your company network. You have a Windows Server 2016 container host. What parameter should you use with the docker run command if you need to start a Hyper-V container?

    A. `--entrypoint`

    B. `--expose`

    C. `--runtime`

    D. `--isolation`

    E. `--privileged`

35. You are the administrator for your company network. You and a colleague are discussing the Azure Container Service and what it can be used for. Which statement is true regarding the Azure Container Service?

    A. Uses commercial scheduling and management tools

    B. Uses open source scheduling and management tools

    C. Uses proprietary scheduling and management tools

    D. Uses registered scheduling and management tools

36. You are the administrator for your company network. The network has a main office and several branch offices and consists of an Active Directory domain. The main office contains three domain controllers and each branch office has one domain controller. You discover that the new settings in the Default Domain Policy are not applied in one of the branch offices, but all other Group Policy Objects (GPOs) are applied. You need to check the replication of the Default Domain Policy for the branch office. What should you do from a domain controller in the main office?

A. Click Default Domain Policy and then open the Details tab from Group Policy Management.

B. Click Default Domain Policy and then open the Scope tab from Group Policy Management.

C. From a command prompt, run `repadmin.exe`.

D. From a command prompt, run `dcdiag.exe`.

37. You are the administrator for your company network. You are discussing Container components with a coworker. This component can be on a physical or virtual machine, and it is the component that is configured with the Windows Container feature. What is being described?

A. Container Host

B. Container Image

C. Container OS Image

D. Container Registry

38. You are the network administrator for your company network. The company has decided that it would like to start using containers. You have installed Docker and now wish to add an image to a container. You check out images that are currently available in your repository. Now, what item is required to turn the image into a container?

A. Image ID

B. Image Info

C. Image Name

D. Image Status

39. You are the administrator for your company network. You and a coworker are discussing using Docker Hub to set up a private repository. What statement is true regarding Docker Hub and a private repository?

A. Only Windows images are allowed in a Docker Hub repository.

B. Once images are added to the Docker Hub, everyone will have access to the images; there is no private option.

C. Administrators can add users and accounts to the Docker Hub to verify that only the organization's users are accessing the images.

D. There is a monthly fee to set up a private Docker Hub repository.

40. You are the network administrator for your company network. You have a two-node Hyper-V cluster named ClusterA. A virtual machine named VM-1 runs the cluster. You need to configure monitoring of VM-1. You have to move VM-1 to a different node if the Print Spooler service on VM-1 stops unexpectedly. What should you use?

A. clussvc.exe command

B. cluster.exe command

C. Computer Management console

D. configurehyperv.exe command

E. Disk Management console

F. Failover Cluster Manager console

G. Hyper-V Manager console

H. Server Manager Desktop app

41. You are the administrator for your company network. The network consists of an Active Directory domain. The domain contains Windows Server 2016 servers named ServerA, ServerB, and ServerC. ServerA and ServerB are nodes in a Hyper-V cluster named Cluster-1. You add a Hyper-V Replica Broker role named Broker-1 to Cluster-1. ServerC is a Hyper-V server and also has a virtual machine named VM-1. Live Migration is enabled on all three servers and they are configured to use Kerberos authentication only. You need to ensure that you can perform the migration of VM-1 to ServerB. What should you do?

A. Add the ServerC computer account to the Replicator group on ServerA and ServerB.

B. Modify the Cluster permissions for Cluster-1.

C. Modify the Delegation settings on the ServerC computer account.

D. Modify the Storage Migration settings on ServerC.

42. You are the administrator for your company network. You have a computer that has the following four hard disk drives installed:

- Drive A—500 GB OS volume
- Drive B—400 GB data volume
- Drive C—400 GB empty volume
- Drive D—500 GB empty volume

You want to create a two-way mirror using Storage Spaces. What drives should you use while at the same time minimizing data loss?

A. Drive A and Drive B

B. Drive A and Drive D

C. Drive B and Drive C

D. Drive C and Drive D

43. You are the administrator for your company network. You purchase a new computer. You have six external USB hard drives and you want to create a single volume by using these USB drives. You want the volume to be expandable, portable, and resilient in the event of simultaneous failure of two USB hard drives. What should you do if you need to create the volume?

    A. Create a new Storage Space across six USB hard drives; set the resiliency type to Three-Way Mirror from the Control Panel.

    B. Create a new Storage Space across six USB hard drives; set the resiliency type to Parity from the Control Panel.

    C. Create a new spanned volume from Disk Management.

    D. Create a new striped volume from Disk Management.

44. You are the administrator for your company network. You have a failover cluster named ClusterA that runs a highly available virtual machine named VM-1 that runs a custom application named App1. You need to configure monitoring of VM-1. If App1 adds an error entry to the Application event log, VM-1 should be automatically rebooted and moved to another cluster node. What tool should you use to accomplish this?

    A. Failover Cluster Manager

    B. Hyper-V Manager

    C. Resource Monitor

    D. Server Manager

45. You are the administrator for your company network. A coworker previously opened Hyper-V Manager, selected a virtual machine, and used the Enable Replication Wizard. The process was completed successfully and replication occurred as expected. However, several weeks later, you decide you want to run a planned failover. How should you first proceed?

    A. Right-click the primary virtual machine and select Replication ➤ Planned Failover.

    B. Right-click the replica virtual machine and select Replication ➤ Planned Failover.

    C. Right-click the primary virtual machine and select Replication ➤ Extend Replication.

    D. Right-click the replica virtual machine and select Replication ➤ Test Failover.

46. You are the administrator for your company network. You have a Windows Server 2016 Hyper-V host named ServerA that hosts two virtual machines named VM-1 and VM-2. On the Hyper-V host, you create two virtual disks named DiskA and DiskB. You plan to create a test environment for Storage Spaces Direct. You need to configure the virtual machines to connect to the virtual disks. What should you use?

    A. An iSCSI target

    B. A virtual SCSI controller

    C. A virtual Fibre Channel adapter

    D. A virtual IDE controller

47. You are the administrator for your company network. You are going to deploy two servers that run Windows Server 2016. You install the Failover Clustering feature on both servers. You plan to create a workgroup cluster. What should you do?

   A. Create matching local administrative accounts on both of the servers. Assign the same primary DNS suffix to both of the servers. Run the New-Cluster cmdlet and specify an administrative access point of None.

   B. Configure both of the servers to be in a workgroup named Workgroup. Configure the Cluster Service to log on as Network Service. Run the New-Cluster cmdlet and specify an administrative access point of DNS.

   C. Create matching local administrative accounts on both of the servers. Assign the same primary DNS suffix to both of the servers. Run the New-Cluster cmdlet and specify an administrative access point of DNS.

   D. Configure both of the servers to be in a workgroup named Workgroup. Configure the Cluster Service to log on as Network Service. Run the New-Cluster cmdlet and specify an administrative access point of None.

48. You are the administrator for your company network. Your network contains an Active Directory domain that contains two Windows Server 2016 servers named ServerA and ServerB. Each server has an operating system disk and four data disks. All of the disks are locally attached SATA disks. Each disk is a basic disk, is initialized as a MBR disk, and has a single NTFS volume. You plan to implement Storage Spaces Direct by using the data disks on ServerA and ServerB. You need to prepare the data disks for the Storage Spaces Direct implementation. What should you do?

   A. Convert the data disks to dynamic disks.

   B. Delete the volumes from the data disks.

   C. Format the volumes on the data disks as exFAT.

   D. Initialize the data disks as GPT disks and create an ReFS volume on each disk.

49. You are the administrator for your company network. You have two Windows Server 2016 Hyper-V hosts named ServerA and ServerB that are nodes in a failover cluster. You have a virtual machine named VM-1 that connects to a virtual switch named vSwitch1. You discover that VM-1 automatically live migrates when vSwitch1 temporarily disconnects. You need to prevent VM-1 from being live migrated when vSwitch1 temporarily disconnects. What should you do?

   A. Run the Set-VMNetworkAdapter cmdlet and set StormLimit to 0.

   B. From the network adapter setting of VM-1, disable the Heartbeat integration service.

   C. Run the Set-VMNetworkAdapter cmdlet and set IsManagementOS to False.

   D. From the network adapter setting of VM-1, disable the Protected network setting.

50. You are the administrator for your company network. You have a Hyper-V failover cluster that contains three nodes. The virtual machines are distributed evenly across the nodes. Which settings should you modify if you need to ensure that if a node loses connectivity from the other nodes that the virtual machines on the node will be transitioned to one of the remaining nodes after one minute?

A. QuarantineDuration and QuarantineThreshold

B. QuorumArbitrationTimeMax and RequestReplyTimeout

C. ResiliencyPeriod and ResiliencyLevel

D. SameSubnetDelay and CrossSubnetDelay

Practice Exam 70-741: Networking with Windows Server 2016

1. You are the administrator for your company network. You have a Windows Server 2016 Hyper-V host. The host contains a resource metering enabled virtual machine named VM-1. You need to use resource metering to track the amount of network traffic that the virtual machine sends to the 10.0.0.0/8 network. What cmdlet should you run?

   A. `Add-VMNetworkAdapterAcl`

   B. `Set-VMNetworkAdapter`

   C. `Set-VMNetworkAdapterRoutingDomainMapping`

   D. `New-VMResourcePool`

2. You are the administrator for your company network. You chose the Group Policy based provisioning method for IPAM. You must also provide a GPO name prefix in the provisioning wizard. After providing a GPO name prefix, the wizard will display the GPO names that must be created in domains that will be managed by IPAM. Given the following PowerShell command, how many GPOs would be created?

   `Invoke-IpamGpoProvisioning -Domain willpanek.com -GpoPrefixName IPAM1-DelegatedGpoUser userA -IpamServerFqdn ipam1.willpanek.com`

   A. 1

   B. 2

   C. 3

   D. 4

3. You are the administrator for your company network. The network contains an Active Directory domain that has a Windows Server 2016 server named ServerA, which is a member server and has the DNS Server role installed. Automatic scavenging of state records is enabled and the scavenging period is set to 15 days. All client computers register their names dynamically in the DNS zone on ServerA. You discover that the names of multiple client computers that were removed from the network several weeks ago can still be resolved. You need to configure ServerA to automatically remove the records of the client computers that have been offline for more than 15 days. What should you do?

   A. Modify the Zone Aging and Scavenging properties.

   B. Run the `dnscmd.exe` command and specify the `/AgeAllRecords` parameter.

   C. Set the Expires After value.

   D. Set the Time to Live (TTL) value of all of the records.

4. You are the administrator for your company network. You and a coworker are discussing socket pools. The socket pool enables a DNS server to use source port randomization when issuing DNS queries. What command offers the greatest protection when working with socket pools?

   A. `dnscmd /config /socketpoolsize 0`

   B. `dnscmd /config /socketpoolsize 1`

   C. `dnscmd /config /socketpoolsize 1000`

   D. `dnscmd /config /socketpoolsize 1000 /socketpoolexcludedportranges 1-65535`

5. You are the administrator for your company network. You have a DHCP server named DHCP1. DHCP1 has an IPv4 scope that serves 80 client computers. When you review the address leases in the DHCP console, you discover that there are several leases for devices that you do not recognize. What should you do if you need to ensure that only the 80 computers can obtain a lease from the scope?

   A. Create a DHCP policy for the scope.

   B. Create and enable a DHCP filter.

   C. Run the `Add-DhcpServerv4ExclusionRange` cmdlet.

   D. Run the `Add-DhcpServerv4OptionDefinition` cmdlet.

6. You are the administrator for your company network. You have a DHCP server named DHCP1 that has an IPv4 scope named Scope1. Users report that when they turn on their computers it takes a long time to access the network. You validate that it takes a long time for the computers to receive an IP address from DHCP1. You monitor the network traffic and discover that DHCP1 issues five ping commands on the network before leasing an IP address. You need to reduce the amount of time it takes for the computers to receive an IP address. What should you do?

   A. Configure the bindings from the properties of IPv4.

   B. Configure Name Protection from the properties of DHCP1.

   C. Create a new filter from IPv4.

   D. Create an exclusion range from the properties of Scope1.

   E. Create a reservation.

   F. Modify the Conflict Detection Attempts setting from the properties of DHCP1.

   G. Modify the properties of Ethernet from Control Panel.

   H. Run the DHCP Policy Configuration Wizard from IPv4.

7. You are the administrator for your company network. Your network contains one Active Directory domain that contains an IP Address Management (IPAM) server named IPAM1. IPAM1 manages several DHCP and DNS servers. From Server Manager on IPAM1, you create a custom role for IPAM. What should you do if you need to assign the role to a group named IP_Administrators?

   A. Using Server Manager, create an access policy.

   B. Using Server Manager, create an access scope.

   C. Using PowerShell, run the `Add-Member` cmdlet.

   D. Using PowerShell, run the `Set-IpamConfiguration` cmdlet.

8. You are the administrator for your company network. You have a Windows Server 2016 DHCP server named DHCP1. You have a single IP subnet and DHCP1 has an IPv4 scope named Scope1. Scope1 has an IP address range of 10.0.1.10 to 10.0.1.200 and a length of 24 bits. You need to create a second logical IP network on the subnet. The subnet will use an IP address range of 10.0.2.10 to 10.0.2.200 and a length of 24 bits. What should you do?

A. Create a second scope and then run the DHCP Split-Scope Configuration Wizard.

B. Create a second scope and then create a superscope.

C. Create a superscope and then configure an exclusion range in Scope1.

D. Create a new scope and then modify the IPv4 bindings.

9. You are the administrator for your company network. You are implementing a new network. The network contains a Windows Server 2016 DHCP server named DHCP1 that contains a scope named ScopeA for the 192.168.0/24 subnet. Your company has the following policies:

   - All server addresses must be excluded from DHCP scopes.

   - All client computers must receive IP addresses from ScopeA.

   - All Windows servers must have IP addresses in the range of 192.168.0.200 to 192.168.0.240.

   - All other network devices must have IP addresses in the range of 192.168.0.180 to 192.168.0.199.

   You deploy a print device named PrintDevice1. You need to ensure that PrintDevice1 adheres to the policies for allocating IP addresses. What command should you run?

A. Add-DhcpServerv4ExclusionRange

B. Add-DhcpServerv4Filter

C. Add-DhcpServerv4Lease

D. Add-DhcpServerv4Reservation

10. You are the administrator for your company network. You and a coworker are discussing the use of network IDs. Because the network ID bits must always be chosen in a contiguous fashion from the high order bits, a shorthand way of expressing a subnet mask is to denote the number of bits that define the network ID as a network prefix using the network prefix notation: /<# of bits>. What is the network prefix for Class C?

A. /8

B. /16

C. /24

D. /64

11. You are the administrator for your company network. The network consists of a single Active Directory domain named willpanek.com. You have a server named ServerA that runs a custom network application. ServerA has the following IP addresses:

   - 192.168.15.10
   - 192.168.15.11

   You need to ensure that a client computer resolves ServerA.willpanek.com to only the 192.168.15.11 IP address. What should you do from the computer?

   A. Edit the HOSTS file.

   B. Edit the LMHOSTS file.

   C. Run ipconfig.exe /flushdns.

   D. Run netsh interface ipv4 reset.

12. You are the administrator for your company network. Your network contains three subnets:

   - SubnetA – Production Servers – a production network
   - SubnetB – Development Servers – a development network
   - SubnetC – Client Computers – a client network

   SubnetB is used to test applications and reproduces servers that are located on SubnetA. SubnetB and SubnetA use the same IP address range. A user, User1, has a client computer on SubnetC. User1 reports that when she attempts to connect to the IP address 10.10.1.6 from her computer, she connects to a server on SubnetA. You need to ensure that when User1 connects to 10.10.1.6, she connects to a server on SubnetB. What should you run?

   A. New-NetNeighbor

   B. New-NetRoute

   C. Set-NetNeighbor

   D. Set-NetTcpSetting

13. You are the administrator for your company network. Your network contains a Windows Server 2016 DNS server named DNS1. The network also contains a Windows Server 2012 R2 server named Server1. You change the IP address of Server1. A few hours later several users report that they cannot connect to Server1. On the users' client computers, you flush the DNS client resolver cache and the users can successfully connect to Server1. You need to reduce the amount of time that the client computers cache DNS records. What value should you modify in the Start of Authority (SOA) record?

   A. Expires After

   B. Minimum (Default) Time to Live (TTL)

   C. Refresh Interval

   D. Retry Interval

14. You are the administrator for your company network. Your company has a single Active Directory domain. All servers run Windows Server 2016. You install an additional DNS server. You need to delete the pointer record for the IP address 10.3.2.127. What should you do?

   A. Delete the 127.in-addr.arpa zone using DNS Manager.

   B. Run the dnscmd /ZoneDelete 127.in-addr.arpa command from the command prompt.

   C. Run the dnscmd /RecordDelete 10.in-addr.arpa. 127.1.2.3 PTR command from the command prompt.

   D. Run the dnscmd /RecordDelete 10.3.2.127 command from the command prompt.

15. You are the administrator for your company network. You administer a server that assigns IP addresses via DHCP. You want to make sure that one of the clients always receives the same IP address from the DHCP server. You create an exclusion for that address, but you find that the computer isn't being properly configured at boot up. What do you need to do to resolve this issue?

   A. You excluded the wrong IP address.

   B. You need to create a superscope for the address.

   C. You need to make a reservation for the client that ties the IP address to the computer's MAC address and then delete the exclusion.

   D. You must configure the client manually. You cannot assign the address via the DHCP server.

16. You are the administrator for your company network. You have a single Active Directory forest and your DNS servers are configured as Active Directory Integrated zones. When you look at the DNS records in Active Directory, you notice that there are many records for computers that do not exist on your domain. What should you do if you want to make sure that only domain computers register with your DNS servers?

   A. Set dynamic updates to Nonsecure and Secure.

   B. Set dynamic updates to Domain Users Only.

   C. Set dynamic updates to None.

   D. Set dynamic updates to Secure Only.

17. You are the administrator for your company network. You have two Windows Server 2016 servers named ServerA and DHCP1. DHCP1 is a DHCP server. You want ServerA to help lease addresses for DHCP1. You add the DHCP role to ServerA. What should you do next?

   A. Run the Configure Failover Wizard in the DHCP console.

   B. Run the Configure Zone Wizard in the DHCP console.

   C. Set the DHCP role to Enabled on DHCP1.

   D. Start the Share Zone Information Wizard on ServerA.

18. You are the administrator for your company network. You are speaking to a coworker regarding using Classless Inter-Domain Routing (CIDR). Which of the following subnet masks are represented with the CIDR of /28?

   A. 255.255.255.224

   B. 255.255.255.240

   C. 255.255.255.248

   D. 255.255.255.254

19. You are the administrator for your company network. You have a Windows Server 2016 server named ServerA that is located on the perimeter network and uses only inbound TCP port 443 to connect from the Internet. You install the Remote Access server role on ServerA. What Virtual Private Network (VPN) protocol should you use if you need to configure ServerA to accept VPN connections over port 443?

   A. Internet Key Exchange Protocol Version 2 (IKEv2)

   B. Layer 2 Tunneling Protocol (L2TP)

   C. Point-to-Point Tunneling Protocol (PPTP)

   D. Secure Socket Tunneling Protocol (SSTP)

20. You are the administrator for your company network. The network contains one Active Directory domain named willpanek.com. You deploy DirectAccess on the network. During the deployment, you enable DirectAccess only for a group called WillPanek\ Test Computers. What should you do if you need to enable DirectAccess for all the client computers in the domain after the initial installation?

   A. From Active Directory Users and Computers, modify the membership of the Windows Authorization Access Group.

   B. From Group Policy Management, modify the security filtering of an object named Direct Access Client Setting Group Policy.

   C. Using PowerShell, run the Set-DAClient cmdlet.

   D. Using PowerShell, run the Set-DirectAccess cmdlet.

21. You are the administrator for your company network. You have a Windows Server 2016 Remote Access server named RAS1 that has DirectAccess enabled. You have a proxy server named Proxy2. All computers on the internal network connect to the Internet by using the proxy. You run the command Set-DAClient -forceTunnel Enabled on RAS1. You need to ensure that when a DirectAccess client connects to the network that the client accesses all the Internet resources through the proxy. What should you do on RAS1?

   A. Set-DAEntryPoint

   B. Set-DnsClientGlobalSetting

   C. Set-DnsClientNrptGlobal

   D. Set-DnsClientNrptRule

22. You are the administrator for your company network. You are discussing Remote Access Service (RAS) Gateway modes with a coworker. One mode allows you to deploy the RAS Gateway as an edge VPN server, an edge DirectAccess server, or both simultaneously. In this configuration, RAS Gateway provides remote employees with connectivity to your network by using either VPN or DirectAccess connections. What mode is being described here?

    A. Multitenant mode

    B. Single tenant mode

    C. Unattached tenant mode

    D. Remote tenant mode

23. You are the administrator for your company network. Your network contains an Active Directory forest that has a functional level of Windows Server 2012. The forest contains five domain controllers and five VPN servers that run Windows Server 2016. The VPN Server has 500 users who connect daily. What should you do first if you need to configure a new RADIUS server named RADIUS1?

    A. Deploy the Network Policy and Access Services role on RADIUS1.

    B. Deploy the Remote Access server role on RADIUS1.

    C. Run the `New-NpsRadiusClient` cmdlet on each VPN server.

    D. Set the forest functional level to Windows Server 2016 on a domain controller.

24. You are the administrator for your company network. The company has employees who work remotely by using a Virtual Private Network (VPN) connection from their computers. They use an application to access the company Intranet database servers. The company decides to distribute the latest version of the application using a public cloud. Some users report that every time they try to download the application by using Internet Explorer they receive a warning message that indicates the application could harm their computers. You need to recommend a solution that prevents this warning message from appearing, without compromising the security protection of the computers. What should you do?

    A. Instruct the employees to disable the SmartScreen Filter using the Internet Explorer settings.

    B. Publish the application using the intranet website.

    C. Publish the application using a public File Transfer Protocol (FTP) site.

    D. Publish the application using the Windows Store.

25. You are the administrator for your company network. Your company has 150 client computers. The client computers are connected to a corporate private network. You deploy a Remote Desktop Gateway, DirectAccess, and a VPN server at the main office. Users are currently unable to connect from their home computers to their work computers by using Remote Desktop. You need to ensure that users can remotely connect to their office computers by using Remote Desktop. The users must not be able to access any other corporate network resources from their home computers. What should you configure?

    A. A Virtual Private Network connection

    B. The Remote Desktop Gateway IP address in the advanced Remote Desktop Connection settings on each client

   C. The local resource settings of the Remote Desktop connection

   D. A DirectAccess connection

26. You are the administrator for your company network. Your network contains a single Active Directory domain. You need to prevent computers from connecting to hosts on subnet 131.107.0.0/24. What should you run?

   A. Run the Add-VpnConnection `Trigger Application` cmdlet.

   B. Run the New-NetFirewallRule cmdlet and specify the `-Direction Outbound` parameter.

   C. Run the New-VpnConnection cmdlet.

   D. Run the Set-NetConnection `Profile` cmdlet.

27. You are the administrator for your company network. You have multiple servers that run Windows Server 2016 and are configured as VPN servers. You deploy a Network Policy Server (NPS) server named Server1. What should you configure on Server1 if you need to configure it to accept authentication requests from the VPN servers?

   A. From Policies, add a connection request policy.

   B. From RADIUS Clients and Servers, add a remote RADIUS server group.

   C. From RADIUS Clients and Servers, add RADIUS clients.

   D. From Policies, add a network policy.

28. You are the administrator for your company network. You have a Windows Server 2016 server named VPN1 that is configured as a VPN server. VPN1 is configured to allow domain users to establish VPN connections from 6:00 a.m. to 6:00 p.m. every day of the week. You need to ensure that domain users can establish VPN connections Monday through Friday only. What should you do?

   A. From Routing and Remote Access, configure the Properties of VPN1.

   B. From Server Manager, modify the Access Policies on VPN1.

   C. From Active Directory Users and Computers, modify the Dial-in Properties of the computer accounts.

   D. From Network Policy Server, modify the Network Policy on Server.

29. You are the administrator for your company network. You have a DirectAccess server that is accessible by using the name directaccess.willpanek.com. On the DirectAccess server you install a new server certificate that has the same subject name. You then configure the DNS records for directaccess.willpanek.com. You need to change the endpoint name for DirectAccess to directaccess.willpanek.com. What command should you run?

   A. Set-DaServer -ConnectToAddress directaccess.willpanek.com

   B. Set-DaEntryPoint -EntrypointName directaccess.willpanek.com

   C. Set-DaEntryPoint -ComputerName directaccess.willpanek.com

   D. Set-DaClient -ComputerName directaccess.willpanek.com

30. You are the administrator for your company network. Your client computers use DirectAccess. You need to ensure that the client computers can communicate to IPv4 resources by name. What should you implement on the client computers?

A. AAAA (Quad A) resource records

B. NAT64/DNS64

C. Teredo relays

D. Teredo tunnels

31. You are the administrator for your company network. Your network contains an Active Directory domain. Network Access Protection (NAP) is deployed to the domain. You need to create NAP event trace log files on a client computer. What should you run?

A. Logman

B. Register-EngineEvent

C. Register-ObjectEvent

D. Tracert

32. You are the administrator for your company network. Your network contains four Network Policy Server (NPS) servers named NPS1, NPS2, NPS3, and NPS4. NPS1 is configured as a RADIUS proxy that forwards connection requests to a remote RADIUS server group named Group1. You need to ensure that NPS2 and NPS3 receive connection requests. NPS4 should receive connection requests only if both NPS2 and NPS3 are unavailable. How should you configure Group1?

A. Change the weight of NPS2 and NPS3 to 10.

B. Change the weight of NPS4 to 10.

C. Change the priority of NPS2 and NPS3 to 10.

D. Change the priority of NPS4 to 10.

33. You are the administrator for your company network. Your network contains an Active Directory domain and all servers run Windows Server 2016. The domain contains a server named NPS1 that has the NPS server role and the Remote Access server role installed. The domain contains a server named Radius1 that is configured as a RADIUS server. NPS1 provides VPN access to external users. You need to ensure that all of the VPN connections to NPS1 are logged to the RADIUS server on Radius1. What should you run?

A. Add-RemoteAccessRadius -ServerName NPS1 - AccountingOnOffMsg Enabled -SharedSecret "Secret" -Purpose Accounting

B. Add-RemoteAccessRadius -ServerName Radius1 -AccountingOnOffMsg Enabled -SharedSecret "Secret" -Purpose Accounting

C. Set-RemoteAccessAccounting -AccountingOnOffMsg Enabled -AccountingOnOffMsg Enabled

D. Set-RemoteAccessAccounting -EnableAccountingType Inbox -AccountingOnOffMsg Enabled

34. You are the administrator for your company network. Your network contains an Active Directory domain. The domain contains a server named RAS1 that has the Remote Access server role installed. By using the default configuration, DirectAccess is implemented on RAS1. You discover that DirectAccess clients do not use DirectAccess when accessing websites on the Internet. You need to ensure that DirectAccess clients access all Internet websites by using their DirectAccess connections. What should you do?

A. Enable force tunneling by configuring DirectAccess.

B. In the DirectAccess Client Settings Group Policy Object (GPO), disable the DirectAccess Passive Mode policy setting.

C. In the DirectAccess Server Settings Group Policy Object (GPO), enable the Route All Traffic Through The Internal Network policy setting.

D. On the DirectAccess clients, configure a DNS suffix search list.

35. You are the administrator for your company network. You plan to deploy several Windows Server 2016 Hyper-V hosts. The deployment will use Software Defined Networking (SDN) and Virtual Extensible LAN (VXLAN). To support the planned deployment, what server role should you install on the network?

A. Host Guardian Service (HGS)

B. Remote Access Service (RAS)

C. Network Controller

D. Network Policy and Access Services (NPAS)

36. You are the administrator for your company network. You have an Active Directory domain that contains several Windows Server 2016 Hyper-V hosts. You plan to deploy network virtualization and to centrally manage Datacenter Firewall policies. For the planned deployment, what component must you install?

A. The Canary Network Diagnostics feature

B. The Data Center Bridging feature

C. The Network Controller server role

D. The Routing role service

37. You are the administrator for your company network. You have a Windows Server 2016 server. What should you install if you need to configure it as a multitenant RAS Gateway?

A. The Data Center Bridging feature

B. The Network Controller server role

C. The Network Policy and Access Services server role

D. The Remote Access server role

38. You are the administrator for your company network. You are planning on setting up NIC Teaming. You want to provide fault protection. What is the minimum number of Ethernet adapters you must have to take advantage of fault protection in NIC Teaming?

A. 1

B. 2

C. 3

D. 4

39. You are the administrator for your company network. You want to deploy the RAS Gateway as an Edge VPN server, an Edge DirectAccess server, or both simultaneously. The RAS Gateway will provide remote employees with connectivity to your network by using either VPN or DirectAccess connections. What RAS Gateway mode type will you be setting up to meet your requirements?

   A. Dual tenant

   B. Lone tenant

   C. Multitenant

   D. Single tenant

40. You are the administrator for your company network. You have an environment that includes two Windows Server 2016 servers. You need to ensure that you can implement SMB Direct between the servers. What feature should the servers support?

   A. Multipath I/O (MPIO)

   B. Remote Direct Memory Access (RDMA)

   C. Single Root I/O Virtualization (SR-IOV)

   D. Virtual Machine Queue (VMQ)

41. You are the administrator for your company network. Your company has 10 offices. Each office has a local network that contains several Windows Server 2016 Hyper-V hosts. All of the offices are connected by high speed, low latency WAN links. You need to ensure that you can use QoS policies for Live Migration traffic between the offices. What component should you install?

   A. The Canary Network Diagnostics feature

   B. The Data Center Bridging feature

   C. The Multipath I/O feature

   D. The Network Controller server role

   E. The Routing role service

42. You are the administrator for your company network. You have a Windows Server 2016 server named Hyperv1 that is a Hyper-V host that hosts a virtual machine named VM-1. Hyperv1 has three network adapter cards that are connected to virtual switches named Ethernet1, Ethernet2, and Ethernet3. NIC Teaming on VM-1 is currently configured as follows:

   Team Name: VM-1 NIC Team

   Member Adapters: Ethernet2   10 Gbps

   　　Ethernet3   10 Gbps

   Teaming Mode: Switch Independent

   Load Balancing Mode: Address Hash

   Standby Adapter: None (all adapters Active)

   Primary Team Interface: VM-1 NIC Team; Default VLAN

What should you do if you need to ensure that VM-1 will retain access to the network if a physical network adapter card fails on Hyperv1?

A. From the properties of the NIC team on VM-1, add the adapter named Ethernet1 to the NIC team.

B. From Hyper-V Manager on Hyperv1, modify the settings on VM-1.

C. From PowerShell on VM-1, run the `Set-VmNetworkAdapterTeamMapping` cmdlet.

D. From PowerShell on Hyperv1, run the `Set-VmNetworkAdapterFailoverConfiguration` cmdlet.

43. You are the administrator for your company network. You and a coworker are discussing how to move virtual machines between host machines. How do you accomplish this?

A. Create a snapshot of the virtual machine and apply it to a different machine.

B. Move the virtual machine files to the target host and add them to Hyper-V.

C. Use the Export and Import Virtual Machine command in Hyper-V.

D. Use the Save command in Hyper-V.

44. You are the administrator for your company network. You and a coworker are discussing Software Load Balancer (SLB). The _____ processes inbound network traffic and maps Virtual IPs (VIPs) to Dynamic IPs (DIPs), then forwards the traffic to the correct DIP. What is this process called? (Fill in the blank.)

A. Host Agent

B. Northbound Application Program Interfaces (API)

C. System Center Virtual Machine Manager (SCVMM)

D. SLB Multiplexer (MUX)

45. You are the administrator for your company network. You have a Windows Server 2016 Hyper-V host named Hyperv1 that hosts several virtual machines. Each virtual machine has two network adapters. Hyperv1 also contains several virtual switches. On Hyperv1, you create a NIC team that has two network adapters. You discover that the NIC team is set to Static Teaming mode. You need to modify the NIC teaming mode to Switch Independent. What cmdlet should you use?

A. `Set-NetLbfoTeam`

B. `Set-NetLbfoTeamNic`

C. `Set-VMNetworkAdapter`

D. `Set-VMSwitch`

46. You are the administrator for your company network. Your network contains an Active Directory domain. The domain contains a Windows Server 2016 server named Hyperv1 that has the Hyper-V server role installed. Hyperv1 has a virtual switch named vSwitch1. You replace all of the network adapters on Hyperv1 with new network adapters that support Single Root I/O Virtualization (SR-IOV). You need to enable SR-IOV for all of the virtual machines on Hyperv1. What actions should you perform? (Choose two.)

    A. Delete and then re-create the vSwitch1 virtual switch.

    B. On each virtual machine, modify the Advanced Features settings of the network adapter.

    C. On each virtual machine, modify the BIOS settings.

    D. On each virtual machine, modify the Hardware Acceleration settings of the network adapter.

    E. Modify the settings of the vSwitch1 virtual switch.

47. You are the administrator for your company network. You and a coworker are discussing NIC Teaming. You know that you can set up NIC Teaming by using Server Manager or PowerShell and that different configuration models are available. What is this configuration called if you want each NIC adapter connected into a different switch?

    A. Switch Dependent

    B. Switch Reliant

    C. Switch Independent

    D. Switch Autonomous

48. You are the administrator for your company network. You have a Windows Server 2016 virtual machine named SDN1 that you plan to use as part of a Software Defined Networking (SDN) solution. What should you install if you need to implement the Border Gateway Protocol (BGP) on SDN1?

    A. The Peer Name Resolution Protocol (PNRP) feature

    B. The Network Device Enrollment Service role service

    C. The Network Policy and Access Services server role

    D. The Remote Access Service (RAS) server role

49. You are the administrator for your company network. You have a Windows Server 2016 Hyper-V host named Hyperv1 that has two network adapters named NIC1 and NIC2. Hyperv2 has two virtual switches named vSwitch1 and vSwitch2. NIC1 connects to vSwitch1. NIC2 connects to vSwitch2. Hyperv1 hosts a virtual machine named VM-1. VM-1 has two network adapters named vmNIC1 and vmNIC1. VmNIC1 connects to vSwitch1. VmNIC2 connects to vSwitch2. What should you run on VM-1 if you need to create a NIC team?

    A. `$var1 = "LACP" $var2 = "Dynamic"`

    B. `$var1 = "Static" $var2 = "HyperVPort"`

    C. `$var1 = "SwitchIndependent" $var2 = "TransportPorts"`

    D. `$var1 = "SwitchIndependent" $var2 = "HyperVPort"`

50. You are the administrator for your company network. You have two Windows Server 2016 Hyper-V servers named Hyperv1 and Hyperv2. You want a dedicated area created on the physical network adapter for each virtual network adapter to use. What is this feature called?

A. Remote Direct Memory Access (RDMA)

B. Multipath I/O (MPIO)

C. Virtual Machine Queue (VMQ)

D. Single Root I/O Virtualization (SR-IOV)

Chapter

13

Practice Exam
70-742: Identity with
Windows Server 2016

1. You are the administrator for your company network. Your company has one Active Directory Domain Services (AD DS) forest that contains two domains. All servers run Windows Server 2016. The company uses iSCSI storage and Fibre Channel storage. You plan to deploy a single Hyper-V failover cluster that uses Cluster Shared Volumes (CSVs). The cluster must include virtual machines from both domains. You need to ensure that you can deploy a failover cluster. What should you do?

   A. Deploy clustered storage spaces.

   B. Deploy Serial Attached SCSI (SAS).

   C. Join each Hyper-V host server to the same AD DS domain.

   D. Join each Hyper-V host server to different AD DS domains.

2. You are the administrator for your company network. Your network contains an Active Directory domain. The domain contains a Read-Only Domain Controller (RODC). You need to retrieve a list of accounts that have their passwords cached on the server. What should you run?

   A. dcdiag.exe

   B. netdom.exe

   C. ntdsutil.exe

   D. repadmin.exe

3. You are the administrator for your company network. Your network contains an Active Directory domain. All users are in an Organizational Unit (OU) named Users. You plan to modify the descriptions of all the users who have a string of 207 in their mobile phone numbers. You need to view a list of the users that will be modified. What PowerShell cmdlet should you run?

   A. `Get-ADUser-Filter "MobilePhone-like '*207*'"`

   B. `Get-ADOrganizationalUnit-Filter "MobilePhone-like '*207* "'`

   C. `Get-ADUser-LDAPFilter "(MobilePhone='*207*)"`

   D. `Get-ADOrganizationalUnit-LDAPFilter "(MobilePhone='*207*')"`

4. You are the administrator for your company network. Your network contains a single Active Directory domain. The domain contains five Windows Server 2008 R2 domain controllers. What should you perform if you plan to install a new Windows Server 2016 domain controller? (Choose two.)

   A. At the command line, run `adprep.exe /rodcprep`.

   B. At the command line, run `adprep.exe /forestprep`.

   C. At the command line, run `adprep.exe /domainprep`.

   D. From Active Directory Domains and Trusts, raise the functional level of the domain.

   E. From Active Directory Users and Computers, prestage the RODC computer account.

5. You are the administrator for your company network. Your network contains an Active Directory domain that contains 1,000 desktop computers and 500 laptops. An Organizational Unit (OU) named Computers1 contains the computer accounts for the desktop computers and the laptops. You create a PowerShell script named PScript1.ps1 that removes temporary files and cookies. You create a Group Policy Object (GPO) named GPO1 and link GPO1 to Computers1. You need to run the script once a week on the laptops only. What should you do?

   A. Add PScript1.ps1 as a startup script and attach a WMI filter to GPO1.

   B. Create a File preference that uses item-level targeting in GPO1.

   C. Create a Scheduled Tasks preference that uses item-level targeting in GPO1.

   D. Configure the File System security policy and attach a WMI filter to GPO1.

6. You are the administrator for your company network. You have an offline root Certification Authority (CA) named CertAuth1 that is hosted on a virtual machine. You only turn on CertAuth1 when the CA must be patched or you must generate a key for subordinate CAs. You start CertAuth1 and discover that the file system is corrupt. You resolve the file system corruption and discover that you must reload the CA root from a backup. When you attempt to run the `Restore-CARoleService` cmdlet, you receive the following error message: "The process cannot access the file because it is being used by another process." What should you do to resolve the issue?

   A. Stop the Active Directory Domain Services (AD DS) service.

   B. Stop the Active Directory Certificate Services (AD CS) service.

   C. Run the `Restore-CARoleService` cmdlet and specify the path to a valid CA key.

   D. Run the `Restore-CARoleService` cmdlet and specify the `Force` parameter.

7. You are the administrator for your company network. Your network contains an Active Directory domain. You have an Organizational Unit (OU) named Computers1 that contains the computer accounts of two servers and the user account of a user named User1. A Group Policy Object (GPO) named GPO1 is linked to Computers1. You have an application named App1 that installs by using an application installer named App1.exe. You need to publish App1 to Computers1 by using Group Policy. What should you do?

   A. Create a Config.zap file and add a file to the File System node to the Computer Configuration node of GPO1.

   B. Create a Config.xml file and add a software installation package to the User Configuration node of GPO1.

   C. Create a Config.zap file and add a software installation package to the User Configuration node of GPO1.

   D. Create a Config.xml file and add a software installation package to the Computer Configuration node of GPO1.

8. You are the administrator for your company network. Your network contains an Active Directory forest named willpanek.com. The forest contains three domains named willpanek.com, corp.willpanek.com, and office.willpanek.com. The forest contains three Active Directory sites named Site1, Site2, and Site3. You have the three administrators as described in the following table.

Administrator Name	Group Membership	Domain
Admin1	Domain Admins	willpanek.com
Admin2	Domain Admins	corp.willpanek.com
Admin3	Enterprise Admins	willpanek.com

You create a Group Policy Object (GPO) named GPO1. Who can link GPO1 to Site2?

- **A.** Admin1 and Admin2 only
- **B.** Admin1 and Admin3 only
- **C.** Admin1, Admin2, and Admin3
- **D.** Admin3 only

9. You are the administrator for your company network. You deploy a new Active Directory forest. What should you do if you need to ensure that you can create a Group Managed Service Account (gMSA) for multiple member servers?

- **A.** On the computer account of each member server, configure Kerberos constrained delegation.
- **B.** On the computer account of each domain controller, configure Kerberos constrained delegation.
- **C.** On a domain controller, run the Set-KdsConfiguration PowerShell cmdlet.
- **D.** On a domain controller, run the Add-KdsRootKey PowerShell cmdlet.

10. You are the administrator for your company network. You have one Active Directory forest in your organization that contains one domain named willpanek.com. You have two domain controllers configured with the DNS role installed. There are two Active Directory Integrated zones named willpanek.com and willpanekAD.com. One of your coworkers, who is not an administrator, needs to be able to modify the willpanek.com DNS server, but you need to prevent this user from modifying the willpanekAD.com SOA record. What should you do?

- **A.** From the DNS Manager snap-in, modify the permissions of the willpanek.com zone.
- **B.** From the DNS Manager snap-in, modify the permissions of the willpanekAD.com zone.
- **C.** In Active Directory, run the Delegation Of Control Wizard.
- **D.** In the DNS snap-in, run the Delegation Of Control Wizard.

11. You are the administrator for your company network. The network contains an Active Directory forest. The forest contains three domain controllers configured as shown:

Server Name	Active Directory Site
Server1	Atlanta
Server2	Atlanta
Server3	Chicago

The company physically relocates Server2 from the Atlanta office to the Chicago office. You discover that both Server1 and Server2 authenticate users who sign in to the client computers in the Atlanta office. Only Server3 authenticates users who sign in to the computers in the Chicago office. You need to ensure that Server2 authenticates the users in the Chicago office during normal network operations. What should you do?

   A. On Server2, modify the Internet Protocol Version 4 (TCP/IPv4) configuration from Network Connections.

   B. From Active Directory Users and Computers, modify the Location Property of Server2.

   C. Run the Move-ADDirectoryServer cmdlet.

   D. Run the Set-ADReplicationSite cmdlet.

12. You are the administrator for your company network. You and a coworker are discussing changing an existing partition's file system to another file system. What command-line utility should you use?

   A. CHANGE

   B. CONVERT

   C. REVERT

   D. TRANSFORM

13. You are the administrator for your company network. Your network contains an Active Directory domain. You create a domain security group named Users1 and add several users to it. What should you do if you need to force all of the users in Users1 to change their passwords every 30 days while not affecting any other users?

   A. From Active Directory Administrative Center, create a Password Settings Object (PSO).

   B. Create a forms authentication provider and then set the forms authentication credentials.

   C. Run the Set-ADDomain cmdlet and then run the Set-ADAccountPassword cmdlet using PowerShell.

   D. Modify the Password Policy settings in a Group Policy Object (GPO) that is linked to the domain and then filter the GPO to Users1 only.

14. You are the administrator for your company network. Your network contains an Active Directory domain that has 3,000 user accounts. You have a Group Policy Object (GPO) named GPO1 that is linked to the domain and a GPO named Users1 that is linked to the Domain Controllers Organizational Unit (OU). You need to ensure that all of the client computers on the network automatically download and install Windows updates. What should you do?

   A. Modify Administrative Templates from the Computer Configuration node of GPO1.

   B. Modify Administrative Templates from the User Configuration node of GPO1.

   C. Modify Folder Redirection from the User Configuration node of GPO1.

   D. Modify Security Settings from the User Configuration node of Users1.

15. You are the administrator for your company network. You have multiple Windows Server 2016 servers. You have a server named DC1 that is configured as a domain controller and a DNS server. You need to create an Active Directory–integrated zone on DC1. What should you run?

   A. dism.exe

   B. dns.exe

   C. dnscmd.exe

   D. netsh.exe

16. You are the administrator for your company network. Your network has a single Windows Server 2016 Active Directory domain. The domain has OUs for Sales, Marketing, Admin, R&D, and Finance. You need the users in the Sales OU only to get Microsoft Office 2016 installed automatically onto their computers. You create a GPO named OfficeApp. What is the next step in getting all of the Sales users Office 2016?

   A. Edit the GPO and assign the OfficeApp application to the users' accounts. Link the GPO to the Sales OU.

   B. Edit the GPO and assign the OfficeApp application to the users' accounts. Link the GPO to the domain.

   C. Edit the GPO and assign the OfficeApp application to the computer accounts. Link the GPO to the domain.

   D. Edit the GPO and assign the OfficeApp application to the computer accounts. Link the GPO to the Sales OU.

17. You are the administrator for your company network. Your network contains an Active Directory forest. The forest contains two Windows Server 2016 domain controllers named Server1 and Server2. Server1 holds all of the operations master roles. Server1 experiences a hardware failure. You plan to use an automated process that will create 1,000 user accounts. You need to ensure that the automated process can complete successfully. What PowerShell command should you run?

   A. `Move-ADDirectoryServerOperationsMasterRole -identity "Server2" -OperationsMasterRole PDCEmulator -Force`

   B. `ntdsutil -identity "Server2" -OperationsMasterRole PDC Emulator Seize PDC`

C. `ntdsutil -identity "Server2" -OperationsMasterRole SchemaMaster -Force`

D. `Move-ADDirectoryServerOperationsMasterRole -identity "Server2" -OperationsMasterRole PDCEmulator Seize pdc`

18. You are the administrator for your company network. Recently, you have been asked to make changes to some of the permissions related to OUs within the domain. To restrict security for the Mass OU further, you remove some permissions at that level. Later, a junior administrator mentions that she is no longer able to make changes to objects within the Boston OU (which is located within the Mass OU). Assuming that no other changes have been made to Active Directory permissions, which of the following characteristics of OUs might have caused the change in permissions?

   A. Delegation

   B. Group Policy

   C. Inheritance

   D. Object properties

19. You are the administrator for your company network. Your network contains an Active Directory domain. The domain contains 30 domain controllers. You find that some Group Policy Objects (GPOs) are not being applied by all the domain controllers. You need to verify whether GPOs replicate successfully to all the domain controllers. What should you do?

   A. Run repadmin.exe for each GPO.

   B. Set BurFlags in the registry and then restart the File Replication Service (FRS). Run dcdiag.exe for each domain controller.

   C. Set BurFlags in the registry and then restart the File Replication Service (FRS). View the Directory Service event log.

   D. View the Status tab for the domain from Group Policy Management.

20. You are the administrator for your company network. You have a server named Svr1. A Microsoft Azure Backup of Svr1 is created automatically every day. You rename Svr1 to Svr2. Then you discover that backups are no longer being created in Azure. You need to back up the server to Azure. What should you do?

   A. From the Azure Management Portal, upload the Svr2 certificate as a management certificate.

   B. On Svr2, run the `Start-OBRegistration` cmdlet.

   C. On Svr2, run the `Add-WBBackupTarget` cmdlet.

   D. From the Azure Management Portal, modify the configuration on the backup vault.

21. You are the administrator for your company network. Your network contains an Active Directory domain. A Group Policy Object (GPO) named Users1 is linked to the domain. Users1 has computer configuration policies, user configuration policies, and user preferences configured. You need to ensure that the user preferences in Users1 apply only to users who sign in to computers that run Windows Server 2016. All the other settings in Users1 must be applied, regardless of the computer to which the users sign in. What should you configure?

    A. Item-level targeting

    B. Security filtering

    C. Security settings

    D. WMI filtering

22. You are the administrator for your company network. The company has multiple branch offices. The network contains an Active Directory domain. In one of the branch offices, a coworker is asked to add computers to the domain. After successfully joining multiple computers to the domain, she fails to join any more computers to the domain. You need to ensure that she can join an unlimited number of computers to the domain. What should you do?

    A. Modify the Security settings of your coworker's user account.

    B. Modify the Security settings of the Computers container.

    C. Configure your coworker's user account as a managed service account.

    D. Run the redircmp.exe command.

23. You are the administrator for your company network. Your network contains an Active Directory forest named willpanek.com. A partner company has a forest named wpanek.com. Each forest contains one domain. You need to provide access for a group named Sales in wpanek.com to resources in willpanek.com. The solution must use the least amount of administrative privilege. What should you do?

    A. Create an external trust from wpanek.com to willpanek.com. Enable Active Directory split permissions in wpanek.com.

    B. Create an external trust from willpanek.com to wpanek.com. Enable Active Directory split permissions in willpanek.com.

    C. Create a one-way forest trust from willpanek.com to wpanek.com that uses selective authentication.

    D. Create a one-way forest trust from wpanek.com to willpanek.com that uses selective authentication.

24. You are the administrator for your company network. Your network contains an Active Directory forest named willpanek.com. You need to add a new domain named wpanek.com to the forest. What command should you run?

    A. `Install-ADDSForest -DomainType TreeDomain - InstallDNS:$true -NewDomainName wpanek.com -ParentDomainName willpanek.com`

    B. `Install-ADDSForest -DomainType ChildDomain - InstallDNS:$true -NewDomainName wpanek.com -ParentDomainName willpanek.com`

   C. `Install-ADDSDomain -DomainType TreeDomain -InstallDNS:$true`
      `-NewDomainName wpanek.com -ParentDomainName willpanek.com`

   D. `Install-ADDSDomain -DomainType ChildDomain -InstallDNS:$true`
      `-NewDomainName wpanek.com -ParentDomainName willpanek.com`

25. You are the administrator for your company network. Your network contains an Active Directory forest. The company is planning to hire 500 temporary employees for a project that will last 60 days. You create a new user account for each employee. An Organizational Unit (OU) named TempsOU contains the user accounts for these temporary employees. You need to prevent the new users from accessing any of the resources in the domain after 60 days. What should you do?

   A. Create a group that contains all of the users in the TempsOU. Create a Password Setting Object (PSO) for the new group.

   B. Create a Group Policy Object (GPO) and link the GPO to the TempsOU. Modify the Password Policy settings of the GPO.

   C. Run the `Get-ADOrganizationalUnit` cmdlet and pipe the output to the `Set-Date` cmdlet.

   D. Run the `Get-ADUser` cmdlet and pipe the output to the `Set-ADUser` cmdlet.

26. You are the administrator for your company network. You have a Windows Server 2016 server named WAP1 that has the Windows Application Proxy (WAP) role service installed. You need to publish Microsoft Exchange ActiveSync services by using the Publish New Application Wizard. The ActiveSync services must use preauthentication. How should you configure WAP1's preauthentication method and preauthentication type?

   A. Configure Active Directory Federation Services (AD FS) preauthentication method and HTTP Basic preauthentication type.

   B. Configure Pass-Through preauthentication method and Web/MS-OFBA preauthentication type.

   C. Configure Active Directory Federation Services (AD FS) preauthentication method and Oath2 preauthentication type.

   D. Configure Pass-Through preauthentication method and HTTP Basic preauthentication type.

27. You are the administrator for your company network. You have a Windows Server 2016 server named WAP1 that has the Web Application Proxy (WAP) role service installed. You publish an application named App1 by using the WAP. You need to change the URL that users use to connect to App1 when they work remotely. What command should you run?

   A. `Set-WebApplicationProxyApplication -ID 874A4543-77A3-1E6D-1163E7419AC1`
      `-ExternalURL https://willpanek.com/`

   B. `Set-WebApplicationProxyConfiguration -ID 874A4543-77A3-1E6D-1163E7419AC1`
      `-ADFSURL https://willpanek.com/`

   C. `Set-WebApplicationProxy -ID 874A4543-77A3-1E6D-1163E7419AC1`
      `-InternalURL https://willpanek.com/`

   D. `Set-WebApplicationProxySslCertificate -ID 874A4543-77A3-1E6D-1163E7419AC1`
      `-BackendServerURL https://willpanek.com/`

28. You are the administrator for your company network. You have a Windows Server 2016 server named WAP1. You need to configure the server as a Web Application Proxy (WAP). Which server role or role service should you install?

   A. Active Directory Federation Services (AD FS)

   B. DirectAccess and VPN (RAS)

   C. Remote Access

   D. Web Server (IIS)

29. You are the administrator for your company network. Your network contains an Active Directory forest. Your company has a custom application named App1. App1 uses an Active Directory Lightweight Directory Services (AD LDS) server named ADLDS1 to authenticate users. You have a Windows Server 2016 member server named MbrSrv2. You install the Active Directory Federation Services (AD FS) server role on MbrSrv2 and create an AD FS farm. You need to configure AD FS to authenticate users from the AD LDS server. What cmdlets should you run?

   A. Run the `Add-AdfsRelyingPartyTrust` and `Set-AdfsEndpoint` cmdlets.

   B. Run the `Set-AdfsEndpoint` and the `Enable-AdfsRelyingPartyTrust` cmdlets.

   C. Run the `Enable-AdfsRelyingPartyTrust` and `New-AdfsLdapServerConnection` cmdlets.

   D. Run the `New-AdfsLdapServerConnection` and `Add-AdfsLocalClaimsProviderTrust` cmdlets.

30. You are the administrator for your company network. The network contains an Active Directory domain. The domain contains an Active Directory Federation Services (AD FS) server named ADFS1. On a standalone server, named Svr2, you install and configure the Web Application Proxy (WAP). You have an internal web application named WebApp1. AD FS has a relying party trust for WebApp1. You need to provide external users with access to WebApp1. You want to publish WebApp1 if authentication to WebApp1 must use AD FS preauthentication. What tool should you use?

   A. AD FS Management on ADFS1

   B. AD FS Management on Svr2

   C. Remote Access Management on ADFS1

   D. Remote Access Management on Svr2

31. You are the administrator for your company network. You have an internal web server that hosts websites. The websites use HTTP and HTTPS. You deploy a Web Application Proxy (WAP) to your perimeter network. You need to ensure that users from the Internet can access the websites by using HTTPS only. You want Internet access to the websites to use the WAP. What actions should you perform? (Choose two.)

   A. Create DNS entries that point to the private IP address of the web server on the external DNS name servers.

   B. Create DNS entries that point to the public IP address of the Web Application Proxy on the external DNS name servers.

   C. Enable HTTP Redirect on the Web Application Proxy server from the web server.

   D. Publish the websites from the Remote Access Management console. Configure pass-through authentication and select Enable HTTP to HTTPS redirection.

   E. Using Oauth2, configure the Web Application Proxy to perform preauthentication.

32. You are the administrator for your company network. Your network contains an Active Directory domain. The domain contains an Active Directory Federation Services (AD FS) server named ADFS1, a Web Application Proxy (WAP) server named WAP1, and a web server named Web1. You need to publish a website on Web1 by using the WAP. Users will authenticate by using OAuth2 preauthentication. What should you do first?

   A. On ADFS1, add a claims provider trust.

   B. On ADFS1, enable an endpoint.

   C. On Web1, add site bindings.

   D. On Web1, add handler mappings.

33. You are the administrator for your company network. The network contains an Active Directory domain. A previous administrator implemented a Proof of Concept installation of Active Directory Rights Management Services (AD RMS) on a server named Svr1. After the Proof of Concept was complete the AD RMS server role was removed. You attempt to deploy AD RMS. During the configuration you receive an error message indicating that an existing AD RMS Service Connection Point (SCP) was found. You need to ensure that clients will only attempt to establish connections to the new AD RMS deployment. What should you do?

   A. Remove the computer object for Srv1 from Active Directory.

   B. Remove the records for Svr1 from DNS.

   C. Increase the priority of the DNS records for the new deployment of AD RMS from DNS.

   D. Remove the Service Connection Point (SCP) from Active Directory.

34. You are the administrator for your company network. You need to ensure that clients check at least every 60 minutes to see whether a certificate has been revoked. Which of the following should you configure to accomplish this goal?

   A. Certificate templates

   B. CRL publication interval

   C. Delta CRL publication interval

   D. Key recovery agent

35. You are the administrator for your company network. You have an Enterprise Certification Authority (CA) named Server1. Recovery agents are configured for Server1. You duplicate the User certificate template and name it UserTemplate. You plan to issue the certificates based on UserTemplate to provide users with the ability to encrypt email messages and files. You need to ensure that the recovery agents can access any user-encrypted files and email messages if the users lose their certificates. What should you do?

   A. Based on a Key Recovery Agent certificate, issue a certificate.

   B. For UserTemplate, modify the Request Handling settings.

   C. For Server1, modify the Recovery Agents settings.

   D. On Server1, configure the Key Recovery Agent template as a certificate template to issue.

36. You are the administrator for your company network. Your network contains an Active Directory forest. The forest contains an Active Directory Federation Services (AD FS) farm. You install Windows Server 2016 on a server named Server1. You need to configure Server1 as a node in the federation server farm. What cmdlets should you run?

   A. `Install-AdfsFarm` and `New-AdfsOrganization`

   B. `Install-AdfsFarm` and `Set-AdfsProperties`

   C. `Install-Package` and `Set-AdfsFarmInformation`

   D. `Install-WindowsFeature` and `Install-AdfsFarm`

37. You are the administrator for your company network. You have an Enterprise Certification Authority (CA) named Server1 that has a certificate template named CertTemp that is based on a User certificate template. Domain users are configured to auto-enroll CertTemp. A user, Sue, has an email address defined in Active Directory, while a user named Scott does not. You discover that Sue was issued a certificate based on the template automatically. A request by Scott for a certificate based on the template fails. You need to ensure that all users can auto-enroll for certificates based on the template. What setting should you configure from the properties on the CertTemp certificate template?

   A. Cryptography

   B. Issuance Requirements

   C. Request Handling

   D. Subject Name

38. You are the administrator for your company network. You and a coworker are discussing Active Directory Federation Services (AD FS). You want to configure AD FS. What server should you deploy on a perimeter network?

   A. Claims-provider server

   B. Federation server

   C. Relying Party server

   D. Web application proxy

39. You are the administrator for your company network. You have users that access web applications by using HTTPS. The web applications are located on the servers in your perimeter network. The servers use certificates obtained from an enterprise root Certification Authority (CA). The certificates are generated by using a custom template named TempWebApps. The Certificate Revocation List (CRL) is published to Active Directory. When users attempt to access the web applications from the Internet, they report that they receive a revocation warning message in their web browsers. The users do not receive the message when they access the web applications from the intranet. You need to ensure that the warning message is not generated when the users attempt to access the web applications from the Internet. What should you do?

- **A.** Install the Certificate Enrollment Web Service role service on a server in the perimeter network.
- **B.** Install the Web Application Proxy (WAP) role service, then create a publishing point for the CA on a server in the perimeter network.
- **C.** Modify the CRL distribution point and then reissue the certificates used by the web application servers.
- **D.** Modify the TempWebApps certificate template, then issue the certificates used by the web application servers.

40. You are the administrator for your company network. The network contains an Active Directory domain. You plan to deploy a new Active Directory Rights Management Services (AD RMS) cluster on a server named Svr1. You need to create the AD RMS service account. The solution must use the principle of least privilege. What should you do?

- **A.** Create a domain user account and add the account to the Account Operators group in the domain.
- **B.** Create a domain user account and add the account to the Domain Users group in the domain.
- **C.** Create a domain user account and add the account to the Administrators group on Svr1.
- **D.** Create a local user account and add the account to the Administrators group on Svr1.

41. You are the administrator for your company network. Your network contains an enterprise root Certification Authority (CA) named Server1. Multiple computers on the network successfully enroll for certificates that will expire in one year. The certificates are based on a template named CertTemp. The template uses schema version 2. You need to ensure that new certificates based on CertTemp are valid for three years. What should you do?

- **A.** For the certificate template, modify the Validity period.
- **B.** For the root CA certificate, modify the Validity period.
- **C.** Instruct users to request certificates by running the certreq.exe command.
- **D.** Instruct users to request certificates by using the Certificates console.

42. You are the administrator for your company network. Your network contains an Active Directory domain. The domain contains an enterprise Certification Authority (CA) named Server1. You duplicate the computer certificate template and you name the template Temp-Computers. You need to ensure that all of the certificates issued based on TempComputers have a key size of 4,096 bits. What should you do?

   A. From the properties of Server1, modify the Security settings.

   B. From the properties of Server1, modify the Request Handling settings.

   C. From the properties of the computer template, modify the Key Attestation settings.

   D. From the properties of TempComputers, modify the Cryptography settings.

43. You are the administrator for your company network. You have a Windows Server 2016 server named ServerA. A Microsoft Azure Backup of ServerA is created automatically every day. You rename ServerA to Server1. You discover that backups are no longer created in Azure. What should you do if you need to back up the server to Azure?

   A. From the Azure Management Portal, upload the Server1 certificate as a management certificate.

   B. From the Azure Management Portal, modify the configuration on the backup vault.

   C. On Server1, run the Add-WBBackupTarget cmdlet.

   D. On Server1, run the Start-OBRegistration cmdlet.

44. You are the administrator for your company network. You deploy a new certification Authority (CA) to a Windows Server 2016 server named Server1. You need to configure the CA to support recovery of certificates on Server1. What should you do?

   A. Configure the Key Recovery Agent template as a certificate template to issue.

   B. Modify the extensions of the OCSP Response Signing template.

   C. Modify the Recovery Agents settings from the properties of the CA.

   D. Assign the Request Certificates permission to the user account that will be responsible for recovering certificates.

45. You are the administrator for your company network. The network contains an Active Directory domain. You deploy a standalone root Certification Authority (CA) named Server1. You need to auto-enroll domain computers for certificates by using a custom certificate template. What should you do first?

   A. Install an enterprise subordinate certificate authority.

   B. Install a standalone subordinate certificate authority.

   C. Modify the Policy Module for Server1.

   D. Modify the Exit Module for Server1.

46. You are the administrator for your company network. Your network contains an Active Directory domain. The domain contains a Windows Server 2016 server named ServerA that has the Active Directory Certificate Services (AD CS) server role installed and is configured to support key archival and recovery. You create a new Active Directory group named GroupA. You need to ensure that the members of GroupA can request a Key Recovery Agent certificate. Which permissions should you assign to GroupA? (Choose all that apply.)

A. Auto-Enroll

B. Enroll

C. Full Control

D. Read

E. Write

47. You are the administrator for your company network. Your network contains an Active Directory domain. The domain contains a Windows Server 2016 server named Server1 that has the Active Directory Certificate Services (AD CS) server role installed and is configured to support key archival and recovery. You need to ensure that a user named Sue can decrypt private keys archived in the AD CS database. You need to prevent Sue from retrieving the private keys from the AD CS database. What should you do?

A. Assign Sue the Issue and Manage Certificates permission to Server1.

B. Assign Sue the Manage Certificate Authority (CA) permission to Server1.

C. Assign Sue the Read permission and the Write permission to all certificate templates.

D. Provide Sue with access to a Key Recovery Agent certificate and a private key.

48. You are the administrator for your company network. Your network contains an Active Directory domain. The domain contains an enterprise Certification Authority (CA) named Server1. You have a test environment that is isolated from the corporate network and the Internet. You deploy a web server to the test environment. On Server1, you duplicate the Web Server template and you name the template WebServer_Test. You need to request a certificate that does not contain the revocation information of Server1 for the web server. What should you do first?

A. From the properties of Server1, allow certificates to be published to the file system.

B. From the properties of Server1, select Restrict enrollment agents and then add WebServer_Test to the restricted enrollment agent.

C. From the properties of WebServer_Test, set the Compatibility setting of Server1 to Windows Server 2016.

D. From the properties of WebServer_Test, assign the Enroll permission to the guest account.

49. You are the administrator for your company network. You and a coworker are discussing adding a certificate template to the Certificate Authority (CA). You need to add a certificate template using PowerShell. What cmdlet should you use?

A. Add-CATemplate

B. Add-CSTemplate

C. Get-CSTemplate

D. New-Template

50. You are the administrator for your company network. You and a coworker are discussing Active Directory Right Management Services (AD RMS). You know that there are different database servers that are used by AD RMS. Which database server type contains information about users, identifiers (such as email addresses), security IDs, group membership, and alternate identifiers?

A. Configuration Database

B. Directory Services Database

C. Logging Database

D. Remote Database

Appendix

Answers to Practice Tests

Chapter 1: Installing Windows Servers in Host and Compute Environments

1. B. Windows Server 2016 Essentials is ideal for small businesses that have as many as 25 users and 50 devices. Windows Server 2016 Essentials has a simpler interface than the other versions and preconfigured connectivity to cloud-based services, but no virtualization rights.

2. C. Windows Server 2016 has introduced a new type of server installation called Nano Server. Nano Server allows an administrator to remotely administer the server operating system. It was primarily designed and optimized for private clouds and datacenters. Nano Server is very similar to Server Core, but the Nano Server operating system uses significantly less hard drive space, has no local logon capability, and supports only 64-bit applications and tools.

3. B. The Remote Access server role provides connectivity through DirectAccess, VPN, and Web Application Proxy. DirectAccess provides an Always On and Always Managed experience. Remote Access provides VPN access, including site-to-site connectivity.

4. D. To log a memory event based on a data collector, you will use the trace type of collector. Counter type is used to record data for a period of time.

5. D. The correct answer is `Cscript C:\windows\system32\slmgr.vbs -ato`. Cscript will start a script so that it runs in a command-line environment. The `-ato` command prompts Windows to try to do an online activation.

6. B. You can install the Internet Information Services (IIS) server role on Nano Server by using the `-Packages` parameter with `Microsoft-NanoServer-IIS-Package`.

7. D. Windows Server 2016 offers a number of ways to perform installations. All of the above are different ways to perform installations.

8. D. This is an example of using Windows PowerShell to create a Nano Server image named Nano1 on the `abc.com` domain that will be used as a virtualization host.

9. C. The `Format-Volume` cmdlet formats one or more existing volumes or a new volume on an existing partition, and the `-FileSystem` switch specifies the filesystem with which to format the volume. The acceptable values for this parameter are NTFS, ReFS, exFAT, FAT32, and FAT.

10. D. A Generation 1 VM cannot boot from a `.vhdx` disk; only a Generation 2 VM can boot from a `.vhdx` disk.

11. A. The `Copy-Item` cmdlet copies an item from one location to another location in the same namespace. For instance, it can copy a file to a folder, but it cannot copy a file to a certificate drive.

12. A. When you run a data collector set, the data that is collected for performance counters is stored to a log file in the location that was defined when the data collector set was created. In Windows Performance Monitor, you can view log files to see a visual representation of performance counter data.

13. A and E. The correct answer is to share the folder and configure the DFSN target. `New-DfsnFolderTarget` adds a target to a DFS namespace folder, whereas `New-SmbShare` creates an SMB share.

14. D. By default, the Windows firewall will be running on the WSUS server. When you installed WSUS, it automatically configured two inbound rules called "WSUS" that allow both TCP ports, 8530 and 8531.

15. A. The only way to change between Server Core and the Desktop Experience is to reinstall the server. The ability to convert by running a PowerShell command from Server Core to Desktop Experience is no longer available.

16. B. Microsoft recommends that to upgrade Windows Server 2012 or Windows Server 2012 R2 Standard with GUI, you use Windows Server 2016 Standard (Desktop Experience).

17. B. The `Get-Package` PowerShell cmdlet will return a list of all software packages that have been installed.

18. D. Nano Server cannot run Active Directory Domain Services, Network Policy and Access Services, or DHCP Server. The recommended role is IIS Web Server. The Web Server (IIS) role in Windows Server 2016 allows an administrator to set up a secure, easy-to-manage, modular, and extensible platform for reliably hosting websites, services, and applications.

19. C. Unattended installations utilize an answer file called `Autounattend.xml` to provide configuration information during the installation process. The answer file allows questions to be answered without user interaction.

20. A, C, and F. You would first want to mount `Disk1.vhdx`, then run the `bootcfg.exe` command, and then restart Server1.

21. D. The `Write-EventLog` cmdlet writes an event to an event log. To write an event to an event log, the event log must exist on the computer and the source must be registered for the event log. The `-EventID` switch specifies the event identifier. This parameter is required.

22. B. The `Resize-IscsiVirtualDisk` cmdlet resizes a virtual disk by either expanding or compacting an existing virtual disk. The `-ComputerName` parameter specifies the computer name, or IP address, of the remote computer, if this cmdlet is run on a remote computer.

23. A and B. Microsoft recommends that if you are using Windows Server 2012 R2, the path you should choose is Windows Server 2016 Standard or Windows Server 2016 Datacenter.

24. B. Windows Defender offers improved security using cloud-based antivirus protection. When enabled, Windows Defender sends information to Microsoft about any problems it finds. This information is then used to gather more information about the problems affecting you and other users. This can be enabled and disabled. The Cloud-Based Protection is also turned on by default, and it gives you "Real-time protection when Windows Defender sends info to Microsoft about potential security threats."

25. C. The `Get-OBPolicy` cmdlet gets the current backup policy that is set for the server, including the details about scheduling backups, files included in the backup, and retention policy.

26. B. The `Start-OBRegistration` cmdlet registers the current computer to the Online Backup Service using the credentials (username and password) created during enrollment.

27. A. Windows Server 2016 Datacenter was designed for organizations that are seeking to migrate to a highly virtualized, private cloud environment. Windows Server 2016 Datacenter has full Windows Server functionality with unlimited virtual instances.

28. A, B, C, and D. All four answers are advantages of using Windows Server 2016. Server Core is a smaller installation of Windows Server and therefore all four answers apply.

29. B. Windows Server 2016 Features On Demand allows an administrator not only to disable a role or feature but also to remove the role's or feature's files completely from the hard disk.

30. C. Windows Server 2016 has a type of domain controller called a Read-Only Domain Controller (RODC). This gives an organization the ability to install a domain controller in an area or location (onsite or offsite) where security may be a concern.

31. D and E. You must import the module for NanoServerImage generation, then use the `New-NanoServerImage` command to create the new image.

32. A, B, F, and G. When Microsoft created Nano Server, they had some very specific ideas of how companies would use this version. For example, Nano Server is a good option for a DNS server, an IIS server, an application server for cloud-based applications, or even a storage machine for file servers.

33. B and D.

    Step 1: `Import-Module`

    Step 2: `New-NanoServerImage`

    The `Import-Module` cmdlet adds modules to the current session. The modules that you import must be installed on the local computer or on a remote computer. The `New-NanoServerImage` cmdlet creates a Nano Server installation image. The `New-NanoServerImage` cmdlet makes a local copy of the necessary files from the installation media and converts the included Nano Server Windows image (.wim) file into a VHD or VHDX image, or reuses the existing .wim file.

34. B. As long as the guest OS can use video GPU cards, the Hyper-V virtual machine must be enabled to use such cards. To do this, you must add the GPU adapter in the settings of the virtual machine.

35. B, F, and G. The `Add-WindowsDriver` cmdlet adds a driver to an offline Windows image. The `Dismount-WindowsImage` cmdlet dismounts a Windows image from the directory it's mapped to. The `Dismount-WindowsImage` cmdlet either saves or discards the changes to a Windows image and then dismounts the image. The `Optimize-WindowsImage` cmdlet configures a Windows image with specified optimizations. It performs specified configurations on an offline image.

36. A, B, and C. Windows Server Backup supports NTFS, ReFS, and FAT32 file systems.

37. D. Microsoft Azure Backup Server is included as a free download with Azure Backup, and it enables cloud backups and disk backups for key Microsoft workloads like SQL,

SharePoint, and Exchange regardless of whether these workloads are running on Hyper-V, VMware, or physical servers.

38. D. Distributed File System Replication (DFSR) staging is a hard drive area that is used for files that need to be replicated from one DFS server to other DFS servers. If the files that you are trying to replicate are larger than your assigned staging area, the replication will fail. When this happens, you must increase the amount of space used in the staging area.

39. B. When an administrator sets up DFS Replication, the replication settings allow you to choose when the replication will take place. If DFS replication is happening during business hours, an administrator can go back into the replication group properties and change when replication will take place.

40. C. To use Windows Server Migration Tools, the feature must be installed on both the source and destination computers.

41. B. Automatic Virtual Machine Activation (AVMA) allows you to install virtual machines on the Windows Server operating system without having to use or manage product keys for each virtual machine.

42. A. Active Directory Certificate Services (AD CS) in Windows Server 2016 is the server role that allows you to build a PKI and provide public key cryptography, digital certificates, and digital signature capabilities for your organization.

43. C. Active Directory Federation Services (AD FS) provides Internet-based clients with a secure identity access solution that works on both Windows and non-Windows operating systems. AD FS gives users the ability to do a Single Sign-On (SSO) and access applications on other networks without needing a secondary password.

44. B. BitLocker is a tool that allows you to encrypt the hard drives of your computers. By encrypting the hard drives, you can provide enhanced protection against data theft or unauthorized exposure of your computers or removable drives that are lost or stolen.

45. B. In the Windows PowerShell session, install Windows Server Migration Tools by using the Windows PowerShell `Install-WindowsFeature` cmdlet.

46. B. To be able to use NIC Teaming, the computer system must have at least one Ethernet adapter. If you want to provide fault protection, an administrator must have a minimum of two Ethernet adapters. One advantage of Windows Server 2016 is that an administrator can set up 32 network adapters in a NIC Team.

47. C. Nano Server has no local logon or GUI capabilities, and it will allow only 64-bit applications and utilities.

48. A and C. Nano Server is available for both Standard and Datacenter editions of Windows Server 2016.

49. E. The first downside to using a Nano Server is that it cannot act as domain controller. Group Policy Objects are also not supported on Nano Servers. Finally, Nano Servers can't be configured to use System Center Configuration Manager, System Center Data Protection Manager, or NIC Teaming, or to be used as proxy servers.

50. C. To configure KMS host systems, you must configure and retrieve Volume Activation information. This is done by using a Software License Manager (referred to as SL Manager) script (`Slmgr.vbs`). The `/ato` switch is used for retail and volume systems editions with a KMS host key or a Multiple Activation Key (MAK) installed. The `/ato` command prompts Windows to try to do an online activation.

51. D. Steps for preparing the WDS server:

1. Make sure that the server meets the requirements for running WDS.
2. Install WDS.
3. Configure and start WDS.
4. Configure the WDS server to respond to client computers (if this was not configured when WDS was installed).

For WDS to work, the server on which you will install WDS must meet the requirements for WDS and be able to access the required network services.

52. B. The Windows Deployment Services (WDS) server must meet several requirements. One is that at least one partition on the server must be formatted as NTFS.

53. B. If you want an easy way to create a Nano Server virtual hard disk (VHD), you can just download Nano Server Image Builder. This software will help you easily create a Nano Server VHD that you can then use to boot up a server with or use in Microsoft's Hyper-V server. Download Nano Server Image Builder at Microsoft's website (`https://www.microsoft.com/en-us/download/details.aspx?id=54065`) by clicking the Download button.

54. B. Key Management Service (KMS) allows your computers to get activated right on your local network without the need to contact Microsoft. To configure KMS host systems, you must configure and retrieve Volume Activation information. This is done by using a Software License Manager (referred to as SL Manager) script (`Slmgr.vbs`). The `/dlv` switch displays the operating system license information.

55. A. To configure KMS host systems, you must configure and retrieve Volume Activation information. This is done by using a Software License Manager (referred to as SL Manager) script (`Slmgr.vbs`). The `/dli` switch allows administrators on the KMS host to view the current KMS activation count.

56. A, B, and C. To run `slmgr.vbs` remotely, administrators must supply additional parameters. They must include the computer name of the target computer as well as a username and password of a user account that has local administrator rights on the target computer.

57. B. For companies running Active Directory, administrators can use ADBA to their advantage when it comes to activation. Active Directory–Based Activation (ADBA) allows administrators to activate computers right through the domain connection.

58. C. Nano Server only supports the Current Branch for Business (CBB) licensing model.

59. A. Windows Server 2016 Nano Server uses the Current Branch for Business (CBB) servicing model. This version of servicing is a more aggressive version, and it was specifically designed with the cloud in mind. As the cloud continues to quickly evolve, the CBB servicing model is meant for that life cycle.

60. D. The /initialize-server switch initializes the configuration of the WDS server.

61. B. One component to which you need to pay attention when using the Windows Deployment Services is the Preboot Execution Environment (PXE) network devices. PXE boot devices are network interface cards (NICs) that can talk to a network without the need for an operating system. As far as creating an image, there is no tool called imgcrt. Microsoft recommends that you use DISM for image creation and management.

62. A, B, C, and D. The following network services must be running on the WDS server or be accessible to the WDS server from another network server:

- TCP/IP installed and configured
- A DHCP server, which is used to assign DHCP addresses to WDS clients
- A DNS server, which is used to locate the Active Directory controller
- Active Directory, which is used to locate WDS servers and WDS clients as well as authorize WDS clients and manage WDS configuration settings and client installation options

63. B. Windows Server 2016 Server Core is a more secure, slimmed-down version of Windows Server. Web versions of Windows Server 2016 are not available. You would use Windows Server 2016 Standard as a web server.

64. D. Windows Server 2016 Essentials is ideal for small businesses that have as many as 25 users and 50 devices. Windows Server 2016 Essentials has a simpler interface than the other versions and preconfigured connectivity to cloud-based services, but no virtualization rights.

65. B. Windows Server 2016 containers allow applications to share the system's kernel with their container and all other containers running on the same host. There are no such things as Windows Full Container or Windows Limited Container.

66. C. The Hyper-V role is Microsoft's virtualization platform. It allows server virtualization.

67. D. The Network Controller provides the point of automation needed for continual configuration, monitoring, and diagnostics of virtual networks, physical networks, network services, network topology, address management, and so on within a datacenter.

68. D. You would use the Sysprep utility. The /generalize option prevents system-specific information from being included in the image.

69. A. The DISM utility with the /get-ImageInfo parameter displays information about images in a WIM or VHD file.

70. D. Windows System Image Manager (Windows SIM) is a graphical utility that can be used to create an answer file. Answer files can be used to automate the installation routine so that no user interaction is required.

71. A. The /unattend option can be used with the Setup.exe command to initiate an unattended installation of Windows Server 2016. You should also specify the location of the answer file to use when using the Setup.exe utility.

72. D. The /reboot option restarts the computer. You can use this option to audit the computer and to verify that the first-run experience operates correctly.

73. B. The /oobe option restarts the computer into Windows Welcome mode. Windows Welcome enables end users to customize their Windows operating system, create user accounts, name the computer, and other tasks. Any settings in the /oobe system configuration passed in an answer file are processed immediately before Windows Welcome starts.

74. D. The setup.exe /unattend:answerfile command will initiate an unattended installation. The /unattend option specifies that you will be using an unattended installation for Windows Server 2016. The answerfile variable points to the custom answer file you will use for installation.

75. B. Once you have a reference computer installed, you can use the System Preparation Tool to prepare the computer to be used with disk imaging. Image Capture Wizard is a utility that can be used to create a disk image after it is prepared using the System Preparation Tool. The image can then be transferred to the destination computer(s).

76. C. When you use the System Preparation Tool to create a disk image, the unique information is stripped out of the installation image. For example, the unique SID that is applied to every computer. Unique information is then generated when the target computer is installed.

77. A. You would need to configure formatting and partitioning information in the Windows PE component of the answer file. The options specified in this configuration pass will occur before the image is copied to the local computer.

78. B. The /generalize option prepares the Windows installation to be imaged. If this option is specified, all unique system information is removed from the Windows installation. The security ID (SID) resets, any system restore points are cleared, and event logs are deleted. The next time the computer starts, a new security ID (SID) is created and the clock for Windows activation resets, if the clock has not already been reset three times.

79. A, B, and D. Microsoft Assessment and Planning (MAP) Toolkit uses multiple utilities like the Windows Management Instrumentation (WMI), the Remote Registry Service, and the Simple Network Management Protocol (SNMP) to obtain inventory information. One advantage of using MAP when determining the need for Windows is that MAP will also determine if any hardware upgrades are needed for a machine or device driver's availability.

80. A and B. Microsoft Assessment and Planning (MAP) generates reports in both Microsoft Excel and Microsoft Word. These reports can provide information in both summary and full detail modes.

81. D. Sysprep is a free utility that comes on all Windows operating systems. By default, the Sysprep utility can be found on Windows Server 2016 operating systems in the \Windows\System32\Sysprep directory.

82. G. Once the image is copied, you should boot the destination computer into the Windows PE. If the computer has been used previously, it may be necessary to reformat the hard drive, which you do by using the Diskpart command in Windows PE.

83. C. The Deployment Image Servicing and Management (DISM.exe) tool is a PowerShell and command-line utility that allows you to manipulate a Windows image. DISM also allows you to prepare a Windows PE image. The /Get-ImageInfo switch will display information about images in a WIM or VHD file.

84. F. There are many advantages to using unattended installations as a method for automating Windows Server 2016 installations:

- Unattended installation saves time and money because users do not have to interactively respond to each installation query.

- It can be configured to provide automated query responses while still selectively allowing users to provide specified input during installations.

- It can be used to install clean copies of Windows Server 2016 or upgrade an existing operating system (providing it is on the list of permitted operating systems) to Windows Server 2016.

- It can be expanded to include installation instructions for applications, additional language support, service packs, and device drivers.

- The physical media for Windows Server 2016 does not need to be distributed to all computers on which it will be installed.

85. C. You can use images to restart the Windows activation clock. The Windows activation clock starts to decrease as soon as Windows starts for the first time. You can restart the Windows activation clock only three times using Sysprep.

Chapter 2: Implement Storage Solutions

1. A, E. The `Remove-PhysicalDisk` cmdlet removes a physical disk from a specified storage pool. The `Set-ResiliencySetting` cmdlet modifies the properties of the specified resiliency setting name.

2. C. The `Redircmp` command is used to redirect the default OU of a newly created object such as a user to another OU.

3. A. The `Set-SRPartnership` command modifies a replication partnership between two replication groups. You can use this cmdlet to add replicated volumes, and you can also change the direction of replication that makes a source volume into a destination volume.

4. C and D. The Windows Server 2016 platform supports two main filesystems: Windows NT File System (NTFS) and Resilient File System (ReFS). Although ReFS was new to Windows Server 2012, NTFS has been around for many years, and NTFS in Windows Server 2016 has been improved for better performance.

5. B. The `Resize-VirtualDisk` cmdlet resizes an existing virtual disk to be larger or smaller. If there is a partition on the virtual disk, then the partition must also be resized in order for the client to have additional space on the disk.

6. C. The `Set-SmbBandwidthLimit` cmdlet adds a Server Message Block (SMB) bandwidth cap for the traffic categories that you specify. SMB bandwidth caps limit the amount of data that the server can send for each traffic category.

7. A. ReFS has the fastest creation times for large, fixed-size VHDX files.

8. B. The `Format-Volume` cmdlet formats one or more existing volumes, or a new volume on an existing partition. This cmdlet returns the object representing the volume that was just formatted, with all properties updated to reflect the format operation. The `Enable-DeDupVolume` cmdlet enables data deduplication on one or more volumes.

9. D. Although the features of the other filesystems will compel most system administrators to use NTFS, additional reasons make using it mandatory. The most important reason is that the Active Directory data store must reside on an NTFS partition.

10. A. The `New-SRPartnership` cmdlet creates a replication partnership between two new or existing replication groups. This cmdlet can create the complete replication topology. It can also tie together separately created replication groups. The `-ReplicationMode` switch specifies the desired mode of replication for this source and destination pair. The acceptable values for this parameter are:

- Synchronous or 1: The synchronous mode requires all writes to commit on the destination server and on the source server, which guarantees data integrity between computers. This is the default value.

- Asynchronous or 2: The asynchronous mode writes to the source server without waiting for the destination server, which allows for replication over high-latency, geographic networks.

11. B. A MBR has a partition table that indicates where the partitions are located on the disk drive, and with this particular partition style, only volumes up to 2 TB (2,048 GB) are supported. A MBR drive can have up to four primary partitions, or it can have three primary partitions and one extended partition that can be divided into unlimited logical drives.

12. A, B, and D.

Step 1: First you will want to create a storage pool. Specify which disks should be included in the storage pool.

Step 2: After creating the storage pool, start creating a virtual disk for the pool you created. When the Storage Pool Wizard finishes, mark the Create A Virtual Disk option to create a virtual disk after this wizard. Select the storage pool to create a virtual disk. When shown in the New Virtual Disk Wizard, select the Storage Layout. Select Parity.

Step 3: After creating the virtual disk, create a volume with the New Volume Wizard. Use the volume you created earlier.

13. D. A mirrored volume duplicates data across two disks. This type of volume is fault tolerant because if one drive fails, the data on the other disk is unaffected.

14. C, E. Data deduplication on volumes must meet the following requirements: The volume must not be a system or boot volume. Deduplication is not supported on operating system volumes. It can be partitioned as a master boot record (MBR) or a GUID Partition Table (GPT), and it must be formatted using the NTFS filesystem. It can reside on shared storage. It can't be smaller than 2 GB or larger than 64 TB in size. It must be exposed to the operating system as nonremovable drives. Remotely mapped drives are not supported. So, that leaves options C and E as acceptable drives to use for deduplication.

15. C. If you want to convert an existing partition from FAT or FAT32 to NTFS, you must to use the convert command-line utility and insert the drive letter where d is in the command.

16. B. The iscsicli removeisnsserver command removes the host from the iSNS server. The iscsicli addisnsserver command manually registers the host server to an iSNS server. Refreshisnsserver refreshes the list of available servers. Listisnsservers lists the available iSNS servers.

17. A. The iscsicli addisnsserver command manually registers the host server to an iSNS server. Refreshisnsserver refreshes the list of available servers. Removeisnsserver removes the host from the iSNS server. Listisnsservers lists the available iSNS servers.

18. B and D. Shared folder permissions apply only across the network (remotely) and can only be placed on folders. NTFS permissions can apply locally and remotely, and NTFS can be placed on files or folders.

19. C. The iSCSI default port is TCP 3260. Port 21 is used for FTP. Port 1433 is used for Microsoft SQL, and port 3389 is used for RDP.

20. A. Permissions are additive among themselves. This means you get the highest level of permissions. But when the two permissions meet, the most restrictive set of permission applies. In this question, the NTFS side would be Full Control (this would be the local permission) and the shared permission would be Deny. But when the two permissions meet, the most restrictive, Deny, would apply.

21. D. User1 is a member of both the Everyone group and the Marketing group and must access C:\Sales from across the network. When accessing a file locally, you combine the NTFS permissions granted to your account either directly or by way of group membership. The "least" restrictive permission is then the permission that applies. In this question, the NTFS permission is the least restrictive of Read/Execute and Modify—so Modify is the effective permission.

22. A, C, and D. Fsutil quota manages disk quotas on NTFS volumes to provide more precise control of network-based storage. The violations switch searches the system and application logs and displays a message to indicate that quota violations have been detected or that a user has reached a quota threshold or quota limit.

23. A and B. A spanned volume is a dynamic volume consisting of disk space on more than one physical disk. If a simple volume is not a system volume or boot volume, you can extend it across additional disks to create a spanned volume, or you can create a spanned volume in unallocated space on a dynamic disk. A GPT disk uses the GUID partition table (GPT) disk partitioning system.

24. A. You must enable the Remote Event Log Management exception in the Windows Firewall settings on the remote computer that you want to connect to.

25. C. The Disk Management utility allows you to set up and create new hard drive volumes. Disk Management can be accessed directly or through Computer Management.

26. A. The Microsoft Windows Performance Monitor is a tool that administrators can use to examine how programs running on their computers affect the computer's performance. The tool can be used in real time and also be used to collect information in a log to analyze the data at a later time. With Performance Monitor, you can set up counter logs and alerts.

27. B. File History allows for easy automated backups of data and works with a number of devices on which data can be stored. File History continuously protects your personal files stored in libraries, desktop, favorites, and contacts folders. It periodically (every hour by default) scans the filesystem for changes and copies changed files to another location.

28. C. A provisioning package (.ppkg) is a container for a collection of configuration settings. An administrator can create provisioning packages that let them quickly and efficiently configure a device without having to install a new image.

29. G. Diskpart is a command-line utility that configures and manages disks, volumes, and partitions on the host computer. It can also be used to script many of the storage management commands.

30. B. BCDBoot is a command-line tool used to configure the boot files on a PC or device to run the Windows operating system. It enables you to quickly set up a system partition or repair the boot environment located on the system partition. The system partition is set up by copying a simple set of Boot Configuration Data (BCD) files to an existing empty partition.

31. C. A Virtual Hard Disk (VHD) is a file format that represents a virtual disk drive. A VHD can be used to store virtual disk data in files that can be easily transferred from one computer to another. It contains what is found on physical HDDs, such as the disk partition and filesystem. Once they are attached, you can treat them like physical disks and use them to store data. To attach the VHD, you use the Computer Management console.

32. E. There are many advantages to using NTFS. Compression, encryption, quotas, and security are just a few of them.

33. B. The convert command is the command-line utility that allows a FAT or FAT32 partition to be upgraded to NTFS. You can also use Disk Management to convert the disk.

34. D. In this question we have a fixed disk, so you would need to "convert" that first to Dynamic to be able to "compact" it later.

35. D. You cannot modify the cache size, but you can specify it at the time that you create a new virtual hard disk. So, in order to do so, you have to delete the virtual disk and then run the New-VirtualDisk PowerShell cmdlet.

36. C. Storage Spaces can combine multiple hard drives into a single virtual drive. To create a Storage Space, you need to connect two or more internal or external drives to the computer to create a storage pool. When the drive begins to fill up and nears the physical limit, Windows will display a notification prompting you to add additional physical Storage Space. Selecting the Parity resiliency type allows Windows to store parity information with the data, thereby protecting you from a single drive failure.

37. D. iSCSI is an industry standard protocol that allows sharing block storage over the Ethernet. The server that shares the storage is called the iSCSI target. The server (machine) that consumes the storage is called the iSCSI initiator.

The target is an object that allows the iSCSI initiator to make a connection. The target keeps track of the initiators that are allowed to be connected to it. The target also keeps track of the iSCSI virtual disks that are associated with it. Once the initiator establishes the connection to the target, all the iSCSI virtual disks associated with the target will be accessible by the initiator.

The iSCSI target server is the server that runs the iSCSI target. It is also the iSCSI Target role name in Windows Server 2016.

38. D. The default port for RDP is port 3389. Port 21 is used for FTP. Port 1433 is used for Microsoft SQL, and iSCSI uses port 3260.

39. B. Permissions are additive among themselves. This means you get the highest level of permissions. But when the two permissions meet, the most restrictive set of permission applies. In this question, the NTFS side would be Read (this would be the local permission) and the shared permission would be Deny. So, when the two permissions meet, the most restrictive, Deny, would apply.

40. D. One of the issues that IT members have had to face over the years is the problem of rapidly growing data sizes. As we continue to rely more and more on computers, our data continues to get larger and larger. This is where ReFS can help an IT department. ReFS was designed specifically with the issues of scalability and performance in mind.

41. C. To restrict the amount of disk space used by users on the network, system administrators can establish disk quotas. By default, Windows Server 2016 supports disk quota restrictions at the volume level. That is, you can restrict the amount of Storage Space that a specific user uses on a single disk volume.

42. D. System administrators can use the Remote Storage features supported by NTFS to offload seldom-used data automatically to a backup system or other devices. The files, however, remain available to users. If a user requests an archived file, Windows Server 2016 can automatically restore the file from a remote storage device and make it available.

43. A. The Active Directory data store must reside on an NTFS partition. Therefore, before you begin installing Active Directory, make sure you have at least one NTFS partition available.

44. A and C. Windows Server 2016 supports two types of disk configurations: basic and dynamic. Basic disks are divided into partitions and can be used with previous versions of Windows. Dynamic disks provide features that basic disks do not, such as the ability to create volumes that span multiple disks (spanned and striped volumes) and the ability to create fault-tolerant volumes (mirrored and RAID-5 volumes).

45. D. The convert command is the command-line utility that allows a FAT or FAT32 partition to be upgraded to NTFS. You can also use Disk Management to convert the disk. Since you want to implement RAID, you must convert the basic disks to dynamic disks.

46. B. A spanned volume is a simple volume that spans multiple disks, with a maximum of 32. Use a spanned volume if the volume needs are too great for a single disk.

47. D. A mirrored volume duplicates data across two disks. This type of volume is fault tolerant because if one drive fails, the data on the other disk is unaffected.

48. E. A RAID-5 volume stores data in stripes across three or more disks. This type of volume is fault tolerant because if a drive fails, the data can be re-created from the parity off the remaining disk drives. Operating system files and boot files cannot reside on the RAID-5 disks.

49. A, B, and F. Windows Server 2016 supports three types of RAID technology: RAID-0, RAID-1, and RAID-5.

50. A. RAID-0 (Disk Striping). Disk striping is using two or more volumes on independent disks created as a single striped set. RAID-0 does not offer the ability to maintain data integrity during a single disk failure. In other words, RAID-0 is not fault tolerant; a single disk event will cause the entire striped set to be lost, and it will have to be re-created through some type of recovery process, such as a tape backup.

51. B. Disk mirroring is two logical volumes on two separate identical disks created as a duplicate disk set. Data is written on two disks at the same time; that way, in the event of a disk failure, data integrity is maintained and available. So, two disks at minimum are needed.

52. C. Mount points are used to surpass the limitation of 26 drive letters and to join two volumes into a folder on a separate physical disk drive. A mount point allows you to configure a volume to be accessed from a folder on another existing disk. A mount point folder can be assigned to a drive instead of using a drive letter, and it can be used on basic or dynamic volumes that are formatted with NTFS.

53. A. In a failover configuration, there is no load balancing. There is a primary path that is established for all requests and subsequent standby paths. If the primary path fails, one of the standby paths will be used.

54. C. In a round-robin configuration, all available paths will be active and will be used to distribute I/O in a balanced round-robin fashion.

55. E. In a dynamic least queue depth configuration, I/O will route to the path with the fewest number of outstanding requests.

56. A. Internet Small Computer System Interface (iSCSI) is an interconnect protocol used to establish and manage a connection between a computer (initiator) and a storage device (target). iSCSI was developed to allow block-level access to a storage device over a network.

57. B. The concept of a Network Attached Storage (NAS) solution is that it is a low-cost device for storing data and serving files through the use of an Ethernet LAN connection. A NAS device accesses data at the file level via a communication protocol such as NFS, CIFS, or even HTTP, which is different from iSCSI or FC (Fibre Channel) storage devices that access the data at the block level. NAS devices are best used in file-storing applications, and they do not require a storage expert to install and maintain the device. In most cases, the only setup that is required is an IP address and an Ethernet connection.

58. A, C, and D. Windows Server 2016 uses the Disk Management snap-in, Diskpart, and DiskRAID. The Disk Management snap-in is an application that allows you to configure and manage the disk drives on the host computer. Diskpart is a command-line utility that configures and manages disks, volumes, and partitions on the host computer. DiskRAID is a scriptable command-line utility that configures and manages hardware RAID storage systems. However, at least one VDS hardware provider must be installed for DiskRAID to be functional.

59. B. `Diskpart /compact` attempts to reduce the physical size of the file.

60. A. If you would like to install and use DCB through PowerShell, you need to complete the following steps:

1. Click the Start button, then right-click Windows PowerShell ➤ More ➤ Run As Administrator.

2. In the Windows PowerShell console, type the following command and press the Enter key:

`Install-WindowsFeature -name data-center-bridging`

61. D. `Get-SmbConnection` retrieves the connections established from the SMB client to the SMB servers.

62. B. `Set-SmbShare` modifies the properties of the SMB share.

63. A. The one advantage of SMB is that it doesn't matter what network protocol you are using (such as TCP/IP); SMB will run on top of the network protocol that is being used on your infrastructure.

64. A and B. If files are encrypted using the Encrypting File System (EFS) and an administrator has to unencrypt the files, there are two ways to do this. First, the administrator can log in using the user's account (the account that encrypted the files) and unencrypt the files. Second, the administrator can become a recovery agent and manually unencrypt the files.

Note: If EFS is used, it is best not to delete users immediately when they leave a company. Administrators have the ability to recover encrypted files, but it is much easier to gain access to the user's encrypted files by logging in as the user who left the company and unchecking the encryption box.

65. A. The default security permission for Users = Read on new folders or shares.

66. A. Permissions are additive among themselves. This means you get the highest level of permissions. But when the two permissions meet, the most restrictive set of permission applies. In this question, the NTFS side would be Full Control (this would be the local permission) and the shared permission is Read. Therefore, the shared folder permission for Sales will need to be changed to Change so that Matt can modify the document.

67. C. NTFS security is additive. In this question Matt is a member of Sales, R&D, and HR. Sales has Read permission, R&D has Modify permission, and HR has Full Control. Since NTFS security is additive, his overall effective NTFS permission will be Full Control.

68. D. NTFS security is additive. In this question Lisa is a member of Sales, R&D, and HR. Sales has Read permission, R&D has Modify permission, and HR has Deny. Since NTFS security is additive, her overall effective NTFS permission will be Deny. Even though NTFS security is additive, the Deny permission overrides all other group settings.

69. C. The default shared permission for Administrators = Full Control. The shared permissions going from lowest to highest are Read, Change, Full Control, and Deny.

70. C. Disk quotas give administrators the ability to limit how much Storage Space a user can have on a hard drive. Disk quotas are an advantage of using NTFS over FAT32. If you decide to use FAT32 on a volume or partition, quotas will not be available. You can set up disk quotas based on volume or on users.

71. D. Quota templates are predefined ways to set up quotas. Templates allow you to set up disk quotas without needing to create a disk quota from scratch.

72. A. Tiered Storage is a feature in Windows Server 2016 that gives administrators the ability to use *both* solid state drives (SSDs) and conventional hard disk drives (HDDs) in the same storage pool.

73. B. To edit the boot options in the BCD store, use the bcdedit utility, which can be launched only from a command prompt.

74. C. Data deduplication involves finding and removing duplicate data within the company network without compromising its integrity. Data deduplication allows redundant copies of data chunks and then it references those multiple copies into a single copy. The data is first compressed and then configured into a filesystem container in the System Volume Information folder.

75. C. To enable data deduplication, you enable a volume for deduplication and then the data is automatically optimized.

76. A, B, C, and D. The correct answer is all of them. With optimized files, the volume will contain files that are optimized, and that means that these files will have pointers to map the data to their respective areas of the chunk store. With unoptimized files, some files will not meet the standards for data duplication. These files will remain as unoptimized files. For example, encrypted files are not eligible to be optimized. The chunk store is the location where the data duplicated files will be stored and optimized. Finally, because data files are optimized and require less space, the volume will have additional free space that the administrator can use.

77. D. The Encrypting File System (EFS) is a component of the NTFS file system on Windows. EFS enables transparent encryption and decryption of files by using cryptographic algorithms. Any individual or program that doesn't possess the appropriate cryptographic key cannot read the encrypted data.

78. A. FTP uses port 21. Port 1433 is used for Microsoft SQL. The iSCSI default port is TCP 3260. Port 3389 is used for RDP.

79. C. Permissions are additive among themselves. This means you get the highest level of permissions. But when the two permissions meet, the most restrictive set of permission applies. In this question, the NTFS side would be Modify (this would be the local permission) and the shared permission would be Full Control. But when the two permissions meet, the most restrictive, Modify, would apply.

80. A. A simple volume uses only one disk or a portion of a disk. When creating simple volumes, keep these points in mind:

- If you have only one dynamic disk, you can create only simple volumes.
- You can increase the size of a simple volume to include unallocated space on the same disk or on a different disk. The volume must be unformatted or formatted by using NTFS. You can increase the size of a simple volume in two ways:
    - By extending the simple volume on the same disk. The volume remains a simple volume, and you can still mirror it.
    - By extending a simple volume to include unallocated space on other disks on the same computer. This creates a spanned volume.

Note: If the simple volume is the system volume or the boot volume, you cannot extend it.

81. B. Failback is similar to failover in that it has primary and standby paths. However, with failback you designate a preferred path that will handle all process requests until it fails, after which the standby path will become active until the primary reestablishes a connection and automatically regains control.

82. C. By using mounted drives, system administrators can map a local disk drive to an NTFS directory name. This helps them organize disk space on servers and increase manageability.

83. A. The Disk Management utility shows you the logical and physical disks that are currently configured on your system. Note that information about the size of each partition is also displayed in the Capacity column within Disk Management.

84. A and D. Once a disk drive has been physically installed, it must be initialized by selecting the type of partition. Different types of partition styles are used to initialize disks: Master Boot Record (MBR) and GUID Partition Table (GPT).

85. C. When a disk is initialized, it is automatically created as a basic disk, but when a new fault-tolerant (RAID) volume set is created, the disks in the set are converted to dynamic disks. Fault-tolerance features and the ability to modify disks without having to reboot the server are what distinguish dynamic disks from basic disks.

Chapter 3: Implement Hyper-V

1. D. The `Optimize-VHD` cmdlet allows an administrator to optimize the allocation of space in virtual hard disk files, except for fixed virtual hard disks. The `Compact` operation optimizes the files. It reclaims unused blocks and rearranges them to be more efficiently packed, which reduces the size of a virtual hard disk file.

2. C. The `Set-VMProcessor` cmdlet allows an administrator to configure the processors of a virtual machine. While the virtual machine is in the OFF state, run the `Set-VMProcessor` cmdlet on the physical Hyper-V host. This enables nested virtualization for the virtual machine.

3. C. The `Set-VMSwitch` cmdlet allows an administrator to configure a virtual switch. Configuring a virtual switch between VM1 and VM2 will prevent them from communicating with Server1.

4. A. The `Get-ShieldedVMProvisioningStatus` cmdlet allows you to view the provisioning status of a shielded virtual machine.

5. B. The `Set-VMNetworkAdapter` cmdlet allows an administrator to configure features of the virtual network adapter in a virtual machine or the management operating system.

6. A and C. To boot a virtual machine from the network, it must be a Generation 2 VM, or a Generation 1 VM connected to a legacy network adapter. Your choice to create a Generation 1 or Generation 2 virtual machine depends on which guest operating system you want to install and the boot method you want to use to deploy the virtual machine. A virtual machine created with Generation 1 supports legacy drivers and uses Hyper-V BIOS-based architecture. Hyper-V BIOS-based virtual machines can only initialize IDE controllers for operating systems to initialize a filesystem. Alternatively, a virtual machine created with Generation 2 supports UEFI-based architecture, in which a subset of Integration Service components has been included to allow SCSI controllers to initialize before the operating system starts loading.

7. F. The `Set-VMProcessor` cmdlet allows an administrator to configure the processors of a virtual machine. While the virtual machine is in the OFF state, run the `Set-VMProcessor` cmdlet on the physical Hyper-V host. This enables nested virtualization for the virtual machine.

8. G. The first thing you need to do is install the Host Guardian feature on the new server by running the `Install-WindowsFeature` cmdlet.

9. C. The `Set-VHD` cmdlet sets the properties associated with a virtual hard disk. The `Set-VHD` cmdlet sets the `ParentPath` or `PhysicalSectorSizeBytes` properties of a virtual hard disk. The two properties must be set in separate operations.

10. B. The question asks to deploy a shielded virtual machine. A shielded virtual machine needs to have at least two partitions. So, the first thing you must do is run the `Diskpart` command to create another partition.

11. A. Desired State Configuration (DSC) is an important part of the configuration, management, and maintenance of Windows Server 2016. Using a PowerShell script specifies the configuration of the machine using a standard way that is easy to maintain and understand.

12. D. Virtual Machine Connection cannot be used to connect to shielded virtual machines, so the answer would be VM3 and VM4 only.

13. B. Make sure to manually delete any virtual disks that were part of the virtual machines to free up disk space. Virtual disks are not deleted when you delete a virtual machine.

14. B. Virtual machines each run in their own child partitions. Child partitions do not have direct access to hardware resources; instead, they have a virtual view of the resources, which are called virtual devices.

15. A. Dynamically expanding is a disk that starts with a small VHD file and expands on demand once an installation takes place. It can grow to the maximum size you define during creation. You can use this type of disk to clone a local hard drive during creation.

16. G. The Hyper-V Manager console allows you to migrate storage of the virtual machine to the cluster. Hyper-V Manager is an administrative tool that allows you to create, change, and delete virtual machines.

17. H. The question does not state that the Failover Cluster feature has been installed, so it would need to be installed on Server1 and Server2 before a cluster can be created. So, for that reason, Server Manager is the option that you must use first. The same result can be achieved by running the command `Install-WindowsFeature -name Failover-Clustering` on Server1 and Server2.

18. C. When you use the Private virtual switch type, the virtual machines can communicate with each other but not with the host system or the physical network; thus, no network packets are hitting the wire. This question states that the virtual machines must be prevented from communicating with Server1 and all other servers on the corporate network.

19. A. When you use the External virtual switch type, any virtual machine connected to this virtual switch can access the physical network. This option is used in production environments where your clients connect directly to the virtual machines. This question states that Hyper-V hosts on the corporate network must be able to connect to the virtual machines.

20. D. By using Windows Server Software Load Balancing (SLB), you can scale out your load balancing capabilities using SLB VMs on the same Hyper-V compute servers that you use for your other virtual machine workloads. Multitenancy for VLANs is not supported by network controllers; however, you can use VLANs with SLB for service provider managed workloads, such as the datacenter infrastructure and high-density web servers.

21. A. The `\Hyper-V Hypervisor\Logical Processors` counter monitors the number of logical processors that are being consumed by Hyper-V and the virtual machines.

22. D. A legacy network adapter is required for Preboot Execution Environment (PXE) boot. Generation 1 virtual machines require a Legacy NIC. Generation 2 virtual machines do not have this requirement.

23. C. `Set-VMNetworkAdapter` configures features of the virtual network adapter in a virtual machine or the management operating system. The `-VMName` switch specifies the name of the virtual machine that has the virtual network adapter that you want to configure.

24. C. The `Set-VMNetworkAdapterIsolation` cmdlet modifies isolation settings for a virtual network adapter. You can isolate a virtual machine adapter by using virtual local area network (VLAN), Hyper-V Network Virtualization, or a third-party virtualization solution. You can specify the isolation method and modify other settings, which include multitenancy settings. The `MultiTenantStack` parameter specifies whether to use multiple isolation IDs for the virtual machine. The acceptable values for this parameter are On and Off. On indicates isolation IDs so that the virtual machine provides services to multiple tenants on different isolation subnets. Off does not indicate isolation IDs to the virtual machine.

25. A. Packet capture software on VM3 would be able to capture the network traffic for VM1 and VM2 if it has network connectivity to the same VLAN. Network virtualization would prevent this.

26. B. PowerShell Direct is a feature for Windows 10 and Windows Server 2016. The virtual machine generation or VHD type do not matter. It is a way of running PowerShell commands inside a virtual machine from the host operating system. To create a PowerShell Direct session on a virtual machine:

- The VM must run at least Windows 10 or Windows Server 2016.
- The VM must be running locally on the host and booted.
- You must be logged into the host computer as a Hyper-V administrator.
- You must supply valid user credentials for the virtual machine.
- The host operating system must run at least Windows 10 or Windows Server 2016.

27. A. To configure the Virtual Subnet ID, you need to configure the virtual switch on the Hyper-V host. A virtual switch allows virtual machines created on Hyper-V hosts to communicate with other computers. You can create a virtual switch when you first install the Hyper-V role on Windows Server 2016.

28. A. You will want to enable Receive Side Scaling (RSS), which allows for multiprocessor use. The `Set-NetAdapterRss` cmdlet sets the RSS properties on a network adapter. RSS is a scalability technology that distributes the received network traffic among multiple processors by hashing the header of the incoming packet.

29. D. The `Compare-VM` cmdlet compares a virtual machine and a virtual machine host for compatibility, returning a compatibility report. This is useful when trying to import or migrate a virtual machine that is incompatible with the target Hyper-V server.

30. C, D, and E. When you set up VMs on a host, the VMs need to be able to connect to the network (or Internet). To do this, you must set up the network adapters, on the host, to be virtual switches for the VMs. The VMs then need to connect to these virtual switches so that they can access the network. Since these VMs are connecting directly to the Internet from Host1, you need Host1 to be set up as a NAT server.

31. B. To see if a network adapter is using certain properties, you open Device Manager and then the properties of the network adapter. You then look under the Advanced tab and see if the network adapter is using SR-IOV.

32. B. Standard checkpoints are used to capture the state, data, and hardware configuration of a running virtual machine and are intended for use in development and test scenarios.

33. A. A private virtual network allows virtual machines to communicate with each other but not with the host system or the physical network; thus, no network packets are hitting the wire. For example, you can use this to define internal virtual networks for test environments.

34. D. To meet the goal, you must use Live Migration. A Hyper-V replica will cause the host to disconnect from the network. To use Live Migration, hosts must be connected to the same virtual switch and have the same brand of processor.

35. B. NIC Teaming allows you to group between 1 and 32 physical Ethernet network adapters into one or more software-based virtual network adapters. These virtual network adapters provide fast performance and fault tolerance in the event of a network adapter failure. NIC Team member network adapters must all be installed in the same physical host computer to be placed in a team.

36. D. Hyper-V Network Virtualization provides "virtual networks" (called VM networks) to virtual machines, similar to how server virtualization (hypervisor) provides "virtual machines" to the operating system. Network Virtualization decouples virtual networks from the physical network infrastructure and removes the constraints of VLAN and hierarchical IP address assignment from virtual machine provisioning.

37. A. The `Merge-VHD` cmdlet merges virtual hard disks in a differencing virtual hard disk chain. The merge is from a specified source child disk to a specified destination child disk. Merge is an offline operation; the virtual hard disk chain must not be attached when the merge is initiated.

38. B. The `Optimize-VHD` cmdlet optimizes the allocation of space in one or more virtual hard disk files, except for fixed virtual hard disks. To use `Optimize-VHD`, the virtual hard disk must not be attached or must be attached in read-only mode.

39. A. Communication between the virtual machine and the local host computer is not configured automatically. Once you install a virtual machine, you need to make sure that the TCP/IP settings are in agreement with the settings you define in the virtual network card. Start with a successful ping from your host machine to the virtual machines to verify that communication is working.

40. C. In this scenario the virtual machine has multiple checkpoints, which will use up a lot of disk space. Virtual machines will go into the Paused-Critical state in Hyper-V if the free space on the drive that contains the checkpoint goes below 200 MB. Once a virtual machine checkpoint has been taken, the base virtual hard disk stops expanding and the checkpoint file stores new data that is written to the disk. So it is critical that there is enough space in the checkpoint storage location.

41. D. An administrator can use PowerShell Direct to run PowerShell cmdlets on a virtual machine from the Hyper-V host. Because Windows PowerShell Direct runs between the host and the virtual machine, there is no need for a network connection or to enable remote management. There are no network or firewall requirements and no special configuration. To create a PowerShell Direct session, use one of the following commands:

```
Enter-PSSession -VMName VMName
Invoke-Command -VMName VMName -ScriptBlock { commands }
```

42. C. In this scenario you will want to attach a VHD using the Computer Management console. To do this, use the following steps:

1. Launch the Computer Management console.
2. Click Disk Management to view the current disk attached.

3. Right-click Disk Management and then click Attach VHD.

4. In the Attach Virtual Hard Disk dialog box, type in the path to the VHD or click Browse and browse to the path of the VHD. Click OK.

The Virtual Hard disk is now mounted and assigned drive letters. Your drive is now ready for use.

43. A. A Media Access Control (MAC) address is a unique identifier assigned to most network adapters or network interface cards (NICs) by the manufacturer for identification. It is used at the Media Access Control protocol sublayer. MAC address filtering is a feature for IPv4 addresses that allows you to include or exclude computers and devices based on their MAC address.

44. C. Hyper-V provides a virtualization layer called the hypervisor that runs directly on the system hardware. It is a software layer responsible for the interaction with the core hardware and works in conjunction with an optimized instance of Windows Server 2016 that allows running multiple operating systems on a physical server simultaneously. Thus, only option C can be the correct answer.

45. B. Automatic Virtual Machine Activation (AVMA) is a feature that allows administrators to install virtual machines on a properly activated Windows Server 2016 system without the need to manage an individual product key for each virtual machine. When using AVMA, virtual machines get bound to the licensed Hyper-V server as soon as the virtual machine starts.

46. B. The size of the VHD file is fixed to the size specified when the disk is created. This option is faster than a dynamically expanding disk. However, a fixed-size disk uses up the maximum defined space immediately. This type is ideal for cloning a local hard drive.

47. C. Any virtual machine connected to an external virtual switch can access the physical network. You would use this option if you want to allow your virtual machines to access, for example, other servers on the network or the Internet. This option is used in production environments where your clients connect directly to the virtual machines.

48. A. Use the Add-VMNetworkAdapter cmdlet to specify which network to enable resource metering on. If no ACLs are specified, metering will occur on all available networks.

49. C. When you use Hyper-V Manager to delete a virtual machine, the virtual machine configuration file will be deleted. All other files, like virtual disks, will still exist and need to be deleted manually.

50. A, B, and D. The minimum CPU requirement in order to run Hyper-V is a x64-compatible processor with Intel VT or AMD-V technology enabled. Hardware Data Execution Prevention (DEP), specifically Intel XD bit (execute disable bit) or AMD NX bit (no execute bit), must be available and enabled. You must have a minimum of 1.4 GHz; 2 GHz or faster is recommended.

51. B. You need to use the Export and Import functions to move virtual machines, including their configuration, between computers.

52. B. Hyper-V allows an organization of any size to act and compete with other organizations of any size. A small company can buy a single server and then virtualize that server into multiple servers. Hyper-V gives a small company the ability to run multiple servers on a single box and compete with a company of any size.

53. B. When you use presentation virtualization, your applications run on a different computer, and only the screen information is transferred to your computer. An example of presentation virtualization is Microsoft Remote Desktop Services in Windows Server 2016.

54. A. Server Virtualization basically enables multiple servers to run on the same physical server. Hyper-V is a server virtualization tool that allows you to move physical machines to virtual machines and manage them on a few physical servers. Thus, you will be able to consolidate physical servers.

55. D. Both 32-bit and 64-bit operating systems can run simultaneously in Hyper-V. Also, different platforms—like Windows, Linux, FreeBSD, and others—are supported.

56. C. Hyper-V supports up to 64 processors in a virtual machine environment, which provides you with the ability to run applications as well as multiple virtual machines faster.

57. A. Automatic Virtual Machine Activation (AVMA) is a feature that allows administrators to install virtual machines on a properly activated Windows Server 2016 system without the need to manage individual product keys for each virtual machine. When using AVMA, virtual machines get bound to the licensed Hyper-V server as soon as the virtual machine starts.

58. B. The minimum is 1 GB RAM to run Hyper-V. However, this question states what is Microsoft's recommended amount, and that would be 4 GB RAM or greater. (Additional RAM is required for each running guest operating system.) The maximum is 1 TB. Plan for at least 4 GB of RAM. More memory is better. You'll need enough memory for the host and all virtual machines that you want to run at the same time.

59. A, B, and D. To use virtualization in Windows Server 2016, you need to consider the basic software requirements for Hyper-V. Hyper-V runs only on the following editions of the Windows Server 2016 operating system:

- Windows Server 2016 Standard Edition
- Windows Server 2016 Datacenter Edition
- Microsoft Hyper-V Server 2012 R2 Edition

60. C. The Internal option allows virtual machines to communicate with each other, as well as the host system, but not with the physical network. When you create an internal network, it also creates a local area connection in Network Connections that allows the host machine to communicate with the virtual machines. You can use this if you want to separate your host's network from your virtual networks. Any virtual machine connected to the External virtual switch can access the physical network. When you use the Private option, virtual machines can communicate with each other but not with the host system or the physical network; thus, no network packets are hitting the wire. Public is not an option.

61. C. The Differencing type of disk is associated in a parent-child relationship with another disk. The differencing disk is the child, and the associated virtual disk is the parent. Differencing disks include only the differences to the parent disk. By using this type, you can save a lot of disk space in similar virtual machines. This option is suitable if you have multiple virtual machines with similar operating systems.

62. D. The virtual machine receives direct pass-through access to the physical disk for exclusive use. This type provides the highest performance of all disk types and thus should be used for production servers where performance is the top priority. The drive is not available for other guest systems.

63. B. The Linux operating systems that run on newer generation virtual machines can boot with the Secure Boot option enabled. Before you boot the virtual machine for the first time, you must configure the virtual machine to use the Microsoft UEFI Certificate Authority. You can do this from Hyper-V Manager, Virtual Machine Manager, or an elevated Windows PowerShell session.

64. B. A Generation 1 VM cannot boot from a VHDX disk; only a Generation 2 VM can boot from a VHDX disk. Therefore, you should recreate Nano1 as a Generation 2 virtual machine.

65. B. To be able to use NIC Teaming, the computer system must have at least one Ethernet adapter. If you want to provide fault protection, an administrator must have a minimum of two Ethernet adapters. One advantage of Windows Server 2016 is that an administrator can set up 32 network adapters in a NIC Team.

66. C and D. NIC Teaming can be configured in different configuration models, including Switch Independent or Switch Dependent. Switch Independent means that each NIC adapter is connected into a different switch. Switch Dependent means that all NIC adapters are connected into the same switch.

67. A, B, and C. You can use Storage QoS in Windows Server 2016 to accomplish the following:

- Relieve problem neighbor issues. By default, Storage QoS ensures that a single virtual machine cannot consume all storage resources and starve other virtual machines of storage bandwidth.

- Monitor end-to-end storage performance. Performance details of all running virtual machines and the configuration of the Scale-Out File Server cluster can be viewed from a single location.

- Manage Storage I/O per workload needs. Storage QoS policies define performance minimums and maximums for virtual machines and ensure that they are met.

68. B. The Export-VM cmdlet exports a virtual machine to disk. This cmdlet creates a folder at a specified location having three subfolders: Checkpoints, Virtual Hard Disks, and Virtual Machines. The Checkpoints and Virtual Hard Disks folders contain the checkpoints of and virtual hard disks of the specified virtual machine, respectively. The Virtual Machines folder contains the configuration XML of the specified virtual machine. The Import-VM cmdlet imports a virtual machine from a file.

69. B, C, and E. The three PowerShell cmdlets would be (in order) `Stop-VM`, `Update-VMVersion`, and `Checkpoint-VM`. The `Update-VMVersion` cmdlet updates virtual machines to the current version. The `Checkpoint-VM` cmdlet creates a checkpoint of a virtual machine. The `Stop-VM` cmdlet shuts down, turns off, or saves a virtual machine.

70. A. `Set-VMNetworkAdapter` configures features of the virtual network adapter in a virtual machine or the management operating system.

71. B. Switch Embedded Teaming (SET) allows an administrator to combine a group of physical adapters (minimum of 1 adapter and a maximum of 8 adapters) into software-based virtual adapters.

72. D. One of the requirements of Switch Embedded Teaming (SET) is that all network adapters that are members of the SET group must be identical adapters. This means that they need to be the same adapter types from the same manufacturers.

73. D. The `New-VMSwitch` cmdlet creates a new virtual switch on one or more virtual machine hosts. To use RDMA capabilities on Hyper-V host virtual network adapters (vNICs) on a Hyper-V virtual switch that supports RDMA teaming, you will want to use the `New-VMSwitch` cmdlet.

74. C. Generation 1 virtual machines must be shut down before you can modify changes to the settings. Generation 2 virtual machines can have changes made while the virtual machine is running.

75. A. You should create an external virtual switch. This will allow you to pass the host's Internet connection through to virtual machines that use the switch. Configuring the MAC Address Range will not work. This setting defines the MAC address range that can be assigned to virtual machines, but it does not configure Internet connectivity. You should not configure NUMA Spanning. This setting allows virtual machines to span Non-Uniform Memory Architecture (NUMA). This gives virtual machines more computing resources, but it does not help with connectivity. Enhanced Session Mode will not work either. This setting allows redirection of local devices and resources from computers running Virtual Machine Connections, but it does not provide Internet access to virtual machines.

76. D. Non-Uniform Memory Access (NUMA) is a multiprocessor memory architecture that allows a processor to access its local memory more quickly than memory located on another processor. NUMA allows a system to access memory quickly by providing separate memory on each processor.

77. A. Hyper-V provides a virtualization layer called a hypervisor that runs directly on the system hardware. The hypervisor is similar to what the kernel is to Windows. It is a software layer responsible for the interaction with the core hardware and works in conjunction with an optimized instance of Windows Server 2016 that allows running multiple operating systems on a physical server simultaneously. The Hyper-V architecture consists of the hypervisor and parent and child partitions.

78. C. Enhanced Session Mode gives administrators the following benefits for local resource redirection:

- Display configuration
- Audio

- Printers
- Clipboard
- Smart cards
- Drives
- USB devices
- Supported Plug and Play (PnP) devices

79. B. Windows Server 2016 has introduced a new feature of Hyper-V called Hyper-V nesting. Hyper-V nesting allows you to run a virtual machine within a virtual machine.

80. A. External virtual networks are used when you want to allow the following types of communicatons:

- Virtual machine to virtual machine on the same physical server
- Virtual machine to parent partition (and vice versa)
- Virtual machine to externally located servers (and vice versa)
- (Optional) Parent partition to externally located servers (and vice versa)

81. A. The `Add-VMNetworkAdapterRoutingDomainMapping` cmdlet adds a routing domain and virtual subnets to a virtual network adapter. The cmdlet adds the information about the routing domain and virtual subnets to connected multitenant virtual machines.

82. C, D, and E. In order, you would want to

1. Run the `Mount-VMHostAssignableDevice` cmdlet on VM1.
2. Run the `Enable-PnPDevice` cmdlet on VM1.
3. Run the `Disable-PnPDevice` cmdlet on Server1.

The `Mount-VMHostAssignableDevice` is used to mount a device globally for the Hyper-V host. The `Enable-PnPDevice` cmdlet enables a Plug and Play (PnP) device. The `Disable-PnPDevice` cmdlet disables a PnP device.

83. C. When a virtual machine is in the Running state, it is currently working. In the Saved state, the virtual machine is saved to disk in its current state. In the Off state, the virtual machine is turned off. In the Paused state, the virtual machine is in a paused state. When you export a running virtual machine from one machine to another, the imported virtual machine will automatically be in a Running state.

84. B and C. Hyper-V provides two tools to manage virtual hard disks: Inspect Disk and Edit Disk. Inspect Disk provides information about the virtual hard disk. It shows not only the type of the disk but also information such as the maximum size for dynamically expanding disks and the parent VHD for differencing disks. Edit Disk provides the Edit Virtual Hard Disk Wizard, which allows an administrator to compact, convert, expand, merge, or reconnect hard disks.

85. A. If you have a virtual machine that has a smaller amount of memory than what it needs for startup memory, when the virtual machine gets restarted, Hyper-V then needs additional memory to restart the virtual machine. Smart Paging is used to bridge the memory gap between minimum memory and startup memory. This allows your virtual machines to restart properly.

Chapter 4: Implement Windows Containers

1. **C.** You would want to connect to Container1, since that is where the web application is located. Container1 has an IP address of 172.16.5.6 and a port mapping from port 80.

2. **D.** You will want to configure Media Access Control (MAC) address spoofing on Server1. If your container host is virtualized, you must enable MAC address spoofing.

3. **A.** Administrators can set any configuration option for the daemon in a JSON format. This would be the daemon.json file. By default, Docker captures the standard output (and standard error) of all your containers and writes them in files using the JSON format. The default file location is C:\ProgramData\docker\config\daemon.json.

4. **B, C, and E.** In order, first you would install the Container feature, then install Docker, and then install the Base Container images.

5. **B.** In a Windows Server Container, the kernel is shared among all the different Windows Containers. This container allows the administrator to isolate applications so that applications can run in their own space and not affect other applications.

6. **C.** Docker can only be administered by an administrator. So, by creating a Docker Administrators group and adding it to the local Administrators group, you allow the Docker Administrators group to administer Docker.

7. **D.** When you are working with Hyper-V Containers in Docker, the settings are identical to managing Windows Server containers. The one difference that you want to include in the Hyper-V Container is the --isolation=hyperv parameter. The following is an example of the Docker command with the Hyper-V parameters: docker run -it --isolation=hyperv microsoft/nanoserver cmd.

8. **B.** The docker run command is used with the -v switch to mount a folder to a container.

9. **C.** A Dockerfile is a text document that contains all the commands a user could call on the command line to assemble an image.

10. **A.** The docker run command executes commands in a Dockerfile and also allows you to delete an image.

11. **B.** The Docker application does need to be installed in order to work with Windows Containers.

12. **C.** The default setting for a container is no. This setting will not automatically restart the container.

13. **B.** You can build your own images using Dockerfiles. When you install Docker, the Docker engine includes tools that can be used to create Dockerfiles. Dockerfiles are just text files that are manually created and they are compiled and turned into image files.

14. **D.** Windows Containers share the system's kernel between all containers and the host. Hyper-V Containers are different because each Hyper-V Container utilizes its own instance of the Windows kernel.

15. C. Once you have installed Docker, there will be three networks that are created automatically. You can see these networks by typing `docker network ls` in PowerShell or at an elevated command prompt. The three networks are bridge, none, and host.

16. B. The Azure Container Service allows you to easily create, configure, and manage your virtual machine cluster of containers. By using open source tools, the Azure Container Service connects you with thousands of other users who are also designing, building, and maintaining container images.

17. D. The `Get-Container` PowerShell cmdlet allows an administrator to view information about containers.

18. A. The `Volume` Dockerfile command allows an administrator to create a mount point and externally mounted volumes from host systems or other containers.

19. B. The `docker create` command gives you the ability to create a new container.

20. B. The `docker images` command gives you the ability to see your images. The `docker info` command allows you to see how many images you have on a host, but it does not give you details about the images.

21. A. The `docker build` command allows you to compile and create an image. The `docker run` command executes commands in a Dockerfile, and the `docker rm` command allows you to delete an image.

22. B. The `docker run` command executes commands in a Dockerfile. The `docker build` command allows you to compile and create an image, and the `docker rm` command allows you to delete an image.

23. D. The `remove-container` command gives you the ability to delete a container.

24. C. The `docker pull microsoft/windowsservercore` command allows you to grab an image of Windows Server Core from the Docker website.

25. D and E. Computer systems (physical or virtual machines) running Windows Server 2016 (Core and with Desktop Experience), Nano Server, or Windows 10 Professional and Enterprise (Anniversary Update) allow you to set up containers.

26. A, B, D, and E. In order, that's E, D, A, and B. First thing you'd want to do is create a `New-Item`, then `Add-Content`, then restart the Docker service, and then create the `New-ContainerNetwork`.

27. C. `repadmin.exe` is a Replication Diagnostics tool. This command-line tool assists administrators in diagnosing replication problems between Windows domain controllers. `repadmin.exe` can also be used for monitoring the relative health of an Active Directory forest.

28. A. Windows Containers are independent and isolated environments that run an operating system. These isolated environments allow an administrator to place an application into its own container, thus not affecting any other applications or containers.

29. A. Hyper-V Containers run within a virtual machine, and the Windows Containers don't need to run in a Hyper-V environment. In a Hyper-V Container, the container host's kernel is not shared between the other Hyper-V Containers.

30. B. The Container Host component can be on a physical or virtual machine, and it's configured with the Windows Container feature. So the Windows Container sits on top of the Container Host.

31. A. Container Image is the component that contains all of the layers of the container. So the Container Image contains the operating system, the application, and all of the services required to make that application function properly.

32. B. The Docker daemon is the component that runs the Docker application. The Docker daemon is automatically installed after you complete the installation of the Docker application. If you need to configure the Docker daemon, you would use the Docker daemon file. This file is in a JSON format.

33. B. A minimum of 4 GB of RAM needs to be available to the virtualized Hyper-V host.

34. C. To see what Windows version you have installed, enter the system's registry (regedit.exe) and do a search for the current version.

35. A, C, and D. Docker is the software package that you install and the Docker daemon is the application that you use to do your configuration and management. After you install Docker, the Docker daemon is automatically installed and configured with default settings. Docker is a third-party application that Microsoft has started using for containers. The Docker application consists of a Docker engine and a Docker client (Docker daemon).

36. D. One way to determine what Windows version you have installed is to enter the system's registry (regedit.exe) and search for the following registry key: HKEY_LOCAL_MACHINE\ Software\Microsoft\Windows NT\CurrentVersion.

37. C. The docker commit command allows an administrator to debug and build a new image.

38. D. Administrators can use the docker deploy command to create and modify a stack.

39. B. Using the docker cp command allows an administrator to copy files and folders between the container and the local computer system.

40. A. The docker ps command allows you to view all of the containers.

41. A. The always setting will always restart the container. When the setting is set to always, Docker will try to restart the container indefinitely. The container will also always start on daemon startup.

42. C. The docker info command allows you to see how many images you have on a host, but it does not give you details about the images. The docker images command gives you the ability to see your images.

43. A. Administrators can use the docker pull command to pull an image from a registry. So, to install a container image such as Microsoft Nano Server from the online package repository, you'd type the following command into PowerShell: docker pull microsoft/nanoserver.

44. D. The docker rm command allows you to delete an image. There may be a time when you need to remove an image from a container.

45. B. You will need the Image ID. Example, the Image ID for my Nano Server is d9bccb9d4cac. You will use this ID to turn the image into a container. Type the following into a PowerShell prompt (your Image ID will be different) and press Enter: docker run d9bccb9d4cac.

46. D. Administrators have the ability to change the tags associated with the images. Administrators use tag names as version names so that they can keep track of the different images on their machines. Having tags that you create allows you to easily access the images later by their tag names. To tag an image, you use the -t parameter. So the following is tagging an image as WillPanekImage: docker build -t WillPanekImage.

47. A, C, and D. If your organization decides that they want to build their own Dockerfiles, then they will get some benefits. Some of the advantages of building your own Dockerfiles are as follows:

- Administrators can store images as code.
- Your organization can have rapid re-creation of images. These images can then be used for maintenance and upgrade cycles.
- Your organization can customize exactly what it wants.

48. B. Using the pound (#) symbol for making comments and stating exactly why each line is included helps someone following you or if someone is trying to learn what you do.

49. C. The Add command will copy new files, directories, or remote file URLs from a source (<src>) location to the filesystem of the image destination <dest>.

50. A. The Expose command tells Docker that the container is listening on the specified network ports during runtime.

51. D. The Volume command allows an administrator to create a mount point and externally mounted volumes from host systems or other containers.

52. B. The Onbuild command allows you to set a trigger that is executed when the image is used as the base for another build.

53. A. A bridge network is an automatically generated network with a subnet and a gateway. Docker connects to the bridge network by default; this allows deployed containers to be seen on your network.

54. D. None is a container-specific network stack that lacks a network interface.

55. A. Docker has a public database of images that you can access. The Docker Hub repository has images for Microsoft, Unix, Linux, and hundreds more. If you want to see what a vendor has out on the repository, just type **docker search <*vendorname*>**.

56. C. Administrators have the ability to set up a private repository so that coworkers can share and use the images that you create. After you create your images using the Docker daemon, you can then push those images to your corporate Docker Hub repository. Administrators can then add users and accounts to the Docker Hub to verify that only the organization's users are accessing the images.

57. D. Before you can create an account, you must first go to the website. When you are ready to start uploading corporate images to the Docker Hub, you will first need to create a Docker Hub user account (https://cloud.docker.com/). After you have created your account, click the Create button and choose Create Repository.

58. B. The Get-Container cmdlet allows an administrator to view information about containers.

59. D. Administrators can use the Get-ContainerImage cmdlet to view local container images.

60. B. The Add-ContainerNetworkAdapter cmdlet allows an administrator to add a virtual network adapter to a container.

61. B. Docker is required in order to work with Windows Containers. Docker consists of the Docker Engine (dockerd.exe) and the Docker client (docker.exe).

62. A and D. Windows Containers are offered with two container base images: Windows Server Core and Nano Server.

63. A. Two virtual processors for the container host virtual machine are required if you are going to be running virtualization with a container.

64. C. The docker kill command allows you to terminate running containers.

65. A. The docker diff command allows an administrator to view changes to files or directories in the containers file system.

66. D. Administrators can use the docker exec command to run a new command in an existing container.

67. A. Any given swarm can have multiple manager nodes, but it must always have at least one.

68. A. Hyper-V Containers and Windows Containers work the same way. The difference between the two is that Hyper-V Containers run within a virtual machine and Windows Containers don't need to run in a Hyper-V environment. In a Hyper-V Container, the container host's kernel is not shared between the other Hyper-V Containers.

69. D. The Docker Hub repositories are where all of your images are stored. By having a central location for stored images, you can share your images with coworkers, customers, or the entire IT population. There are Docker Hub repositories on the Internet, and these locations allow you to grab and use images for your organization.

70. D. The unless-stopped command will always restart the container unless the container was stopped before the restart.

71. A. The ENV command allows you to add an environmental variable.

72. C. The From command shows the location of the container image that will be used during the image creation process.

73. A. Type **docker search Microsoft** to search the repository for Microsoft images.

74. B. The docker push command allows you to push an image to a registry. After you have created your repository, you can push images to the repository by providing the name of your image, your Docker Hub username, the repository name that you created, and an image tag. You'd type the following command: **docker push <hub-user>/<repo-name>:<tag>**.

75. B. The host network adds a container on the host's network stack. As far as the network is concerned, there is no isolation between the host machine and the container. For instance, if you run a container that runs a web server on port 80 using host networking, the web server is available on port 80 of the host machine.

76. B. Using the --expose option allows you to expose a port or a range of ports.

77. A. Using the --ip option allows you to configure an IPv4 address (e.g., 172.30.100.104).

78. C. To view the current list of Docker networks, use the docker network ls command.

79. A. Use the docker network create to create the new network. Then assign the options --driver=bridge, --subnet=192.168-5.0/24, --gateway-192.168.5.10, and the new name of new_subnet1.

80. D. You need to use Install-WindowsFeature - Name Hyper-V. You only need to use -ComputerName <computer_name> if you are connected remotely.

81. B. To set the metadata on a container, use the --label or -l command.

82. C. An Azure Container Registry stores and manages private Docker container images, similar to the way Docker Hub stores public Docker images. Azure Container Registry allows you to store Docker container images in repositories. This allows you to store groups of images (or versions of images) in isolated environments.

83. D. If your application will be built for the cloud and uses .NET Core, then you should use Nano Server. This is because Nano Server was built with the intention of having as small a footprint as possible, and several nonessential libraries were removed. If you find that your application needs full compatibility with the .NET Framework, then you should use Windows Server Core.

84. A. Administrators can use Install-Package to install a software package on a computer.

85. C. Administrators can use Stop-Container to stop a container.

Chapter 5: Implement High Availability

1. A. The PowerShell cmdlet `Enable-ClusterStorageSpacesDirect` enables Storage Spaces Direct (S2D). This cmdlet enables highly available Storage Spaces that use directly attached Storage Spaces Direct on a cluster.

2. F. To configure a virtual machine for high availability:

    1. Install Hyper-V.

    2. In the Failover Cluster Manager snap-in, if the cluster that you want to configure is not displayed, in the console tree right-click Failover Cluster Manager, click Manage a Cluster, and then select or specify the cluster that you want.

3. F. Using the Failover Cluster Manager console, select the replica virtual machine you want to test and select Replication > Test Failover.

4. F. The Failover Cluster Manager console is the tool that you'd want to use if the Print Spooler service on one virtual machine stops unexpectedly. You can move the virtual machine to another node. Failover Cluster Manager, also called *VM monitoring*, allows you to monitor the health state of applications that are running within a virtual machine and then reports that to the host level so that it can take recovery actions. You can monitor any Windows service (such as the Print Spooler service) in your virtual machine. When the condition you are monitoring gets triggered, the Cluster Service logs an event and takes recovery actions.

5. B. The `Set-VMHost` cmdlet allows an administrator to configure a Hyper-V host. These settings include network settings for network adapters. Using the `Set-VMHost` cmdlet, you can ensure that Server1 uses all available networks to perform the Live Migration of VM2.

6. E. The Data Center Bridging (DCB) feature provides hardware-based bandwidth allocation for a specific type of traffic and improves Ethernet transport reliability with the use of priority-based flow control.

7. C. If you use Kerberos to authenticate live migration traffic, be sure to configure constrained delegation. To configure constrained delegation, open the Active Directory Users and Computers snap-in. Kerberos constrained delegation eliminates the need for requiring users to provide credentials twice.

8. C. If you have decided to use Kerberos to authenticate Live Migration traffic, configure constrained delegation before you proceed. To configure constrained delegation:

    1. Open the Active Directory Users and Computers snap-in.

    2. From the navigation pane, select the domain and double-click the `Computers` folder.

    3. From the `Computers` folder, right-click the computer account of the source server and then click Properties.

    4. In the Properties dialog box, click the Delegation tab.

    5. On the Delegation tab, select Trust this Computer for Delegation to the Specified Services Only. Under that option, select Use Kerberos only.

9. B, C, and E. First you need to need to update the VM version to enable the Production Checkpoints feature.

   1. Stop-VM. The virtual machine should be shut down before upgrading it.

   2. Update-VMVersion. Use this cmdlet to upgrade the virtual machine configuration.

   3. Checkpoint-VM. This cmdlet creates a checkpoint of a virtual machine.

10. B and D. Hyper-V Live Migration is a Microsoft Hyper-V feature that allows an administrator to move virtual machines (VMs) between clustered hosts without noticeable service interruption. Live Migration can be initiated through the Failover Cluster Manager, PowerShell, or the Microsoft System Center Virtual Machine Manager (SCVMM). Live Migration from AMD to Intel or vice versa cannot be done, so options A and C are incorrect. That would leave B (Xeon to Xeon) and D (Intel i7 to Intel i7).

11. D. Since you are creating a two-way mirror, you will require at least two disks. This writes two copies of your data on the drives, which can protect your data from a single drive failure. Since you want to minimize data loss, you should use drives C and D, as there is nothing on them.

12. A. Storage Spaces supports four types of resiliency: single, two-way mirror, three-way mirror, and parity. This question states failure of two USB drives. So the answer would be a three-way mirror. This option works similar to the two-way mirror, but it writes three copies of your data on the drives, which will help you to protect your data from two simultaneous drive failures. Three-way mirror requires at least three drives.

13. B. Storage Spaces supports four types of resiliency: single, two-way mirror, three-way mirror, and parity. This question states failure of an individual USB drive. So the answer would be to set resiliency type to parity. Selecting the parity resiliency type allows Windows to store parity information with the data, thereby protecting you from a single drive failure.

14. D. There are prerequisites for multi-domain or workgroup clusters in Windows Server 2016. One of those is the need for a primary DNS suffix. The exhibit shows that this is blank. So, each cluster node needs to have a primary DNS suffix. For multi-domain clusters, the DNS suffix for all the domains in the cluster should be present on all cluster nodes.

15. D. Run the Enable-VMReplication cmdlet. This allows an administrator to enable virtual machine migration on a virtual machine host.

16. A. The Optimize-VHDSet cmdlet optimizes the allocation of space used by virtual hard disk (VHD) set files.

17. B. Failover Cluster Manager is a management tool within the Windows Server operating system, and it's used to create, validate, and manage failover server clusters running Windows Server. Administrators can open the Failover Cluster Manager by clicking Start ➤ Administrative Tools ➤ Failover Cluster Manager.

18. C. Before enabling Storage Spaces Direct, you must create a new cluster using the New-Cluster cmdlet. The New-Cluster cmdlet creates a new failover cluster. "New-Cluster –Name Cluster1 –Node 'Server1', 'Server2', 'Server3', 'Server4' –NoStorage" is the correct syntax code to create a new storage cluster that uses Storage Spaces Direct. This creates a four-node cluster named Cluster1. The cluster will not have any clustered storage or disk resources.

19. A. Planned Failover is an operation initiated on the primary virtual machine. Planned Failover is used when you want to perform host maintenance on the primary virtual machine and would like to run from the replica site.

20. D. To prevent the virtual machine from being live migrated automatically, you need to go into the network adapter settings of the virtual machine and disable the Protected network setting.

21. A. When you create a new SET team, you must configure the member adapters and Load Balancing Mode team properties. The options for SET team load balancing distribution mode are Hyper-V Port and Dynamic. The Dynamic Load Balancing Mode provides the following:

  - Outbound loads are distributed based on a hash of the TCP ports and IP addresses. Dynamic mode also re-balances loads in real time so that a given outbound flow can move back and forth between SET team members.

  - Inbound loads are distributed in the same manner as the Hyper-V Port mode.

    This question is asking about load balancing—thus, the answer would be Dynamic mode.

22. B. Each virtual machine needs a virtual disk that is used as a boot/system disk, and two or more virtual disks to be used for Storage Spaces Direct. Disks used for Storage Spaces Direct must be connected to the virtual machines using a virtual SCSI controller.

23. C. The quorum arbitration time setting is used to set the limit of the time period that is allowed for quorum arbitration. Quorum arbitration is the process that occurs when the controlling node of the cluster is no longer active and other nodes of the cluster attempt to gain control of the quorum resource and thus control of the cluster. QuorumArbitrationTimeMax specifies the maximum number of seconds a node is allowed to spend arbitrating for the quorum resource in a cluster. RequestReplyTimeout describes the length of time a request from a node with a cluster state update will wait for replies from the other healthy nodes before the request times out.

24. C. Before you resize a volume, make sure you have enough capacity in the storage pool to accommodate the larger footprint. You will need to add 3 TB to the coordinator node.

25. B. To set up a cluster in a workgroup, you need to configure both of the servers to be in a workgroup. You then need to configure the Cluster Service to log on as Network Service and specify an administrative access point of DNS.

26. C. Use the Pause option on a node to prevent resources from being failed over or moved to the node. You typically would pause a node when the node is involved in maintenance or troubleshooting. After a node is paused, it must be resumed to allow resources to be run on it again.

27. A. Eviction is an irreversible process. Once you evict the node, it must be re-added to the cluster. You would evict a node when it is damaged beyond repair or is no longer needed in the cluster. If you evict a damaged node, you can repair or rebuild it and then add it back to the cluster using the Add Node Wizard.

28. D. You will need to set `ResiliencyLevel`. This defines how unknown failures are handled. Level 1 allows the node to be in an isolated state only if the node gave a notification and it went away for a known reason; otherwise, it fails immediately. Known reasons include a Cluster Service crash or Asymmetric Connectivity between nodes. Level 2 always lets a node go to an isolated state and gives it time before taking over ownership of the VMs. This is the default value: `(Get-Cluster).ResiliencyLevel = <value>`.

29. B and D. The `New-Cluster` cmdlet creates a new failover cluster. The `-Name` parameter specifies the name of the cluster to create. The `-Node` parameter specifies a comma-separated list of cluster node names, or server names, on which to create the cluster. The `-AdministrativeAccessPoint` specifies the type of administrative access point that the cmdlet creates for the cluster. The DNS cmdlet creates an administrative access point for the cluster. The administrative access point is registered in DNS but is not enabled in Active Directory Domain Services. Using the WMI command-line (WMIC) utility provides a command-line interface for WMI. WMIC is compatible with existing shells and utility commands. In this question you are adding both servers to Workgroup2.

30. A. Microsoft recommends using the Resilient File System (ReFS) for Storage Spaces Direct. ReFS is the premier filesystem purpose-built for virtualization and offers many advantages, including dramatic performance accelerations and built-in protection against data corruption.

31. B. To update the cluster functional level, open an administrative PowerShell session and enter the following cmdlet: `Update-ClusterFunctionalLevel`. The `Update-ClusterFunctionalLevel` cmdlet updates the functional level of a mixed-version cluster.

32. D. Network Controller provides a centralized, programmable point of automation to manage, configure, monitor, and troubleshoot virtual and physical network infrastructure in your datacenter. Using Network Controller, you can automate the configuration of network infrastructure instead of performing manual configuration of network devices and services.

33. A. You can restore objects from the Active Directory Recycle Bin by using Active Directory Administrative Center. Active Directory Recycle Bin allows you to restore a user, computer, or organizational unit (OU) account that has been accidentally deleted.

34. B. The `Suspend-NlbClusterNode` cmdlet suspends a specific node in a Network Load Balancing (NLB) cluster. A node in a cluster may need to be suspended to override any remote control cmdlets, or non-Windows PowerShell operations, that are issued for maintenance work.

35. B. Drainstop is the function that allows the current session to end before stopping the cluster on the node. Evict is used to remove a node completely from a failover cluster. Stop will immediately end the cluster service on the NLB cluster node, not allowing the current session to complete. Pause is used to keep resources from failing over to a failover cluster node.

36. A. Network Load Balancing requires all hosts to be on the same subnet and all hosts to use multicast or unicast (not a combination of the two), and requires static IP addresses. Dynamic IP (DHCP) is not supported by NLB.

37. B. Single affinity is the default setting that the wizard uses when you create an NLB cluster. This affinity is used primarily when the bulk of the client traffic originates from intranet addresses. Single affinity is also useful for stateful Internet (or intranet) applications where session stickiness is important.

38. C. A checkpoint is a snapshot in time from when an administrator can recover a virtual machine. Checkpoints can be accessed from up to 24 hours ago.

39. F. Network Load Balancing is a form of clustering where the nodes are highly available for a network-based service. Windows Server 2016 NLB is designed to work with web servers, FTP servers, firewalls, proxy servers, and virtual private networks (VPNs).

40. B. A single cluster can support up to 32 computers.

41. C. Hypertext Transfer Protocol (HTTP) uses port 80. File Transfer Protocol (FTP) uses ports 20 and 21. Simple Mail Transfer Protocol (SMTP) uses port 25. Hypertext Transfer Protocol Secure (HTTPS) uses port 443.

42. B. There are network requirements that must be met for failover clustering:

- Cluster nodes should be connected to multiple networks for communication redundancy.
- Network adapters should be the same make, use the same driver, and have the firmware version in each cluster node.
- Network components must be marked with the "Certified for Windows Server 2016" logo.

43. A and D. The two types are as follows:

- Public Network: This is the network through which clients are able to connect to the clustered service application.
- Private Network: This is the network used by the nodes to communicate with each other.

44. C. The quorum configuration in a failover cluster determines the number of failures that the cluster can sustain. The cluster quorum settings will tell the cluster which physical server(s) should be active at any given time.

45. A. The <*value*> input can be 1, 2, or 3. 1 is equivalent to the Low setting (move the host when showing more than 80 percent loaded), 2 is equivalent to Medium (move the host when more than 70 percent loaded), and 3 is equivalent to High (move the host when showing more than 5 percent above the average).

46. B. Configure DHCP failover on the server that created the scope. In this case, Server1 created Scope1, therefore DHCP Failover should be configured on Server1. The DHCP Failover feature allows high availability of the service without using cluster services.

47. A and B. The quorum configuration in a failover cluster determines the number of failures that the cluster can sustain. There are four quorum types:

- The Majority Node option is recommended for clusters with an odd number of nodes. This configuration can handle a loss of half of the number of cluster nodes rounded off downward.

- The No Majority: Disk Only option requires only one active cluster node to keep the cluster active; the quorum is stored on a disk. This disk becomes a single point of failure and therefore a risk.

- The Node and Disk Majority option is recommended for clusters with an even number of nodes and provides multiple possibilities regarding the failure of nodes and therefore the maximum number of nodes that may fail before the cluster goes down.

- The Node and File Share Majority option is similar to Node and Disk Majority, but in this case the disk is replaced by a file share (also called the File Share Witness Resource).

48. D. The `Set-NetAdapterRss` cmdlet sets the Receive Side Scaling (RSS) properties on a network adapter. RSS is a scalability technology that distributes the receive network traffic among multiple processors by hashing the header of the incoming packet.

49. C. To create a new NLB cluster, you would use the PowerShell cmdlet `New-NlbCluster`.

50. C. RAS Gateway is a software router and gateway that you can use in either single tenant mode or multitenant mode. For multitenant mode, it is recommended that you deploy RAS Gateway on VMs that are running Windows Server 2016. Software Load Balancing allows administrators to have multiple servers hosting the same virtual networking workload in a multitenant environment. This allows an administrator to set up high availability.

51. D. If you want to stop the entire cluster from running, while in the NLB Manager (choose Start ➤ Run and then type **NLBmgr**), you would right-click the cluster, point to Control Hosts, and then choose Stop. If you're using the Stop command, the cluster stops immediately and any current connections to the NLB cluster are killed. This question states that all connections must be terminated immediately; hence, you would want to use Stop.

52. A. The PowerShell cmdlet `Stop-VMReplication` will stop virtual machine replication from happening. So, the `Stop-VMReplication` cmdlet cancels an ongoing virtual machine resynchronization.

53. B. To use unicast communication between NLB cluster nodes, each node must have a minimum of two network adapters.

54. D. Setting the cluster affinity to Single will send all traffic from a specific IP address to a single cluster node. Using this affinity will keep a client on a specific node where the client should not have to authenticate again. Setting the filtering mode to Single would remove the authentication problem but would not distribute the load to other servers unless the initial server was down.

55. C. When setting the affinity to Class C, NLB links clients with a specific member based on the Class C part of the client's IP address. This allows an administrator to set up NLB so that clients from the same Class C address range can access the same NLB member. This affinity is best for NLB clusters using the Internet.

56. A and B. The first PowerShell command, (Get-Cluster).CrossSiteDelay, is used to set the amount of time between the heartbeats sent to nodes. This value is in milliseconds (the default is 1,000).

The second PowerShell command, (Get-Cluster).CrossSiteThreshold, is the value that you set for the number of missed heartbeats (the default is 20) before the node is considered offline.

57. D. A Windows Server 2016 cluster consisting of servers running the x64 version can contain up to 64 nodes.

58. A. The Enable-ClusterStorageSpacesDirect cmdlet allows an administrator to enable highly available Storage Spaces that use directly attached storage, Storage Spaces Direct (S2D), on a cluster.

59. B. The storage tests require the clustered disk resource to be offline. If you need to run the storage tests, the Validate a Configuration Wizard will prompt you to make sure you want to take the resources offline.

60. A and C. SQL Server and Exchange Server are supported only on failover clusters. Websites and VPN services are network-based services, so they are better suited for NLB clusters.

61. A. You would want use the Test-Cluster cmdlet to complete validation tests for a cluster. The Test-Cluster cmdlet runs validation tests for failover cluster hardware and settings. Tests can be run both before and after a cluster is set up.

62. B. The cluster heartbeat is a signal sent between servers so they know that the machines are up and running. Servers send heartbeats and, after five nonresponsive heartbeats, the cluster assumes that the node was offline. Cross-Site Heartbeating is the same signal but with longer timeouts to allow for cluster nodes in remote locations.

63. B. Up to two votes can be lost before quorum can no longer be achieved. These votes can come from the file share witness or a cluster node.

64. B. In a three-node cluster, only one node can be offline before quorum is lost; a majority of the votes must be available to achieve quorum.

65. B and D. Answers B and D are the only versions that are real. There is no 2016 Small Business Server or Virtual Edition. So, Network Load Balancing (NLB) can be installed on Windows Server 2016 Standard and Windows Server 2016 Datacenter Edition.

66. C. To be able to use NIC Teaming, the computer system must have at least one Ethernet adapter. If you want to provide fault protection, an administrator must have a minimum of two Ethernet adapters. One advantage of Windows Server 2016 is that an administrator can set up 32 network adapters in a NIC Team.

67. B and D. Websites and Terminal Services are designed to work with NLB clusters. Database servers like SQL Server do not work on NLB clusters.

68. A. To keep the failed resource from causing the entire application to fail over, the option to allow the resource to fail over the service or application must be unchecked. Removing the possible owners from the clustered application would keep the application from failover even when needed. Running the resource in a separate resource monitor does not change how it affects the failover of the application.

69. B. A Service Level Agreement (SLA) defines the services and metrics that must be met for the availability and performance of an application or service. SLAs are usually expressed in percentages of the time the application is available. These percentages are also often referred to by the number of nines the percentage includes.

70. A and C. Windows Server 2016 provides two types of high availability: Failover Clustering and Network Load Balancing (NLB). Failover Clustering is used for applications and services such as SQL Server and Exchange Server. Network Load Balancing is used for network-based services such as web and FTP servers.

71. C. Administrators can choose two types of authentication: Kerberos or Credential Security Support Provider (CredSSP). CredSSP allows an administrator to set up better security but requires constrained delegation for Live Migration. Administrators have the ability to sign in to the source server. Administrators can sign in to the source server by using a local console session, a Remote Desktop session, or a remote Windows PowerShell session.

72. A. Windows Server 2016 Cloud Witness is a new type of Failover Cluster quorum witness that leverages Microsoft Azure as the intercession point. The Cloud Witness gets a vote just like any other quorum witness. Administrators can set up the Cloud Witness as a quorum witness using the Configure a Cluster Quorum Wizard.

73. A, C, and D. Shared virtual hard disks are extremely useful in providing highly available shared storage for the following virtualized workloads: SQL Server, Virtual Machine Manager, and Exchange Server. Shared virtual hard disks can reside on a Scale-Out File Server failover cluster or cluster CSV volumes.

74. C. In Hyper-Converged, there is only one cluster for storage and compute. The Hyper-Converged deployment option runs the Hyper-V virtual machines or SQL Server databases directly on the servers delivering the storage, storing all files on the local volumes.

75. A. In Converged, there are separate clusters for each storage and compute. The Converged deployment option, also called Disaggregated, puts a Scale-Out File Server (SoFS) on top of Storage Spaces Direct to provide Network Attached Storage (NAS) over SMB3 file shares. This allows for scaling computer/workloads separately from the storage cluster.

76. D. Storage Spaces Direct requires a minimum of 2 servers and a maximum of 16 servers. All servers should be the same make and model.

77. A. The NLB feature uses the TCP/IP networking protocol to distribute traffic. For web servers and other necessary servers, NLB can provide performance and consistency when two or more computers are combined into a single virtual cluster.

78. C. Use Test Failover to verify that the replica virtual machine can successfully start in the secondary site. It will create a copy test virtual machine during failover and does not affect standard replication. After the test failover, if the administrator selects Failover on the replica test virtual machine, the test failover will be deleted. There are several types of manually initiating failover—Test Failover, Planned Failover, and Unplanned Failover.

79. D. Dynamic quorum management automatically manages the vote assignment to nodes. With this feature enabled, votes are automatically added or removed from nodes when that node either joins or leaves a cluster. Dynamic quorum management is enabled by default.

80. A, B, C, and D. One nice new advantage of using Windows Server 2016 is the ability to set up a cluster on systems not part of the same domain. Windows Server 2016 allows you to set up a cluster without using Active Directory dependencies. Administrators can create clusters in the following situations:

- Single-domain cluster
- All nodes in a cluster are part of the same domain
- Multidomain cluster
- Nodes in the cluster are part of different domains
- Workgroup cluster
- Nodes are member servers and part of a workgroup

81. B. You should run the Validate A Configuration Wizard before creating a cluster or after making any major hardware or software changes to the cluster. Doing so will help you identify any misconfigurations that could cause problems with the failover cluster.

82. A. Storage Spaces Direct recommends two NICs for redundancy and performance.

83. D. Administrators have the ability to set Network Health Detection at the virtual machine level for a Hyper-V host cluster. This is configured as a Protected Network. When you select the Protected Network check box, the virtual machine will be moved to another cluster node if a network disconnection is detected. If the health of a network connection is showing as disconnected, the VM will be automatically moved.

84. B. Switch Embedded Teaming (SET) can be an alternative to using NIC Teaming in environments that include Hyper-V and the Software Defined Networking (SDN) stack in Windows Server 2016. SET does use some of the functionality of NIC Teaming in the Hyper-V Virtual Switch, but SET allows an administrator to combine a group of physical adapters (a minimum of one adapter and a maximum of eight adapters) into software-based virtual adapters.

85. C. The `Set-VMReplicationServer` PowerShell cmdlet allows an administrator to configure a host as a replica server.

Chapter 6: Implement Domain Name System (DNS)

1. B. The `Enable-WindowsOptionalFeature` is used to add the DNS Server role to a Nano Server. The `Enable-WindowsOptionalFeature` cmdlet enables or restores an optional feature in a Windows image.

2. D. The `Add-VMNetworkAdapterAcl` cmdlet creates an access control list (ACL) to apply to the traffic through a virtual machine network adapter. When a virtual network adapter is created, there is no ACL on it. Given a list of IP-based ACL entries to be applied to traffic in the same direction, the longest match rule decides which one of the entries is most appropriate to apply to a specific packet.

3. A. dnscmd.exe is a command-line tool for managing DNS servers. This utility is useful in scripting batch files to help automate routine DNS management tasks, or to perform simple unattended setup and configuration of new DNS servers on your network.

4. C. The refresh interval is the time in seconds that a secondary name server should wait between zone file update checks. The interval should not be so short that the primary name server is overwhelmed by the update checks and not so long that propagation of changes to the secondary name servers is delayed.

5. C. This example creates three GPOs (IPAM1_DHCP, IPAM1_DNS, and IPAM1_DC_NPS) and links them to the abc.com domain. These GPOs enable access to the ipam1.abc.com server using the domain administrator account user1.

6. B. The Set-IpamConfiguration cmdlet modifies the IP Address Management (IPAM) server configuration, including the TCP port over which the computer that runs the IPAM Remote Server Administration Tools (RSAT) client connects and communicates with the computer that runs the IPAM server. The -GpoPrefix<String> parameter specifies the unique Group Policy Object (GPO) prefix name that IPAM uses to create the Group Policy Objects. Use this parameter only when the value of the ProvisioningMethod parameter is set to Automatic.

7. B. The IPAM MSM Administrators are users who are in the IPAM Users IPAM security group and who have the privileges to manage DHCP and DNS server instance–specific information. Such users are Multi Server Management (MSM) Administrators.

8. B. You will need to modify the Zone Aging and Scavenging properties. When you set zone-level properties for a specified zone, these settings apply only to that zone and its resource records. Unless you otherwise configure these zone-level properties, they inherit their default settings from comparable settings that AD DS maintains in the Aging and Scavenging properties for the DNS server.

9. D. DHCP server in Windows Server 2016 allows you to group clients based on their fully qualified domain names. Using wildcards, you can use this criterion to group clients based on their DNS suffixes or based on their host names. Setting up the DNS suffix is done using the DHCP Policy Configuration Wizard.

10. A. ipconfig /release sends a DHCPRELEASE message to the DHCP server to release the current DHCP configuration and discard the IP address configuration. This parameter disables TCP/IP for adapters configured to obtain an IP address automatically. To specify an adapter name, type the adapter name that appears when you use ipconfig without parameters.

11. B. A stub zone is a copy of an authoritative DNS zone that only contains the records needed to reach the authoritative server. When a zone that is a DNS server hosts a stub zone, this DNS server is a source only for information about the authoritative name servers for this zone. The zone at this server must be obtained from another DNS server that hosts the zone. This DNS server must have network access to the remote DNS server to copy the authoritative name server information about the zone.

12. B. The -DnssecOk parameter sets the DNSSEC OK bit for this query. When DO=1, the client indicates that it is able to receive DNSSEC data if available. Because the secure.abc.com zone is signed, an RRSIG resource record is included with the DNS response when DO=1.

13. C. The DNS socket pool enables a DNS server to use source port randomization when it issues DNS queries. When the DNS service starts, the server chooses a source port from a pool of sockets that are available for issuing queries. Instead of using a predicable source port, the DNS server uses a random port number that it selects from the DNS socket pool. The DNS socket pool makes cache-tampering attacks more difficult because a malicious user must correctly guess both the source port of a DNS query and a random transaction ID to successfully run the attack. When you configure the DNS socket pool, you can choose a size value from 0 to 10,000. The larger the value, the greater the protection you will have against DNS spoofing attacks.

14. D, E. When setting DHCP options for WDS PXE booting, you will want to use 060 Option 60, which is the client identifier. You should set this to the string PXEClient. This only applies if DHCP is on the same server as Windows Deployment Services. You will also want to use O66 Boot Server Host Name, which is the boot server's host name.

15. B, C. DNS attacks can be very serious in a company. Shutting down a DNS server or even changing the records can prevent your users from accessing proper information. By signing the zone, you allow DNS to use certificates, and by locking the DNS cache, you prevent hackers from changing cache entries. These simple steps can help administrators secure their DNS servers.

16. A. A DHCP superscope is a collection of individual scopes that are grouped together for administrative purposes. This configuration allows client computers to receive an IP address from multiple logical subnets even when the clients are located on the same physical subnet. You can create a superscope only if you have already created two or more IP scopes in DHCP. You can use the New Superscope Wizard to select the scopes that you wish to combine to create a superscope. A DHCP superscope is useful if a scope runs out of addresses, and you cannot add more addresses from the subnet.

17. B. DHCP polices allow an administrator to determine scope for specific types of equipment coming in that correspond to different characteristics. An administrator needs to ensure that different types of devices are provisioned appropriately for network connectivity. You want different types of clients to get IP addresses from different IP address ranges within the subnet. By specifying a different IP address range for different device types, you can more easily identify and manage devices on the network.

18. A. The next step is to run the Configure Failover Wizard from the DHCP console. The Load Balance Percentage feature specifies the percentage of the IP address range to reserve for each server in the failover relationship. Each server will use its assigned range of addresses prior to assuming control over the entire IP address range of a scope when the other server transitions into a "partner down" state and the Maximum Client Lead Time passes.

19. G. By default, the service bindings on the server depend on whether the first network connection is configured dynamically or statically for TCP/IP. Since the question uses a manually specified IP address, the connection is enabled in the service bindings on the server. The DHCP server will bind to the first static IP address configured on each adapter.

20. B. When conflict detection attempts are set, the DHCP server uses the ping process to test available scope IP addresses before including these addresses in DHCP lease offers to clients. A successful ping means the IP address is in use on the network. Therefore, the DHCP server does not offer to lease the address to a client. If the ping request fails and times out, the IP address is not in use on the network. In this case, the DHCP server offers to lease the address to a client.

21. D. Name squatting occurs when a non-Windows-based computer registers in Domain Name System (DNS) with a name that is already registered to a Windows-based computer. The use of name protection in Windows Server prevents name squatting by non-Windows-based computers. Name squatting does not present a problem on a homogeneous Windows network where Active Directory Domain Services (AD DS) can be used to reserve a name for a single user or computer. Name protection can be configured for IPv4 and IPv6 at the network adapter level or scope level. Name protection settings configured at the scope level take precedence over the setting at the IPv4 or IPv6 level.

22. C. The `Get-DhcpServerInDC` cmdlet retrieves the list of authorized computers that run the Dynamic Host Configuration Protocol (DHCP) server service from Active Directory. Only a computer that runs a DHCP server service that is authorized in Active Directory can lease IP addresses on the network.

23. A. The correct answer is to modify the lease duration; 169.254.0.0/16 is an APIPA address. You cannot create a DHCP scope in that range. Every computer that is connected to a network needs an IP address so that it can send and receive data over the network. Each network has a limited number of addresses to assign to devices. The total number of addresses varies based on the network configuration. The network administrator determines the DHCP lease time. The optimum length depends on the number and kinds of devices on the network. A network with more dynamic clients than IP addresses might require a shorter lease period so that addresses are recycled more frequently.

24. D. The `Set-IpamConfiguration` cmdlet modifies the IP Address Management (IPAM) server configuration, including the TCP port over which the computer that runs the IPAM Remote Server Administration Tools (RSAT) client connects and communicates with the computer that runs the IPAM server.

25. C. A role is a collection of IPAM operations. You can associate a role with a user or group in Windows using an access policy. Several built-in roles are provided, but you can also create customized roles to meet your requirements. You can create an access policy for a specific user or for a user group in Active Directory. When you create an access policy, you must select either a built-in IPAM role or a custom role that you have created.

26. A. The Name Resolution Policy Table (NRPT) provides a means for configuring both DNSSEC and DirectAccess policies. It is stored in Group Policy, so its settings can be applied at the domain, site, OU, or local level. Before a security-aware DNS client issues a query, it checks the NRPT to determine whether DNSSEC should be used.

27. D. The `Set-DnsServerCache` cmdlet modifies cache settings for a Domain Name System (DNS) server. When using the `-LockingPercent` parameter, it specifies a percentage of the original Time to Live (TTL) value that caching can consume. Cache locking is configured as a percent value. By default, the cache locking percent value is 100. This value means that the DNS server will not overwrite cached entries for the entire duration of the TTL.

28. D. The `Resolve-DnsName` cmdlet performs a DNS query for the specified name. This cmdlet is functionally similar to the Nslookup tool, which allows users to query for names. The `Resolve-DnsName` cmdlet will return a maximum of 25 A and AAAA records from NS servers.

29. C, E, F. To disable recursion on the DNS server:

1. Open DNS Manager.
2. In the console tree, right-click the applicable DNS server; then click Properties.
3. Click the Advanced tab.
4. In Server Options, select the Disable Recursion check box, and then click OK.

Disable recursion on DNS servers that do not respond to DNS clients directly and that are not configured with forwarders. A DNS server requires recursion only if it responds to recursive queries from DNS clients or if it is configured with a forwarder. DNS servers use iterative queries to communicate with each other. The DNS server has root DNS servers in its configuration, so it returns the root DNS server details each time it is queried for a non-existent domain name. To prevent this, we need to create a forward lookup zone with the name "".

Another option is to run `dnscmd.exe` with the `/config` parameter. `dnscmd.exe` is a command-line interface for managing the DNS servers. Using `dnscmd.exe` and specifying the `/config` parameter will reset the DNS server or zone configuration and allow you to disable recursion.

30. D. Before a DHCP server can provide clients with IP addresses, the server must be configured with a scope. A scope is a range of IP addresses that can be leased to DHCP clients on a given subnet. You can also create a second type of scope known as a superscope. In an environment that has multiple logical IP subnets defined on a single physical network, superscopes allow a DHCP server to assign leases to clients on multiple subnets.

31. C. The `Add-DhcpServerv4ExclusionRange` cmdlet adds a range of excluded IP addresses for an IPv4 scope. The excluded IP addresses are not leased out by the Dynamic Host Configuration Protocol (DHCP) server service to any DHCP clients. The only exception to this is reservation. If an IP address is reserved, the same IP address is leased to the designated client even if it falls in the exclusion range.

32. A. Virtual Machine Manager (VMM) must be granted permission to view and modify IP address space in IPAM and to perform remote management of the IPAM server. VMM uses a Run As account to provide these permissions to the IPAM network service plug-in. The Run As account must be configured with appropriate permissions on the IPAM server. To assign permissions to the VMM user account, in the upper navigation pane of the IPAM server console, click Access Control. Then right-click Access Policies in the lower navigation pane and click Add Access Policy.

33. B. Network prefixes are determined directly from the subnet mask of the network. A Class B subnet mask would be 255.255.0.0. To determine the network prefix on a Class B subnet, you would need to convert each octet of the subnet mask to a binary value. So for Class B it would be 11111111.11111111.00000000.00000000. Count the consecutive 1s to determine the prefix. So, the answer would be /16.

34. B. RFC 1918 was used to create the standards by which networking equipment assigns IP addresses in a private network. A private network can use a single public IP address. The RFC reserves the following ranges of IP addresses that cannot be routed on the Internet:

- 10.0.0.0 - 10.255.255.255 (10/8 prefix)
- 172.16.0.0 - 172.31.255.255 (172.16/12 prefix)
- 192.168.0.0 - 192.168.255.255 (192.168/16 prefix)

35. A. First turn both numbers into their binary equivalents and line them up. Then perform the AND operation on each bit and write down the result.

    10000001 00111000 10111101 00101001 IP Address

    11111111 11111111 11110000 00000000 Subnet Mask

    10000001 00111000 10110000 00000000 Network ID

The result of the bit-wise logical AND of the 32 bits of the IP address and the subnet mask is the network ID 129.56.176.0.

36. D. Internet connection sharing is not supported in Windows Server 2016. To do Internet connection sharing, you must set up a NAT server. The correct answer is to install the Routing role service, configure NAT, and then set it to use Server2's internal address.

37. C. You set up a NAT server using the Routing and Remote Access role. To do this, you can install the role using either Server Manager or PowerShell.

38. B. The New-NetRoute cmdlet creates an IP route in the IP routing table. Specify the destination prefix and specify an interface by using the interface alias or the interface index. IP routing is the process of forwarding a packet based on the destination IP address. Routing occurs at TCP/IP hosts and at IP routers. The sending host or router determines where to forward the packet. To determine where to forward a packet, the host or router consults a routing table that is stored in memory. When TCP/IP starts, it creates entries in the routing table. You can add entries either manually or automatically.

39. B. The New-NetIPAddress cmdlet creates and configures an IP address. To create a specific IP address object, specify either an IPv4 address or an IPv6 address, and an interface index or interface alias. We recommend that you define the prefix length, also known as a subnet mask, and a default gateway. If you run this cmdlet to add an IP address to an interface on which DHCP is already enabled, then DHCP is automatically disabled. If Duplicate Address Detection (DAD) is enabled on the interface, the new IP address is not usable until DAD successfully finishes, which confirms the uniqueness of the IP address on the link.

40. C. The Set-DnsServerResponseRateLimiting cmdlet enables Response Rate Limiting (RRL) on a Windows DNS server.

41. A. The Netlogon service creates a log file that contains all the locator resource records stored in Netlogon. When you promote a server to a domain controller using DCPROMO, a text file containing all of the appropriate records the domain controller will register in DNS is created. This text file is stored in the %systemroot%\system32\config folder and is called netlogon.dns. Whenever a domain controller starts, the Netlogon service registers these records or refreshes these records in the primary zone held by DNS.

42. B. Time to Live (TTL) is used for computer data, including DNS servers. It is the amount of time or number of transmissions that a packet can experience before it is discarded. The Minimum (Default) Time to Live (TTL) is the default or minimum amount of time for a newly created record.

43. A. Make sure that a reverse lookup zone that is authoritative for the pointer (PTR) resource record exists. PTR records contain the information that is required for the server to perform reverse name lookups. A reverse lookup is when a DNS client queries a DNS server for the name of a host when it has the IPv4 or IPv6 address of the host.

44. C. The HOSTS file is a common way to resolve a host name to an IP address through a locally stored text file that contains IP-address-to-host-name mappings. The HOSTS file is used to map host names to IP addresses.

45. A. Round robin is used by DNS servers as a local balancing mechanism to share and distribute network resource loads. You can use it to rotate all resource record (RR) types contained in a query if multiple RRs are found. By default, DNS uses round robin to rotate the order of RR data returned in query answers where multiple RRs of the same type exist for a queried DNS domain name. So, in this case, you would want to create two resource records for intranet.abc.com. Point one record to Web1 and point one record to Web2.

46. C. If you choose to delete all PTR records at the node, use dnscmd.exe to delete them. So, to delete all PTR records at the 10.3.2.1 address you would type the following command at the command prompt: dnscmd /RecordDelete 10.in-addr.arpa. 127.2.3 PTR.

47. D. Adding a secondary DNS server to a zone involves three steps:

1. Add the prospective secondary DNS server to the list of name servers that are authoritative for the zone on the primary DNS server.

2. Verify that the transfer settings for the zone permit the zone to be transferred to the prospective secondary DNS server on the primary DNS server.

3. Add the zone as a secondary zone on the prospective secondary DNS server.

48. B. The Conflict Detection value specifies how many ICMP echo requests (pings) the server sends for an address it is about to offer. The default is 0. Conflict Detection is a way to verify that the DHCP server is not issuing IP addresses that are already being used on the network. So, an administrator should set the Conflict Detection Attempts to a value other than 0. The value you enter determines the number of times the DHCP server checks an IP address before leasing it to a client. The DHCP server checks IP addresses by sending a ping request over the network.

49. A. Microsoft's jetpack.exe utility allows you to compact a JET database. Microsoft JET databases are used for WINS and DHCP databases.

50. C. An exclusion just marks addresses as excluded; the DHCP server doesn't maintain any information about them. A reservation marks an address as reserved for a particular client. So, create a client reservation on a DHCP server if you want the server to always assign the same IP address to a specific machine on the network.

51. A. When the DHCP server crashed, the scope was effectively deactivated. Deactivating a scope has no effect on the client until it needs to renew the lease.

52. B, C, E, F. The acronym to remember is DORA. The DHCP operation stages are often abbreviated as DORA for discovery, offer, request, and acknowledgment. IP lease discovery is used when a DHCP-enabled IP stack is initialized to locate a DHCP server with this specialized broadcast. When a DHCP server receives the discover packet, it sends out an IP lease offer containing an available address. The client responds to the DHCP offer with an IP lease acceptance message showing that this address is acceptable. Finally, when the DHCP request is received, the server sends out an IP lease acknowledgment, which contains configuration options for the IP stack and adds the information to the DHCP database.

53. B. The client has been manually configured with a different set of DNS servers. Manual settings will override the DHCP options.

54. C. During lease renewal, the client gets all configuration information offered by the server. Since the client machine has received different configurations during the last few times the lease was renewed, this is an indication that an administrator is changing the configuration information between the lease durations.

55. D. The Secure Only option is for DNS servers that have an Active Directory Integrated zone. When a computer tries to register with DNS dynamically, the DNS server checks Active Directory to verify that the computer has an Active Directory account. If the computer that is trying to register has an account, DNS adds the host record. If the computer trying to register does not have an account, the record gets tossed away and the database is not updated.

56. A. If you need to complete a zone transfer from Microsoft DNS to a BIND (Unix) DNS server, you need to enable BIND secondaries on the Microsoft DNS server. BIND secondaries determine whether to use fast transfer format for transfer of a zone to DNS servers running legacy BIND implementations. By default, all Windows-based DNS servers use a fast zone transfer format.

57. D. Active Directory Integrated zones store their records in Active Directory. Because this company has only one Active Directory forest, it's the same Active Directory that both DNS servers are using. This allows Server1 to see all of the records of Server2 and Server2 to see all the records of Server1.

58. B. On a Windows Server 2016 DNS machine, debug logging is disabled by default. When it is enabled, you have the ability to log DNS server activity, including inbound and outbound queries, packet type, packet content, and transport protocols.

59. C. Windows Server 2016 DNS supports two features called DNS Aging and DNS Scavenging. These features are used to clean up and remove stale resource records. DNS zone or DNS server aging and scavenging flags old resource records that have not been updated in a certain amount of time (determined by the scavenging interval). These stale records will be scavenged at the next cleanup interval.

60. B. The `dnscmd /zoneexport` command creates a file using the zone resource records. This file can then be given to the Compliance team as a copy.

61. D. Stub zones are very useful for slow WAN connections. These zones store only three types of resource records: NS records, glue host (A) records, and SOA records. These three records are used to locate authoritative DNS servers.

62. D. To calculate the network mask, you need to figure out which power number (2x) is greater than or equal to the number you need. Since we are looking for 1,000, 210 = 1,024. You then add the power (10) to the current network mask (53 + 10 = 63).

63. A. When you look at an IPv6 address, the first sections tell you the IPv6 address space prefix. Fd00:: /8 is the unique local unicast prefix, and this allows the server to communicate with all local machines within your intranet.

64. C. A Class B address with a default subnet mask of 255.255.0.0 will support up to 65,534 hosts. To increase the number of networks that this network will support, you need to subnet the network by borrowing bits from the host portion of the address. The subnet mask 255.255.252.0 uses 6 bits from the host's area, and it will support 64 subnets while leaving enough bits to support 1,022 hosts per subnet. The subnet mask 255.255.248.0 uses 5 bits from the hosts and will support 32 subnetworks while leaving enough bits to support 2,046 hosts per subnet. Option C, 255.255.252.0, is the best answer because it leaves quite a bit of room for further growth in the number of networks while still leaving room for more than 1,000 hosts per subnet, which is a fairly large number of devices on one subnet. The subnet mask 255.255.254.0 uses 7 bits from the host's area and will support 126 networks, but it will leave only enough bits to support 500 hosts per subnet. The subnet mask 255.255.240.0 uses 4 bits from the hosts and will support only 16 subnetworks, even though it will leave enough bits to support more than 4,000 hosts per subnet.

65. A. The CIDR /27 tells you that 27 1s are turned on in the subnet mask. Twenty-seven 1s equals 11111111.11111111.11111111.11100000. This would then equal 255.255.255.224.

66. B. You need to configure a subnet mask that can accommodate 1,600 clients. The way to figure this out is to use the formula 2x − 2 = Mask Number. So, a total of 1,600 clients means that it is 211 − 2 = 2048, and 2,048 is the first power number that is greater than 1,600. So since it is 211, that means that our subnet mask has 11 zeros. So it looks like the following: 11111111.11111111.11111000.00000000. This translates to 255.255.248.0.

67. B, D. If the first word of an IPv6 address is FE80 (actually the first 10 bits of the first word yields 1111 1110 10 or FE80:: /10), then the address is a link-local IPv6 address. If it's in EUI-64 format, then the MAC address is also available (unless it's randomly generated). The middle FF:FE is the filler and indicator of the EUI-64 space, with the MAC address being 00:03:FF:11:02:CD. Remember that the 00 of the MAC becomes 02 in the link-local IPv6 address, flipping a bit to call it local.

68. A. You need to configure a subnet mask that can accommodate 600 clients. The way to figure this out is to use the formula 2x − 2 = Mask Number. So a total of 600 clients means that it is 210 − 2 = 1,022, and 1,022 (power of 10) is the first power number that is greater than 600. So since it is 210, that means that our subnet mask has 10 zeros. So it looks like the following: 11111111.11111111.11111100.00000000. This translates to 255.255.252.0.

69. A. You need to configure a subnet mask that can accommodate 3,500 clients. The way to figure this out is to use the formula 2x − 2 = Mask Number. So, a total of 3,500 clients means that it is 212 − 2 = 4094, and 4,094 (power of 12) is the first power number that is greater than 3,500. So since it is 212, that means that our subnet mask has 12 zeros. So it looks like the following: 11111111.11111111.11110000.00000000. This translates to 255.255.240.0.

70. A, C, F. There is no such IP address type as simulcast or staticast. Broadcast is an IPv4 address type. Unicast is the one-to-one address type. Anycast is the one-to-"one of many" address type. Multicast is the one-to-many address type.

71. D. The `ipconfig /all` command shows you all of the network configuration data, including TCP/IP settings.

72. C, D. Teredo is designed to give IPv4/IPv6 users access to the IPv6 Internet and network resources when the client machines are behind a NAT. There are some caveats and extra implementation steps, but the Teredo implementation in conjunction with a dual-stack node (which supports Teredo, like Windows Server 2016) are the required components.

73. A. Remember the rules: Use `::` only once to replace a word or complete words (four 0s between colons). Use `:0:` as a compressed format for one complete word of 0s. You can leave out preceding 0s, but not trailing 0s; options B and C violate this rule.

74. D. Out of the possible answers provided, the only DHCP configuration option that would be both fault-tolerant and redundant is DHCP failover.

75. C. Administrators can use the `Set-DhcpServerv4Scope` cmdlet to configure the settings of an existing IPv4 scope. This cmdlet sets the properties of an existing IPv4 scope on the Dynamic Host Configuration Protocol (DHCP) server service.

76. D. Microsoft recommends the 80/20 rule for redundancy of DHCP services in a network. Implementing the 80/20 rule calls for one DHCP server to make approximately 80 percent of the addresses for a given subnet available through DHCP, while another server makes the remaining 20 percent of the addresses available.

77. A. DHCP can become a single point of failure within a network if there is only one DHCP server. If that server becomes unavailable, clients will not be able to obtain new leases or renew existing leases. For this reason, it is recommended that you have more than one DHCP server in the network. However, more than one DHCP server can create problems if they both are configured to use the same scope or set of addresses. Microsoft recommends the 80/20 rule for redundancy of DHCP services in a network. To do this, you run the Configure Failover Wizard.

78. A. 003 Router is used to provide a list of available routers or default gateways on the same subnet.

79. B. 006 DNS is used to provide a list of available DNS servers to your scope settings or to your server settings.

80. C. You would want to set up a scope level policy to apply to just that IP range. If you set up a server level policy, it would apply to all scopes. Administrators can configure policies to provide an IP address from a specified range of the scope.

81. B. DHCP Name Protection ensures that DNS host A records are never overwritten during DNS dynamic updates. The other three options would not fulfill this question's requirements.

82. D. Active Directory Integrated zones give you many benefits over using primary and secondary zones, including less network traffic, secure dynamic updates, encryption, and reliability in the event of a DNS server going down. The Secure Only option is for dynamic updates to a DNS database.

83. B. The `Invoke-IpamGpoProvisioning` cmdlet creates and links three group policies speci-fied in the `-Domain` parameter for provisioning required access settings on the server roles managed by the computer running the IP Address Management (IPAM) server. The `-GpoPrefixName` parameter specified should be the same as the prefix configured in the IPAM Provisioning Wizard. The three Group Policy Objects (GPOs) are created with the suffixes `_DHCP`, `_DNS`, and `_DC_NPS` appended to the `GpoPrefixName` parameter value. These suffixes signify the three different types of access settings that are propagated by them, depending on the type of server role managed by the computer running the IPAM server.

84. D. The `Set-DnsServerForwarder` cmdlet changes forwarder settings on a Domain Name System (DNS) server. This cmdlet sets or resets IP addresses to which the DNS server forwards DNS queries when it cannot solve them locally. This cmdlet overwrites existing server level forwarders. The `-UseRootHint` parameter specifies whether to prevent the DNS server from performing iterative queries. If you set `UseRootHint` to `$false`, the DNS server forwards unresolved queries only to the DNS servers in the forwarders list and does not try iterative queries if the forwarders do not resolve the queries.

85. B, E, F. To manually start discovery of the servers that IPAM can manage, run the follow-ing cmdlets:

Step 1: `Invoke-IpamServerProvisioning`. Choose a provisioning method. The `Invoke-IpamGpoProvisioning` cmdlet creates and links three group policies specified in the Domain parameter for provisioning required access settings on the server roles managed by the computer running the IP Address Management (IPAM) server.

Step 2: `Add-IpamDiscoveryDomain`. Configure the scope of discovery. The `Add-IpamDiscoveryDomain` cmdlet adds an Active Directory discovery domain for an IP Address Management (IPAM) server. A discovery domain is a domain that IPAM searches to find infrastructure servers. An IPAM server uses the list of discovery domains to determine what type of servers to add. By default, IPAM discovers all domain controllers, Dynamic Host Configuration Protocol (DHCP) servers, and Domain Name System (DNS) servers.

Step 3: `Start-ScheduledTask`. Start server discovery. To begin discovering servers on the network, click Start Server Discovery to launch the IPAM ServerDiscovery task or use the `Start-ScheduledTask` cmdlet.

Chapter 7: Implement Network Connectivity and Remote Access Solutions

1. A. VPN Reconnect uses the Internet Key Exchange v2 (IKEv2) tunneling protocol. VPN Reconnect can be used in conjunction with DirectAccess.

2. D. Secure Socket Tunneling Protocol (SSTP) is a form of VPN tunnel that provides a mech-anism to transport Point-to-Point Protocol (PPP) traffic through a Secure Sockets Layer/ Transport Layer Security (SSL/TLS) channel. SSL/TLS provides transport-level security with key negotiation, encryption, and traffic integrity checking. The use of SSL/TLS over TCP port 443 allows SSTP to pass through virtually all firewalls and proxy servers except for authenticated web proxies.

3. A. Routing and Remote Access Service (RRAS) supports Internet Key Exchange version 2 (IKEv2), a VPN tunneling protocol. The primary advantage of IKEv2 is that it tolerates interruptions in the underlying network connection. If the connection is temporarily lost, or if a user moves a client computer from one network to another, IKEv2 automatically restores the VPN after the network connection is reestablished without intervention on the part of the user.

4. A. When you select the RADIUS Authentication option from the Authentication Provider drop-down menu, you are enabling a RADIUS client that passes authentication duties to a RADIUS server.

To configure a RADIUS server to be the authentication provider:

1. Open the Routing and Remote Access MMC snap-in.
2. Right-click the server name for which you want to configure RADIUS authentication and then click Properties.
3. On the Security tab, in Authentication Provider, click RADIUS Authentication and then click Configure.
4. In the RADIUS Authentication dialog box, click Add.
5. In the Add RADIUS Server dialog box, configure the settings for your RADIUS authentication server and then click OK.

5. B. Deploying Remote Access requires a minimum of two Group Policy Objects: one Group Policy Object contains settings for the Remote Access server and one contains settings for DirectAccess client computers. When you configure Remote Access, the wizard automatically creates the required Group Policy Object. However, if your organization enforces a naming convention, or you do not have the required permissions to create or edit Group Policy Objects, they must be created prior to configuring Remote Access.

6. C. The Name Resolution Policy Table (NRPT) contains rules configured by an administrator for either names or namespaces and the settings for the required special handling. When performing a DNS name resolution, the DNS Client service compares the requested name against each rule in the NRPT before sending a DNS name query. Queries and responses that match an NRPT rule get the specified special handling applied. You can configure the NRPT with Group Policy.

7. A. The `Set-DAEntryPoint` cmdlet configures entry point settings, including the name of the server in the entry point, the name of the entry point, and the IP address used for global load balancing on the specified entry point.

8. B. In the single tenant mode, administrators can deploy RAS Gateways as an edge VPN server, an edge DirectAccess server, or both simultaneously. Using RAS Gateways this way provides remote users with connectivity to your network by using either VPN or DirectAccess connections. Also, single tenant mode allows administrators to connect offices at different physical locations through the Internet.

9. A, B, D. To set up a RADIUS server, the components needed on the RADIUS server include the RADIUS client and a RADIUS group. Microsoft recommends that you set up RADIUS connection policies as well.

10. C. Network Policy Server (NPS) is Microsoft's solution for enforcing company-wide access policies, including remote authentication. NPS is a role service of the Network Policy and Access Services (NPAS) server role. Other role services of NPAS are the Routing and Remote Access Service, Health Registration Authority, and Host Credential. These help you safeguard the health and security of a network.

11. B. Use Network Policy Server (NPS) configured as a RADIUS proxy to load balance connection requests between multiple NPS servers or other RADIUS servers. On the NPS proxy, configure load balancing so that the proxy evenly distributes the connection requests among the RADIUS servers. This method of load balancing is best for medium and large organizations that have many RADIUS clients and servers.

12. C. When you add a new network access server (VPN server, wireless access point, authenticating switch, or dial-up server) to your network, you must add the server as a RADIUS client in NPS so that NPS is aware of and can communicate with the network access server. On the NPS server, in the NPS console, double-click RADIUS Clients and Servers.

13. C. Create a VPN connection for the users by following User Configuration/Preferences/ Control Panel Settings/Network Options.

14. A. Intranet is the generic term for a collection of private computer networks within an organization. The intranet uses network technologies as a tool to facilitate communication between people or work groups to improve the data-sharing capability and overall knowledge base of an organization's employees. The Internet utilizes standard network hardware and software technologies like Ethernet, Wi-Fi, TCP/IP, web browsers, and web servers. An organization's intranet typically includes Internet access but is firewalled so that its computers cannot be reached directly from the outside. Because all the users can connect via VPN, this would allow access to the intranet website and the published application.

15. C. The Control Panel application from which most of the networking settings and tasks can be launched is the Network and Sharing Center. The Network and Sharing Center is one of the most important Control Panel apps for managing your network connections.

16. B. The solution is to deploy Remote Desktop Gateway in the office. Remote users can then connect to their computers on the office network by using Remote Desktop client on their home computers configured with the IP address of the Remote Desktop Gateway. Remote Desktop Gateway (RD Gateway) is a role service that enables authorized remote users to connect to resources on an internal corporate or private network, from any Internet-connected device that can run the Remote Desktop Connection (RDC) client. VPN connections would enable remote access to the office network, but this solution would not prevent users from accessing other corporate network resources. Remote Desktop local resources determine which local resources (printers, drives, etc.) are available in a Remote Desktop connection. However, this solution makes no provision for actually connecting to the office network. DirectAccess connections would enable remote access to the office network, but this solution would not prevent users from accessing other corporate network resources.

17. D. The `Add-VpnConnectionTriggerApplication` cmdlet adds applications to a VPN connection object. The applications automatically trigger a VPN connection when launched. This setting allows App1 to automatically request the VPN connection to ensure it can access the required data.

18. H. The `Set-VpnConnection` cmdlet changes the configuration settings of an existing VPN connection profile. If the VPN profile specified does not exist, you see an error. If errors occur when you modify the VPN profile, the cmdlet returns the error information.

19. H. The `Set-VpnConnection` cmdlet changes the configuration settings of an existing VPN connection profile.

20. G. The `Set-NetConnectionProfile` cmdlet changes the network category setting of a connection profile. A connection profile represents a network connection.

21. E. The `New-NetFirewallRule` cmdlet creates an inbound or outbound firewall rule and adds the rule to the target computer. The `-Direction` parameter specifies that matching firewall rules of the indicated direction are created. This parameter specifies which direction of traffic to match with this rule. The acceptable values for this parameter are Inbound or Outbound. The default value is Inbound.

22. D. Remote Access is a server role that provides administrators with a dashboard for managing, configuring, and monitoring network access. The Remote Access server role is a logical grouping of Remote Access Service (RAS), Routing, and Web Application Proxy. These technologies are the role services of the Remote Access server role. When you install the Remote Access server role with the Add Roles and Features Wizard or with Windows PowerShell, you can install one or more of these role services.

23. B, D. Connection request policies are sets of conditions and settings that allow administrators to designate which RADIUS servers authenticate and authorize the connection requests that the server running Network Policy Server (NPS) receives from the RADIUS clients. The default connection request policy uses NPS as a RADIUS server and processes all authentication requests locally. If you do not want the NPS server to act as a RADIUS server and process connection requests locally, you can delete the default connection request policy.

24. G. Deploying the application as a published application on the Remote Desktop server will use no disk space on the tablets. Users will be able to access the application by using Remote Desktop Connections. This will also ensure that the application is isolated from other applications on the tablets. You can use Remote Desktop Connection "redirection" to ensure that the application can access files stored on an internal SSD on the tablets. The redirection enables access to local resources such as drives and printers in a Remote Desktop Connection.

25. B. Access policies are a list of roles and the resources with which roles are to be provisioned or deprovisioned. Access policies are used to automate the provisioning of target systems to users.

26. D. The `Set-DAClient` cmdlet configures the properties related to a DirectAccess (DA) client. The `-ComputerName` parameter specifies the IPv4 or IPv6 address, or host name, of the computer on which the Remote Access server computer–specific tasks should be run.

27. D. Teredo traffic uses UDP port 3544. UDP Port 3544 must be open to ensure that Teredo clients can successfully communicate with the Teredo server.

28. B. 6to4 traffic uses Internet Protocol (IP) ID 41. 6to4 is a special usage of protocol 41. A 6to4 address starts with the digits 2002, followed by the IPv4 address of its router. Here's an example of a 6to4 address: 2002:CB00:71FF:0:fe64:3486:d398:3346.

29. C. Internet Protocol - Hypertext Transfer Protocol Secure (IP-HTTPS) traffic uses Transmission Control Protocol (TCP) 443. HTTPS URLs begin with https:// and use port 443. HTTP Secure (HTTPS) is an extension of the Hypertext Transfer Protocol (HTTP) for secure communication over a computer network and is widely used on the Internet.

30. C. You will first install the Routing and Remote Access Service (RRAS). In the wizard you have to select NAT and then add an interface for NAT. Then, add the public interface to the NAT configuration, right-click NAT, and click New Interface. Select the interface connected to the network, and then click OK.

31. B. The route.exe command is an MS-DOS executable for Windows. It is used to block IP connections to the system by adding IP addresses to a routing table. The syntax is Route [*command*] [*destination*] [*subnet mask*] [*gateway*] [*metric*].

add: Adds a route.

destination: Specifies the host.

subnet mask: Specifies the subnet mask value for the route entry. The default is 255.255.255.255.

gateway: Specifies the gateway.

metric: Specifies the metric (the cost for the destination). Metrics are cost values used by routers to determine the best path to a destination network.

32. B, C, F. In order, you would want to deploy a site-to-site VPN, configure BGP Peering, and then advertise all of the routes on all of the BGP routers. A site-to-site VPN connection lets branch offices use the Internet as a means for accessing the main office's intranet. BGP is the standard routing protocol commonly used on the Internet to exchange routing and reachability information between two or more networks. BGP enables the Azure VPN gateways and your on-premises VPN devices, called BGP peers or neighbors, to exchange "routes" that will inform both gateways on the availability and reachability of those prefixes to go through the gateways or routers. For each prefix in the routing table, the routing protocol process selects a single best path, called the *active path*. Unless you configure BGP to advertise multiple paths to the same destination, BGP advertises only the active path. Peering is a process by which two Internet networks connect and exchange traffic. It allows them to directly hand off traffic between each other's customers, without having to pay a third party to carry that traffic across the Internet for them.

33. C. NAT64 is an IPv6 transition mechanism that facilitates communication between IPv6 and IPv4 hosts by using a form of Network Address Translation (NAT). The NAT64 gateway is a translator between IPv4 and IPv6 protocols. It needs at least one IPv4 address and an IPv6 network segment comprising a 32-bit address space. DNS64 describes a DNS server that synthesizes the AAAA records from the A records. The first part of the synthesized IPv6 address points to an IPv6/IPv4 translator, and the second part embeds the IPv4 address from the A record. The translator in question is usually a NAT64 server.

34. B. The `Get-BgpRouter` PowerShell cmdlet allows you to see the configuration information for BGP routers.

35. B. The `Get-DAClient` cmdlet allows you to see the list of client security groups that are part of the DirectAccess deployment and the client properties.

36. A. The `logman.exe` utility can be used to create and manage Event Trace Session and Performance logs and allows an administrator to monitor many different applications through the use of the command line.

37. B. The `Get-RemoteAccess` cmdlet shows the configuration of a DirectAccess and VPN server.

38. D. The higher the RADIUS priority number, the less often the RADIUS server gets used. To make sure that RADIUS Server4 is used only when Server2 and Server3 are unavailable, you would set the RADIUS priority from 1 to 10. This way, it will be used only when Server2 and Server3 are having issues or are unresponsive.

39. B. The `Set-DAServer` cmdlet allows an administrator to set the properties specific to the DirectAccess server. This cmdlet configures properties that are applicable globally to the entire DA deployment; properties that are applicable per-server or per-cluster in a load-balancing scenario; or properties that are applicable per-site, such as in a multisite deployment.

40. C. The `Set-VpnAuthType` cmdlet is used only to toggle from one authentication type to another. This cmdlet cannot be used to explicitly add any RADIUS servers if RADIUS authentication is being used. Administrators use the `Set-VpnAuthType` cmdlet to set the authentication type to be used for a VPN connection.

41. B. `Add-RemoteAccessRadius` adds a new external RADIUS server for VPN authentication, accounting for DirectAccess (DA) and VPN, or one-time password (OTP) authentication for DA. The `AccountingOnOffMsg<String>` indicates the enabled state for sending accounting on or off messages. The acceptable values for this parameter are Enabled or Disabled. Disabled is the default value. This parameter is applicable only when the RADIUS server is being added for remote access accounting.

42. C. The `Add-RemoteAccessRadius` cmdlet adds a new external RADIUS server. This cmdlet allows an administrator to add a new external RADIUS server for VPN or DirectAccess connectivity.

43. D. The Link Control Protocol (LCP) handles the details of establishing and configuring the lowest-level PPP link. In that regard, you can think of LCP as if it were almost part of the Physical layer.

44. A. You can configure DirectAccess clients to send all of their traffic through the tunnels to the DirectAccess server with force tunneling. When force tunneling is configured, DirectAccess clients detect that they are on the Internet, and they remove their IPv4 default route. With the exception of local subnet traffic, all traffic sent by the DirectAccess client is IPv6 traffic that goes through tunnels to the DirectAccess server.

45. D. Layer 2 Tunneling Protocol (L2TP) is more secure than Point-to-Point Tunneling Protocol (PPTP). PPTP uses Microsoft Point-to-Point Encryption (MPPE) for security, which is less secure than the IPsec encryption method, which is what L2TP uses for security.

46. E. Secure Socket Tunneling Protocol (SSTP) is the tunneling protocol that uses the HTTPS protocol over TCP port 443 to pass traffic through firewalls and web proxies that might block PPTP and L2TP/IPsec traffic.

47. D. By default, each server logs its data in `systemroot\system32\LogFiles`. You can change this location to wherever you want.

48. A. The General tab of the Connection Properties dialog box is where you specify either the IP address of the VPN server or the modem and phone number to use with this particular connection. With the General tab, you can set VPN options by entering the VPN server address or host name and specifying whether to dial another connection automatically first and then specify the connection to dial.

49. B. The Network Policy Server (NPS) snap-in allows you to set up RADIUS servers and determine which RADIUS server would accept authentication from other RADIUS servers. You can do your entire RADIUS configuration through the NPS snap-in.

50. A. When an administrator chooses Multitenant mode, Cloud Service Providers (CSPs) and Enterprise networks can use RAS Gateways to allow datacenter and cloud network traffic routing between both virtual and physical networks. For multitenant mode, it is recommended that you deploy RAS Gateways on virtual machines that are running Windows Server 2016.

51. B. The `Disconnect-VpnUser` cmdlet disconnects a VPN connection originated by a specific user or originating from a specific client computer. A VPN connection can be disconnected in one of the following two ways: by the username of the user who originated the connection, or by the tunnel IP address assigned by the VPN server. Just note that only one of these methods can be used at a time.

52. B. SHVs settings define the requirements for client computers that connect to your network. They are configured using the Network Policy Server console. Using this feature allows you to specify different network policies for different sets of health requirements based on a specific configuration of the SHV.

53. C, E. MS-CHAPv2 provides encrypted and mutual authentication between the respective RRAS locations. MPPE works with MS-CHAPv2 and provides encryption for all of the data between the locations. CHAP provides encrypted authentication, but MS-CHAPv2 is needed for MPPE to work. PAP is the lowest level of authentication providing passwords, but it sends passwords in clear text, which is not the most secure solution. L2TP needs to team up with IPsec to provide the data encryption for the secure transfer of information between the locations.

54. A. Windows Server 2016 comes with EAP-TLS. This allows you to use public key certificates as an authenticator. TLS is similar to the familiar Secure Sockets Layer (SSL) protocol used for web browsers and 802.1X authentication. When EAP-TLS is turned on, the client and server send TLS-encrypted messages back and forth. EAP-TLS is the strongest authentication method you can use. EAP-TLS supports smartcards. EAP-TLS requires your NPS server to be part of the Windows Server 2016 domain.

55. D, E. PEAP-MS-CHAP v2 is an EAP type protocol that is easier to deploy than EAP-TLS. It is easier because user authentication is accomplished by using password-based credentials (username and password) instead of digital certificates or smartcards. Both PEAP and EAP use certificates with their protocols.

56. D. One advantage of NPS is that you can use the accounting part of NPS so that you can keep track of what each department does on your NPS server. This way, departments pay for the amount of time they use on the SQL server database. Configuring Network Policy Server Accounting, you can use the following log types:

- *Event logging*: Used primarily for auditing and troubleshooting connection attempts. You can configure NPS event logging by obtaining the NPS server properties in the NPS console.

- *Logging user authentication and accounting requests to a local file*: Used primarily for connection analysis and billing purposes. Also used as a security investigation tool because it provides you with a method of tracking the activity of a malicious user after an attack. You can configure local file logging using the Accounting Configuration Wizard.

- *Logging user authentication and accounting requests to a Microsoft SQL Server XML-compliant database*: Used to allow multiple servers running NPS to have one data source. Also provides the advantages of using a relational database. You can configure SQL Server logging by using the Accounting Configuration Wizard.

57. A. Connection request policies are sets of conditions and settings that allow network administrators to designate which RADIUS servers perform the authentication and authorization of connection requests that the server running NPS receives from RADIUS clients. NPS allows you to set up policies on how your users could log into the network. NPS allows you to set up policies that systems need to follow, and if they don't follow these policies or rules, they will not have access to the full network.

58. C. CHAP—as well as MS-CHAPv2 and PAP—allow the client to authenticate itself to the server. This authentication functions much like a regular network logon; once the client presents its logon credentials, the server can figure out what access to grant.

59. D. Encapsulation allows the client to take a packet with some kind of private content, wrap it inside an IP datagram, and send it to the server. The server, in turn, processes the IP datagram, routing real datagrams normally and handling any encapsulated packets with the appropriate protocol.

60. C, D. A VPN Device IP Address is a public-facing IPv4 address of your on-premises VPN device that you'll use to connect to Azure. The VPN device cannot be located behind a NAT. You need at least one or preferably two publicly visible IP addresses. One of the IP addresses is used on the Windows Server 2016 machine that acts as the VPN device by using RRAS. The other optional IP address is to be used as the default gateway for outbound traffic from the on-premises network.

61. B. Windows Server 2016's VPN support includes several worthwhile features; one is that you can set up account lockout policies for dial-up and VPN users. This capacity has existed for network and console users for some time. When you're using Windows Server

2016 and enabling the VPN client access, a system policy rule named Allow VPN Clients to Firewall is enabled. This allows a maximum of 1,000 VPN clients to connect simultaneously in Standard Edition and 16,000 in Enterprise Edition. VPNs do not auto-connect to a network, DirectAccess does auto-connect, and you can connect to a RADIUS server using most Windows clients (not just Windows 10).

62. D. The client sends a VPN connection request to the server. The exact format of the request varies, depending on whether the VPN is using PPTP, L2TP, or SSTP.

63. A. Software at each level of the OSI model has to see header information to figure out where a packet is coming from and where it's going. However, the payload contents aren't important to most of those components, and the payload is what's encapsulated. By fabricating the right kind of header and prepending it for whatever you want in the payload, you can route foreign traffic types through IP networks with no trouble.

64. B. The answer to this question would be phase 2, the client answers with an encrypted response.

    The phases are as follows:

    1. The server sends a challenge message to the client.
    2. The client answers with an encrypted response.
    3. The server checks the response to see whether the answer is right. The challenge-response process allows the server to determine which account is trying to make a connection.
    4. The server determines whether the user account is authorized to make a connection.
    5. If the account is authorized, the server accepts the inbound connection; any access controls or remote access restrictions still apply.

65. C. The answer to this question would be phase 2: during the TCP session, SSL negotiation takes place.

    The phases are as follows:

    1. The client connects to the server through the Internet using port 443.
    2. During the TCP session, SSL negotiation takes place.
    3. During the SSL authentication phase, the client machine receives the server certificate.
    4. The client machine will send HTTPS requests on top of the encrypted SSL session.
    5. The client machine will then also send SSTP control packets on top of the HTTPS session.
    6. PPP negotiation now takes place on both ends of the connection.
    7. After PPP is finished, both ends are ready to send IP packets to each other.

66. A. You can use the PPP tab of the RRAS server's Properties dialog box to control the PPP layer options available to clients that call in. The settings you specify here control whether the related PPP options are available to clients; you can use remote access policies to control whether individual connections can use them.

67. D. The Multilink Connections check box is selected by default. It controls whether the server will allow clients to establish multilink connections when they call in.

68. B. A VPN sits between your internal network and the Internet, accepting connections from clients in the outside world.

69. C. The General tab of the server's Properties dialog box allows you to specify whether your RRAS server is a router, a Remote Access server, or both. The first step in converting your existing RRAS server to handle VPN traffic is to make sure that the IPv4 Remote Access Server or the IPv6 Remote Access Server check box is selected on this tab.

70. A. The Remote Access Connections (Inbound Only) check box must be activated in order to accept VPN connections with this port type. To disable a VPN type (for instance, if you want to turn off L2TP), deselect this box.

71. B. The Maximum Ports control lets you set the number of inbound connections that this port type will support. By default, you get 5 PPTP and 5 L2TP ports when you install RRAS; you can use from 0 to 250 ports of each type by adjusting the number here.

72. C. Sometimes the simplest solutions are overlooked. The first thing you will want to check is that your clients can make the underlying connection to their ISP.

73. B. A standard RRAS installation will always log some data locally, but that's pretty useless unless you know what gets logged and where it goes. Each RRAS server on your network has its own set of logs, which you manage through the Remote Access Logging folder. Within that folder, you'll usually see a single item labeled Local File, which is the log file stored on that particular server.

74. A. The Log Errors Only radio button instructs the server to log errors and nothing else. This gives you an adequate indication of problems after they happen, but it doesn't point out potential problems noted by warning messages.

75. D. The huge advantage of NAT is the ability for you to share a single public IP address and a single Internet connection between multiple locations using private IP addressing schemes. The nodes on the private network use nonroutable private addresses. NAT maps the private addresses to the public address.

76. B. To program the route, you would need to use the Route command. To add a route, you would type Route add and the parameters of the route path. route.exe is an MS-DOS executable for Windows. It is used to block IP connections to the system by adding IP addresses to a routing table.

77. A. Microsoft uses the Routing Information Protocol (RIP) to automatically program routes. RIP is a broadcast-based protocol that can be added to any Microsoft router. The downside to using RIP is the extra broadcast traffic. So if you have only a few routers, it's best to configure the routes manually. On a large network with many subnets, you may want to consider using RIP.

78. B. The General tab has a field where you enter the VPN server address or host name. The First Connect group lets you specify which dial-up connection, if any, you want brought up before the VPN connection is established.

79. D. The Web Application Proxy feature allows applications running on servers inside the corporate network to be accessed by any device outside the corporate network. The process of allowing an application to be available to users outside of the corporate network is known as publishing.

80. B. Active Directory Federation Services (AD FS) must always be deployed with WAP. AD FS gives you features such as Single Sign-On (SSO), which allows you to log in one time with a set of credentials and use that set of credentials to access the applications over and over. AD FS also allows you to set up security so that only authorized users can access the applications through AD FS.

81. C. To establish this connection, DirectAccess uses IPsec and IPv6. IPsec provides a high level of security between the client and the server, and IPv6 is the protocol that the machines use.

82. A. As with any software package, role, or feature, when you install any one of these, there are always prerequisites that you must deal with. DirectAccess is no different. With DirectAccess Server with Advanced Settings, a public key infrastructure must be deployed.

83. B. By using Ad Hoc mode, wireless network computers connect directly to each other without the use of an access point (AP) or bridge.

84. D. The Password Authentication Protocol (PAP) is the simplest authentication protocol. It transmits all authentication information in clear text with no encryption, which makes it vulnerable to snooping if attackers can put themselves between the modem bank and the Remote Access server. However, this type of attack is unlikely in most networks. PAP is the most widely supported authentication protocol, and therefore you may find that you need to leave it enabled.

85. C. The `Add-DAAppServer` cmdlet allows an administrator to add a new application server security group to DirectAccess.

Chapter 8: Implement an Advanced Network Infrastructure

1. D. SDN provides all of the listed capabilities.

2. A. The Host Guardian Service (HGS) is the centerpiece of the guarded fabric solution. It is responsible for ensuring that Hyper-V hosts in the fabric are known to the host or enterprise and running trusted software and for managing the keys used to start up shielded VMs.

3. A. Microsoft Dynamic Access Control (DAC) is a data governance tool in Windows Server 2016 that lets administrators control access settings. DAC uses centralized policies to let administrators review who has access to individual files. Files can be manually or automatically classified.

4. A, D. NIC Teaming, also known as Load Balancing/Failover (LBFO), allows multiple network adapters to be placed into a team for the purposes of bandwidth aggregation, and/or traffic failover to maintain connectivity in the event of a network component failure.

5. C. Network controllers are new to Windows Server 2016. Network controllers allow an administrator to have a centralized virtual and physical datacenter infrastructure. This allows administrators to manage, configure, and troubleshoot all of their infrastructure components from one location. The Network Controller feature allows you to configure and manage allow/deny firewall Access Control rules for your workload VMs for both East/West and North/South network traffic in your datacenter.

6. D. To install a multitenant RAS Gateway, you must install the Remote Access server role first. You can deploy RAS Gateway as a multitenant, software-based edge gateway and router when you are using Hyper-V Network Virtualization or you have VM networks deployed with Virtual Local Area Networks (VLANs). With the RAS Gateway, tenants can use Point-to-Site VPN connections to access their VM network resources in the datacenter from anywhere.

7. D. Remote Access Service (RAS) Gateways are used for bridging traffic between virtual and non-virtual networks. Organizations can use Software Load Balancing (SLB) to evenly distribute network traffic between the virtual network resources.

8. B. To be able to use NIC Teaming, the computer system must have at least one Ethernet adapter. But if you want to provide fault protection, you must have a minimum of two Ethernet adapters.

9. D. In single tenant mode, the RAS Gateway is used as the exterior or Internet-facing VPN or DirectAccess edge server. Single tenant mode allows organizations of any size to deploy the gateway as an exterior, or Internet-facing edge virtual private network (VPN) and DirectAccess server. In single tenant mode, you can deploy RAS Gateway on a physical server or virtual machine running Windows Server 2016.

10. A. The `Set-NetAdapterRss` cmdlet sets the RSS properties on a network adapter. RSS is a scalability technology that distributes the receive network traffic among multiple processors by hashing the header of the incoming packet.

11. B. RDMA allows computers in a network to exchange data in main memory without involving the processor, cache, or operating system of either computer. RDMA improves throughput and performance because it frees up resources and uses a faster data transfer rate and low-latency networking. It can be implemented for networking and storage applications.

12. B. SET is an alternative NIC Teaming solution that you can use in environments that include Hyper-V and the SDN stack in Windows Server 2016. SET allows you to group between one and eight physical Ethernet network adapters into one or more software-based virtual network adapters. These virtual network adapters provide fast performance and fault tolerance in the event of a network adapter failure.

13. D. The `Get-VMSwitch` cmdlet gets the virtual switches from a Hyper-V host. If you specify no parameters, this cmdlet returns all virtual switches from the local Hyper-V host. This will show you whether SET is enabled.

14. A. NIC Teams within a virtual machine must have their Teaming mode configured as Switch Independent. In addition, Load Balancing Mode for the NIC Team in a VM must be configured with the Address Hash distribution mode. You can configure NIC Teaming in the Guest OS; however, before NIC Teaming will work in a virtual machine, you need to enable NIC Teaming in the Advanced Features section of the VM settings. In this question, Ethernet1 has not been added to the NIC Team, so you must add the missing adapter to the NIC Team.

15. D. In order of highest to lowest priority, the access categories are: Voice (VO), Video (VI), Best Effort (BE), and Background (BK). Voice (VO) is the highest with a DSCP range of 48–63, while Background (BK) is the lowest with a range of 8–23.

16. B. You can enable and configure network QoS with the Data Center Bridging (DCB) feature. QoS can help manage network traffic by configuring rules that can detect congestion or reduced bandwidth, and then to prioritize, or throttle, traffic accordingly. You can use QoS to prioritize voice and video traffic, which is sensitive to latency. DCB provides bandwidth allocation to specific network traffic and helps to improve Ethernet transport reliability by using flow control based on priority.

17. D. The `New-VMSwitch` command creates a new virtual switch on one or more virtual machine hosts. The `-EnableEmbeddedTeaming` parameter specifies whether this cmdlet enables teaming for the virtual switch.

18. C. The `New-NetworkControllerNodeObject` PowerShell cmdlet allows you to set up a new network controller. The `New-NetworkControllerNodeObject` cmdlet creates a network controller node object. This cmdlet is used for configuring a network controller for the first time.

19. B, C. Hyper-V Manager supports copying a physical disk to a virtual disk by using only dynamically expanding or fixed-size virtual hard disks. You can perform this task in the New Virtual Hard Disk Wizard. Differencing and physical disks are not available with this feature.

20. C. One advantage of Windows Server 2016 is that an administrator can set up 32 network adapters in a NIC Team.

21. B. The only supported way to move virtual machines between host machines is to use Export and Import Virtual Machine. The option to move the virtual machine files cannot be used anymore because you will lose the configuration of your virtual machines. You cannot apply a snapshot to a different host machine. The Save command is not an available option in Hyper-V.

22. C. The `Add-VMHardDiskDrive` cmdlet adds a hard disk drive to a virtual machine.

23. B. NIC Teaming, also known as Load Balancing and Failover (LBFO), gives an administrator the ability to allow multiple network adapters on a system to be placed into a team.

24. C. The storage tests require the clustered disk resource to be offline. If you need to run the storage tests, the Validate a Configuration Wizard will prompt you to make sure you want to take the resources offline.

25. D. The `Set-SmbBandwidthLimit` cmdlet adds a Server Message Block (SMB) bandwidth cap for the traffic categories that you specify. SMB bandwidth caps limit the amount of data that the server can send for each traffic category.

26. D. The SLB Multiplexer (MUX) processes inbound network traffic and maps Virtual IPs (VIPs) to Dynamic IPs (DIPs), then forwards the traffic to the correct DIP. Each MUX also uses Border Gateway Protocol (BGP) to publish VIP routes to edge routers. BGP Keepalive notifies MUXs when a MUX fails, which allows active MUXs to redistribute the load. This essentially provides load balancing for the load balancers.

27. A. The Generic Routing Encapsulation (GRE) keys must match. To separate the traffic between the two virtualized networks, the GRE headers on the tunneled packets include a GRE Key that provides a unique Virtual Subnet ID for each virtualized network.

28. C. Remote Direct Memory Access (RDMA) allows one computer to directly access memory from the memory of another computer without the need of interfacing with either one's operating system. This gives systems the ability to have high throughput and low-latency networking. This is very useful when it comes to clustering systems (including Hyper-V).

29. D. The `Set-VMNetworkAdapter` cmdlet configures features of the virtual network adapter in a virtual machine or the management operating system.

30. A. The `Set-NetLbfoTeam` cmdlet sets the TeamingMode or LoadBalancingAlgorithm parameters on the specified NIC Team.

31. C. One of the requirements of SET is that all network adapters that are members of the SET group be identical adapters. This means that they need to be the same adapter types from the same manufacturer.

32. A. Redirected traffic will be sent to the NIC with the lowest metric, but in Server 2016 CSVs use SMB Multichannel (which enables traffic to be redirected using multiple NICs), so you also need to disable SMB Multichannel to prevent redirected traffic from being sent elsewhere on one of the other NICs.

33. A. Switch Dependent means that all NIC adapters are connected into the same switch. There are no such models as Switch Reliant or Switch Autonomous.

34. A, D. The first step when allowing a virtual machine to have connectivity to a physical network is to create an external virtual switch using Virtual Switch Manager in Hyper-V Manager. The additional step that is necessary when using SR-IOV is to ensure the check box is selected when the virtual switch is being created. Once a virtual switch has been created, the next step is to configure a virtual machine and enable the SR-IOV. At the bottom is a check box to enable SR-IOV.

35. C, D. The SLB Host Agent: When you deploy SLB, you must use System Center, Windows PowerShell, or another management application to deploy the SLB Host Agent on every Hyper-V host computer. You can install the SLB Host Agent on all versions of Windows Server 2016 that provide Hyper-V support, including Nano Server.

The SLB MUX: Part of the Software Load Balancer (SLB) on Windows Server 2016, the SLB MUX processes inbound network traffic and maps Virtual IPs (VIPs) to Datacenter IPs (DIPs), then forwards the traffic to the correct DIP. Each MUX also uses BGP to publish VIP routes to edge routers. This will need to be installed on the virtual machines (SLB-VM1 and SLB-VM2).

36. C. Switch Independent means that each NIC adapter is connected into a different switch. If you use Switch Independent NIC Teaming, you must connect your NICs to different switches, but both switches must be on the same subnet. There are no such models as Switch Reliant or Switch Autonomous.

37. D. To use Border Gateway Protocol (BGP) routing, you must install the Remote Access Service (RAS) and/or the Routing Role service of the Remote Access server role on a computer or virtual machine (VM). BGP reduces the need for manual route configuration on routers because it is a dynamic routing protocol, and it automatically learns routes between sites that are connected by using site-to-site VPN connections.

38. C. With Switch Independent mode, the switch or switches to which the NIC Team members are connected are unaware of the presence of the NIC Team and do not determine how to distribute network traffic to NIC Team members. Instead, the NIC Team distributes inbound network traffic across the NIC Team members. When you use Switch Independent mode, the network traffic load is distributed based on the TransportPorts address hash as modified by the Dynamic load balancing algorithm.

39. B. The `Get-NetQosDcbxSetting` command gets Data Center Bridging Exchange (DCBX) settings. The only thing you need to configure is whether the network adapters in the computer that runs Windows Server 2012 or later accepts Data Center Bridging (DCB) configurations from the computer or from a remote device.

40. A. When you create a new SET team, you must configure the member adapters and Load Balancing Mode team properties. The options for SET team Load Balancing distribution mode are Hyper-V Port and Dynamic. The options Dynamic Hyper-V and Outbound are not valid distribution modes.

The Dynamic Load Balancing Mode provides the following:

- Outbound—Loads are distributed based on a hash of the TCP Ports and IP addresses. Dynamic mode also re-balances loads in real time so that a given outbound flow can move back and forth between SET team members.

- Inbound—Loads are distributed in the same manner as the Hyper-V Port mode.

41. B. SET can be an alternative to using NIC Teaming in environments that include Hyper-V and the Software Defined Networking (SDN) stack in Windows Server 2016. SET allows an administrator to combine a group of physical adapters (minimum of one adapter and a maximum of eight adapters) into software-based virtual adapters.

42. C. Windows Server 2016 Hyper-V includes a feature called Virtual Machine Queue (VMQ). VMQ uses packet filtering to provide data from an external virtual machine network directly to virtual machines. This helps reduce the overhead of routing packets from the management operating system to the virtual machine.

43. A. Receive Side Scaling (RSS) allows a system's network adapter to spread the network processing between multiple processor cores in systems that have a multicore processor. Due to the fact that RSS can distribute the networking load across multiple processors, the system can handle more network traffic.

44. E. vRSS works with many different types of technologies, including

- IPv4 and IPv6
- TCP and UDP
- LBFO (NIC Teaming)

- Live Migration
- Network Virtualization using Generic Routing Encapsulation (NVGRE)

45. D. RSS has the ability to work with systems that have more than 64 processors. RSS can do this because it spreads the load across all of the processors. Since RSS can spread the network load, you end up with TCP load balancing. RSS also has the ability to load balance non-TCP traffic like UDP and multicast messages. RSS also allows an administrator to have better auditing and management capabilities.

46. B. To enable vRSS using PowerShell, you need to run one of the following commands from PowerShell. Either PowerShell command will enable vRSS.

```
Enable-NetAdapterRSS -Name "AdapterName"
```

or

```
Set-NetAdapterRSS -Name "AdapterName" -Enabled $True
```

The `Enable-NetAdapterRSS` command enables either RSS or vRSS on a network adapter, and the `Set-NetAdapterRSS` cmdlet sets either RSS or vRSS on a network adapter. `-$True` indicates whether RSS or vRSS on an interface is enabled.

47. A. To disable vRSS using PowerShell, you will need to run one of the following commands from PowerShell. Either PowerShell command will disable vRSS.

```
Disable-NetAdapterRSS -Name "AdapterName"
```

or

```
Set-NetAdapterRSS -Name "AdapterName" -Enabled $False
```

The `Disable-NetAdapterRSS` cmdlet disables either RSS or vRSS on a network adapter, and the `Set-NetAdapterRSS` cmdlet sets either RSS or vRSS on a network adapter. `-$False` indicates whether RSS or vRSS on an interface is disabled.

48. D. Virtual Machine Multi-Queue (VMMQ) allocates multiple queues to a single virtual machine. Each queue will have its own affinity settings to a core. For this to operate properly, the virtual machine must have the ability to work with multiple virtual CPUs (vCPUs).

49. C. Virtual Machine Quality of Service (vmQoS) allows an administrator to set the bandwidth limits generated by a virtual machine so that you can control the traffic that is generated by a virtual machine. Administrators have the ability to set minimum and maximum bandwidth limits.

50. B. To enable Data Center Bridging (DCB), you would use the following PowerShell cmdlet:

```
Install-WindowsFeature -Name Data-Center-Bridging -IncludeManagementTools
```

By using DCB, administrators can unite multiple types of network traffic onto a single network adapter. This allows administrators to have a guaranteed level of service for every type of network traffic.

51. B, C, E. The `New-NetworkControllerAccessControlList` command creates a new access control list for allowing/denying traffic to/from a particular subnet or network interface. Each access control list can contain multiple rules. In this given scenario, you will want to add:

- The `$ruleproperties.SourceAddressPrefix` to the IP address indicated as `"10.10.10.0/24"` as the source address
- The `$ruleproperties.Protocol = "ALL"`, which will allow all protocols
- The `$ruleproperties.DestinationAddressPrefix = "*"`, which is the wildcard and will allow all destination addresses

52. A. When it comes to SLB and Network Address Translation (NAT), you may sometimes hear the terms North-South or East-West. These terms just refer to the way that your application traffic patterns go in the context of your datacenter. This question refers to "applications that send data to other applications within the same datacenter or between datacenters," so it has an East-West traffic pattern.

53. B. You would want to install the Network Controller feature. Network Controller provides a centralized, programmable point of automation to manage, configure, monitor, and troubleshoot virtual and physical network infrastructure in your datacenter. Using the Network Controller feature, you can automate the configuration of network infrastructure instead of performing manual configuration of network devices and services.

54. A. Datacenter Firewalls are new Windows Server 2016 network layer, stateful, multitenant firewalls. Network administrators who work with virtual network tenants can install and then configure firewall policies. These firewall policies can help protect their virtual networks from unwanted traffic from Internet and intranet networks. Windows Server 2016 Datacenter Firewalls give you the following tenant benefits:

- Administrators have the ability to define firewall rules to protect data between virtual machines on the same Layer 2 (L2) or different Layer 2 (L2) virtual subnets.
- Administrators have the ability to define firewall rules that help protect Internet-facing workloads on virtual networks.
- Administrators have the ability to define firewall rules to protect and isolate network traffic between tenants on a virtual network from a service provider.

55. A, C, D. In this scenario, the three actions you should perform in order are:

- Deploy a Site-to-Site (S2S) VPN.
- Configure Border Gateway Protocol (BGP) peering.
- Advertise all the routes on all the Border Gateway Protocol (BGP) routers.

56. C. When it comes to SLB and Network Address Translation (NAT), you may sometimes hear the terms North-South or East-West. These terms just refer to the way that your application traffic patterns go in the context of your datacenter. In this question, it states that "if your organization has an older datacenter where clients simply request data from a single server," so it has a North-South traffic pattern.

57. A. Generic Routing Encapsulation (GRE)–based tunnels enable connectivity between tenant virtual networks and external networks. Since the GRE protocol is lightweight and support for GRE is available on most network devices, it becomes an ideal choice for tunneling where encryption of data is not required. GRE support in S2S tunnels solves the problem of forwarding between tenant virtual networks and tenant external networks using a multitenant gateway.

58. C. Layer 3 (L3) forwarding enables connectivity between the physical infrastructure in the datacenter and the virtualized infrastructure in the Hyper-V network virtualization cloud. Using L3 forwarding, tenant network virtual machines can connect to a physical network through the Windows Server 2016 SDN Gateway, which is already configured in an SDN environment. In this case, the SDN gateway acts as a router between the virtualized network and the physical network.

59. D. By using virtual adapters, you get better performance and greater fault tolerance in the event of a network adapter failure. For SET to be enabled, all the physical network adapters must be installed on the same physical Hyper-V host.

60. B. The `Remove-VMSwitch` cmdlet deletes a virtual switch. `Remove-VMSwitch "VSwitch1"` is the correct cmdlet to use to remove the virtual switch.

61. A. Storage QoS gives an administrator the ability to guarantee that the storage throughput of a single VHD cannot adversely affect the performance of another VHD on the same host. It does this by giving administrators the ability to specify the maximum and minimum I/O loads based on I/O operations per second (IOPS) for each virtual disk in your virtual machines.

62. D. Storage QoS provides the ability to specify a maximum IOPS value for your virtual hard disk. An administrator can throttle the storage I/O to stop a tenant from consuming excessive storage resources that may impact another tenant. Administrators can also set a minimum IOPS value. They will be notified when the IOPS to a specified virtual hard disk is below a threshold that is needed for its optimal performance.

63. D. Software Defined Networking (SDN) allows an administrator to centrally manage and control all of your virtual and physical network devices. These devices include things like datacenter switches, routers, and gateways. SDN also allows administrators to manage virtual elements like Hyper-V virtual switches and gateways. Administrators can easily manage their entire networks centrally.

64. B. The Southbound API allows network controllers to communicate with the network. Network controllers use API languages to control all of the different hardware on your network. The Northbound API allows you to communicate with the network controller.

65. D. The `New-NetworkControllerNodeObject` cmdlet creates a Network Controller node object. This cmdlet is used for configuring a Network Controller for the first time:

```
New-NetworkControllerNodeObject -Name <String> -Server <String> -FaultDomain
<String> -RestInterface <String> [-NodeCertificate <X509Certificate2>]
[-WhatIf] [-Confirm] [<CommonParameters>]
```

66. C. Multitenant mode is used for CSPs or enterprise networks to allow datacenter or cloud network traffic routing between virtual and physical networks. This includes traffic that goes over the Internet. In multitenant mode, administrators will deploy the RAS Gateway on a Windows Server 2016 virtual machine.

67. A. If the computers or virtual machines for Network Controller and the management client are domain-joined, you configure security groups for Kerberos authentication. A security group defines who can access particular resources.

68. A. Border Gateway Protocol (BGP) provides you with the ability to manage the routing of network traffic between your tenants' virtual machine networks and their remote sites. BGP reduces the need for manual route configuration on routers because it is a dynamic routing protocol, and it automatically learns routes between sites that are connected by using site-to-site VPN connections.

69. D. Windows Server Containers are a lightweight operating system virtualization method used to separate applications or services from other services that are running on the same container host. Windows Containers are independent and isolated environments that run an operating system. These isolated environments allow an administrator to place an application into its own container, thus not affecting any other applications or containers. With Windows Server 2016, you can now connect Windows Server Containers to virtual networks.

70. B. An Inbound NAT forwards the external traffic to a specific virtual machine in a virtual network.

NAT allows virtual machines (VMs) in an isolated SDN virtual network to obtain external connectivity. Virtual Machine Manager (VMM) configures a Virtual IP (VIP) to forward the traffic to and from an external network. The following two NAT types are supported by VMM:

- Outbound NAT—Forwards the VM network traffic from a virtual network to external destinations
- Inbound NAT—Forwards the external traffic to a specific virtual machine in a virtual network

71. C. NIC Teaming gives an administrator the ability to allow a virtual machine to use virtual network adapters in Hyper-V. The advantage of using NIC Teaming in Hyper-V is that the administrator can connect to more than one Hyper-V switch.

72. A. An administrator can configure NIC Teaming using either Server Manager or PowerShell. Membership in the Administrators group, or equivalent, is a minimum requirement.

73. D. Datacenter Firewall is a new service included with Windows Server 2016. It is a network layer, 5-tuple (protocol, source and destination port numbers, source and destination IP addresses), stateful, multitenant firewall. 5-tuple refers to a set of five different values that comprise a Transmission Control Protocol/Internet Protocol (TCP/IP) connection.

74. B. Multitenant mode allows Cloud Service Providers (CSPs) and Enterprises to use RAS Gateway to enable datacenter and cloud network traffic routing between virtual and physical networks, including the Internet. Multitenancy is the ability of a cloud infrastructure to support the virtual machine workloads of multiple tenants, yet isolate them from each other, while all of the workloads run on the same infrastructure.

75. C. You cannot use the Windows interface to install Remote Access when you want to deploy Remote Access Service (RAS) Gateway in multitenant mode for use with Software Defined Network (SDN). You must use Windows PowerShell.

76. A. Before you can install RAS Gateway by using PowerShell, you must use PowerShell to add the RemoteAccess Windows feature. To do this, run the following command at the PowerShell prompt:

```
Add-WindowsFeature -Name RemoteAccess -IncludeAllSubFeature
-IncludeManagementTools
```

This command adds the RemoteAccess feature and the PowerShell commands for the feature. After you have added RemoteAccess to your server, you can install Remote Access as a RAS Gateway with multitenant mode and BGP.

77. A. The Northbound API allows the network to communicate with the network controller. Network controllers use different application programming interface (API) languages to control all of the different hardware on your network. The Southbound API allows network controllers to communicate with the network.

78. B. To deploy Network Controller, you must install the Network Controller server role on a Hyper-V virtual machine (VM) that is installed on a Hyper-V host. Do not deploy the Network Controller server role on physical hosts. Membership in Administrators, or equivalent, is the minimum required to perform this procedure.

79. C. Internal DNS Service (iDNS) for SDN-hosted virtual machines (VMs) and applications requires DNS to communicate within their own networks and with external resources on the Internet. With iDNS, you can provide tenants with DNS name resolution services for their isolated, local name space, and for Internet resources.

80. C. For Windows Server 2016 deployments, you can deploy Network Controller on one or more computers, one or more VMs, or a combination of computers and VMs. All VMs and computers planned as network controller nodes must be running Windows Server 2016 Datacenter edition.

81. C. The `Install-NetworkControllerCluster` cmdlet creates a network controller cluster. Configuration of the network controller involves creating a network controller cluster and then creating a network controller application on top of the cluster. You can create a network controller application by using the `Install-NetworkController` cmdlet.

82. D. You can disable vRSS for a VM on the Hyper-V Virtual Switch port by using the following Windows PowerShell cmdlet on the Hyper-V host: `Set-VMNetworkAdapter -VrssEnabled $FALSE`.

83. F. Administrators can use Windows PowerShell to communicate with the Representational State Transfer (REST) API (this is the management application) to manage their network infrastructure components. These components include the following:

- Physical switches
- Physical routers
- Hyper-V switches and Virtual Machines (VMs)
- Datacenter Firewalls
- VPN Gateways
- Load Balancing components

84. B. The following are the key features of iDNS:

- iDNS provides shared DNS name resolution services for tenant workloads.
- iDNS is an authoritative DNS service for name resolution and DNS registration within the tenant name space.
- iDNS is a recursive DNS service for resolution of Internet names from tenant VMs.
- If desired, you can configure simultaneous hosting of fabric and tenant names.
- iDNS provides a cost-effective DNS solution because tenants do not need to deploy their own DNS infrastructure.
- iDNS provides high availability with Active Directory integration, which is required.

85. B. Software Load Balancer (SLB) allows an administrator to set up multiple servers that can host the same workload. This gives an organization the ability to have high availability and scalability between the server's workload.

Chapter 9: Install and Configure Active Directory Domain Services (AD DS)

1. C. All servers in the cluster must be in the same Active Directory domain. As a best practice, all clustered servers should have the same domain role (either member server or domain controller). The recommended role is member server.

2. D. `repadmin.exe` is a command-line tool that can assist administrators in diagnosing replication problems between Windows domain controllers. Administrators can use Repadmin to retrieve a list of accounts that have their passwords cached on an RODC. Repadmin.exe can also be used for monitoring the relative health of an Active Directory forest.

3. A. The `Get-ADUser` cmdlet gets a specified user object or performs a search to get multiple user objects. To search for and retrieve more than one user, use the `Filter` or `LDAPFilter` parameters. `-Filter` specifies a query string that retrieves Active Directory objects.

4. C. LDAP Data Interchange Format Directory Exchange (LDIFDE.exe) is a powerful utility that can be useful in adding, deleting, and modifying user accounts in Active Directory. This utility enables you to import/export information from/to Active Directory. LDIFDE queries any available domain controller to retrieve or update AD information.

5. B. You can open an elevated command prompt and execute the command netdom query fsmo. This will list the FSMO role holder server. It will show you the five FSMO roles:

- Schema Master—Forest-wide and one per forest
- Domain Naming Master—Forest-wide and one per forest
- RID Master—Domain-specific and one for each domain
- PDC—Domain-specific and one for each domain
- Infrastructure Master—Domain-specific and one for each domain

6. B. This is a trick question, because a group has been modified but nothing has been deleted. Therefore, options A and D will not work. Option C would work if it was an authoritative restore, but it won't work for a nonauthoritative restore. The solution is to recover an earlier copy of the group from a backup or Active Directory checkpoint by using Dsamain.

7. A, B, C, D. To install an RODC, ensure that the forest and functional levels are Windows 2003 or newer.

8. B. A domain controller can contain Active Directory information for only one domain. If you want to use a multidomain environment, you must use multiple domain controllers configured in either a tree or a forest setting.

9. B, C. You need to run the adprep command when installing your first Windows Server 2016 domain controller onto a Windows Server 2008 R2 domain. If you are doing an in-place upgrade of an existing domain controller to the Windows Server 2016 operating system, you will need to run adprep /forestprep and adprep /domainprep manually. adprep /forestprep needs to be run only once in the forest. adprep /domainprep needs to be run once in each domain in which you have domain controllers that you are upgrading to Windows Server 2016. adprep /rodcprep gets the network ready to install a read-only domain controller and not a GUI version.

10. B. A computer account and the domain authenticate each other by using a password. The password resets every 30 days. Since the machine has not connected to the domain for eight weeks, the computer needs to be rejoined to the domain.

11. C. Item-level targeting is a feature of Group Policy preferences that allows preference settings to be applied to individual users and/or computers within the scope of the GPO that contains the preferences. Item-level targeting allows an administrator to specify a list of conditions that must be met in order for a preference setting to be applied to a user or computer object. The Scheduled Tasks preference items let you create, replace, update, and delete scheduled tasks and their associated properties.

12. D. To prevent replicating data between a broken domain controller and the rest, you will need to perform a metadata cleanup. This can be done using ntdsutil.exe on any workstation/server in a network. Metadata cleanup removes all the references to the domain controller from Active Directory so that tasks like replication continue to work without any errors.

13. B. You will need to stop the Active Directory Certificate Services (AD CS) service prior to running the `Restore-CARoleService` cmdlet. If you're using the `Restore-CARoleService` cmdlet and you receive the error message "The process cannot access the file because it is being used by another process," you need to stop the Active Directory Certificate Services (AD CS) service first.

14. D. You can use Active Directory and Active Directory Domain Services (AD DS) to implement limitations on the number of objects that a security principal (a user, computer, and group) can create in a directory node. You can define these limitations through Active Directory quotas. `dsadd_quota` adds a quota specification to a directory partition. A quota specification determines the maximum number of directory objects a given security principal can own in a specified directory partition.

15. C. The Group Policy Software installation extension allows administrators to use the Group Policy Object Editor to centrally manage the installation of software on all client computers in an organization. When Group Policy is used to deploy software and the software is included in the GPO linked to a site, domain, or OU, the software is referred to as being advertised to the user and computer. If you're assigning the application to a user, use the Software Installation node under the User Configuration node, Software Settings. If you're assigning the application to a computer, use the Software Installation node under Computer Configuration, Software Settings. A .zap package is a simple text wrapper around a setup command. This information is extracted directly by the Group Policy Software installation extension.

16. B. By default, only domain administrators and enterprise administrators have this privilege for domains and OUs. Enterprise administrators and domain administrators of the forest root domain have this privilege for sites.

17. E. You would want to modify the security settings from the Computer Configuration node of the GPO named DomainPolicy. Configuring Group Policy settings enables you to customize the configuration of a user's desktop, environment, and security settings. The actual settings are divided into two subcategories: Computer Configuration and User Configurations. The subcategories are referred to as Group Policy nodes. A node is simply a parent structure that holds all related settings. In this case, the node is specific to Computer Configurations and User Configurations.

18. A. You can restore objects from the Active Directory Recycle Bin by using Active Directory Administrative Center. Starting with Windows Server 2012, the Active Directory Recycle Bin feature was enhanced with a new graphical user interface for users to manage and restore deleted objects. Users can now visually locate a list of deleted objects and restore them to their original or desired locations.

19. H. Ntdsutil is the primary method by which system administrators can do offline maintenance. It is a command-line tool that is run at an elevated command prompt. The main utility we use for offline maintenance is Ntdsutil. You can use the defragmentation process to compact the Active Directory database when it's offline. Offline defragmentation helps return free disk space and check Active Directory database integrity. When you perform a defragmentation of the Active Directory database, a new, compacted version of the database is created. This new database file can be created on the same machine (if space permits) or on a network location. After the new file is created, copy the compacted `Ntds.dit` file back to the original location.

20. **A.** To enable Fine-Grained Password Policies (FGPPs), you need to open the Active Directory Administrative Center. Using FGPPs, you specify multiple password policies in a single domain and apply different restrictions for password and account lockout policies to different sets of users in a domain. You can apply stricter settings to privileged accounts and less strict settings to the accounts of other users.

21. **D.** NTFS has file-level security and makes efficient use of disk space. Since this machine is to be configured as a domain controller, the configuration requires at least one NTFS partition to store the SYSVOL information.

22. **D.** The first step in creating a gMSA is to create the KDS Root Key. Use the Add-KdsRootKey cmdlet to generate a new root key for the Microsoft Group Key Distribution Service (KdsSvc) within Active Directory. The Microsoft Group KdsSvc generates new group keys from the new root key.

23. **C.** The HOSTS file is a text-file-based database of mappings between host names and IP addresses. It works like a file-based version of DNS. DNS resolves a host name to an IP address.

24. **A.** You only need to give them rights to the abc.com zone using the DNS snap-in. If they do not have any rights to the abcAD.com zone, they will not be able to configure this zone in any way.

25. **B, E.** The use of DNS and TCP/IP is required to support Active Directory. TCP/IP is the network protocol favored by Microsoft, which determined that all Active Directory communication would occur on TCP/IP. DNS is required because Active Directory is inherently dependent on the domain model. DHCP is used for automatic address assignment and is not required. Similarly, NetBEUI and IPX/SPX are not available network protocols in Windows Server 2016.

26. **D.** The Set-ADReplicationSite cmdlet is used to set the properties for an Active Directory site that is being used for replication. Sites are used in Active Directory to either enable clients to discover network resources (published shares, domain controllers) close to the physical location of a client computer or to reduce network traffic over wide area network (WAN) links. Sites can also be used to optimize replication between domain controllers.

27. **A.** An SPN is a unique identifier of a service instance. SPNs are used by Kerberos authentication to associate a service instance with a service logon account. This allows a client application to request that the service authenticate an account even if the client does not have the account name. To see if the SPNs are registered, you can use Active Directory Users and Computers.

28. **B.** Administrative Template files are divided into .admx files and language-specific .adml files for use by Group Policy administrators. To create a central store for .admx and .adml files, create a new folder in File Explorer that is named PolicyDefinitions on the domain controller—for example, \\abc.com\SYSVOL\abc.com\policies\PolicyDefinitions.

29. **B.** The Copy-Item cmdlet copies an item from one location to another in the same namespace. This cmdlet does not cut or delete the items being copied. Copy-Item can copy files and directories in a filesystem drive and registry keys and entries in the registry drive.

30. C. By making the server a Server Core based server, you prevent users from changing the Windows Server by using the graphical user interface (GUI). Server Core has no GUI installed on it. Then by making the domain controller an RODC, you prevent changes to Active Directory.

31. B. If you want to convert an existing partition from one filesystem to another, you will need to use the CONVERT command-line utility. For example, to convert the C: partition from FAT to NTFS, you would use the following command: CONVERT c: /fs:ntfs.

32. A, B. The Update action will, if a drive mapping exists, be updated with the settings specified. The Replace action will remove whatever drive mapping exists for this share and create a new one with these settings.

33. C. Windows Server 2016 allows you to install a domain controller using the IFM method by using the Ntdsutil utility. The Ntdsutil utility allows you to create installation media for an additional domain controller in a domain.

34. D. Shortcut trusts are trusts that are set up between two domains in the same forest. Shortcut trusts are one-way or two-way transitive trusts that can be used when administrators need to optimize the authentication process.

35. A. PSOs are created so that you can create fine-grained password policies. You create PSOs using the Active Directory Service Interfaces (ADSI) editor, and then you can use those PSOs to create your fine-grained password policies. Fine-grained password policies allow you to specify multiple password policies in a single domain.

36. A, D. There are a few ways to join a computer to a domain. You can do it using the System icon in Control Panel or you can do it using the djoin.exe command. If you pre-created all of the computers in Active Directory, this would take a lot of extra time. Option C is incorrect because if you add the computer to the domain using the System icon, you would not need to use the netdom command.

37. A. When you configure the Group Policy settings for WSUS, use a GPO linked to an Active Directory container appropriate for your environment. Here are the steps in automatically downloading and installing Windows Updates:

1. In the Group Policy Object Editor, expand Computer Configuration, expand Administrative Templates, expand Windows Components, and then click Windows Update.

2. In the details pane, click Configure Automatic Updates.

3. Click Enabled and then select how you would like the updates to be installed.

4. Click OK.

38. D. The wbadmin command allows you to back up and restore your operating system, volumes, files, folders, and applications from a command prompt. You must be a member of the Administrators group to configure a backup schedule. You must be a member of the Backup Operators or the Administrators group (or you must have been delegated the appropriate permissions) to perform all other tasks using the wbadmin command. To use the wbadmin command, you must run it from an elevated command prompt.

39. C. dnscmd.exe is a command-line interface for managing DNS servers. This utility is useful in scripting batch files to help automate routine DNS management tasks, or to perform simple unattended setup and configuration of new DNS servers on your network. Here is an example:

```
dnscmd <ServerName> <command> [<command parameters>]
```

40. B, C, D. You can install Active Directory by using the Windows Server 2016 installation disk (Install from Media [IFM]), or by using Server Manager or Windows PowerShell.

41. B, C, E. In order, you'd want to create a new site object, create a new subnet object, and then promote the member server to a domain controller.

42. C. Dcgpofix re-creates the default GPOs for a domain. It will restore the Default Domain Controllers Policy GPO to its original state. You will lose any changes that you have made to the GPO.

43. D. If you assign an application to a user, the application does not get automatically installed. To have an application automatically installed, you must assign the application to the computer account. Since Finance is the only OU that should receive this application, you would link the GPO to Finance only.

44. D. The Invoke-GPUpdate cmdlet refreshes Group Policy settings, including security settings that are set on remote computers by scheduling the running of the GPUpdate cmdlet on a remote computer. The refresh can be scheduled to immediately start a refresh of policy settings or wait for a specified period of time.

45. B, C, D. In order to run adprep /forestprep and to add the first Windows Server 2016 domain controller to an existing forest, the command must be run by an administrator who is a member of the Enterprise Admins group, the Schema Admins group, or the Domain Admins group of the domain that hosts the schema master.

46. A, C, D, E. SRV records show that a machine is running a specific service. There are a few services that are needed for the network to properly function. DNS must have service records for the domain controllers, global catalogs, PDC emulator, and the Kerberos KDC service. The easiest way to configure the SRV records is to have these machines all be DNS clients. DNS clients will send their client information to the DNS server by default.

47. D. In the Active Directory Sites and Services console, the Server NTDS settings are where you would activate and deactivate Global Catalogs.

48. A. The Move-ADDirectoryServerOperationMasterRole cmdlet moves one or more operation master roles to a directory server. You can move operation master roles to a directory server in a different domain if the credentials are the same in both domains. The -identity parameter specifies the directory server that receives the roles. The -OperationMasterRole parameter is used to specify the roles for transfer. Operation roles include PDCEmulator, RIDMaster, InfrastructureMaster, SchemaMaster, and DomainNamingMaster. In this scenario we are using the PDCEmulator. The -Force parameter indicates that the cmdlet is used for seize operations on domain controllers with the flexible single master operations (FSMO) role.

49. B. To set up domain controller cloning, you must be a member of the Domain Admins group or have the equivalent permissions. The administrator must then run PowerShell from an elevated command prompt. The following example is used to create a clone domain controller named TestClone with a static IP address of 10.0.0.5 and a subnet mask of 255.255.0.0. This command also configures the DNS Server and WINS server configurations.

```
New-ADDCCloneConfigFile -CloneComputerName "TestClone" -Static -IPv4Address
"10.0.0.5" -IPv4DNSResolver "10.0.0.1" -IPv4SubnetMask "255.255.0.0" -
PreferredWinsServer "10.0.0.1" -AlternateWinsServer "10.0.0.2"
```

50. C. Inheritance is the process by which permissions placed on parent OUs affect child OUs. In this example, the permissions change for the higher-level OU (Texas) automatically caused a change in permissions for the lower-level OU (Austin).

51. C. The Resultant Set of Policy (RSoP) utility displays the exact settings that apply to individuals, users, computers, OUs, domains, and sites after inheritance and filtering have taken effect. Desktop wallpaper settings are under the User section of the GPO, so you would run the RSoP against the user account.

52. B. Repadmin is used to troubleshoot replication issues in Active Directory. This command-line tool assists administrators in diagnosing replication problems between domain controllers. Repadmin can be used to manually create the replication topology to force replication events between domain controllers. Repadmin can also be used for monitoring the relative health of an Active Directory forest.

53. A, B, E. In order, you would, from the Files context, run `compact`. Then, run `ntdsutil.exe` and then run `activate instance ntds`. Active Directory servers must be restored offline. The system must be restarted in Directory Services Restore mode. DSRM is a safe mode boot option for Windows Server domain controllers. DSRM allows an administrator to repair or restore an Active Directory database. Performing an offline defragmentation creates a new version of the database file without internal fragmentation. It also re-creates all indexes. Depending on how fragmented the original database file was, the new file may be much smaller.

54. B. The `Start-OBRegistration` cmdlet needs to be run because it registers the server using the vault credentials downloaded during enrollment.

55. A. The Local Group Policy Editor (`gpedit.msc`) is a Microsoft Management Console (MMC) snap-in that provides a single user interface through which all the Computer Configuration and User Configuration settings of Local Group Policy objects can be managed. To modify the Group Policy setting on Server1, use the File menu and then select the Options settings.

56. D. The `Invoke-GPUpdate` cmdlet refreshes Group Policy settings, including security settings that are set on remote computers, by scheduling the running of the `GPUpdate` command on a remote computer.

57. A. Administrators have the ability to apply individual preference items only to selected users or computers using a GPO feature called item-level targeting. Item-level targeting allows an administrator to select specific items that the GPO will look at and then apply that GPO only to the specific users or computers.

58. C. Group Policy loopback is a computer configuration setting that enables different Group Policy user settings to apply based on the computer from which logon occurs. This policy directs the system to apply the set of GPOs for the computer to any user who logs on to a computer affected by this policy. This policy is intended for special-use computers where you must modify the user policy based on the computer that is being used.

59. D. Redircmp redirects the default container for newly created computers to a specified, target organizational unit (OU) so that newly created computer objects are created in the specific target OU instead of in CN=Computers. You must run the `redircmp` command from an elevated command prompt.

60. C. By checking the box Account Never Expires, you stop this user's account from expiring again.

61. B, E. Enabling the Advanced Features item in the View menu will allow Sue to see the `LostAndFound` and `System` folders. The `LostAndFound` folder contains information about objects that could not be replicated among domain controllers.

62. C. In one-way relationships, the trusting domain allows resources to be shared with the trusted domain but not the other way around. Selective authentication means that users cannot authenticate to a domain controller or resource server in the trusting forest unless they are explicitly allowed to do so.

63. C. The `Install-ADDSDomain` cmdlet installs a new Active Directory domain configuration. If the value set for `-DomainType` is `TreeDomain`, this parameter can be used to specify the fully qualified domain name (FQDN) for the new domain tree (for example, `abc.com`). `-InstallDns:$true` indicates that the DNS Server service will be installed and configured for the domain or domain tree. `-NewDomainName` indicates the new name domain to be added, and `-ParentDomainName` specifies the FQDN of an existing parent domain.

64. D. The `Search-ADAccount` cmdlet retrieves one or more user, computer, or service accounts that meet the criteria specified by the parameters. Search criteria include account and password status. `-AccountDisabled` specifies a search for accounts that are disabled. An account is disabled when the `ADAccount Enabled` property is set to false. `-TimeSpan` specifies a time interval. This parameter is used to specify a time value. `-UsersOnly` indicates that this cmdlet searches for user accounts only. `Format-TableName, UserPrincipalName` is the output format for the results.

65. E. The `Set-ADReplicationSite` cmdlet is used to set the properties for an Active Directory site that is being used for replication. Sites are used in Active Directory to either enable clients to discover network resources (published shares, domain controllers) close to the physical location of a client computer or to reduce network traffic over wide area network (WAN) links. Sites can also be used to optimize replication between domain controllers. You would want to use the `-ProtectedFromAccidentalDeletion` parameter, which specifies whether to prevent the object from being deleted. When this property is set to $True, you cannot delete the corresponding object without changing the value of the property. The acceptable values for this parameter are:

- `$False or 0`
- `$True or 1`

66. C. The `Set-ADUser` cmdlet modifies the properties of an Active Directory user. You can modify commonly used property values by using the cmdlet parameters. The parameter `-UserPrincipalName` specifies a UPN in the format `<user>@<DNS-domain-name>`. The UPN is independent of the user object's distinguished name, so a user object can be moved or renamed without affecting the user logon name. When logging on using a UPN, users don't have to choose a domain from a list in the logon dialog box.

67. E. Through the use of filtering, you can choose which types of objects you want to see using the Active Directory Users and Computers tool. Several of the other choices may work, but they require changes to Active Directory settings or objects.

68. D. The Delegation of Control Wizard is designed to allow administrators to set up permissions on specific Active Directory objects. The Delegation of Control Wizard is a tool for delegating routine tasks without having to learn the complex details of Active Directory object permissions.

69. A. By decreasing the replication interval for the `DEFAULTIPSITELINK` object, you will decrease the replication latency for all sites using `DEFAULTIPSITELINK`.

70. D. Preferred bridgehead servers receive replication information for a site and transmit this information to other domain controllers within the site. By configuring one server at each site to act as a preferred bridgehead server, you can ensure that all replication traffic between the two sites is routed through the bridgehead servers and that replication traffic will flow properly between the domain controllers.

71. B. A service, like any process, has a primary security identity that determines the granted access rights and privileges for local and network resources. If you want a service to use a different account, you need to go into the services properties and change which account starts the service.

72. D. The `Get-ADUser` cmdlet gets a specified user object or performs a search to get multiple user objects. The `Set-ADUser` cmdlet modifies the properties of an Active Directory user. You can use the `Get-ADUser` cmdlet to retrieve a user object and then pass the object through the pipeline to the `Set-ADUser` cmdlet.

73. B. The easiest way to configure the SRV records is to have these machines all be DNS clients. DNS clients will send their client information to the DNS server by default. But if the servers are not DNS clients or for some reason they do not register with DNS, you may need to manually create these SRV records.

1. Open the DNS management tool by clicking Start ➤ Administrative Tools ➤ DNS.
2. Expand the Forward Lookup Zone and expand your zone name.
3. Right-click _TCP and choose Other New Record.
4. Choose the SRV record.
5. Enter the SRV record information.

74. A. The dsadd command allows you to add an object (user's account) to the Active Directory database. To use dsadd, you must run it from an elevated command prompt. dsadd user will add a single user to the directory.

75. B. The Active Directory Domains and Trusts tool is used to view and change information related to the various domains in an Active Directory environment. This MMC snap-in also allows you to set up shortcut trusts.

76. A. The NTDS settings for the site level are where you would activate and deactivate Global Catalogs. To create a Global Catalog server, simply expand the Server object in the Active Directory Sites and Services tool, right-click NTDS Settings, and select Properties to bring up the NTDS Settings Properties dialog box. To configure a server as a Global Catalog server, simply place a check mark in the Global Catalog box.

77. C. When you delegate the ability to log on to an RODC to a user or a security group, the user or group is not added to the Domain Admins group and therefore does not have additional rights to perform directory service operations. A delegated RODC administrator can do the following on the RODC:

- Install hardware devices, such as network adapters and disk drives
- Manage disk drives and other devices
- Install software updates and drivers
- Stop and start Active Directory Domain Services (AD DS)
- Install and remove other server roles and features
- View logs in Event Viewer
- Manage shares and other applications and services

By default, a delegated RODC administrator cannot make updates to SYSVOL contents. In addition, any updates that are made to the SYSVOL contents on an RODC are not replicated to other domain controllers because RODCs do not perform outbound replication.

78. C. Distribution groups are for emails only and cannot be assigned rights and permissions to objects. Security groups allow you to manage user and computer access to shared resources. You can also control who receives group policy settings. Security groups allow you to set permissions once on multiple computers, then to change the membership of the group as needed. The change in group membership automatically takes effect everywhere.

79. B. DC1 successfully transfers the PDC emulator role to DC2. So, that is correct. DC1 fails before transferring the schema master and RID master roles to DC2. So those are incorrect. You cannot add other domains to forest, because DC1 is offline.

80. D. `repadmin.exe` is a command-line tool used to assist administrators in diagnosing replication problems between domain controllers. Administrators can use repadmin to view the replication topology. Repadmin can be used to manually create the replication topology to force replication events between domain controllers and to view the replication metadata. Repadmin can also be used for monitoring the relative health of an Active Directory forest. The operations `replsummary`, `showrepl`, `showrepl /csv`, and `showvector /latency` can be used to check for replication problems.

81. A. By default, connection objects are automatically created by the Active Directory replication engine. You can choose to override the default behavior of Active Directory replication topology by manually creating connection objects, but this step is not required.

82. C. Domain local groups are used to authorize permission for access to resources. You can assign these permissions only in the same domain in which you create the domain local group. Members from any domain may be added to a domain local group.

83. B. The Knowledge Consistency Checker (KCC) is responsible for establishing the replication topology and ensuring that all domain controllers are kept up to date. Replication is the process by which replicas are kept up to date. Application data can be stored and updated on designated servers in the same way basic Active Directory information (such as users and groups) is synchronized between domain controllers. Application data partition replicas are managed using the KCC, which ensures that the designated domain controllers receive updated replica information.

84. D. Site link bridges are designed to allow site links to be transitive. That is, they allow site links to use other site links to transfer replication information between sites. By default, all site links are bridged. However, you can turn off transitivity if you want to override this behavior. A site link is created to define the types of connections that are available between the components of a site. Site links can reflect a relative cost for a network connection and can also reflect the bandwidth that is available for communications.

85. D. SMTP was designed for environments in which persistent connections may not always be available. SMTP uses the store-and-forward method to ensure that information is not lost if a connection cannot be made. SMTP is perhaps best known as the protocol that is used to send and receive email messages on the Internet. SMTP was designed to use a store-and-forward mechanism through which a server receives a copy of a message, records it to disk, and then attempts to forward it to another email server. If the destination server is unavailable, it holds the message and attempts to resend it at periodic intervals. DHCP is a protocol used to provide quick, automatic, and central management for the distribution of IP addresses within a network. Options B and C do not exist.

Chapter 10: Implement Identity Federation and Access Solutions

1. E. The Dsamain tool exposes Active Directory data that is stored in a snapshot or backup as an LDAP server. Dsamain.exe is available if you have the Active Directory Domain Services (AD DS) or Active Directory Lightweight Directory Services (AD LDS) server role installed. To use Dsamain, you must run it from an elevated command prompt.

2. B. Federation Proxy services are installed under Remote Access as a Web Application Proxy (WAP) server in Windows Server 2016. A domain controller can contain Active Directory information for only one domain. If you want to use a multidomain environment, you must use multiple domain controllers configured in either a tree or a forest setting.

3. C. The Single Sign-On (SSO) feature allows users to enter their credentials only once to be authenticated to all supported published applications. SSO is a feature that is used heavily when connecting your corporate network to another network (like the cloud). Users sign in once but have access to both networks.

4. B, C. To log modifications of the Certification Authority role service, you will need to enable AD FS auditing. You must check the boxes for Success Audits and Failure Audits on the Events tab of the Federation Service Properties dialog box. You must also enable Object Access Auditing in Local Policy or Group Policy.

5. B. You will need to use Active Directory Federation Services (AD FS) in order to implement federated identity management. Federated identity management is a standards-based and information technology process that will enable distributed identification, authentication, and authorization across organizational and platform boundaries. The AD FS solution in Windows Server 2016 helps administrators address these challenges by enabling organizations to share a user's identity information securely.

6. C. The pass-through preauthentication method is when users are not required to enter credentials before they are allowed to connect to published web applications. The HTTP Basic preauthentication type is the authorization protocol used by many protocols, including ActiveSync, to connect to smartphones or to your Exchange mailbox. Publishing an app using HTTP Basic provides support for ActiveSync clients in Web Application Proxy (WAP) by caching the token that is received from AD FS and serving it from the cache. In this way, WAP enables the HTTP app to receive a non-claims Relying Party Trust for the application to the Federation Service.

7. B, E. AD FS provides features such as Single Sign-On (SSO). SSO allows you to log in one time with a set of credentials and use that set of credentials to access the applications over and over. To use a Web Application Proxy (WAP), you should set your firewall to allow for ports 443 and 49443.

8. C. The `Set-WebApplicationProxyApplication` cmdlet modifies settings of a web application published through Web Application Proxy. Specify the web application to modify by using its ID. The `-ID` parameter specifies the GUID of a web application. The `-ExternalUrl` parameter specifies the external address, as a URL, for the web application. Include the trailing slash (/).

9. B. Administrative Template files are divided into .admx files and .adml files for use by Group Policy administrators. Windows uses a Central Store to store Administrative Templates files. To create a Central Store for .admx and .adml files, create a new folder named `PolicyDefinitions` in File Explorer.

10. C. To use the WAP, you must install the Remote Access role. One of the advantages of using the Remote Access role service in Windows Server 2016 is the WAP. Normally, your users access applications on the Internet from your corporate network. The WAP reverses this feature, and it allows your corporate users to access applications from any device outside the network.

11. B. The AD FS configuration database stores all of the configuration data. It contains information that a federation service requires to identify partners, certificates, attribute stores, claims, and so forth. You can store this configuration data in either a Microsoft SQL Server or the Windows Internal Database feature that is included with Windows Server 2008/2008 R2, Windows Server 2012/2012 R2, and Windows Server 2016. The Windows Internal Database supports only up to five federation servers in a farm.

12. B. The `New-AdfsLdapServerConnection` cmdlet creates a connection object that represents the Lightweight Directory Access Protocol (LDAP) folder that serves as a claims provider trust. The `Add-AdfsClaimsProviderTrust` cmdlet adds a new claims provider trust to the Federation Service. In order for AD FS to authenticate users from an LDAP directory, you must connect this LDAP directory to your AD FS farm by creating a local claims provider trust. A local claims provider trust is a trust object that represents an LDAP directory in your AD FS farm. So to configure a connection to your LDAP directory, you would use the `New-AdfsLdapServerConnection` cmdlet. Then you must register the LDAP store with AD FS as a local claims provider trust by using the `Add-AdfsLocalClaimsProviderTrust` cmdlet.

13. A. When using pass-through preauthentication, users are not required to enter credentials before they are allowed to connect to published web applications. Pass-through will let WAP act like a reverse proxy.

14. E. AD FS preauthentication requires the user to authenticate directly with the AD FS server. After the AD FS authentication happens, WAP then redirects the user to the published web application. This guarantees that traffic to your published web applications is authenticated before a user can access them. You will do this using the Remote Access Management console.

15. A. The Certificate Authorities (CA) certificate of the forest should be added to the GPO. The Forest Certificate Authorities (CA) certificate is the only certificate that is automatically trusted; it does not require user interaction or a digital signature, and it does not change in this scenario. CAs issue certificates, revoke certificates they've issued, and publish certificates for their clients.

16. A, E. For your users to gain access, you need to allow them to have access and set up DNS so that they can find the access point. So, you would publish the websites from the Remote Access Management console. Configure Pass-Through Authentication and select Enable HTTP to HTTPS redirection. You would also create DNS entries that point to the public IP address of the WAP on the external DNS name servers.

17. C. To install WAP, you must first install Active Directory Federation Service (AD FS). AD FS is Microsoft's claims-based identity solution providing browser-based clients (internal or external to your network) with transparent access to one or more protected Internet-facing applications. WAP functions as an AD FS federation server proxy. WAP provides reverse proxy functionality for web applications inside your corporate network to enable users on any device to access them from outside the corporate network.

18. B. A claims provider is a federation server that processes trusted identity claims requests. A federation server processes requests to issue, manage, and validate security tokens. Security tokens consist of a collection of identity claims, such as a user's name or role or an anonymous identifier.

19. A. To upgrade the farm behavior level from Windows Server 2012 R2 to Windows Server 2016, use the `Invoke-AdfsFarmBehaviorLevelRaise` cmdlet. This raises the behavior level of an Active Directory Federation Services (AD FS) farm to enable the new features that are available in later versions of the Windows operating system. AD FS for Windows Server 2016 introduces the ability to have role separation between server administrators and AD FS service administrators. After upgrading an AD FS server to Windows Server 2016, the last step is to raise the Farm Behavior Level using the `Invoke-AdfsFarmBehaviorLevelRaise` PowerShell cmdlet.

20. A, B, E. You would do them in this order: A, E, B.

The `Connect-MsolService` cmdlet attempts to initiate a connection to Azure Active Directory. The `Set-MsolADFSContext` cmdlet sets the credentials to connect to Microsoft Online and to the Active Directory Federation Services (AD FS) server. The `-Computer` parameter specifies the computer name of the primary AD FS server. The `Convert-MSOLDomainToFederated` cmdlet converts the specified domain from standard authentication to Single Sign-On. The `-DomainName` parameter specifies the name of the domain to convert to Single Sign-On.

21. B. Administrators can use the `Get-CACrlDistributionPoint` cmdlet to view all the locations set for the CRL distribution point (CDP). The `Get-CACRLDistributionPoint` cmdlet gets all the locations set on the CDP extension of the certification authority (CA) properties.

22. D. The AD RMS Service Connection Point (SCP) is an object in Active Directory that holds the web address of the AD RMS certification cluster. AD RMS–enabled applications use the SCP to discover the AD RMS service; it is the first connection point for users to discover the AD RMS web services. Only one SCP can exist in your Active Directory forest. If you try to install AD RMS and an SCP already exists in your forest from a previous AD RMS installation that was not properly removed, the new SCP will not install properly. The pre-existing SCP must be removed before you can establish the new SCP.

23. A. The AD RMS super user group is a special group that has full control over all rights-protected content managed by the cluster. Its members are granted full owner rights in all use licenses that are issued by the AD RMS cluster on which the super users group is configured.

24. B. Since you are planning to issue certificates based on a User certificate template, you need to first copy that template so that you can alter it to the new settings. The built-in templates support auto-enrollment. You need to duplicate the template and then modify the permissions on the new template.

25. C. A Delta CRL is a Certificate Revocation List (CRL) that contains all non-expired certificates that have been revoked since the last base CRL was published. You can set a time interval for how often the servers check the CRL. This is referred to as the Delta CRL publication interval.

26. A. Network Load Balancing (NLB) is the only supported Microsoft solution for providing high availability across an AD FS server farm. Windows Failover Clustering does not currently support AD FS, as one master server is allowed to write to the configuration database per farm.

27. C. You can take a stand-alone root CA offline and it functions as the top of a CA hierarchy. A stand-alone root CA is also the topmost CA in the certificate chain. A stand-alone root CA is not dependent on Active Directory and can be removed from the network. This makes a stand-alone root CA the solution for implementing a secure offline root CA.

28. A. Online Certificate Status Protocol (OCSP) is a lightweight HTTP protocol that responds more quickly and efficiently than downloading a traditional CRL. An online responder is a trusted server that receives and responds to individual client requests for the status of a certificate. An OCSP responder retrieves CRLs and provides digitally signed real-time certificate revocation status responses to clients based on a given certificate authority's CRL.

29. A. There can be only one Active Directory Rights Management Services (AD RMS) root cluster per Active Directory forest. After a root cluster is deployed, there is the option of installing additional licensing-only clusters, which issue licenses to clients for publishing their content.

30. D. The Request Handling tab in the Certificate Templates Management console has the Renew With Same Key Certificate Template Configuration option. This certificate template option becomes visible in the user interface when you configure the Certification Authority and Certificate Recipient options to Windows Server 2016 and Windows 8/8.1, and Windows 10, respectively.

31. A. To configure the computer as a hosted cache server after the BranchCache feature is installed, and to register an SCP in AD DS, use the `Enable-BCHostedServer` PowerShell cmdlet. The `Enable-BCHostedServer` cmdlet configures BranchCache to operate in hosted cache server mode.

32. B. The `Install-WindowsFeature` installs one or more roles, role services, or features on either the local or a specified remote server that is running Windows Server 2016. The `Install-AdfsFarm` cmdlet creates the first node of a new federation server farm.

33. C. The Online Responder service retrieves revocation status requests for specific certificates and the status of these certificates, and it returns a signed response with the requested certificate status information. Online Responders are used to validate requests sent by network users. Instead of downloading huge CRLs, a user will send a request to the local Online Certificate Status Protocol (OCSP) service to verify the authenticity of an entity. You can deploy one Online Responder to verify the revocation status for one or multiple CAs.

34. D. If you want to enable automatic certificate approval and automatic user certificate enrollment, use enterprise CAs to issue certificates. You would need to open the template properties and select the Subject Name tab. If the Email name field is populated in the Active Directory user object, that email name will be used for user accounts. The email name is required for user certificates. If the email name is not populated for a user in AD DS, the certificate request by that user will fail.

35. C. To install Active Directory Certificate Services (AD CS) using PowerShell, follow these steps:

1. Open an elevated PowerShell console.

2. Use the `Get-WindowsFeature` cmdlet to ensure that the Active Directory Certificate Services role's installation state is available.

3. In the PowerShell console, type the following command and press Enter:
`Install-WindowsFeature adcs-cert-authority -IncludeManagementTools`.

4. Use the `Get-WindowsFeature` cmdlet to verify the installation.

36. B. An AD RMS root cluster manages all of the AD RMS licensing and certificate provisions for the forest. There can be only one AD RMS root cluster per AD forest.

37. D. With the Web Application Proxy, an organization can make on-premises web resources available for external access while at the same time managing the risk of this access by controlling authentication and authorization policies on the AD FS. Since you are discussing the perimeter network, you would need to deploy a WAP.

38. B.   The `New-NpsRadiusClient` cmdlet creates a Remote Authentication Dial-In User Service (RADIUS) client. A RADIUS client uses a RADIUS server to manage authentication, authorization, and accounting requests that the client sends. A RADIUS client can be an access server, such as a dial-up server or WAP, or a RADIUS proxy. To add a new RADIUS client, use `New-NpsRadiusClient -Address <address> -Name <Name> -SharedSecret <shared secret>`. This command adds a WAP as a RADIUS client to the NPS configuration. The `-Address` parameter specifies a fully qualified domain name (FQDN) or IP address of the RADIUS client. The `-Name` parameter specifies a name for the RADIUS client. This name must be unique. The `-SharedSecret` parameter specifies a shared secret key that is configured at the RADIUS client.

39. C.   Active Directory Sites and Services is a tool to create and manage Active Directory sites and services to map to an organization's physical network infrastructure. Using this tool, you can create objects called sites, place servers in sites, and create connections between sites. You can graphically create and manage sites in much the same way that you create and manage OUs. To create a global catalog, expand the Server object in the Active Directory Sites and Services tool.

40. C.   Certificate revocation uses CRLs, which contain a list of certificates that are no longer valid. CRLs can become large. They are accessed through CRL Distribution Points (CDPs), which are part of a CA role in Windows Server 2016. HTTP, FTP, LDAP, or file-based addresses may be used as URLs.

41. C.   Service Principal Names (SPNs) are registered by services in order for clients to identify them in a domain. Before a client can connect to a service, it must compose the SPN for that instance of service, connect to the service, and finally present the SPN for authentication via Kerberos. SPN is a unique identifier of a service instance. A SPN must be registered with Active Directory, which assumes the role of the Key Distribution Center (KDC) in a Windows domain.

42. D.   In this scenario, from AD RMS in `abc.com`, you would configure `xyz.com` as a trusted publisher domain. Trusted Publishing Domains (TPDs) allow an AD RMS cluster to issue end-use licenses for content that was originally published by a different AD RMS cluster. A TPD does not restrict the applications and distribution channels that clients use to protect and consume content. It also presents two advantages. First, configuring a TPD requires less administrative effort to enable users to protect documents for groups that contain partner users. Second, you do not need to connect to your partner's AD RMS cluster to consume content, reducing network overhead. A TPD allows a cluster to decrypt content it did not publish. Therefore, the original cluster does not have to be accessible in order for partner users to consume content. By configuring a TPD, users can still access all documents published by the partner cluster, even after that cluster has been decommissioned.

43. B.   For Workplace Join to work, a certificate is placed on the mobile device. AD FS challenges the device as a claims-based authentication to applications or other resources without requiring administrative control of the device. Workplace Join is supported by the Device Registration Service (DRS) included with the Active Directory Federation Services role in Windows Server 2016. When a device is set up with Workplace Join, the DRS registers a device as an object in Active Directory and sets a certificate on the consumer device that is used to represent the device identity. The DRS is meant to be both internal and external facing.

44. C. Considerations for installing AD RMS on Windows Server 2016 include creating an AD RMS Service account by creating a domain user account that has no additional permissions that can be used as the AD RMS service account. Use a group-managed service account to ensure that the account password is managed by Active Directory and that it does not require a manual password change by an administrator. If you are registering the AD RMS Service Connection Point (SCP) during installation, the user account installing AD RMS must be a member of the AD DS Enterprise Admins group or equivalent.

45. A, B, C. Active Directory Rights Management Services (AD RMS) uses three database servers:

- Configuration Database—This is a critical component of an AD RMS installation. The database stores, shares, and retrieves all configuration data and other data that the service requires to manage account certification, licensing, and publishing services for a whole cluster.

- Directory Services Database—This contains information about users, identifiers (such as email addresses), security IDs, group membership, and alternate identifiers. This information is a cache of directory services data.

- Logging Database—This is all of the historical data about client activity and license acquisition. For each root or licensing-only cluster, by default AD RMS installs a logging database in the same database server instance hosting the configuration database.

46. C. You would modify the Validity period for the certificate template. All certificates issued by a CA have a validity period. The validity period is a time range that specifies how long public key infrastructure (PKI) clients can accept the certificate as an authoritative credential based on the identity stated in the subject of the certificate.

47. D. To manage certificate templates, open a CA console, right-click Certificate Templates, and select Manage. Key size is modified in the Cryptography settings for the template. On the Cryptography tab, you can choose the minimum key size and the Cryptographic Service Provider (CSP). CSP is a library that contains algorithms to encrypt or unencrypt information. For this scenario, you would modify the Cryptography settings from the properties of Cert_Computers.

48. B, D. To configure Active Directory Federation Services (AD FS) you can select Start ➤ Run and type `FsConfigWizard.exe`, or you can click the `FsConfigWizard.exe` file located in the `C:\windows\adfs` folder.

49. D. The key archive stores a certificate's subject name, public key, private key, and supported cryptographic algorithms in its CA database. Key archiving can be performed manually or automatically, depending on the configuration. If the certificate template requires key archiving, then the process requires no manual intervention. However, key archiving can also be performed manually if the private key is exported and then sent to an administrator for import into the CA database.

50. B, C. To enable the Device Registration Service:

On your federation server, open a PowerShell command window and type `Enable-AdfsDeviceRegistration`.

Repeat this step on each federation farm node in your AD FS farm.

Enable seamless second factor authentication. Seamless second factor authentication is an enhancement in AD FS that provides an added level of access protection to corporate resources and applications from external devices that are trying to access them. When a personal device is Workplace Joined, it becomes a "known" device and administrators can use this information to drive conditional access and gate access to resources. To enable seamless second factor authentication, persistent Single Sign-On (SSO), and conditional access for Workplace Joined devices:

1. In the AD FS Management console, navigate to Authentication Policies.
2. Select Edit Global Primary Authentication.
3. Select the check box next to Enable Device Authentication.
4. Click OK.

51. C. Microsoft Passport allows your users to set up a key-based authentication that allows them to authenticate by using more than just their password (biometrics or PIN numbers). Your users would then log on to their systems using a biometric or PIN number that is linked to a certificate or an asymmetrical key pair.

52. A, B. The relying-party server is a member of the Active Directory forest that hosts resources that a user in the partner organization wants to access. In this case, the relying party server should be the abc.com AD FS server. A claims provider provides users with claims. These claims are stored within digitally encrypted and signed tokens. In this case, xyz.com is the claims provider.

53. B. The Start-OBRegistration cmdlet registers the server using the vault credentials downloaded during enrollment. The cmdlet registers the server by uploading a backup certificate to the vault. This cmdlet supports the -WhatIf and -Confirm parameters. The cmdlet prompts the user for confirmation by default.

54. B. The Get-OBPolicy cmdlet gets the current backup policy that is set for the server, including the details about scheduling backups, files included in the backup, and retention policy.

55. C. Azure Active Directory (Azure AD) enables Single Sign-On to devices, apps, and services from anywhere. Through devices, users are getting access to the corporate assets. To protect the corporate assets, you want to have control over these devices. This enables you to make sure that your users are accessing your resources from devices that meet your standards for security and compliance. Getting control of devices through Azure AD is done by registering and joining devices. Joining a device is an extension of registering a device. This means it provides you with all the benefits of registering a device, and in addition to this it changes the local state of a device. Changing the local state enables your users to sign in to a device using an organizational work or school account instead of a personal account.

56. B. A Key Recovery Agent (KRA) is able to extract the private key from an issued certificate from the certificate services database on a CA. The KRA is a user account that is able to perform key recovery. You can configure your CA to enable key archival, and then you can specify that your certificate templates will have key archival enabled. Your private keys can be copied to the CA so that you can recover them when needed.

57. A. In AD RMS, rights can be assigned to users who have a federated trust with Active Directory Federation Services (AD FS). This enables an organization to share access to rights-protected content with another organization without having to establish a separate Active Directory trust or AD RMS infrastructure.

58. D. You will want to install an Enterprise Subordinate Certificate Authority (CA). This CA needs Active Directory and is used to issue certificates to users and computers. You cannot create templates or configure auto-enrollment on a stand-alone CA.

59. D. The `Set-ADReplicationSite` cmdlet is used to set the properties for an Active Directory site that is being used for replication. Sites are used in Active Directory to either enable clients to discover network resources (published shares, domain controllers) close to the physical location of a client computer or to reduce network traffic over wide area network (WAN) links. Sites can also be used to optimize replication between domain controllers.

60. C. The `Add-AdfsFarmNode` cmdlet allows administrators to add a computer to an existing federation server farm.

61. B, D. In Template, type a new template display name and then modify any other optional properties as needed. On the Security tab, click Add, type the name of the users you want to issue the KRA certificates to, and then click OK. Under Group or Usernames, select the usernames that you just added. Under Permissions, select the Read and Enroll check boxes, and then click OK.

62. A. Active Directory Migration Tool (ADMT) allows an administrator to migrate users, groups, and computers from a previous version of the server to a current version of the server. Administrators can also use ADMT to migrate users, groups, and computers between Active Directory domains in different forests (interforest migration) and between Active Directory domains in the same forest (intraforest migration). By default, OUs inherit the permissions of their new parent container when they are moved. By using the built-in tools provided with Windows Server 2016 and Active Directory, you can move or copy OUs only within the same domain. You cannot use the Active Directory Users and Computers tool to move OUs between domains.

63. A, B, D. You can implement exclusion policies to deny certain entities the ability to acquire certificate and license requests. There are three ways to exclude these entities: by user, by application, and by lockbox version. When an entity is excluded, you use licenses that are created by servers in the AD RMS cluster. If, after a period of time, you decide to remove an entity that you have previously included in an exclusion policy, you can delete the entity from the exclusion list. Any new certification or licensing requests will not consider this entity as excluded. Lockboxes are used to store a user's private key.

64. C. Key Recovery Agents (KRAs) are administrators who can decrypt users' archived private keys. An organization can assign KRAs by issuing KRA certificates to designated administrators and configure them on the CA. The KRA role is not one of the default roles defined by the Common Criteria specifications, but a virtual role that can provide separation between Certificate Managers and the KRAs. This allows the separation between the Certificate Manager, who can retrieve the encrypted key from the CA database but not decrypt it, and the KRA, who can decrypt private keys but not retrieve them from the CA database.

65. A. In this scenario, for Template1, modify the Security settings within the CA. You need to enable users to automatically obtain a certificate based on the template. Then, you will want to set the security permissions to grant a specific User/Authenticated Users to issue and manage certificates, manage CAs, and request certificates. This can be done manually by opening the CA MMC, right-clicking the Server name, selecting Properties from the context menu, selecting the Security tab, and then adding the user and setting permissions.

66. A, D. An online responder is a trusted server that receives and responds to individual client requests for the status of a certificate. An OCSP responder retrieves CRLs and provides digitally signed real-time certificate revocation status responses to clients based on a given certificate authority's CRL.

Configuring the CA to support the Online Responder service includes these steps:

1. Run `certsrv.msc`.
2. Navigate to your CA.
3. Right-click on the CA and click Properties.
4. Select the Extensions tab. In the Select extension list, click Authority Information Access (AIA).
5. Click Add, and in the Add Location dialog box, type in the URL for the location. Click OK.
6. On the Extensions tab, make sure the URL that was just added to the locations area is highlighted. Then make sure the check boxes next to Include in the AIA extension of issued certificates and Include in the Online Certificate Status Protocol (OCSP) extension are checked.
7. Click Apply, let the service restart, and then click OK.
8. In Certification Authority, right-click Certificate Templates, and then click New Certificate Templates to Issue.
9. Select your CA, and in the right pane, right-click on Certificate Templates.
10. In Enable Certificates Templates, select the OCSP Response Signing template and any other certificate templates that you configured previously, and then click OK.
11. Open Certificate Templates in the CA and verify that the modified certificate templates appear in the list.

67. D. The Compatibility tab helps to configure the options that are available in the certificate template. The options available in the certificate template properties change depending on the operating system versions that are selected for the CA and certificate recipient. The option "Do not include revocation information in issued certificates" check box is available only with the compatibility mode set to Windows Server 2008 R2 or later.

68. C. When a user or group is created in Active Directory, the Mail attribute is an optional attribute that can be set to include a primary email address for the user or group. For AD RMS to work properly, this attribute must be set because all users must have an email attribute to protect and consume content. This can be done by setting the Email Address field in the properties for the user or group using any of the following tools:

- The Active Directory Users and Computers console
- The Active Directory Administrative Center
- Windows PowerShell

69. A, E. First, you configure what exactly needs to be audited on the object level (in this case, on the level of the CA object). Second, you must also configure the audit policy and enable success or failure auditing for a given set of audit policy categories or subcategories. So, in this scenario, modify the Certificate Manager settings for the CA from the Certification Authority console and then configure auditing for policy change from the Local Group Policy Editor.

70. A. The `Add-CATemplate` cmdlet adds a certificate template to the CA for issuing. A certificate template is a preconfigured list of certificate settings that allows users and computers to enroll for certificates without having to create complex certificate requests. Certificate templates allow for the customization of a certificate that can be issued by the CA. The template defines items such as the cryptographic types, validity and renewal periods, and certificate purposes.

71. D. The Online Responder service retrieves revocation status requests for specific certificates and the status of these certificates, and it returns a signed response with the requested certificate status information. The Online Responder uses a lightweight HTTP protocol that responds more quickly and efficiently than downloading a traditional CRL.

72. A. To view the installation state of AD FS using PowerShell, open an elevated PowerShell console, type the following command, and press Enter: `Get-WindowsFeature "adfs*","*fed*"`.

73. D. A relying party is a federation server that receives security tokens from a trusted federation partner claims provider. In turn, the relying party issues new security tokens that a local relying party application consumes.

74. C. Endpoints provide access to the federation server functionality of AD FS, such as token issuance, information card issuance, and the publishing of federation metadata. Based on the type of endpoint, you can then enable or disable the endpoint or control whether the endpoint is published to AD FS proxies.

75. B. The Message AD FS security mode allows the client credentials to be included in the header of a SOAP message. Confidentiality is preserved by encryption inside the SOAP message.

76. D. The correct syntax would be `Install-WindowsFeature Web-Application-Proxy -IncludeManagementTools`.

The `Install-WindowsFeature` installs one or more roles, role services, or features on either the local or a specified remote server that is running Windows Server 2016. `Web-Application-Proxy` installs the Federation Service Proxy role and using the `-IncludeManagementTools` parameter installs the management tools such as snap-ins on a target server.

77. A. DRS requires at least one global catalog server in the forest root domain. The global catalog server is needed to run the PowerShell cmdlet `Initialize-ADDeviceRegistration` during AD FS authentication.

78. B. In this question, we can see that the Backend Server SPN has been left blank. We need to enter the Backend Server SPN, so enter the Service Principal Name (SPN) for the backend server. For example, type HTTP/owa.abc.com.

To publish an Integrated Windows authenticated application, follow these steps:

1. On the Web Application Proxy (WAP) server, in the Remote Access Management console, in the Navigation pane, click Web Application Proxy, and then in the Tasks pane, click Publish.

2. In the Publish New Application Wizard, on the Welcome page, click Next.

3. On the Pre-authentication page, click Active Directory Federation Services (AD FS), and then click Next.

4. On the Relying Party page, in the list of relying parties, select the relying party for the application that you want to publish, and then click Next.

5. On the Publishing Settings page, do the following, and then click Next:

   - In the Name box, enter a friendly name for the application. This name is used only in the list of published applications in the Remote Access Management console.

   - In the External URL box, enter the external URL for this application; for example, https://owa.yourdomain.com/.

   - In the External certificate list, select a certificate whose subject covers the external URL.

   - In the Backend Server URL box, enter the URL of the backend server. Note that this value is automatically entered when you enter the external URL and you should change it only if the backend server URL is different; for example, http://owa/.

   - In the Backend Server SPN box, enter the service principal name for the backend server; for example, HTTP/owa.yourdomain.com.

6. On the Confirmation page, review the settings, and then click Publish.

7. On the Results page, make sure that the application published successfully, and then click Close.

79. C. The Edit right is being discussed. If this right is established, the AD RMS client enables protected content to be decrypted and re-encrypted by using the same content key. Usually, when this right is established, the RMS-aware application will allow the user to change protected content and then save it to the same file. This right is effectively identical to the Save right.

80. A. Trust policies are implemented to define how content licensing requests are processed throughout the enterprise, including rights-protected content from other AD RMS clusters. A Trusted User Domains (TUD) is the boundary mechanism for the AD RMS root cluster to process client licensor certificates or use licenses from users whose RACs were issued by another AD RMS root cluster. You must import the server licensor certificate of the AD RMS cluster to be trusted, in order to define your TUD.

81. D. One of the advantages of using the Remote Access role service in Windows Server 2016 is the Web Application Proxy (WAP) feature. Normally, your users access applications on the Internet from your corporate network. WAP reverses this feature, and it allows your corporate users to access applications from any device outside the network.

82. C. The Web Application Proxy feature allows applications running on servers inside the corporate network to be accessed by any device outside the corporate network. The process of allowing an application to be available to users outside of the corporate network is known as publishing.

83. B. When using pass-through preauthentication, users are not required to enter credentials before they are allowed to connect to published web applications.

84. D. To publish service-specific data in the directory database, the Active Directory Schema helps define an SCP object class for a service. Clients of the service use the data in an SCP to locate, connect to, and authenticate an instance of your service.

85. A. The `Add-AdfsClaimsProviderTrust` cmdlet adds a new claims provider trust to the Federation Service. Use this cmdlet when users from a partner organization need to access resources (relying parties) protected by the AD FS service.

Chapter 11: Practice Exam 70-740: Installation, Storage, and Compute with Windows Server 2016

1. D. The Remote Access server role provides connectivity through DirectAccess, VPNs, and Web Application Proxies (WAPs). DirectAccess provides an Always On and Always Managed experience. Remote Access provides VPN access, including site-to-site connectivity.

2. A. The correct answer is `Cscript C:\windows\system32\slmgr.vbs -ato`. `Cscript` will start a script so that it runs in a command-line environment. The `-ato` parameter command prompts Windows to try to do an online activation.

3. C. You can install the Internet Information Services (IIS) server role on Nano Server by using `-Packages Microsoft-NanoServer-IIS-Package`. The NanoServer folders contain a .wim image and a subfolder called `Packages`. The `Packages` subfolder is needed when you want to add server roles and features to the image.

4. D. The `Format-Volume` cmdlet formats one or more existing volumes or a new volume on an existing partition, and the `-FileSystem` switch specifies the filesystem with which to format the volume. The acceptable values for this parameter are NTFS, ReFS, exFAT, FAT32, and FAT.

5. D. By default, Windows Firewall will be running on the WSUS server; when you installed WSUS, it automatically configured two inbound rules called WSUS that allow both ports TCP 8530 and 8531.

6. D. A Nano Server cannot run Active Directory Domain Services (AD DS), Network Policy and Access Services, or a DHCP server. The recommended role is IIS Web Server. The Web Server (IIS) role in Windows Server 2016 allows an administrator to set up a secure, easy-to-manage, modular, and extensible platform for reliably hosting websites, services, and applications.

7. C. The `Write-EventLog` cmdlet writes an event to an event log. To write an event to an event log, the event log must exist on the computer and the source must be registered for the event log. The `-EventID` switch specifies the event identifier. This parameter is required.

8. C. Windows Defender offers improved security using cloud-based antivirus protection. When enabled, Windows Defender sends information to Microsoft about any problems it finds. This information is then used to gather more information about the problems affecting you and other users. This can be enabled and disabled. The cloud-based protection is also turned on by default and it provides real-time protection when Windows Defender sends information to Microsoft about potential security threats.

9. D, E. You must import the module for NanoServerImage generation, and then use the `New-NanoServerImage` command to create the new image. The `New-NanoServerImage` cmdlet makes a local copy of the necessary files from the installation media and converts the included Nano Server Windows image (.wim) file into a VHD or VHDX image, or reuses the existing .wim file. It then makes a copy of the converted VHD or VHDX image in the specified path. The `-Edition` parameter specifies the edition of the operating system. Valid values are Standard and Datacenter. The `-DeploymentType` parameter specifies the type of Nano Server deployment image. Valid values are Guest and Host. The `-MediaPath` parameter specifies the path of the source media. The `-TargetPath` parameter specifies the path of the final, modified image. The `-Computer` parameter indicates that this operation adds the Compute package. The `Import-Module` cmdlet adds one or more modules to the current session. The modules that you import must be installed on the local computer or a remote computer.

10. C. Distributed File System Replication (DFSR) staging is a hard drive area that is used for files that need to be replicated from one DFS server to other DFS servers. If the files that you are trying to replicate are larger than your assigned staging area, the replication will fail. When this happens, you must increase the amount of space used in the staging area.

11. B, C. The `Remove-PhysicalDisk` cmdlet removes a physical disk from a specified storage pool. The `Set-ResiliencySetting` cmdlet modifies the properties of the specified resiliency setting name.

12. B. The `Set-SRPartnership` command modifies a replication partnership between two replication groups. You can use this cmdlet to add replicated volumes, and you can also change the direction of replication, which makes a source volume into a destination volume.

13. B. The `Format-Volume` cmdlet formats one or more existing volumes, or a new volume on an existing partition. This cmdlet returns the object representing the volume that was just formatted, with all properties updated to reflect the format operation. The `Enable-DeDupVolume` cmdlet enables Data Deduplication on one or more volumes.

14. C. The `New-SRPartnership` cmdlet creates a replication partnership between two new or existing replication groups. This cmdlet can create the complete replication topology. It can also tie together separately created replication groups. The `-ReplicationMode` parameter specifies the desired mode of replication for this source and destination pair. The acceptable values for this parameter are:

- Synchronous or 1—The synchronous mode requires all writes to commit on the destination server and on the source server, which guarantees data integrity between computers. This is the default value.

- Asynchronous or 2—The asynchronous mode writes to the source server without waiting for the destination server, which allows for replication over high-latency, geographic networks.

15. A. A mirrored volume duplicates data across two disks. This type of volume is fault tolerant because if one drive fails, the data on the other disk is unaffected.

16. D. The `iscsicli removeisnsserver` command removes the host from the iSNS server. The `iscsicli addisnsserver` command manually registers the host server to an iSNS server. `refreshisnsserver` refreshes the list of available servers. `listisnsservers` lists the available iSNS servers.

17. A. Permissions are additive among themselves. This means you get the highest level of permissions. But when the two permissions meet, the most restrictive set of permission applies. In this question, the NTFS side would be Full Control (this would be the local permission) and the Shared permission would be Deny. But when the two permissions meet, the most restrictive, Deny, would apply.

18. C. The Microsoft Windows Performance Monitor is a tool that administrators can use to examine how programs running on their computers affect the computer's performance. The tool can be used in real time and can also be used to collect information in a log to analyze the data at a later time. With Performance Monitor, you can set up counter logs and alerts.

19. C. Virtual Hard Disk (VHD) is a file format that represents a virtual disk drive. A VHD can be used to store virtual disk data in files that can be easily transferred from one computer to another. It contains what is found on a physical HDD, such as disk partition and filesystem. Once attached, they can be treated like physical disks and you can use them to store data. To attach the VHD, you would use the Computer Management console.

20. D. Storage Spaces can combine multiple hard drives into a single virtual drive. To create a Storage Space, you need to connect two or more internal or external drives to the computer to create a storage pool. When the drive begins to fill up and nears the physical limit, Windows will display a notification prompting you to add additional physical Storage Space. Selecting the Parity resiliency type allows Windows to store parity information with the data, thereby protecting you from a single drive failure.

21. C. The `Optimize-VHD` cmdlet allows an administrator to optimize the allocation of space in virtual hard disk files, except for fixed virtual hard disks. The Compact operation is used to optimize the files. This operation reclaims unused blocks as well as rearranges the blocks to be more efficiently packed, which reduces the size of a virtual hard disk file.

22. C. Desired State Configuration (DSC) is an important part of the configuration, management, and maintenance of Windows Server 2016. Using a PowerShell script specifies the configuration of the machine using a standard way that is easy to maintain and understand.

23. B. Dynamically expanding is a disk that starts with a small VHD file and expands on demand once an installation takes place. It can grow to the maximum size you define during creation. You can use this type of disk to clone a local hard drive during creation.

24. A. When you use the External Virtual Switch type, any virtual machine connected to this virtual switch can access the physical network. This option is used in production environments where your clients connect directly to the virtual machines. This question states that Hyper-V hosts on the corporate network must be able to connect to the virtual machines.

25. D. By using a RAS Gateway and Windows Server Software Load Balancing (SLB), you can scale out your load balancing capabilities using SLB VMs on the same Hyper-V compute servers that you use for your other virtual machine workloads. Multitenancy for VLANs is not supported by Network Controller; however, you can use VLANs with SLB for service provider managed workloads, such as the datacenter infrastructure and high-density web servers.

26. C. The `Set-VmNetworkAdapterIsolation` cmdlet modifies isolation settings for a virtual network adapter. You can isolate a virtual machine adapter by using a virtual local area network (VLAN), Hyper-V Network Virtualization, or a third-party virtualization solution. You can specify the isolation method and modify other settings, which include multitenancy settings. The `-MultiTenantStack` parameter specifies whether to use multiple isolation IDs for the virtual machine. The acceptable values for this parameter are: On, indicate isolation IDs so that the virtual machine provides services to multiple tenants on different isolation subnets, and Off, do not indicate isolation IDs to the virtual machine.

27. B. PowerShell Direct is a feature for Windows 10 and Windows Server 2016. The virtual machine generation or VHD type do not matter. It is a way of running PowerShell commands inside a virtual machine from the host operating system. To create a PowerShell Direct session on a virtual machine:

- The VM must run at least Windows 10 or Windows Server 2016.
- The VM must be running locally on the host and booted.
- You must be logged into the host computer as a Hyper-V administrator.
- You must supply valid user credentials for the virtual machine.
- The host operating system must run at least Windows 10 or Windows Server 2016.

28. B. NIC Teaming allows you to group between 1 and 32 physical Ethernet network adapters into one or more software-based virtual network adapters. These virtual network adapters provide fast performance and fault tolerance in the event of a network adapter failure. NIC Team member network adapters must all be installed in the same physical host computer to be placed in a team. In this case, you would modify the settings on VM-1 from Hyper-V Manager on ServerA.

29. A. The `Merge-VHD` cmdlet merges virtual hard disks in a differencing virtual hard disk chain. The merge is from a specified source child disk to a specified destination child disk. Merge is an offline operation; the virtual hard disk chain must not be attached when the merge is initiated.

30. D. An administrator can use PowerShell Direct to run PowerShell cmdlets on a virtual machine from the Hyper-V host. Because Windows PowerShell Direct runs between the host and virtual machine, there is no need for a network connection or to enable remote management. There are no network or firewall requirements or special configuration. To create a PowerShell Direct session, use one of the following commands:

```
Enter-PSSession -VMName VMName
Invoke-Command -VMName VMName -ScriptBlock { commands }
```

31. A. You would want to connect to ContainerA since that is where the web application is located. ContainerA has an IP address of 172.16.5.6 and a port mapping from port 80.

32. B. You will want to configure Media Access Control (MAC) address spoofing on ServerA. If your container host is virtualized, you must enable MAC address spoofing. The `Get-VMNetworkAdapter` cmdlet gets the virtual network adapters of the specified virtual machine, snapshot, or management operating system. The `-VMName` parameter specifies the virtual machine whose virtual network adapters are to be retrieved. The `Set-VMNetworkAdapter` cmdlet configures features of the virtual network adapter in a virtual machine or the management operating system. The `-MacAddressSpoofing` parameter specifies whether virtual machines may change the source MAC address in outgoing packets to one not assigned to them. Allowed values are On (allowing the virtual machine to use a different MAC address) and Off (allowing the virtual machine to use only the MAC address assigned to it).

33. B. Administrators can set any configuration option for the daemon in a JSON format. This would be the `daemon.json` file. By default, Docker captures the standard output (and standard error) of all your containers, and writes them in files using the JSON format. The default file location is `C:\ProgramData\docker\config\daemon.json`.

34. D. When you are working with Hyper-V containers in Docker, the settings are identical to managing Windows Server containers. The one difference that you want to include in the Hyper-V Container is using the `--isolation=hyperv` parameter. The following is an example of the `docker` command with the Hyper-V parameters: `docker run -it --isolation=hyperv microsoft/nanoserver cmd`.

35. B. The Azure Container Service allows you to easily create, configure, and manage your virtual machine cluster of containers. By using open source tools, the Azure Container Service connects you with thousands of other users who are also designing, building, and maintaining container images.

36. C. `repadmin.exe` is the Replication Diagnostics Tool. This command-line tool assists administrators in diagnosing replication problems between Windows domain controllers. `repadmin.exe` can also be used for monitoring the relative health of an Active Directory forest.

37. A. The Container Host component can be on a physical or virtual machine and it's configured with the Windows Container feature. So the Windows Container sits on top of the Container Host.

38. A. You will need the Image ID. For example, the Image ID for my Nano Server is d9bccb-9d4cac. You will use this ID to turn the image into a container. Type the following into a PowerShell prompt (your Image ID will be different) and press Enter: docker run d9bccb9d4cac.

39. C. Administrators have the ability to set up a private repository so that coworkers can share and use the images that you create. After you create your images using the Docker daemon, you can then push those images to your corporate Docker Hub repository. Administrators can then add users and accounts to the Docker Hub to verify that only the organization's users are accessing the images.

40. F. Failover Cluster Manager is also called "VM Monitoring." It allows you to monitor the health state of applications that are running within a virtual machine and then reports that to the host level so that it can take recovery actions. You can monitor any Windows service (such as the Print Spooler service) in your virtual machine. When the condition you are monitoring gets triggered, the Cluster Service logs an event and takes recovery actions.

41. C. If you use Kerberos to authenticate Live Migration traffic, make sure to configure constrained delegation. To configure constrained delegation, open the Active Directory Users and Computers snap-in. Kerberos constrained delegation eliminates the need for requiring users to provide credentials twice. In this case, you would modify the Delegation settings on the ServerC computer account.

42. D. Since you are creating a two-way mirror, you will require at least two disks. This writes two copies of your data on the drives, which can protect your data from a single drive failure. Since we want to minimize data loss, you will use Drives C and D because there is nothing in them.

43. A. Storage Spaces supports four types of resiliency: single, two-way mirror, three-way mirror, and parity. This question states that two USB drives have failed. So the answer would be a three-way mirror. This option works similar to the two-way mirror, but it writes three copies of your data on the drives, which will help protect your data from two simultaneous drive failures. Three-way mirror requires at least three drives.

44. A. Failover Cluster Manager is a management tool within the Windows Server operating system that is used to create, validate, and manage failover server clusters running Windows Server. Administrators can open the Failover Cluster Manager by clicking Start ➤ Administrative Tools ➤ Failover Cluster Manager.

45. A. Planned Failover is an operation initiated on the primary virtual machine. Planned Failover is used when you want to perform host maintenance on the primary virtual machine and would like to run from the replica site.

46. B. Each virtual machine needs a virtual disk that is used as a boot/system disk, and two or more virtual disks to be used for Storage Spaces Direct. Disks used for Storage Spaces Direct must be connected to the virtual machines using a virtual SCSI controller.

47. B. To set up a cluster in a workgroup, you need to configure both of the servers to be in a workgroup. You then need to configure the Cluster Service to log on as Network Service and specify an administrative access point of DNS. The New-Cluster cmdlet creates a new failover cluster. Before you create a cluster, the hardware (servers, networks, and storage) must be connected, and the validation tests must be run. The -AdministrativeAccessPoint parameter specifies the type of administrative access point that the cmdlet creates for the cluster. DNS creates an administrative access point for the cluster. The administrative access point is registered in DNS but is not enabled in Active Directory Domain Services (AD DS).

48. D. Microsoft recommends using the Resilient File System (ReFS) for Storage Spaces Direct. ReFS is the premier filesystem built for virtualization and offers many advantages, including dramatic performance accelerations and built-in protection against data corruption.

49. D. To prevent the virtual machine from being live migrated automatically, you need to go into the network adapter settings of the virtual machine and disable the protected network setting.

50. B. The quorum arbitration time setting is used to set the limit of the time period that is allowed for quorum arbitration. Quorum arbitration is the process that occurs when the controlling node of the cluster is no longer active and other nodes of the cluster attempt to gain control of the quorum resource and thus control of the cluster. QuorumArbitrationTimeMax specifies the maximum number of seconds a node is allowed to spend arbitrating for the quorum resource in a cluster. RequestReplyTimeout describes the length of time a request from a node with a cluster state update will wait for replies from the other healthy nodes before the request times out.

Chapter 12: Practice Exam 70-741: Networking with Windows Server 2016

1. A. The Add-VMNetworkAdapterAcl cmdlet creates an access control list (ACL) to apply to the traffic through a virtual machine network adapter. When a virtual network adapter is created, there is no ACL on it. Given a list of IP-based ACL entries to be applied to traffic in the same direction, the longest match rule decides which one of the entries is most appropriate to apply to a specific packet.

2. C. This example creates three GPOs (IPAM1_DHCP, IPAM1_DNS, and IPAM1_DC_ NPS) and links them to the willpanek.com domain. These GPOs enable access for the server ipam1.willpanek.com using the domain administrator account userA.

3. A. You will need to modify the Zone Aging and Scavenging properties. When you set zone-level properties for a specified zone, these settings apply only to that zone and its resource records. Unless you otherwise configure these zone-level properties, they inherit their default settings from comparable settings that AD DS maintains in the Aging and Scavenging properties for the DNS server.

4. C. The DNS socket pool enables a DNS server to use source port randomization when it issues DNS queries. When the DNS service starts, the server chooses a source port from a pool of sockets that are available for issuing queries. Instead of using a predictable source port, the DNS server uses a random port number that it selects from the DNS socket pool. The DNS socket pool makes cache-tampering attacks more difficult because a malicious user must correctly guess both the source port of a DNS query and a random transaction ID to successfully run the attack. When you configure the DNS socket pool, you can choose a size value from 0 to 10,000. The larger the value, the greater the protection you will have against DNS spoofing attacks.

5. A. DHCP polices allow you to determine scope for specific types of equipment coming in that correspond to different characteristics. An administrator needs to ensure that different types of devices are provisioned appropriately for network connectivity. You want different types of clients to get IP addresses from different IP address ranges within the subnet. By specifying a different IP address range for different device types, you can more easily identify and manage devices on the network.

6. F. When the Conflict Detection Attempts option is set, the DHCP server uses the ping process to test available scope IP addresses before including these addresses in DHCP lease offers to clients. A successful ping means the IP address is in use on the network. Therefore, the DHCP server does not offer to lease the address to a client. If the ping request fails and times out, the IP address is not in use on the network. In this case, the DHCP server offers to lease the address to a client.

7. A. A role is a collection of IPAM operations. You can associate a role with a user or group in Windows using an access policy. Several built-in roles are provided, but you can also create customized roles to meet your requirements. You can create an access policy for a specific user or for a user group in Active Directory. When you create an access policy, you must select either a built-in IPAM role or a custom role that you have created.

8. B. Before a DHCP server can provide clients with IP addresses, the server must be configured with a scope. A scope is a range of IP addresses that can be leased to DHCP clients on a given subnet. You can also create a second type of scope known as a superscope. In an environment that has multiple logical IP subnets defined on a single physical network, superscopes allow a DHCP server to assign leases to clients on multiple subnets.

9. A. The Add-DhcpServerv4ExclusionRange cmdlet adds a range of excluded IP addresses for an IPv4 scope. The excluded IP addresses are not leased out by the Dynamic Host Configuration Protocol (DHCP) server service to any DHCP client. The only exception to this is reservation. If an IP address is reserved, the same IP address is leased to the designated client even if it falls in the exclusion range.

10. C. Network prefixes are determined directly from the subnet mask of the network. A Class C subnet mask would be 255.255.255.0. To determine the network prefix on a Class C subnet, you would need to convert each octet of the subnet mask to a binary value. So for a Class C, it would be 11111111.11111111.11111111.00000000. Count the consecutive 1s to determine the prefix. So, the answer would be /24.

11. A. The HOSTS file is a common way to resolve a host name to an IP address through a locally stored text file that contains IP-address-to-host-name mappings. The HOSTS file is used to map host names to IP addresses.

12. B. The New-NetRoute cmdlet creates an IP route in the IP routing table. Specify the destination prefix and specify an interface by using the interface alias or the interface index. IP routing is the process of forwarding a packet based on the destination IP address. Routing occurs at TCP/IP hosts and at IP routers. The sending host or router determines where to forward the packet. To determine where to forward a packet, the host or router consults a routing table that is stored in memory. When TCP/IP starts, it creates entries in the routing table. You can add entries either manually or automatically.

13. B. Time to Live (TTL) is used for computer data including DNS servers. It is the amount of time or number of transmissions that a packet can experience before it is discarded. The Minimum (Default) Time to Live (TTL) is the default or minimum amount of time for a newly created record.

14. C. If you choose to delete all PTR records at the node, use dnscmd.exe to delete them. So, to delete all PTR records at the 10.3.2.127 address you would type the following command at the command prompt: dnscmd /RecordDelete 10.in-addr.arpa. 127.1.2.3 PTR.

15. C. An exclusion just marks addresses as excluded; the DHCP server doesn't maintain any information about them. A reservation marks an address as reserved for a particular client. So, create a client reservation on a DHCP server if you want the server to always assign the same IP address to a specific machine on the network.

16. D. The Secure Only option is for DNS servers that have an Active Directory Integrated zone. When a computer tries to register with DNS dynamically, the DNS server checks Active Directory to verify that the computer has an Active Directory account. If the computer that is trying to register has an account, DNS adds the host record. If the computer trying to register does not have an account, the record gets tossed away and the database is not updated.

17. A. DHCP can become a single point of failure within a network if there is only one DHCP server. If that server becomes unavailable, clients will not be able to obtain new leases or renew existing leases. For this reason, it is recommended that you have more than one DHCP server in the network. However, more than one DHCP server can create problems if they both are configured to use the same scope or set of addresses. Microsoft recommends the 80/20 rule for redundancy of DHCP services in a network. To do this, you run the Configure Failover Wizard.

18. B. The CIDR /28 tells you that 28 1s are turned on in the subnet mask. Twenty-eight 1s equals 11111111.11111111.11111111.11110000. This would then equal 255.255.255.240.

19. D. Secure Socket Tunneling Protocol (SSTP) is a form of VPN tunnel that provides a mechanism to transport Point-to-Point (PPP) traffic through a Secure Sockets Layer/Transport Layer Security (SSL/TLS) channel. SSL/TLS provides transport-level security with key negotiation, encryption, and traffic integrity checking. The use of SSL/TLS over TCP port 443 allows SSTP to pass through virtually all firewalls and proxy servers except for authenticated web proxies.

20. B. Deploying Remote Access requires a minimum of two Group Policy Objects: one Group Policy Object contains settings for the Remote Access server and one contains settings for DirectAccess client computers. When you configure Remote Access, the wizard automatically creates the required Group Policy Object. However, if your organization enforces a naming convention, or you do not have the required permissions to create or edit Group Policy Objects, they must be created prior to configuring Remote Access.

21. A. The Set-DAEntryPoint cmdlet configures entry point settings, including the name of the server in the entry point, the name of the entry point, and the IP address used for global load balancing on the specified entry point.

22. B. In the single tenant mode, administrators can deploy RAS Gateways as an edge VPN server, an edge DirectAccess server, or both simultaneously. Using RAS Gateways this way provides remote users with connectivity to your network by using either VPN or DirectAccess connections. Also, single tenant mode allows administrators to connect offices at different physical locations through the Internet.

23. A. Network Policy Server (NPS) is Microsoft's solution for enforcing company-wide access policies, including remote authentication. NPS is a role service of the Network Policy and Access Services (NPAS) server role. Other role services of NPAS are the Routing and Remote Access Service, Health Registration Authority, and Host Credential. These help you safeguard the health and security of a network.

24. B. Intranet is the generic term for a collection of private computer networks within an organization. An intranet uses network technologies as a tool to facilitate communication between people or workgroups to improve the data-sharing capability and overall knowledge base of an organization's employees. The Internet uses standard network hardware and software technologies like Ethernet, Wi-Fi, TCP/IP, web browsers, and web servers. An organization's intranet typically includes Internet access but is firewalled so that its computers cannot be reached directly from the outside. Because all the users can connect via VPN, this would allow access to the intranet website and the published application.

25. B. The solution is to deploy Remote Desktop Gateway (RD Gateway) in the office. Remote users can then connect to their computers on the office network by using Remote Desktop client on their home computers configured with the IP address of the Remote Desktop Gateway. Remote Desktop Gateway is a role service that enables authorized remote users to connect to resources on an internal corporate or private network, from any Internet-connected device that can run the Remote Desktop Connection (RDC) client. VPN connections would enable remote access to the office network, but this solution would not prevent users from accessing other corporate network resources. Remote Desktop local resources determine which local resources (printers, drives, etc.) are available in a Remote Desktop connection. However, this solution makes no provision for actually connecting to the office network. DirectAccess connections would enable remote access to the office network, but this solution would not prevent users from accessing other corporate network resources.

26. B. The `New-NetFirewallRule` cmdlet creates an inbound or outbound firewall rule and adds the rule to the target computer. The `-Direction` parameter specifies that matching firewall rules of the indicated direction are created. This parameter specifies which direction of traffic to match with this rule. The acceptable values for this parameter are `Inbound` or `Outbound`. The default value is `Inbound`.

27. C. When you add a new network access server (VPN server, wireless access point, authenticating switch, or dial-up server) to your network, you must add the server as a RADIUS client in NPS so that NPS is aware of and can communicate with the network access server. On the NPS server, in the NPS console, double-click RADIUS Clients and Servers.

28. B. Access policies are a list of roles and the resources with which roles are to be provisioned or deprovisioned. Access policies are used to automate the provisioning of target systems to users. In this case, from Server Manager, you would modify the Access Policies on VPN1.

29. D. The `Set-DaClient` cmdlet configures the properties related to a DirectAccess (DA) client. The `-ComputerName` parameter specifies the IPv4 or IPv6 address, or host name, of the computer on which the Remote Access server computer–specific tasks should be run.

30. B. NAT64 is an IPv6 transition mechanism that facilitates communication between IPv6 and IPv4 hosts by using a form of network address translation (NAT). The NAT64 gateway is a translator between IPv4 and IPv6 protocols. It needs at least one IPv4 address and an IPv6 network segment comprising a 32-bit address space. DNS64 describes a DNS server that, when asked for a domain's AAAA records but only finds A records, synthesizes the AAAA records from the A records. The first part of the synthesized IPv6 address points to an IPv6/IPv4 translator, and the second part embeds the IPv4 address from the A record. The translator in question is usually a NAT64 server.

31. A. The `logman.exe` utility can be used to create and manage Event Trace Session and Performance logs and allows an administrator to monitor many different applications through the use of the command line.

32. D. The higher the RADIUS priority number, the less the RADIUS server gets used. To make sure that RADIUS NPS4 is used only when NPS2 and NPS3 are unavailable, you would set the RADIUS priority from 1 to 10. This way, it will get used only when NPS2 and NPS3 are having issues or are unresponsive.

33. B. `Add-RemoteAccessRadius` adds a new external RADIUS server for VPN authentication, accounting for DirectAccess (DA) and VPN, or one-time password (OTP) authentication for DA. `AccountingOnOffMsg<String>` indicates the enabled state for sending of accounting on or off messages. The acceptable values for this parameter are `Enabled` or `Disabled`. `Disabled` is the default value. This parameter is applicable only when the RADIUS server is being added for Remote Access accounting.

34. A. You can configure DirectAccess clients to send all of their traffic through the tunnels to the DirectAccess server with force tunneling. When force tunneling is configured, DirectAccess clients detect that they are on the Internet, and they remove their IPv4 default route. With the exception of local subnet traffic, all traffic sent by the DirectAccess client is IPv6 traffic that goes through tunnels to the DirectAccess server.

35. A. The HGS is the centerpiece of the guarded fabric solution. It is responsible for ensuring that Hyper-V hosts in the fabric are known to the host or enterprise and running trusted software and for managing the keys used to start up shielded VMs.

36. C. Network Controllers are new to Windows Server 2016. Network Controllers allow an administrator to have a centralized virtual and physical datacenter infrastructure. This enables administrators to manage, configure, and troubleshoot all of their infrastructure components from one location. The Network Controller feature allows you to configure and manage allow/deny firewall Access Control rules for your workload VMs for both East/West and North/South network traffic in your datacenter.

37. D. To install a multitenant RAS Gateway, you must install the Remote Access Server role first. You can deploy RAS Gateway as a multitenant, software-based edge gateway and router when you are using Hyper-V Network Virtualization or you have VM networks deployed with virtual Local Area Networks (VLANs). With the RAS Gateway, tenants can use point-to-site VPN connections to access their VM network resources in the datacenter from anywhere.

38. B. To be able to use NIC Teaming, the computer system must have at least one Ethernet adapter. But, if you want to provide fault protection, an administrator must have a minimum of two Ethernet adapters.

39. D. In single tenant mode, the RAS Gateway is used as the exterior or Internet-facing VPN or DirectAccess edge server. Single tenant mode allows organizations of any size to deploy the gateway as an exterior, or Internet-facing, edge virtual private network (VPN) and DirectAccess server. In single tenant mode, you can deploy RAS Gateway on a physical server or virtual machine (VM) running Windows Server 2016.

40. B. Remote Direct Memory Access (RDMA) allows computers in a network to exchange data in main memory without involving the processor, cache, or operating system of either computer. RDMA improves throughput and performance because it frees up resources and also uses a faster data transfer rate and low-latency networking. It can be implemented for networking and storage applications.

41. B. You can enable and configure network QoS with the Data Center Bridging (DCB) feature. QoS can help manage network traffic by configuring rules that can detect congestion or reduced bandwidth, and then to prioritize, or throttle, traffic accordingly. You can use QoS to prioritize voice and video traffic, which is sensitive to latency. DCB provides bandwidth allocation to specific network traffic and helps to improve Ethernet transport reliability by using flow control based on priority.

42. A. NIC Teams within a virtual machine must have their Teaming mode configured as Switch Independent. In addition, Load Balancing Mode for the NIC Team in a VM must be configured with the Address Hash distribution mode. You can configure NIC Teaming in the Guest OS; however, before NIC Teaming will work in a virtual machine, you need to enable NIC Teaming in the Advanced Features section of the VM settings. In this question, Ethernet1 has not been added to the NIC team, so you must add the missing adapter to the NIC team.

43. C. The only supported way to move virtual machines between host machines is to use Export and Import Virtual Machine. The option to move the virtual machine files cannot be used anymore because you will lose the configuration of your virtual machines. You cannot apply a snapshot to a different host machine. The Save command is not an available option in Hyper-V.

44. D. The SLB Multiplexer (MUX) processes inbound network traffic and maps VIPs to DIPs, then forwards the traffic to the correct DIP. Each MUX also uses Border Gateway Protocol (BGP) to publish VIP routes to edge routers. BGP Keep Alive notifies MUXs when a MUX fails, which allows active MUXs to redistribute the load in case of a MUX failure—essentially providing load balancing for the load balancers.

45. B. The `Set-NetLbfoTeam` cmdlet sets the `TeamingMode` or `LoadBalancingAlgorithm` parameters on the specified NIC team.

46. A, D. The first step when allowing a virtual machine to have connectivity to a physical network is to create an external virtual switch using Virtual Switch Manager in Hyper-V Manager. The additional step that is necessary when using SR-IOV is to ensure the check box is selected when the virtual switch is being created. Once a virtual switch has been created, the next step is to configure a virtual machine is to enable the SR-IOV—at the bottom is a check box to enable SR-IOV.

47. C. Switch Independent means that each NIC adapter is connected into a different switch. If you use Switch Independent NIC Teaming, then you must connect your NICs to different switches, but both switches must be on the same subnet. There are no models called Switch Reliant or Switch Autonomous.

48. D. To use BGP routing, you must install the Remote Access Service (RAS) and/or the Routing role service of the Remote Access server role on a computer or virtual machine (VM). BGP reduces the need for manual route configuration on routers because it is a dynamic routing protocol, and it automatically learns routes between sites that are connected by using site-to-site VPN connections.

49. C. With Switch Independent mode, the switch or switches to which the NIC Team members are connected are unaware of the presence of the NIC team and do not determine how to distribute network traffic to NIC Team members—instead, the NIC Team distributes inbound network traffic across the NIC Team members. When you use Switch Dependent mode, the network traffic load is distributed based on the TransportPorts address hash as modified by the dynamic load balancing algorithm.

50. C. Windows Server 2016 Hyper-V includes a feature called Virtual Machine Queue (VMQ). VMQ uses packet filtering to provide data from an external virtual machine network directly to virtual machines. This helps reduce the overhead of routing packets from the management operating system to the virtual machine.

Chapter 13: Practice Exam 70-742: Identity with Windows Server 2016

1. C. Domain role: All servers in the cluster must be in the same Active Directory domain. As a best practice, all clustered servers should have the same domain role (either member server or domain controller). The recommended role is member server.

2. D. Repadmin.exe is a command-line tool that can assist administrators in diagnosing replication problems between Windows domain controllers. Administrators can use Repadmin to retrieve a list of accounts that have their passwords cached on a Read-Only-Domain Controller (RODC). Repadmin.exe can also be used for monitoring the relative health of an Active Directory forest.

3. A. The Get-ADUser cmdlet gets a specified user object or performs a search to get multiple user objects. To search for and retrieve more than one user, use the Filter parameter. The -Filter specifies a query string that retrieves Active Directory objects.

4. B, C. You need to run the Adprep command when installing your first Windows Server 2016 domain controller onto a Windows Server 2008 R2 domain. If you are doing an in-place upgrade of an existing domain controller to the Windows Server 2016 operating system, you will need to run adprep /forestprep and adprep /domainprep manually. Adprep /forestprep needs to be run only once in the forest. Adprep /domainprep needs to be run once in each domain in which you have domain controllers that you are upgrading to Windows Server 2016. Adprep /rodcprep actually gets the network ready to install a read-only domain controller and not a GUI version.

5. C. Item-level targeting is a feature of Group Policy preferences that allows preference settings to be applied to individual users and/or computers within the scope of the Group Policy Object (GPO) that contains the preferences. Item-level targeting allows an administrator to specify a list of conditions that must be met in order for a preference setting to be applied to a user or computer object.

6. B. You will need to stop the Active Directory Certificate Services (AD CS) service prior to running the `Restore-CARoleService` cmdlet. If using the `Restore-CARoleService` cmdlet and you receive the error message: "The process cannot access the file because it is being used by another process." You need to stop the Active Directory Certificate Services (AD CS) service first.

7. C. The Group Policy Software installation extension allows administrators to use the Group Policy Object Editor to centrally manage the installation of software on all client computers in an organization. When Group Policy is used to deploy software and the software is included in the GPO linked to a site, domain, or OU, the software is referred to as being advertised to the user and computer. If assigning the application to a user, use the Software Installation node under User Configuration node, Software Settings. If assigning the application to a computer, use the Software Installation node under Computer Configuration, Software Settings. A .zap package is a simple text wrapper around a setup command. This information is extracted directly by the Group Policy Software installation extension.

8. B. By default, only domain administrators and enterprise administrators have this privilege for domains and OUs. Enterprise administrators and domain administrators of the forest root domain have this privilege for sites.

9. D. The first step to creating a Group Managed Service Account (gMSA) is to create the KDS Root Key. Use the `Add-KdsRootKey` cmdlet to generate a new root key for the Microsoft Group Key Distribution Service (KdsSvc) within Active Directory. The Microsoft Group KdsSvc generates new group keys from the new root key.

10. A. You only need to give them rights to the willpanek.com zone using the DNS snap-in. If they do not have any rights to the willpanekAD.com zone, they will not be able to configure this zone in any way.

11. D. The `Set-ADReplicationSite` cmdlet is used to set the properties for an Active Directory site that is being used for replication. Sites are used in Active Directory to either enable clients to discover network resources (published shares, domain controllers) close to the physical location of a client computer or to reduce network traffic over wide area network (WAN) links. Sites can also be used to optimize replication between domain controllers.

12. B. If you want to convert an existing partition from one filesystem to another, you will need to use the `CONVERT` command-line utility. Example: To convert the C: partition from FAT to NTFS you would use the following command: `CONVERT c: /fs:ntfs`.

13. A. Password Settings Objects (PSOs) are created so that you can create fine-grained password policies. You create PSOs using the ADSI editor and then you can use those PSOs to create your fine-grained password policies. Fine-grained password policies allow you to specify multiple password policies within a single domain.

14. A. When you configure the Group Policy settings for WSUS, use a Group Policy Object (GPO) linked to an Active Directory container appropriate for your environment. Here are the steps in automatically downloading and installing Windows updates:

1. In Group Policy Object Editor, expand Computer Configuration, expand Administrative Templates, expand Windows Components, and then click Windows Update.
2. In the details pane, click Configure Automatic Updates.
3. Click Enabled, then select how you would like the updates to be installed.
4. Click OK.

15. C. Dnscmd.exe is a command-line interface for managing DNS servers. This utility is useful in scripting batch files to help automate routine DNS management tasks, or to perform simple unattended setup and configuration of new DNS servers on your network.

```
dnscmd <ServerName> <command> [<command parameters>]
```

16. D. If you assign an application to a user, the application does not get automatically installed. To have an application automatically installed, you must assign the application to the computer account. Since Sales is the only OU that should receive this application, you would link the GPO to Sales only.

17. A. The `Move-ADDirectoryServerOperationMasterRole` cmdlet moves one or more operation master roles to a directory server. You can move operation master roles to a directory server in a different domain if the credentials are the same in both domains. The `-identity` parameter specifies the directory server that receives the roles. The `-OperationMasterRole` parameter is used to specify the roles for transfer. Operation roles include PDCEmulator, RIDMaster, InfrastructureMaster, SchemaMaster, or DomainNamingMaster. In this scenario we are using the PDCEmulator. The `-Force` parameter indicates that the cmdlet is used for seize operations on domain controllers with the flexible single master operations (FSMO) role.

18. C. Inheritance is the process by which permissions placed on parent OUs affect child OUs. In this example, the permissions change for the higher-level OU (Mass) automatically caused a change in permissions for the lower-level OU (Boston).

19. A. Repadmin is used to troubleshoot replication issues in Active Directory. This command-line tool assists administrators in diagnosing replication problems between domain controllers. Repadmin can be used to manually create the replication topology to force replication events between domain controllers. Repadmin.exe can also be used for monitoring the relative health of an Active Directory forest.

20. B. The `Start-OBRegistration` cmdlet needs to be run because it registers the server using the vault credentials downloaded during enrollment.

21. A. Administrators have the ability to apply individual preference items only to selected users or computers using a GPO feature called item-level targeting. Item-level targeting allows an administrator to select specific items that the GPO will look at and then apply that GPO only to the specific users or computers.

22. D. Redircmp redirects the default container for newly created computers to a specified, target Organizational Unit (OU) so that newly created computer objects are created in the specific target OU instead of in CN=Computers. You must run the redircmp command from an elevated command prompt.

23. C. In one-way relationships, the trusting domain allows resources to be shared with the trusted domain but not the other way around. Selective authentication means that users cannot authenticate to a domain controller or resource server in the trusting forest unless they are explicitly allowed to do so.

24. C. The Install-ADDSDomain cmdlet installs a new Active Directory domain configuration. If the value set for -DomainType is set to "TreeDomain", this parameter can be used to specify the fully qualified domain name (FQDN) for the new domain tree (for example, "willpanek.com"). The -InstallDns:$true indicates that the DNS Server service will be installed and configured for the domain or domain tree. -NewDomainName indicates the new name domain to be added and the -ParentDomainName specifies the fully qualified domain name (FQDN) of an existing parent domain.

25. D. The Get-ADUser cmdlet gets a specified user object or performs a search to get multiple user objects. The Set-ADUser cmdlet modifies the properties of an Active Directory user. You can use the Get-ADUser cmdlet to retrieve a user object and then pass the object through the pipeline to the Set-ADUser cmdlet.

26. D. The Pass-through preauthentication method is when a user is not required to enter credentials before they are allowed to connect to published web applications. The HTTP Basic preauthentication type is the authorization protocol used by many protocols, including ActiveSync, to connect rich clients, including smartphones, with your Exchange mailbox. Publishing an app using HTTP basic provides support for ActiveSync clients in Web Application Proxy by caching the token that is received from AD FS and serving the token from the cache to overcome this limitation and avoid a high load on AD FS. In this way Web Application Proxy enables the HTTP app to receive a non-claims Relying Party Trust for the application to the Federation Service.

27. A. The Set-WebApplicationProxyApplication command modifies the settings of a web application published through Web Application Proxy. Specify the web application to modify by using its ID. The -ID parameter specifies the GUID of a web application. The -ExternalURL parameter specifies the external address, as a URL, for the web application. Include the trailing slash (/).

28. C. To use the Web Application Proxy (WAP), you must install the Remote Access role. One of the advantages of using the Remote Access role service in Windows Server 2016 is the WAP. Normally, your users access applications on the Internet from your corporate network. The WAP reverses this feature and allows your corporate users to access applications from any device outside the network.

29. D. The New-AdfsLdapServerConnection cmdlet creates a connection object that represents the Lightweight Directory Access Protocol (LDAP) folder that serves as a claims provider trust. The Add-AdfsClaimsProviderTrust cmdlet adds a new claims provider trust to the Federation Service. In order for AD FS to authenticate users from an LDAP directory, you must connect this LDAP directory to your AD FS farm by creating a local claims provider

trust. A local claims provider trust is a trust object that represents an LDAP directory in your AD FS farm. So to configure a connection to your LDAP directory you would use the New-AdfsLdapServerConnection cmdlet. Then you must register the LDAP store with AD FS as a local claims provider trust by using the Add-AdfsLocalClaimsProviderTrust cmdlet.

30. D. AD FS preauthentication requires the user to authenticate directly with the AD FS server. After the AD FS authentication happens, the Web Application Proxy then redirects the user to the published web application. This guarantees that traffic to your published web applications is authenticated before a user can access them. You will do this using the Remote Access Management console on Svr2.

31. B, D. For your users to gain access, you need to allow them to have access and also set up DNS so that they can find the access point. So, you would publish the websites from the Remote Access Management console. Configure Pass-Through Authentication and select Enable HTTP to HTTPS redirection. You would also create DNS entries that point to the public IP address of the Web Application Proxy on the external DNS name servers.

32. A. A claims provider is a federation server that processes trusted identity claims requests. A federation server processes requests to issue, manage, and validate security tokens. Security tokens consist of a collection of identity claims, such as a user's name or role or an anonymous identifier.

33. D. The Active Directory Rights Management Services (AD RMS) Service Connection Point (SCP) is an object in Active Directory that holds the web address of the AD RMS certification cluster. AD RMS-enabled applications use the SCP to discover the AD RMS service; it is the first connection point for users to discover the AD RMS web services. Only one SCP can exist in your Active Directory forest. If you try to install AD RMS and an SCP already exists in your forest from a previous AD RMS installation that was not properly removed, the new SCP will not install properly. The pre-existing SCP must be removed before you can establish the new SCP.

34. C. A Delta CRL is a CRL that contains all non-expired certificates that have been revoked since the last base CRL was published. You can set a time interval for how often the servers check the CRL. This is referred to as the Delta CRL publication interval.

35. B. The Request Handling tab in the Certificate Templates Management console has the Renew With Same Key Certificate Template Configuration option. This certificate template option becomes visible in the user interface when you configure the Certification Authority and the Certificate Recipient options to Windows Server 2016 and Windows 8/8.1 or Windows 10, respectively.

36. D. The Install-WindowsFeature installs one or more roles, role services, or features on either the local or a specified remote server that is running Windows Server 2016. The Install-AdfsFarm cmdlet creates the first node of a new federation server farm.

37. D. If you want to enable automatic certificate approval and automatic user certificate enrollment, use enterprise CAs to issue certificates. You would need to go to the template properties and go to the Subject Name tab. If the Email name field is populated in the Active Directory user object, that email name will be used for user accounts. The email name is required for user certificates. If the email name is not populated for a user in AD DS, the certificate request by that user will fail.

38. D. With the Web Application Proxy (WAP), an organization can make on-premises web resources available for external access while at the same time managing the risk of this access by controlling authentication and authorization policies on the AD FS. Since we are discussing the perimeter network, we would need to deploy a WAP.

39. C. Certificate revocation uses Certificate Revocation Lists (CRL). CRLs contain a list of certificates that are no longer valid, and the CRL can become large. CRLs are accessed through CRL Distribution Points (CDPs), which are part of a CA role in Windows Server 2016. HTTP, FTP, LDAP, or file-based addresses may be used as URLs.

40. B. A consideration for installing Active Directory Rights Management Service (AD RMS) on Windows Server 2016 is to create an AD RMS Service account by creating a domain user account that has no additional permissions that can be used as the AD RMS service account. It is recommended to use a group-managed service account to ensure that the account password is managed by Active Directory and that it does not require a manual password change by an administrator. If you are registering the AD RMS Service Connection Point (SCP) during installation, the user account installing AD RMS must be a member of the AD DS Enterprise Admins group or equivalent. The solution here is to create a domain user account and add the account to the Domain Users group in the domain.

41. A. All certificates issued by a certification authority have a validity period. The validity period is a time range that specifies how long PKI clients can accept the certificate as an authoritative credential based on the identity stated in the subject of the certificate.

42. D. To manage certificate templates, open a certification authority console and right-click on Certificate Templates and select Manage. Key size is modified in the Cryptography settings for the template. On the Cryptography tab you can choose the minimum key size and the Cryptographic Service Provider (CSP). CSP is a library that contains algorithms to encrypt or unencrypt information.

43. D. The Start-OBRegistration cmdlet registers the server using the vault credentials downloaded during enrollment. The cmdlet registers the server by uploading a backup certificate to the vault. This cmdlet supports the -WhatIf and the -Confirm parameters. The cmdlet prompts the user for confirmation by default.

44. A. A Key Recovery Agent (KRA) is able to extract the private key from an issued certificate from the certificate services database on a Certificate Authority (CA). The key recovery agent is a user account that is able to perform key recovery. You can configure your CA to enable key archival and then you can specify that your certificate templates will have key archival enabled and your private keys can be copied to the CA so you can recover them when needed.

45. A. You will want to install an Enterprise Subordinate Certificate Authority (CA). This CA needs Active Directory and is used to issue certificates to users and computers. You cannot create templates or configure auto-enrollment on a standalone CA.

46. B, D. In Template, type a new template display name and then modify any other optional properties as needed. On the Security tab, click Add, type the name of the users you want to issue the key recovery agent certificates to, and then click OK. Under Group or user names, select the usernames that you just added. Under Permissions, select the Read and Enroll check boxes, and then click OK.

47. D. Key Recovery Agents (KRAs) are administrators who can decrypt users' archived private keys. An organization can assign Key Recovery Agents by issuing KRA certificates to designated administrators and configure them on the CA. The KRA role is not one of the default roles defined by the Common Criteria specifications but a virtual role that can provide separation between Certificate Managers and the KRAs. This allows the separation between the Certificate Manager, who can retrieve the encrypted key from the CA database but not decrypt it, and the KRA, who can decrypt private keys but not retrieve them from the CA database. In this case, you should provide Sue with access to a Key Recovery Agent certificate and a private key.

48. C. The Compatibility tab helps to configure the options that are available in the certificate template. The options available in the certificate template properties change depending upon the operating system versions that are selected for the certification authority (CA) and certificate recipient. The option "Do not include revocation information in issued certificates checkbox" is only available with the compatibility mode set to Windows Server 2008 R2 or later.

49. A. The `Add-CATemplate` cmdlet adds a certificate template to the certificate authority (CA) for issuing. A certificate template is a preconfigured list of certificate settings that allows users and computers to enroll for certificates without having to create complex certificate requests. Certificate templates allow for the customization of a certificate that can be issued by the CA. The template defines items such as the cryptographic types, validity and renewal periods, and certificate purposes.

50. B. Active Directory Rights Management Services (AD RMS) uses three database servers. The Directory Services Database contains information about users, identifiers (such as email addresses), security IDs, group membership, and alternate identifiers. This information is a cache of directory services data. The Configuration Database is a critical component of an AD RMS installation. The database stores, shares, and retrieves all configuration data and other data that the service requires to manage account certification, licensing, and publishing services for a whole cluster. The Logging Database is all of the historical data about client activity and license acquisition. For each root or licensing-only cluster, by default AD RMS installs a logging database in the same database server instance hosting the configuration database.

Index

Comprehensive Online Learning Environment

Register on Sybex.com to gain access to the comprehensive online interactive learning environment and test bank to help you study for your MCSA Windows Server certification.

The online test bank includes:

- **Practice Test Questions** to reinforce what you learned
- **Bonus Practice Exams** to test your knowledge of the material

Go to http://www.wiley.com/go/sybextestprep to register and gain access to this comprehensive study tool package.

Register and Access the Online Test Bank

To register your book and get access to the online test bank, follow these steps:

1. Go to bit.ly/SybexTest.
2. Select your book from the list.
3. Complete the required registration information including answering the security verification proving book ownership. You will be emailed a pin code.
4. Go to http://www.wiley.com/go/sybextestprep and find your book on that page and click the "Register or Login" link under your book.
5. If you already have an account at testbanks.wiley.com, login and then click the "Redeem Access Code" button to add your new book with the pin code you received. If you don't have an account already, create a new account and use the PIN code you received.